The Official America Online Tour Guide

The Official America Online Tour Guide

Tour Guide

PC Edition

Version 1.5

Tom Lichty & Kathy Parks

VENTANA
PRESS

The Official America Online Tour Guide—PC Edition
Copyright© 1992 by Tom Lichty & Kathy Parks

Library of Congress Cataloging-in-Publication Data

Lichty, Tom.
      The official America online membership kit & tour guide: PC
  edition / Tom Lichty & Kathy Parks. --1st ed.
            p.   cm.
      Includes bibliographical references and index.
      ISBN 1-56604-025-6 (pbk.)
      1. America Online (Videotex system) 2. PC-DOS
  (Computer file) 3. MS-DOS (Computer file) I. Parks, Kathy.
  II. Title
  QA76.57.A43L53 1992
  004.69—dc20   92-32081
                                          CIP

Technical review: Kate Chase, Jay Levitt and Kathy Ryan; America Online
Book design: Karen Wysocki
Cover design: Cassell Design
Index services: Dianne Bertsch, Answers Plus
Editorial staff: Diana Cooper, Rebecca Johns, Linda Pickett, Ruffin Prevost, Pam Richardson
Production staff: Rhonda Angel, Brian Little, Charles Overbeck, Karen Wysocki

First Edition 9 8 7 6 5 4 3 2 1
Printed in the United States of America

Ventana Press, Inc.
P.O. Box 2468
Chapel Hill, NC 27515
919/942-0220
FAX 919/942-1140

Limits of Liability and Disclaimer of Warranty

# About the Authors

Tom Lichty is Senior Consultant and Instructor for the University of Oregon Portland Center, and author of six computer books, including *Desktop Publishing With Word for Windows*, published by Ventana Press. An eager member of the online community since 1987, he may be reached at MajorTom on America Online, or majortom@aol.com on the Internet.

Kathy Parks owns a computer consulting and training business as well as teaches and consults for the University of Oregon Portland Center. She has written several computer application program manuals. She can be reached via America Online at CoolKath or on the Internet at coolkath@ aol.com.

They *love* mail!

Trademarks

Trademarked names appear throughout this book. Rather than list the names and entities that own the trademarks or insert a trademark symbol with each mention of the trademarked name, the publisher states that it is using the names only for editorial purposes and to the benefit of the trademark owner with no intention of infringing upon that trademark.

Acknowledgments

First and foremost, kudos to Kate Chase (aka PC Kate) for lending her technical expertise to this project, especially to Chapter 7, "Computing & Software," her home turf. Special thanks to Annette Aldous, Theresa Browning, David Butler, Jan Delucian, Bob Greenlee, Janet Hunter, Ken Huntsman, James Jones, Sheri Lesesne, Denise Mueller, Mark Prendergast, Jerry Shi, Bob Stoerrle and Scott Taub, who wrote what may be the most advanced, easy-to-use telecommunications software in the industry today.

Thanks also to Steve Case, Kathy Ryan, Joe Woodman and Larry Levitsky, who envisioned this project and agreed to produce software documentation that would appear in this most unusual form.

At America Online, Jay Levitt answered thousands of questions, responding within 12 hours even when he was on vacation. The man must never sleep. Tom de Boor, Nancy Gralow, Tim Barwick and Julia Wilkenson are producers who are not only escalating AOL to eminence, they're personable, witty, enthusiastic and always willing to help.

Contributors Robin Williams, Cliff Stoll, Raymond Lau, Christian Nelson, Don Rittner, Andy Baird, Tom Clancy, Patrick Wynne, Kai Krause, Kate Chase, Todd Caruthers, Brent Deverman, David Palermo, Jim Leftwich, Kasey K.S. Chang and the people at the Library of Congress are to be thanked for their altruistic willingness to participate in this project. We supplied the cream and flour; they supplied the sugar and spice.

At Ventana Press, Ruffin Prevost and Pam Richardson generously gave of themselves and encouraged us so we continuously felt that our picky little details were as important to them as they were to us; Karen Wysocki wrapped the project in its cloak of poetic design; Diane Lennox orchestrated a Wagnerian promotional effort; while Brian Little, Charles Overbeck and Rhonda Angel (winner of the 1992 award for Beveled Excellence) produced the book in record time. All the while, Elizabeth Woodman stood at the helm, steering the ship with confidence, vision and élan.

At Waterside Productions, Matt Wagner managed finances and negotiated deadlines with aplomb and equality.

At home, Victoria and Mel supplied unceasing support and enthusiasm even when our confidence and composure faltered.

The volume of names appearing in the paragraphs above is notable indication of the complexity of a project like this. This was a community effort; we thank you all.

Tom Lichty and Kathy Parks

Contents

Foreword 21

Chapter 1 Starting the Tour   1

What is America Online?   2
    It's a telecommunications service   4
    It's one big Thunder-Lizard computer   5
        The Stratus ▲ Common carriers
    It's software installed in your computer   8
    It's a resource   10
    It's a community   12

How to use this book   14
    How to use this book as documentation   14
        Finding answers ▲ Departmental listings
        ▲ Subject listings ▲ A documentation strategy
    How to use this book as a book   17

Chapter 2 Making the Connection 21

Things you'll need 22
    The computer 22
    The telephone line 23
    The starter kit 23
    The modem 23
    The money 26
    The screen name 26
    The password 27

Installing the software   28
The initial online session   41
   Configuring the telephone connection   41
   Selecting access numbers   43
   The certificate number & password   44
   Providing your billing information   45
   Choosing a screen name & password   47
   A letter from the President   49
Where to go from here   50

Chapter 3   Online Help & the Members   51

Getting help   51
   Off-line help   53
      Choosing help from the menu bar
   Online help   55
      Members' Online Support ▲ Saving help ▲ Printing help
      ▲ The Directory of Services ▲ Searching the Directory of Services
      ▲ Locating the Directory of Services ▲ Customer Service Live
      ▲ Members Helping Members ▲ Message boards ▲ The value
      of member help
Guides   68
Members   70
   The Member Directory   70
   Member profiles   72

Chapter 4   Entertainment   75

An overview   75
Book Bestsellers   76
Cartoons   77
The Grandstand   79
The Comedy Club   82

RockLink Forum 84
The Trivia Club 86
Movie & video reviews 87
The Online Gaming Forums 89
Neverwinter Nights 90
RabbitJack's Casino 93
Play-by-mail games 94

Chapter 5 News & Finance 97

Your personal stock portfolio 98
StockLink 98
Finding a stock symbol ▲ Building the portfolio
▲ Charting the portfolio ▲ Market News
▲ The TradePlus gateway ▲ The Bulls & Bears Game
Your Money 104
News Search 107
The Microsoft Small Business Center 108
Free of extra charges 113

Chapter 6 Lifestyles & Interests 115

Forums defined 116
Reference materials 117
Articles & folders ▲ Online databases
Bulletin boards 124
Editing the Go To menu 125
Reading messages ▲ Browsing, finding & reading
messages ▲ Posting messages
Libraries 137
The forums at Lifestyles & Interests 139
The Environmental Club 139
Real Estate Online 141
The Bicycling Forum 143

Chapter 7 **Computing & Software** **147**

PC World Online **148**
Computer news & reference sources **150**
Industry connection **156**
The forums **161**
    The DOS Forum   161
    The PC Animation & Graphics Forum   164
    The Windows Forum   166
    The PC Games Forum   169
Downloading files **171**
    What is downloading?   171
    A downloading session   172
        The online file database ▲ Reading a file description
        ▲ The downloading process
    File formats   181
    File compression & decompression   182
        PKZip ▲ StuffIt
Uploading files **186**
    The uploading process   186
        The Upload File Information form
    Concluding the uploading process   188

Chapter 8 **Travel & Shopping** **191**

The EAASY SABRE gateway **192**
    Finding a flight   194
    Finding the cost   195
    Booking the reservations   196
The Independent Traveler **196**
Computer Express **199**
AutoVantage **201**

Chapter 9 **Learning & Reference** **205**

Learning & Reference for everyone **206**
Compton's Encyclopedia   206
National Geographic Online   209
The Online Russian Archives   210
The Electronic University Network   212
The Career Center   213
Learning & Reference for the student **217**
Student Access   217
The Academic Assistance Center   219
College Board Online   221
Learning & Reference for the teacher **224**
Teachers' Information Network   224
NEA Online   227
ASCD Online   228
Learning & Reference for the parent **229**

Chapter 10 **People Connection** **233**

The Lobby **234**
Entering the Lobby   234
Guides   236
Exploring other public rooms **237**
The Event Rooms Guide   237
The Event Rooms Schedule   242
Finding other rooms   242
The New Member Lounge   243
Private rooms **244**
Chat-room technique **245**
Cut & paste   245
Getting information about people in a room   246
Locating a Member Online   247
Highlighting & excluding members   248
Instant Messages **249**
Center Stage **253**

Chapter 11   Electronic Mail   257

What exactly is electronic mail?   258
Why use e-mail?   259
A circular exercise   259
The Mail menu   263
    Composing your mail   263
        Preparing mail off-line
    Addressing a memo   266
    Reading new mail   268
        Replying to Mail ▲ Replying to all ▲ Forwarding mail
    Checking mail you've read   272
    Checking mail you've sent   273
        Checking the status of read mail
    The Address Book   275
        Adding a name to the Address Book
Gorilla food   279
    Saving your mail   279
        The process ▲ Filing strategies ▲ File-naming conventions
        ▲ Accessing these files
    Attaching files to messages   281
    E-mail alternatives   284
        Paper mail ▲ Sending a fax
    The Internet mail gateway   287

Chapter 12   The Download Manager   291

The Download Manager at Work   292
    Selecting files for downloading   292
    Running the Download Manager   295

Chapter 13 **Ten Best   301**

Ten best tips   302
Ten best downloads   305
Ten most frequently asked questions of
        Customer Relations   308
Ten best ways to make friends online   311
Ten best smileys   313
Best Ten-Best list   314
Everybody out!   314

Appendix A: Keywords   317

General Keywords   318
Keywords (Sorted by forum)   318
Keywords (Sorted by category)   326

Appendix B: Using the Keyboard   335

To select buttons...   335
To access a department...   335
To enter an area of a department...   335
To pull down a menu...   336
Keyboard shortcuts...   336
Scrolling text with Page Up/Page Down   336
Control keys   336
Ctrl-X   337

Appendix C: The Menu Bar   339

The Help menu   339
The File menu   339
    New (Ctrl-N)   339
    Open (Ctrl-O)   340
    Save (Ctrl-S)   340
    Save As...   340
    Disk Utilities (Ctrl-U)   340
    Print   340
    Logging   340
    Download Manager   341
    File Transfer Log   341
    Stop Incoming Text (Ctrl-X)   341
    Exit   341
The Edit menu   341
    Copy Text   342
    Cut Text   342
    Paste (Shift+Ins)   342
The Go To menu   342
    Set Up & Sign On   342
    Departments   343
    Keyword... (Ctrl-K)   343
    Directory of Services   343
    Lobby (Ctrl-L)   343
    Members' Online Support   343
    Network News   344
    Edit Go To Menu   344
The Mail menu   344
    Compose Mail (Ctrl-M)   344
    Address Memo (Ctrl-A)   345
    Read New Mail (Ctrl-R)   345
    Check Mail You've Sent   345
    Check Mail You've Read   346

Mail Gateway   346
        FAX/Paper Mail   346
        Edit Address Book   346
The Members menu   347
        Send Instant Message (Ctrl-I)   347
        Get a Member's Profile (Ctrl-G)   347
        Locate a Member Online (Ctrl-F)   348
        Search Member Directory   348
        Edit Your Online Profile   348
        Preferences   348
                General Preferences ▲ Downloading Preferences
                ▲ Font & Color Preferences
        Edit Screen Names   350
The Window menu   350

Appendix D: On the Road   351

Changing your Setup   351
Solving common connection problems   353
Using America Online on the road   354
Signing on as a Guest   354

Appendix E: Running AOL Under GeoWorks   357

Switching between applications   357
Switching to GeoWorks applications while downloading   358
Using GeoWrite documents in AOL Mail   358
Running AOL under Microsoft Windows   359
        Installing America Online into the Program Manager   360
        Modifying your America Online PIF file   360

Glossary   363

Bibliography   377

Index   381

Foreword

My interest in online services dates back to the early 1980s. I didn't know much about them then, but I knew enough to realize they had incredible potential. So when I bought my first personal computer in 1982, I decided to buy a modem and go "online." This proved to be a frustrating experience. It took several months before I had all the equipment properly configured so that I could connect for the first time.

Once online, I found the services expensive and difficult to use. Nevertheless, despite all the hassles and shortcomings, I was a true believer: I knew that a wealth of information and hundreds, maybe even thousands, of services were out there, just waiting to be tapped.

That was ten years ago. Since then, a lot has happened to make online services accessible and relevant to users with a wide range of interests and computer skills. Namely, America Online, which joined the fray in 1985, was founded with the specific mandate to create an online service that offers ease-of-use, affordability, usefulness and fun. Moreover, we set out to create a true online community: a "place" where people could meet, learn, explore, make friends and share the wonders of telecommunicating.

It worked. As a gauge of our success, America Online now serves more than 200,000 customers and is among the fastest-growing companies in the country. In fact, when we took the company public in March 1992, it was one of the hottest new stock offerings on Wall Street.

What continues to differentiate America Online from other online services, though, is our strong commitment to offering an online service that's accessible to everyone. For example, in designing America Online, we didn't want people to have to read a book in order to get connected. Ever mindful of my agonizing experience of signing on to a service a decade ago, we made the America Online software a breeze to install. As a result, people are usually up and running in less than 15 minutes.

We've done a great job of making the process of connecting to America Online hassle-free. But once you're online, what do you do? America Online has grown so quickly and offers such a diversity of information and services—from the latest sports news to classes on leading software packages—that navigating your way around AOL can be quite a challenge.

That's where *The Official America Online Tour Guide* comes in. Think of it as your personal map, highlighting key features and services that will help you get the most out of America Online.

When Ventana Press first contacted us about publishing an America Online book, we thought it was a great idea. Our members had been asking for a book for some time, so we knew the interest was there. And, we felt that by working with an independent publisher, we would end up with a better, friendlier guide to AOL than if we published our own manual.

Ventana's choice of authors Tom Lichty and Kathy Parks was inspired. Tom has written a number of popular computer books and is known for communicating information in an interesting and humorous manner. (A lot of computer books are deathly dull; Tom's are funny and engaging.) Kathy has served as a technical advisor for several computer books and has an impressive amount of expertise in the DOS world. Together they bring to this AOL tour all the insight and perspective of guides you can trust. Their objective is to take you on a tour that will help you realize the full potential of America Online.

As they lead you through AOL, pointing out the landmarks and detours, you'll soon discover that America Online is more than easy-to-use software and a collection of useful, fun services. It's a living, breathing "electronic community" populated with thousands of dynamic people who do much more than read the information that scrolls across their screens. They're active members of the America Online community; they get involved and participate—exchanging ideas, information and opinions on topics ranging from movies to entrepreneurism. We provide the basic framework; beyond that, America Online is shaped by the collective imagination and interests of its members.

As this interactive communications medium emerges, it is changing the way we inform, educate, work and play. America Online is at the forefront of this exciting revolution. Come join us as we work together to shape this growing community.

Steve Case, President, America Online, Inc.
AOL E-Mail Address: SteveCase

Starting
the Tour

As we embark on our tour of America Online, we're reminded of the story a friend related a year or two ago about his tour-guide experience:

"I'll never forget my first visit to the San Diego Zoo. The cabby who drove me there told me to take the tour bus immediately upon arrival. After that, he reasoned, I would have an idea of how the zoo was organized and know what exhibits I would want to visit. I took his advice and hopped on the bus first thing.

"The San Diego Zoo's buses are of the double-decker variety, and I sat on the top deck, baronially surveying the fauna below. The tour guide—wise San Diegan that he was—sat below, out of the sun and away from the family of miscreants who shared the top deck with me, littering it with profanity, malcontent children and various artificially sweetened beverages. I never saw the tour guide, but I heard him. In anticipation of the Odious Family Robinson, the zoo had installed a megaphonelike loudspeaker on the top deck that immersed me in tsunamis of sound capable of drowning out not only the complaints of small children, but the bellows of elephants and screeches of orangutans alike. I left the tour at the first stop, wondering if my insurance covered auditory prosthetics."

With that preamble, allow us to welcome you to the America Online Tour. We have good news: there are no orangutans, no megaphones

---

Frontispiece graphic: "Green Hornet," Macintosh Graphics Forum, America Online's Computing & Software Department. Many of the graphics appearing in this forum are in .TIF or .GIF formats, and thus available for use on PCs.

and no tickets on this tour. There's not even a bus. There are no signs warning you to keep your hands and feet inside, and artificially sweetened beverages are permitted. Though this is a tour, you can take it without ever leaving home or fraternizing with miscreants, and though we are tour guides, we're here for your singular employ. We will endeavor to inform, entertain and enlighten—forever vigilant and always *sotto voce*. When the tour has concluded, you're welcome to explore on your own, secure in your familiarity with the territory and the attractions therein.

Best of all, the territory we're about to explore is every bit as diverse and wondrous as the San Diego Zoo. It's always at your fingertips, and about the most threatening creature you will find there is a mouse.

What is America Online?

This isn't as easy a question as it seems. A term like "America Online" doesn't give many clues as to its composition. We can safely deduce its country of origin (it's in America, all right: Vienna, Virginia, to be exact—just outside Washington, DC). But what's this "online" business? The word's not even in the dictionary.

Figure 1-1: America Online nestles snugly in this office building in the Virginia forests just outside Washington, DC.

There are lots of ways to define America Online. It is, after all, a great many things. It offers abundant resources: the latest news, weather reports, stock quotes, movie and book reviews, databases to research everything from wine to hardware prices, online discussions of everything from politics to system software—even a service for reserving airline tickets, rental cars and hotel rooms.

America Online is an electronic mail service. You can exchange electronic mail with nearly anyone who uses e-mail, regardless of whether they subscribe to AOL. If they don't use e-mail, you can use AOL to send them a fax. If they don't use fax, you can use AOL to send them printed mail via the US Postal Service.

America Online is also a community. In Chapter 4, "Entertainment," we compare AOL to the small town in Oregon where we live. People are friendly there. They say hello when they pass you on the street, they invite you to their house for a chat, and they go out of their way to be of assistance. AOL does all these things: *Instant Messages* allow people who are online at the same time to say hello and hold "passing on the street" conversations; *chat rooms* are electronic "rooms"—public or private—where groups of members hold real-time conversations about subjects of their choosing; and *Members Helping Members* is a message board where members help one another with questions regarding AOL.

But how does all this happen? We can recall when the first CD players hit the market; they offered more features than a 1973 Cadillac and sounded like the Boston Symphony on the bridge of your nose.

At first we were enamored with its technology. CDs were new. Their mega bass and "surround sound" commanded our respect; their aurora borealis of indicator lights illuminated our curiosity, and their scores of controls rivaled those of the Starship Enterprise.

In the end, however, it's the music we enjoy. Mozart, Haydn, Chopin—these are our companions, and it is their company we treasure more than the gadgets.

AOL is much the same. At first it's hard to ignore the technology; but in the end AOL is people, and in the end it will be their company you will treasure the most.

We are going to pursue the definition of America Online much as one might pursue any new technological acquisition: we'll allow its technology to dazzle us; but most of all, we'll venerate AOL for its people—for the community that awaits at the end of our journey. For those who use America Online regularly, community is the reward.

It's a telecommunications service

Now there's a polysyllabic mouthful: "telecommunications." As the term is used here, telecommunications refers to two-way communications via telephone lines. A phone call, in other words, is a form of telecommunicating. Telephone lines are good for things other than phone calls. Fax machines use telephone lines to transfer documents, video phones use them to transmit pictures, and *modems* use them to transfer computer data (more about modems in Chapter 2, "Making the Connection"). We're not talking about expensive, dedicated telephone lines here—we're talking about the very same telephone lines that are already in our homes and offices.

Now we're getting somewhere. If you have a computer and someone else has a computer and you both have modems, you can use your existing telephone lines to connect your computers to one another. Once connected this way, your computers can exchange data: text, graphics, sounds, animation—even other computer programs.

Of course, you have to be at your computer and the other person has to be at his or hers—at the same time—and you both have to know how to make your computers talk to one another, and you both have to check for errors encountered in the transmission; and you're just you and the other person is not *technologically* extraordinary; and there's only so much computer data two people can exchange with one another before the whole thing gets pretty dull.

What we need is a *service* that will store our data so everybody doesn't have to be at their computers at the same time. Instead of calling your friend's computer, you just have your computer call the service and store your data there. When your friend is ready for that data, he or she can instruct his or her computer to call the service and retrieve the data.

As long as we're imagining a service, we might imagine it to automate all the electronic technicalities as well. If we do it right, the service can mediate communications between the two computers, check for errors (and fix them when necessary) and even dial the phone.

And who's to say that you and your friend should have the service all to yourselves? We can let everyone else with a computer in on it as well, regardless of the type of computer they may own. Carried to its extreme, this scenario might result in hundreds of thousands—perhaps millions—of people utilizing the service, exchanging and storing thousands of computer files. Most of this data can be public rather than private, so the exchange becomes multilateral.

Which is precisely what telecommunications services—and America Online—are: a vast network of "members," each of whom uses a computer, a modem and a telephone line to connect with a common destination—to go "online." Public and private files can be exchanged, electronic mail can be sent and received, and members who are online at the same time can "chat" in real time—they can even play online games with one another.

And what does all this cost? The economies of scale allow expenses to be distributed among the members. The only cost is a small monthly membership fee, typically less than $10. Moreover, even though America Online (AOL) is in Washington, DC, few members pay for long-distance calls. AOL has local telephone numbers in nearly every city in the contiguous United States. Even if you live in the sticks, chances are there's a local number you can call, or one that's a "short" long-distance call away.

It's one big Thunder-Lizard computer

Another way of defining America Online is by describing its hardware. Simultaneously coordinating thousands of phone calls and storing tens of thousands of files requires one Thunder Lizard of a computer. No little Stegosaurus will do. We're talking T-Rex here, a beastie who relocates continents whenever he gets the urge to scratch an itch. Forget prefixes like kilo and mega. Think giga and googol. When they turn on the power to this thing, lights dim along the entire Eastern seaboard.

The Stratus

We hate to disappoint you, but miniaturization has dwarfed America Online just as it has dwarfed Newton, Apple's hand-held personal digital assistant. AOL's computer is more of a field mouse than a Thunder Lizard. It's not a single computer either: when we last were there, AOL was using nine computers, each about the size of Jay Leno on a motorcycle. These computers (see Figure 1-2), manufactured by the Stratus Corporation in Marlboro, MA, are collectively and affectionately (if one ever feels affection for nine Jay Leno-sized computers) referred to as "The Stratus" by those who are Way Cool around AOL.

More than anything else, the Stratus is remarkable for its reliability. Everything—memory, disk storage, even processors—is redundant. All data are stored twice. If the primary unit hiccups, the secondary unit covers. Diesel generators are on perpetual standby in case there's a power failure. AOL even has a contract with diesel-oil suppliers to keep its tanks filled. (We're not making this up, honest.) The banking industry uses Stratus computers for the same reason America Online does: these things simply don't fail.

Figure 1-2:
A number of individual computers team up to form "The Stratus," the mechanical heart of AOL. Those are 3 1/2" disk boxes atop the unit in the foreground.

Common carriers

If you wanted to send a package across the country, you could probably hop in your car and drive it there yourself. Compared to the alternatives, it would be a perilous journey and would cost a fortune.

More likely, you'd hire a *common carrier*—a service like UPS or Federal Express—to deliver the package for you. For a fraction of what it would cost you to do the job yourself, common carriers can do it more reliably, less expensively and much more conveniently.

For much the same reason, America Online hires common carriers to deliver goods to its members. And typical of AOL, it hires multiple common carriers to ensure reliability. SprintNet, a service of US Sprint, is the common carrier that AOL most often uses in the United States. Datapac—a subsidiary of Bell Canada—serves Canadian members. These common carriers offer "nodes"—local telephone numbers—in most cities in North America. They charge AOL for phone calls (placed or received) just as Federal Express would charge you to deliver a package.

Again the economies of scale operate to our advantage. Thousands of clients use these long-distance providers, of which AOL is only one. Chances are when you're not using one of your local nodes, some corporate computer is, phoning data to a parent mainframe in New

Figure 1-3: SprintNet's equipment bay at America Online headquarters leaves plenty of room for expansion. This cabinet is about the size of a refrigerator.

Jersey or Chicago. The cost of this service is so insignificant that it's covered by your membership. No matter how many hours you're online per month, AOL never charges extra for the call. Indeed, the only connect charges are to those members who have to make a long-distance call to reach a node, which isn't very often.

It's software installed in your computer

Conceptualizing America Online as nodes and mainframe computers isn't very comforting. AOL is much more parochial than that. For many of us, AOL is software in our PCs—software that arrived on that disk provided from AOL or included in the AOL Membership Kit.

Figure 1-4:
America Online's
logo appears
whenever we run
the software
installed on our
computer.

This is more like it. The software you use on your computer to sign on to AOL more accurately represents the personality of the service than anything we've discussed so far. It communicates in plain English, it's resplendent with windows and icons, and it automates those tasks and procedures that formerly were responsible for excluding most semi-normal people from using an online service.

Here's what we mean. Nearly every telecommunications program assumes you know how to set certain arcane but necessary attributes and protocols like data bits, stop bits, parity or flow. Frankly, though we've both used telecommunications software for years and though we've adjusted our data bits and parity, neither of us really has any idea what they are, and we've always been kind of nervous about making changes in the dark like that. America Online, on the other hand, uses its own custom software at both ends of the line. Once you install the software on your computer (a simple process we describe in the next chapter), all the technicalities are coordinated by the Stratus and your PC. They simply talk things over and make adjustments as they're required. This is as it should be. People should never be asked to do these things. That's why we have machines.

Figure 1-5: America Online's highly advanced software automatically configures itself to your PC and modem settings. Happiness is never having to worry about data bits, flow control or parity.

We're getting closer to the mark. The phrase "user friendly" is properly used to describe this service. America Online's PC software is predictable and comfortable. If you are familiar with the software concept of windows, you'll feel right at home. And, if you're using the GeoWorks interface, you *are* at home. If all these environments are new to you, don't despair. The reason they're so popular is their ease of use. You'll find America Online very enticing.

Amazingly, the software is self-configuring. Whenever you sign on, a behind-the-scenes dialog transpires between your PC and the Stratus. In effect, your PC says, "Hey Stratus! Are there any new features I should know about?" If there are, your PC will request those features from the Stratus and add them to its version of the local software (the copy of America Online that resides on your hard drive). This feature is significant: at any point, AOL can add features to the service and incorporate them immediately. No new software releases have to be sent out. No interminable decimal places have to be added to the version number. That convenience means AOL's software development crew can add features whenever they please. No disk duplication and mass mailings are required. Upgrade costs to you are nonexistent, and they hardly amount to anything at AOL either. AOL's programmers operate in an environment that encourages, rather than stifles, improvement. Perhaps best of all, you don't have to lift a finger to take advantage of whatever changes or additions AOL makes to its service. You just sign on as usual and they're immediately available to you.

Another unique aspect of the AOL software is its interface and communication strategy. Though it's highly graphical, none of those graphical elements are transferred to your PC online. Transferring graphics online takes time—much more than transferring text, for instance—and doing so would make the service seem as sluggish as a hound in July. Instead, all of AOL's graphical components are stored on your hard disk. Only text is transferred. This makes America Online much faster than other graphically oriented services, and saves you money in connect-time charges.

The point is this: AOL is one of the most advanced and aggressive telecommunications services to which you can subscribe. It's growing daily and it contains the features necessary to accommodate that growth. The software features we have described reflect a progressive attitude, and that attitude is a better way of defining America Online.

It's a resource

News, sports, weather—sure, you can get them on radio and television, but not necessarily when you need or want them. You can get them in a newspaper too, but it's going to cost the environment a tree or two, the pictures are fuzzy, and about all you can do with a newspaper after you've read it is throw it away (consult the Environmental Forum—

described in Chapter 6, "Lifestyles & Interests"—for recycling information). America Online offers the news, sports and weather as well, available at your convenience and without sacrificing any trees. It's in electronic form too, so you can file it, search it and include it in documents of your own.

This past spring, we kept up with the Perot (non) candidacy in the News & Finance Department (discussed in Chapter 5), tracked the meager investments in our portfolios (also discussed in Chapter 5) and monitored a devastating series of earthquakes in California. We researched the purchase of a new hard disk for a computer in the Computing & Software Department (discussed in Chapter 7) and booked both airplane and auto rentals for a trip to the Catskills this fall using EAASY SABRE (discussed in Chapter 8, "Travel & Shopping").

We're constantly searching the online video reviews before we rent a tape (the Entertainment Department is discussed in Chapter 4), and we check Wine & Dine Online for recommendations before we hazard the racks of wines at the shop down the street. Past issues of *PC World* and *National Geographic* are online for review, as is *Compton's Encyclopedia*.

We recently sold an old car (after consulting AutoVantage, described in Chapter 8, "Travel & Shopping") and bought a new hard disk (using the Comp-u-Store, also described in Chapter 8). As professional members of the desktop publishing community, we're constantly collecting graphics (AOL has thousands of files online—described in Chapter 7), fonts and utilities.

In other words, you could describe America Online as a resource of almost infinite potential. You don't have to drive anywhere to use it, it's perpetually maintained and updated, and it's all electronic— available for any use you can imagine. Many members find the resource potential alone to be ample justification for signing on to America Online, but to limit your participation this way would be a disservice to AOL and to yourself. Above all, America Online is people: friends, associates, consultants—even lovers. It's a resource all right, but it's also a community, and therein lies its greatest value.

Figure 1-6: Just a few of the thousands of graphics available in AOL's file libraries. ("Lise2" by David Palermo; "Dragonfly" from the Graphics Forum; and "High-Tech Laurel & Hardy" by Lou Moccia.)

A Graphics Gold Mine

It's a community

We've taken the easy way out. Yes, AOL is a telecommunications service. Yes, it's the Stratus. Yes, it's software in your PC, and yes, it's a resource. But that's like saying that Christmas is just another day of the year. There's much more to it than that. Christmas is reverence and good things; but for many of us, Christmas means people: family, friends and community. This is what really defines America Online: its people. AOL is really a *community*. One dictionary defines community as, "A social group sharing common characteristics or interests," and that is no doubt the best definition we can imagine for America Online.

As members, we have common interests, we all have computers, and we love to share. *That's* what AOL is all about. After a few weeks, the novelty of tele-connected computers and graphical images wears off. After a few weeks, we stop wondering about the Stratus and data bits. After a few weeks, we all discover the true soul of America Online, and that soul is its people.

Steve Case

We've never asked AOL President Steve Case where he lives. It would be surprising and disappointing to learn that he doesn't live in the suburbs: Steve Case is a character study of the suburban next-door neighbor. He's a clean-cut, casual guy. He wears rumpled chinos, cotton sportshirts and no tie. He looks as if he's about to mow the lawn. He took us to lunch at the Ringmaster's Pub in the Barnum and Bailey building next door. (AOL is next door to the world headquarters of the Ringling Brothers Circus.) We had iced tea and sandwiches. That's Steve's idea of a business lunch.

Steve's personality is reflected everywhere at AOL. We've never seen a necktie or a closed office door during our visits there. More important, the people there reflect the spirit of community. Titles are never used. No one wears ID badges, not even guests. Everyone calls everyone else by their first name. Conferences happen in hallways.

Steve's eyes sparkle when the conversation turns to community. He sends electronic mail to every new member and hopes for a reply. He's the president of the company, yet he spends as much time conversing with members as he does with his staff. Everyone calls him Steve.

With Steve Case steering the ship, AOL considers itself, foremost, a community. All corporate decisions are based on that concept; every change benefits the community. That's the way Steve wants it to be. If he could have his way, he'd have us all out to Virginia for a barbecue on the greens. You'd know who he was the moment you walked in: he'd be the one turning burgers on the grill. One couldn't ask for a better neighbor.

When we first signed on to write this book, community was the last thing on our minds. We've been telecommunicators for years. We thought we'd seen it all. Now, however, we both spend as much of our online time corresponding with friends—new friends in every part of the country—as we do conducting research. In Chapter 11 ("Electronic Mail"), we admit to getting despondent if we don't hear a musical double-beep notifying us that we have mail when the Welcome screen comes up. Throughout this book, we'll offer tips on making friends online; follow these tips, and you'll become a part of this community.

You really couldn't do much better.

How to use this book

This book serves two purposes: 1) it's the official documentation for America Online; and 2) it's a guidebook for the explorer. As documentation, the book should be thoroughly indexed, strictly organized and pithy. As a guide, the book should offer entertainment, insight and advice. These are somewhat disparate, but not necessarily incompatible goals for such a book.

Fortunately, the people at AOL have an altruistic attitude toward the documentation for their service. This is a book, not a manual. We're independent authors, not staff technical writers. And America Online chose a traditional publisher—Ventana Press—to produce and distribute this book; it's not an AOL production. All of this means that we have the autonomy and elbow room to explore the subject with you independently, thoroughly and candidly. The people at America Online are to be commended for their courage in choosing this path. It could be perilous. Confidence in their product, however, emboldens them, and rightfully so.

How to use this book as documentation

As you no doubt already know, documentation can be dull. Few people take a software manual to the hammock for a lazy afternoon of reading. The universe of technical documentation is far from the universe America Online inhabits. AOL is diverse, abstract and personable— hardly documentation material. Nonetheless, we've included a number of organizational and reference tools to serve the documentation need.

Finding answers

We want you to be able to turn to this book whenever you have a question about America Online. We want you to be able to find that answer with a minimum of effort, no matter how many different places the subject may appear in the book. Pursuant to that, a number of tools are at your disposal:

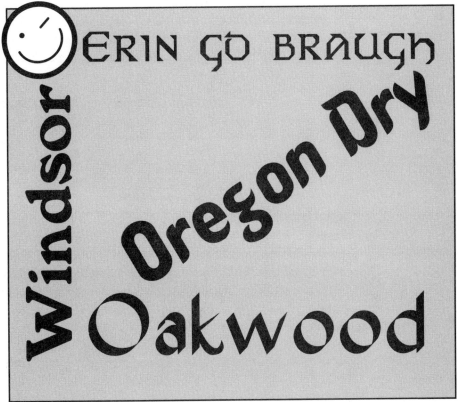

Figure 1-7:
A quintet of fonts, all downloaded from the Desktop Publishing Forum. At top, "Eire" is by Paul Glomski, "Oregon Dry" is by Pat Snyder, Jim Pearson's ""Oakwood ProFont" is particularly elegant, Brian Hendrix's "Windsor" is a traditional, Old World font, and Jonathan Macagba's "Smiley Face" is great for illuminating electronic mail. Most are shareware and cost about $5 each.

- The *table of contents* lists titles, section heads and subheads for every chapter. When you need information on a specific subject, turn first to the table of contents. Nine times out of ten, it will be all you need.

- A thorough *index* appears at the end of the book, with references to subjects, procedures and departments. If the subject you're after doesn't appear in the table of contents, turn to the index.

- A listing of primary *keywords* is the first appendix item. Keywords are the interstate highway system at AOL. If you want to get somewhere in a hurry, use a keyword. As you discover places that appeal to you, grab your yellow pen and highlight the keyword corresponding to that location. Eventually, you'll commit a number of keywords to memory (or place them on your Go To menu, described in Chapter 6, "Lifestyles & Interests"), and the keyword appendix will have served its purpose.

A *listing of keyboard control combinations* follows the listing of keywords. Few people memorize every Control-key combination for every program they use, but most people memorize some. The text of this manual places emphasis on execution of commands via the mouse. However, if you're an occasional (or frequent) user of Control keys, or if you're not a mouse user at all, refer to this section of the book.

A *glossary* of terms used in the book is the last appendix item. The glossary is especially thorough in its inclusion of telecommunications terminology. We may never define "parity" in the text—with AOL, you never have to bother with it—but we want you to be able to find out what it means if you're curious.

Departmental listings

Starting with Chapter 4 ("Entertainment"), each chapter explores a department available online at AOL. If Entertainment is your game (forgive the pun), read Chapter 4. If you're interested in the Computing & Software Department, read Chapter 7. Because America Online is infinitely too large and diverse to explore these departments thoroughly, we've attempted to capture the personality of each department with glimpses into a few areas of particular interest. Wherever possible, we offer insight into the department's features: where to find the really good stuff.

Subject listings

Departments are also vehicles for exploring specific subject areas. In Chapter 6, "Lifestyles & Interests," we introduce the concept of the forum; in Chapter 7, "Computing & Software," we explore the subject of downloading. These can be complex subjects, and to document them without some relief could be as dry as white bread. Instead, we've made a sandwich of each technical subject, flavoring the presentation with the diversity of a department.

This, we hope, will make for more effective documentation: if you're enjoying yourself, you'll learn more about the subject. Associating subjects with departments also provides a context that's practical rather than theoretical; learning by doing is always more effective than listening to a lecture.

A documentation strategy
Our personal strategy for the use of software documentation is to first spend a half-hour browsing. With no specific need and in no particular order, thumb through the manual, trying to get a feeling for its contents and organization. Look for organizational signposts (chapter titles, icons, sidebars, heads and subheads); peek at the index; read a paragraph or two from sections that strike your fancy. This kind of random orientation can instill confidence and help you orient your perspective.

If you're a new member and haven't yet installed the software or signed on, read Chapter 2, "Making the Connection," next. It's a "handholder." Every step of the installation and initial sign-on process is documented there, including a suggested initial online session.

From then on—perhaps once a week—pick a department and tour it with us at your own pace. While we're there, we'll explore a procedural subject as well as the department itself. Each chapter should take about an hour. When we're finished, you'll not only be familiar with the department, you'll learn about a feature that will make your online experience more productive and fun.

How to use this book as a book
We would be flattered if you would read this book for the pleasure of it. As we spend time on America Online, we're both struck by its diversity. One night you can visit the Desktop Publishing Forum for some fonts you need. The next night you can take a class at the Online Campus (which we explore in Chapter 9, "Learning & Reference"). Online visits are often unstructured. Your rhythm is syncopated and your interests wander.

We have tried to organize this book in much the same fashion. We have liberally splashed gobbets of material throughout the book, often with no other intention in mind than to relieve the page of textual tedium. We want your thoughts to wander, we want to pique your curiosity, we want to delight and provoke and intrigue you. That's what AOL does: it discourages linearity and encourages randomness. It demands your regard and rewards your return.

We hope this book does the same.

Figure 1-8: A video review, the title screen for the Online Gaming Forums and a daily horoscope. This is just a tiny slice of the spectrum of opportunity that awaits you on America Online.

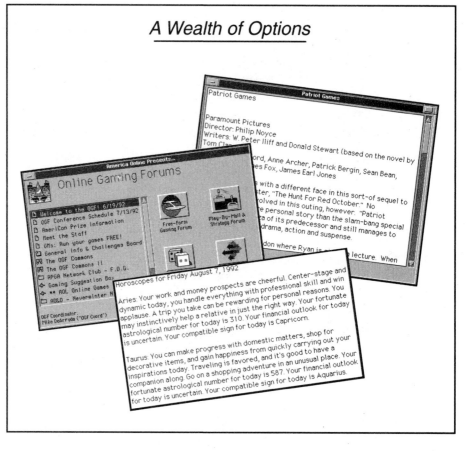

Coming up

Are you comfortable? Our journey is about to begin. Reach into that pocket in the seat in front of you and pull out the program. Here's where we're about to go:

🜂 Chapter 2, "Making the Connection," walks you through the set up and initial sign-on process. Just as it relieves you from worrying about the complexities of most of the other technical aspects of telecommunications, America Online automates most of the process of getting started as well. So Chapter 2 is one of the shortest chapters in the book. You'll be up and running in no time.

🜂 Chapter 3, "Online Help & the Members," serves as an introduction to the AOL software. We'll pull down menus and peek at dialog boxes. We'll do most of this off-line, but you'll need your PC handy. Eventually we'll sign on, visit the Lobby and get to know an online guide. They're usually there, waiting to help. We'll examine the Member Directory and see if we can make a friend.

🜂 Chapter 4, "Entertainment," is simply for the fun of it. This will be our first visit to one of AOL's seven departments. We'll read a few movie reviews, laugh at a few jokes and play a game or two.

🜂 Chapter 5 takes us to the News & Finance Department. There, we'll peruse *USA Today*, start our portfolio of investments (cash optional) and look at tomorrow's weather. We'll keep a log of our visit for review later, when we're off-line and rested.

🜂 Chapter 6, "Lifestyles & Interests," explores America Online's clubs. There are more than 40 of them, so we'll only visit a few. Perhaps we'll try Wine & Dine Online, the Environmental and Star Trek Forums and Real Estate Online. We'll learn about forums, read a few messages and post one of our own.

🜂 Chapter 7 goes for the heart: the Computing & Software Department. We'll look over *PC World* magazine, catch up on the latest computing news and opinion, and solicit some assistance from a software vendor. Along the way, we'll explore the process of downloading files. We'll download a few for ourselves, decompress those that require it and perhaps upload a file in return.

🜂 In Chapter 8 we'll plan a dream vacation in the Travel & Shopping Department. Perhaps we'll buy or sell a car—or at least find out what one's worth. While we're in a spending mood, we'll visit the Comp-u-Store and pump up our PCs with some nifty toys.

🜂 Chapter 9 explores the Learning & Reference Department. *Compton's Encyclopedia* is here, of course, but so is the Online Campus. Perhaps we'll enroll in a class or check out *National Geographic* magazine.

🜂 Chapter 10 lightens the load with the People Connection. We'll wipe the sweat from our palms, walk into the Lobby and say hello. We'll check out a few of America Online's "chat rooms" and see who we can find there. Perhaps we'll visit the Center Stage and participate in a game show.

- Chapter 11 teaches you everything you need to know to master AOL's electronic mail feature. We'll put some names into our Address Book, send (and receive) some mail, attach a file to be uploaded to a friend and delve into the international service that allows AOL users to send and receive e-mail worldwide.

- Chapter 12 explores the Download Manager. This is the heavy-weight stuff, but it's also some of the best telecommunications software ever offered. Even if you never use it, you've got to read this chapter just to appreciate one of AOL's high-end features.

- Chapter 13 offers our ten-best lists—the ten best AOL secrets, the ten most frequently asked questions of the AOL customer support team, the ten best files for downloading—that kind of thing. You'll be among the online illuminati once you've finished this chapter.

- Five appendices conclude the book. "On the Road" teaches you how to change access numbers and baud rates. It's full of good information for travellers who want to access AOL away from home. A keyword listing offers warp-speed navigation through the AOL universe. The keyboard appendix helps you work with AOL using your keyboard, instead of or in addition to your mouse. Another appendix guides you through the AOL menu bar. And the final one explores using AOL under GeoWorks or Windows.

- The glossary promises to define all those nerdy words that have become requisite adjuncts to the telecommunications lexicon.

You'd better fasten your seat belt. Sometimes it gets a little bumpy, and when we get to talking we forget to steer—hand gestures and all that, you know. Don't worry: we haven't lost a passenger yet. Have your camera ready, there's lots of stuff to see. And relax. Smile a bit. You're five years old again and Christmas morning is only a turn of the page away.... Next

Making the Connection

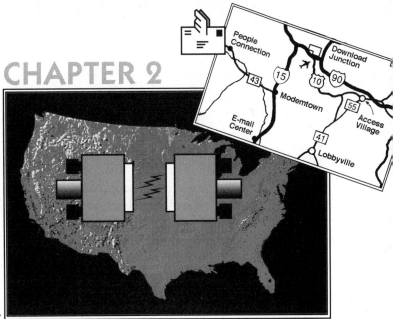

I f you have never used America Online—if you have never even installed the software—this chapter's for you. It's written for the agnostic, the novice—those who hold disks in their sweaty palms and wonder if they are stalwart enough to connect their PC to the outside world.

For most of us, computers are autonomous and independent. The only external device we've ever encountered is a printer. Our dialog with the computer has always been a singular one—isolated and solitary. We may personify our computers. We may give them names and even voices, and we may think of their error messages and dialog boxes as "communication," but we know better.

Computers don't think. Computers don't respond with imagination or indignation or intelligence. There are no threats to us here. Connecting to America Online will put human intelligence at the other end of the line. AOL isn't just a computer in Virginia named "The Stratus," it's people, and people online expect a dialog. People respond, with innovation and humor. This is not the isolation we have come to expect of our PC.

So far, our ordered universe has been predictable and familiar. Why mess with it?

Because there's more to life, that's why. Think of your first car, your first love, your first child. Each was shrouded in anxiety, and each was resplendent with reward. We're talking about discovery here, and

Frontispiece terrain map by Gail P. Thelin and Richard J. Pike, published by the US Geological Survey. Superimposed are the connector icons from the AOL sign-on screen. The terrain map is online. Use the keywords: File Search; search with the criteria "geological survey."

while the AOL opportunity may not rank with love and birth, it's an opportunity one should not deny.

Before you read any further, we want you to understand that this chapter describes the process of installing the America Online software and making the first connection with AOL. If you already have an established AOL account, then you probably won't need to read much of this chapter. Feel free to skim or skip ahead to another part of the tour—we'll catch up with you soon.

Things you'll need

Let's take inventory here. There are a few things you need before you can connect with America Online. No doubt, you already have them, but let's be sure.

The computer

You need a PC, of course. Almost any DOS-based PC will do—an XT or better. That's one of the benefits of telecommunications: nearly any computer is adequate. A friend of ours—and an avid America Online user—bought his computer in 1984. It's a bandaged relic, but it works.

You will need 512k of RAM (Random Access Memory); a hard disk with a couple of megabytes of free space; a 3.5" floppy drive (see the back of this book for details on obtaining 5.25" diskettes); EGA, VGA, SVGA or Hercules video adapter card and monitor (although you should really use a VGA monitor or better to get the most from the service's graphical interface); MS-DOS or PC-DOS 2.0 or higher; and a LogiTech, Microsoft or Mouse Systems compatible mouse—that's about it.

As we write this, America Online communicates at 2400 baud. Don't worry about the semantics: 2400 baud translates to a transfer rate of about a page of text every 20 seconds. It's a lot slower than your average hard disk, which could probably save this entire chapter in just a few seconds. But, it's not your computer (or the Stratus) that's slowing things down. The bottleneck is the telephone system.

While telephones are well suited for voice communication, no one ever envisioned using them for data communication, at least not 60 years ago when the Bell system was first designed. Even the lowliest PC is perhaps a hundred times faster than telephone lines—therefore an XT or better will do. (AOL may have upgraded its service to 9600 baud by the time you read this. Even if it has, the bottleneck will still be the phone lines: even 9600 baud is slower than an XT.)

The telephone line

Speaking of telephone lines, you need one of those, too. Your standard residential phone line is fine. A multiline business telephone may be more of a challenge. What's really important is that your telephone plugs into a modular telephone jack (called an RJ-11 jack by industry know-it-alls), which is a square hole with quarter-inch dimensions.

Whenever you're online, your telephone is out of commission. It's as if someone is on an extension phone, except that you'll *never* want to eavesdrop on an AOL session. The screeching sound that modems make when communicating with each other is about as pleasant as fingernails on a blackboard—and about as intelligible. In addition, picking up an extension when someone is online can easily garble modem communications or corrupt file transfers, so notify anyone who might accidentally interfere with your call before you go online.

The starter kit

AOL starter kits come in a number of forms, but they all have two things in common: they include a disk and a certificate. The certificate (it may just be a label) contains a temporary account number and a temporary password. Find the disk, the account number and the password, and set them by your PC. Keep this book nearby as well.

Make a copy of the America Online disk right now. It's not copy-protected: standard disk-copying routines work just fine. Your DOS manual contains the necessary instructions for copying a floppy, if you don't already know how. Put the original AOL disk away somewhere safe. You never know when you might need it again.

The modem

A modem (short for *modulator/demodulator*) is a device that converts computer data into audible tones that the telephone system can understand. Modems are required at both ends of the line: the Stratus has one, too.

Modems are rated according to their data-transmission speed. If you're shopping for a modem, get one rated at 2400 baud (or faster, if you're looking toward the future). Though you'll find 1200-baud modems for less money, there isn't much of a price difference, and the higher speed will pay for itself soon enough.

Baud rates

The term *baud rate* means bits of data per second. Since it takes eight bits to make a byte, a baud rate of 2400 translates to about 300 bytes per second. A byte is the amount of data required to describe a single character of text. In other words, a baud rate of 2400 should transmit 300 characters—about five lines—of text per second.

Alas, the world is an imperfect place—especially the world of phone lines. If static or interference of any kind occurs on the line, data transmission is garbled. And even one misplaced bit could destroy the integrity of an entire file. To address the problem, AOL uses error-checking methods to validate the integrity of received data. In plain English, this means that the Stratus sends a packet of information (a couple of seconds' worth) to your PC, then waits for the PC to say, "I got that!" before it sends the next packet. Validation like this means things run a little slower than they would without validation, but it's necessary. We're probably down to 200 characters per second once we factor in the time it takes to accommodate data validation.

Then there's noise. You've heard it: static on the line. If you think it interferes with voice communication, it's murder on data. Often your PC says, "That packet was no good. Send it again," and the Stratus complies. The reliability of any particular telephone connection is capricious. Some are better than others. Noise, however, is a definite factor, and packets have to be re-sent once in a while. Now we're probably down to 150 characters per second—a little over two lines of text at 2400 baud.

In other words, a 2400-baud modem isn't twice as fast as a 1200-baud model. Since the lower baud rate is more reliable, fewer packets have to be sent again. A 1200-baud modem can probably transmit or receive about 100 characters per second—about 65 percent the speed of a 2400-baud modem under the same conditions.

Though 2400-baud modems are not twice as fast as 1200-baud modems, they are not twice the price either. Often, the difference is $25 or so. For $25, the increase in performance is worth the money.

Although many new PCs are being shipped with internal modems, we prefer external modems with speakers and lights. A speaker lets you hear the phone being dialed and the modem at the other end answering—very reassuring stuff. At that point—when the connection is established—most modem speakers become silent so you don't have to listen to the screeching sound of two computers talking to each other. Most external modems have several lights on them, and while we don't claim to understand most of them, they look important. The one marked "RD" (receiving data) is worth watching when you're downloading a file (we discuss downloading in Chapter 7, "Computing & Software"). It should stay on almost continuously. If, during a download, your "RD" light is off more often than it's on, you've got a noisy phone line or the system is extremely busy. Whatever the cause, it's best to halt the download (AOL always leaves a Cancel Transfer button on the screen for that purpose) and resume it another time. That's why we advise buying a modem with lights: if you don't have them, how can you tell what's going on?

Your modem needs power of some kind. Some modems get it from the computer and a few others use batteries; but most use AC power and plug into the wall. Be sure an electrical socket is available.

Most important, be sure you have the proper cables. You need two: one to connect the modem to the PC and another to connect the modem to the phone jack. One end of the modem-to-PC cable plugs into a serial port on the back of your PC (that's the male port with 9 or 25 pins), and the other end of that cable plugs into the modem. Some modems aren't sold with these cables, so be sure you have one before you leave the store, and check your PC before you go modem shopping so you know whether your serial port has 9 or 25 pins.

You also need a cable to connect the modem to the phone jack. Most modems come with these, but they rarely exceed six feet. If your phone isn't near your computer, get an extension cable. Again, phone, electronics and hardware stores carry modular extension cables. They're standard equipment and are inexpensive.

It's less complicated if the modem has a jack for your phone. In that case, you can plug the modem into the phone jack, then plug the phone into the modem. The jacks on the back of the modem should be marked for this.

Most modems are marked "line" or "wall" and "phone." Plug the phone line from the wall into your modem at the jack marked "line"— plug your phone into the "phone" jack. If there are no markings, you have a 50 percent chance of getting it right on your first guess. If things don't work right, simply reverse the lines, plugging them into opposite jacks on your modem. Your phone will work, even if power to the modem is off. If no jack is offered for the phone, you'll need a splitter (see the sidebar on the next page).

Splitters

Assuming your modem only has a single jack and you want to continue using your phone as well as your modem, you may also want to invest in a modular "splitter," which plugs into the phone jack on your wall, making two jacks out of one. You then plug your phone into one of the splitter's jacks and your modem into the other. Plugging both devices into the same jack won't interfere with everyday telephone communications; incoming calls will continue to go to your phone, just as they did before.

You should be able to find a splitter at phone, electronics or hardware stores for less than $3.

If all this sounds like a lot of wires to keep track of and you have trouble plugging in a toaster, don't worry. Most modems come with good instructions, and the components are such that you can't connect anything backwards. Just follow the instructions and you'll be all right.

The money

Before you sign on to AOL for the first time, there's something else you'll need: money. AOL wants to know how you plan to pay the balance on your account each month. Cash won't do. Instead, you can provide a credit card number: VISA, MasterCard, Discover Card or American Express are all acceptable. Or, have your checkbook handy: you can make arrangements so that your bank can make your payments to AOL directly from your checking account.

The screen name

We're almost ready, but right now we want you to get all other thoughts out of your mind and decide what you want to call yourself. Every AOL member has a unique screen name. Screen names are how AOL tells us apart. You must have one and it has to be different from everybody else's.

A screen name must be three to ten characters in length—letters, spaces or numbers. Hundreds of thousands of people use America Online, and they all have screen names of ten or fewer characters. Ten isn't many characters; chances are the screen name you want most is taken. Have a number of alternates ready ahead of time, and prepare for disappointment. Hardly anyone ever gets his or her first choice.

There's no going back, by the way. Once AOL accepts your initial screen name, it's yours as long as you remain a member. Though your account can have as many as five screen names (to accommodate other people in your family or your alter egos), your initial screen name is the one AOL uses to establish your identity. For this reason, your initial screen name can't be changed. Be prepared with a zinger (and a half-dozen alternates), or AOL will assign you something like TomLi5437, and you'll forever be known by that name. People have a hard time relating to a name like that.

MajorTom & CoolKath

Tom worked his way through college as a traffic reporter for an Oregon radio station. He was both reporter and pilot. It was a great job: perfect hours for a student, easy work and unlimited access to a flashy plane. It didn't pay much, but somehow that wasn't important—not in the halcyon days of bachelorhood.

David Bowie was an ascending force on the music scene in those days. Impertinent, perhaps—a little too androgynous and scandalous for the conservative element of the Nixon era—but definitely a hit-maker. The station played Bowie, and on Tom's first day, the morning-show disk jockey switched on his microphone and hailed "Ground Control to Major Tom"—a line from Bowie's *Space Oddity*—to get Tom's attention. The name stuck. He was known as Major Tom from then on.

When the time came for Tom to pick his AOL screen name, it suggested TomLi5437 and he balked. "How about just plain Tom?" he asked. "It's in use," said the Stratus. He tried four others and the Stratus continued to remind him of his lack of imagination. In desperation, he tried MajorTom, and the Stratus accepted it. Once an initial screen name is accepted, there's no going back. He's MajorTom on AOL now, and will be forever more.

Kathy's screen name, "CoolKath," comes with far less romanticism. She just picked it out of the air on the first try and it worked.

The password

Oh yes, you need a password. Without a password, anyone knowing your screen name can log on using that name and have a heyday on your nickel. Passwords must be from four to eight characters in length, and any combination of letters or numbers is acceptable. You're asked for your password every time you sign on, so choose something easy for you to remember—something that's not a finger-twister to type. It should be different from your screen name, phone number, address or real name—something no one else would ever guess, even if they know you well.

A case for elaborate passwords

In his book *The Cuckoo's Egg*, Cliff Stoll describes computer hackers' methods for breaking passwords. Since most computers already have a dictionary on disk—all spelling checkers use dictionaries—the hackers simply program their computers to try every word in the dictionary as a password. It sounds laborious, but computers don't mind.

In other words, we're making a case for elaborate passwords here. Don't make it personal, don't write it down, and select something that's not in a dictionary. That'll foil the rascals.

Installing the software

Finally, we're ready to get our hands dirty. Installing the America Online software is a straightforward process, since an installation program does all the work for you.

- Again, be sure you have at least 2 Mb of space available on your hard disk, and at least 512k of memory. Your DOS manual will tell you how to check on these things if you don't know how.

- Assuming you made a copy of the America Online disk, insert that copy into your floppy disk drive. (The original AOL disk works just as well, but making—and using—a copy is just SPP: standard paranoid procedure.)

- Change to the desired drive (at the DOS prompt, type "a:" or "b:" without the quotes and press Enter).

- Type "install" without the quotes and press Enter.

- A greeting screen appears, identifying the installation program (see Figure 2-1). It simply states that installation will now begin. It also lists the Customer Relations phone numbers for technical assistance. Press Enter to continue.

Figure 2-1: The installation greeting screen appears as soon as the install program is running.

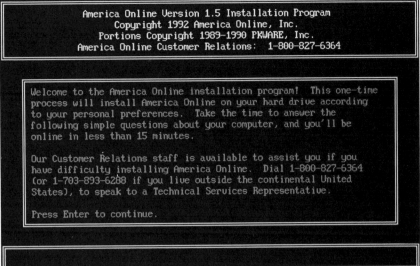

```
America Online Version 1.5 Installation Program
        Copyright 1992 America Online, Inc.
   Portions Copyright 1989-1990 PKWARE, Inc.
America Online Customer Relations:  1-800-827-6364


Welcome to the America Online installation program!  This one-time
process will install America Online on your hard drive according
to your personal preferences.  Take the time to answer the
following simple questions about your computer, and you'll be
online in less than 15 minutes.

Our Customer Relations staff is available to assist you if you
have difficulty installing America Online.  Dial 1-800-827-6364
(or 1-703-893-6288 if you live outside the continental United
States), to speak to a Technical Services Representative.

Press Enter to continue.
```

During the installation process, you will encounter questions to answer. The up and down arrow keys highlight responses, the Enter key makes the selection. The Escape key can be pressed at any time to return to the first screen.

You are now asked if you have ever installed America Online before on your computer. The answer is probably no, so highlight "No" and press the Enter key.

You are next asked if you have GeoWorks Ensemble on your hard drive. (GeoWorks Ensemble is a graphical environment that interfaces programs like America Online. AOL can be run under Geo-Works Ensemble or straight from DOS. Using GeoWorks is optional because AOL includes a special version of GeoWorks designed to be used specifically with AOL.) If you are using Ensemble 1.2 or greater, you should choose Yes. Under every other condition, choose No. Answer appropriately and continue. (For more information about running AOL under GeoWorks, see Appendix E.)

If you answered Yes to the GeoWorks Ensemble question, you are then given the choice of installing AOL as a GeoWorks application or as a stand-alone DOS application. (This book is written from the standpoint that AOL is a stand-alone application.) The screen describes differences when choosing one over the other.

The installation program now scans for hard drives in your computer that have adequate space for the AOL program and prompts you to enter the destination drive where you want the America Online files to be copied. If more than one hard drive/partition is listed, select the destination for the AOL files and press Enter (see Figure 2-2).

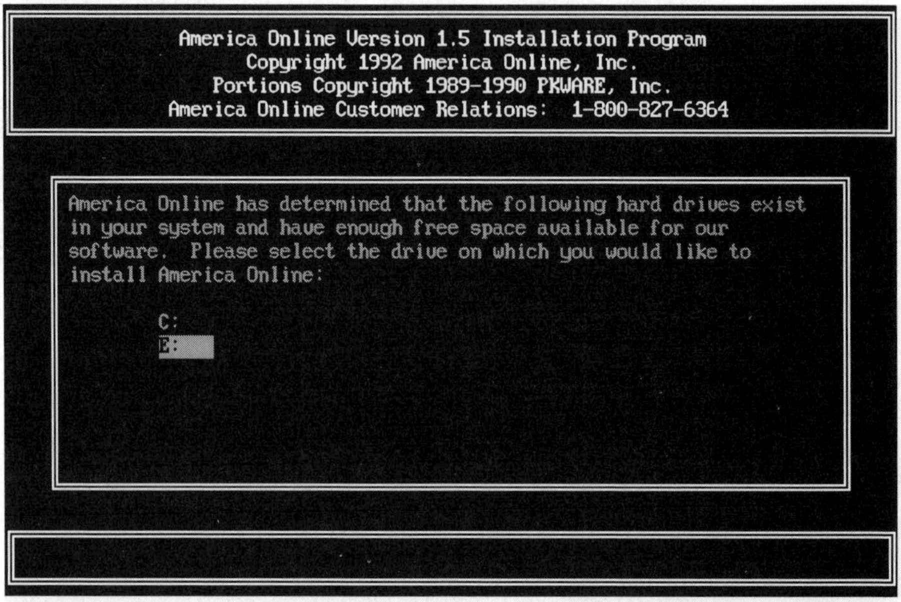

Figure 2-2: At this screen, indicate the drive where you want to install the America Online program files.

```
America Online Version 1.5 Installation Program
          Copyright 1992 America Online, Inc.
      Portions Copyright 1989-1990 PKWARE, Inc.
  America Online Customer Relations:  1-800-827-6364



  America Online has determined that the following hard drives exist
  in your system and have enough free space available for our
  software.  Please select the drive on which you would like to
  install America Online:

        C:
        D:
```

Once the drive is chosen, you are prompted to enter the desired subdirectory name where America Online will be installed. You may accept the default directory name (AOL) by pressing Enter (see Figure 2-3). If you choose to load the program as a GeoWorks application, the question refers to the location of GeoWorks on your computer. Respond here as appropriate. You may enter another name for the AOL directory by deleting the default name and typing the new name. If the subdirectory box is left empty, the program will install America Online into the default directory, which is AOL. If a subdirectory with that name already exists, you must choose another name.

Figure 2-3: Verify
the name of the
subdirectory
where you want
AOL installed. If
AOL is a
satisfactory
directory name,
press Enter.

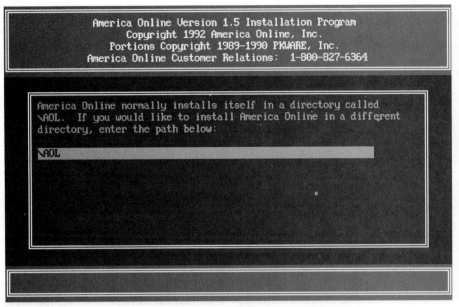

The installation program now goes to work (see Figure 2-4). This takes a couple of minutes.

Figure 2-4: The
installation
process is
automatic. All you
have to do is
watch.

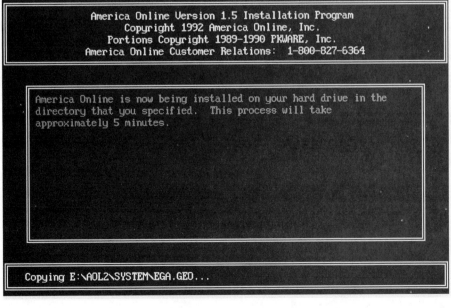

⚠ Once all the files have installed properly, the installation program will read your computer's AUTOEXEC.BAT and CONFIG.SYS files and analyze them for compatibility with America Online. If changes are advised, a message will give you the option of having the program make all or some changes for you, or you may skip this process (see Figure 2-5). Unless you typically customize the AUTOEXEC.BAT and CONFIG.SYS files yourself, you should be fine using the program's automatic suggested adjustments.

Figure 2-5:
Select "Yes" if
you want your
AUTOEXEC.BAT
file automatically
updated.

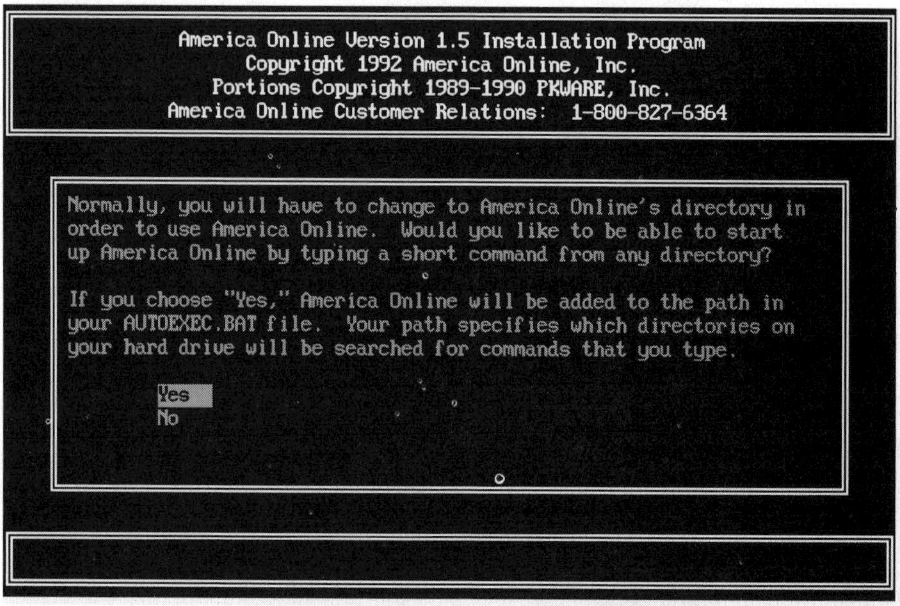

```
America Online Version 1.5 Installation Program
          Copyright 1992 America Online, Inc.
      Portions Copyright 1989-1990 PKWARE, Inc.
   America Online Customer Relations:   1-800-827-6364



  Normally, you will have to change to America Online's directory in
  order to use America Online.  Would you like to be able to start
  up America Online by typing a short command from any directory?

  If you choose "Yes," America Online will be added to the path in
  your AUTOEXEC.BAT file.  Your path specifies which directories on
  your hard drive will be searched for commands that you type.

      Yes
      No
```

⚠ The next message you receive will announce the completion of the installation process. But, we're not quite finished yet; you must make your video, mouse, modem and printer selections so America Online will be completely set up for your system.

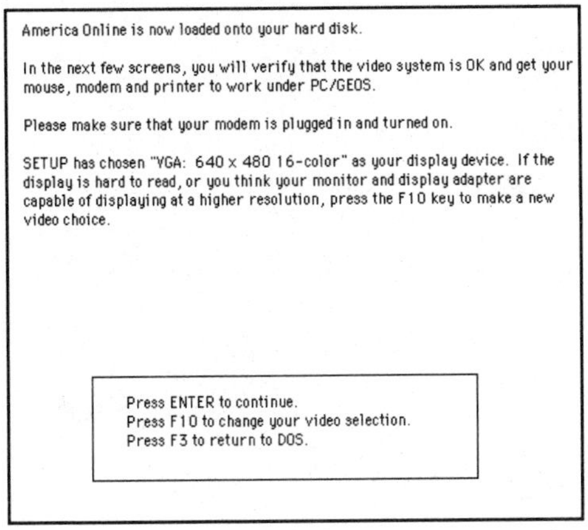

Figure 2-6:
Press Enter to
continue through
the verification
process.

> America Online is now loaded onto your hard disk.
>
> In the next few screens, you will verify that the video system is OK and get your mouse, modem and printer to work under PC/GEOS.
>
> Please make sure that your modem is plugged in and turned on.
>
> SETUP has chosen "VGA: 640 x 480 16-color" as your display device. If the display is hard to read, or you think your monitor and display adapter are capable of displaying at a higher resolution, press the F10 key to make a new video choice.
>
> Press ENTER to continue.
> Press F10 to change your video selection.
> Press F3 to return to DOS.

⚠ At the next screen, you are asked to verify your video adapter (see Figure 2-7). The program will search your system and make a recommendation for the option you should choose. Press Enter if this is correct or F10 if you would like to view the 49 other choices you have. You may need to consult your computer, monitor and video card manuals for assistance. When you have chosen an option, press Enter.

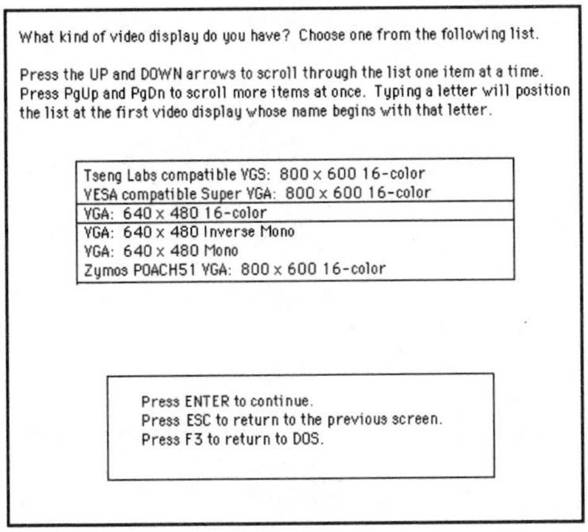

Figure 2-7: If
necessary, scroll
through the list to
select your video
display, then press
Enter.

> What kind of video display do you have? Choose one from the following list.
>
> Press the UP and DOWN arrows to scroll through the list one item at a time. Press PgUp and PgDn to scroll more items at once. Typing a letter will position the list at the first video display whose name begins with that letter.
>
> Tseng Labs compatible VGS: 800 x 600 16-color
> VESA compatible Super VGA: 800 x 600 16-color
> VGA: 640 x 480 16-color
> VGA: 640 x 480 Inverse Mono
> VGA: 640 x 480 Mono
> Zymos POACH51 VGA: 800 x 600 16-color
>
> Press ENTER to continue.
> Press ESC to return to the previous screen.
> Press F3 to return to DOS.

⚠ Next, you will see a screen with an arrow in each corner (see Figure 2-8). This screen confirms that your monitor is working properly with the America Online software. If this screen is sharp and clear, press Enter to continue. Otherwise, press F10 to select another video choice.

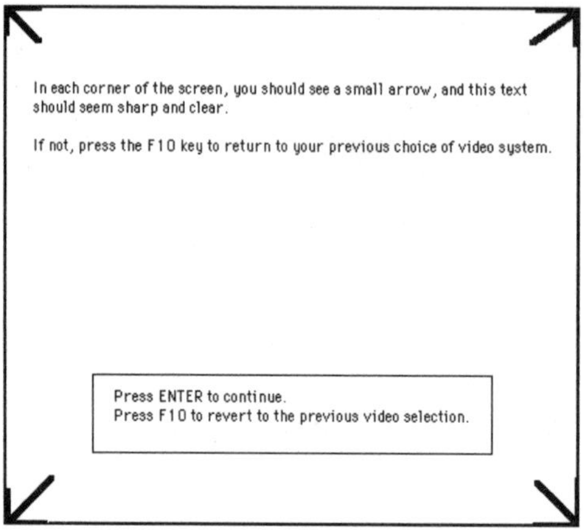

Figure 2-8: If you chose the correct video display, this screen should appear sharp and clear. Choose a different option if it does not look correct.

In each corner of the screen, you should see a small arrow, and this text should seem sharp and clear.

If not, press the F10 key to return to your previous choice of video system.

Press ENTER to continue.
Press F10 to revert to the previous video selection.

⚠ A second confirmation of the correct video driver appears on the next screen, which displays 16 colors or shades of gray (see Figure 2-9). If you do not see these colors or gray variations, you should press F10 to select another video driver.

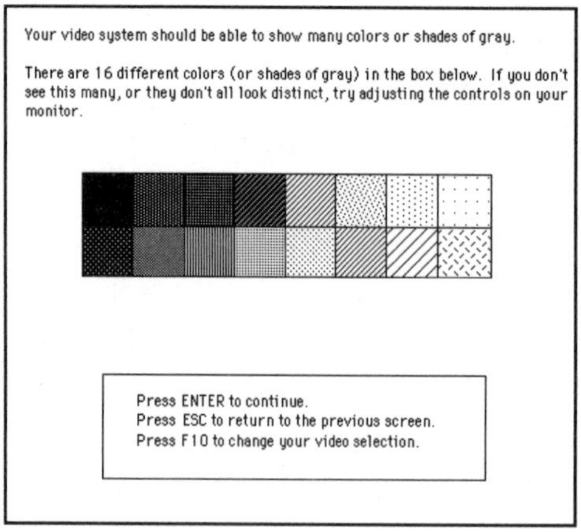

Figure 2-9: Adjust your monitor settings or change your video selection if the 16 variations shown here do not appear as clear and distinct colors or patterns of gray.

Your video system should be able to show many colors or shades of gray.

There are 16 different colors (or shades of gray) in the box below. If you don't see this many, or they don't all look distinct, try adjusting the controls on your monitor.

Press ENTER to continue.
Press ESC to return to the previous screen.
Press F10 to change your video selection.

☝ The selection of a mouse is next (see Figure 2-10). While use of a mouse isn't mandatory, it is highly recommended and this book assumes you are using one. (Keyboard commands are listed in Appendix B.)

Figure 2-10: Select the mouse you're using from the 74 options available on this screen. Choose "No Idea" or "None, or add later" as appropriate.

```
What kind of mouse do you have?  Choose one from the following list.

If you're not sure, check the box the mouse came in, or look at the label on its
bottom.  If you have no idea, choose "No idea."

Press the UP and DOWN arrows to scroll through the list one item at a time.
Press PgUp and PgDn to scroll more items at once.  Typing a letter will position
the list at the first mouse whose name begins with that letter.

    No idea
    None, or add later
    Acer Serial
    Artec AM-21 Plus (Microsoft Mode)
    Artec AM-21 Plus (Mouse Systems Mode)


    Press ENTER to continue.
    Press ESC to return to the previous screen.
    Press F3 to return to DOS.
```

☝ If you selected "No Idea," the next screen informs you of the requirement of a previously installed mouse driver on your computer (see Figure 2-11). Otherwise, selecting "No idea" is not a viable option.

Figure 2-11: You'll see this screen if you selected "No idea" from the previous screen.

```
PC/GEOS will work with any mouse that came with a Microsoft compatible
driver.  You must make sure that you have fully installed the mouse, as it
won't work if you haven't loaded the mouse driver software (usually called
MOUSE.COM or MOUSE.SYS).

The installation manual that came with the mouse will tell you how to install
the driver software.  If this software isn't correctly installed, the pointer
(a small arrow that moves on the screen when you move the mouse) will not
appear when you press ENTER to continue.


    Press ENTER to continue.
    Press ESC to return to the previous screen.
    Press F10 to change your mouse selection.
    Press F3 to return to DOS.
```

▲ If you selected "None, or add later" for the mouse selection, you'll
see the screen depicted in Figure 2-12.

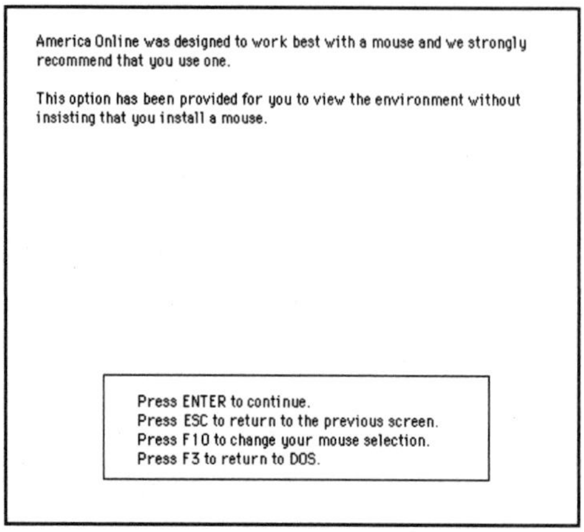

Figure 2-12: This
screen encourages
you to use a
mouse with
America Online. A
mouse greatly
increases AOL's
ease of use and
productivity.

> America Online was designed to work best with a mouse and we strongly
> recommend that you use one.
>
> This option has been provided for you to view the environment without
> insisting that you install a mouse.
>
> Press ENTER to continue.
> Press ESC to return to the previous screen.
> Press F10 to change your mouse selection.
> Press F3 to return to DOS.

▲ If you selected a serial mouse driver, the screen in Figure 2-13 asks
you to indicate which port the mouse is using.

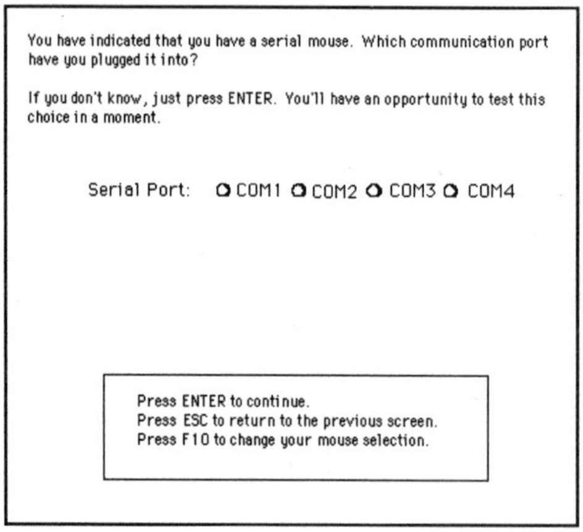

Figure 2-13:
Indicate the serial
port for your
mouse or press
Enter to let the
Installer take a
guess.

> You have indicated that you have a serial mouse. Which communication port
> have you plugged it into?
>
> If you don't know, just press ENTER. You'll have an opportunity to test this
> choice in a moment.
>
> Serial Port: ○ COM1 ○ COM2 ○ COM3 ○ COM4
>
> Press ENTER to continue.
> Press ESC to return to the previous screen.
> Press F10 to change your mouse selection.

👆 If you chose COM3 or COM4 ports for your mouse, you'll see the screen in Figure 2-14. Again, if you don't know the answer, AOL will be happy to guess.

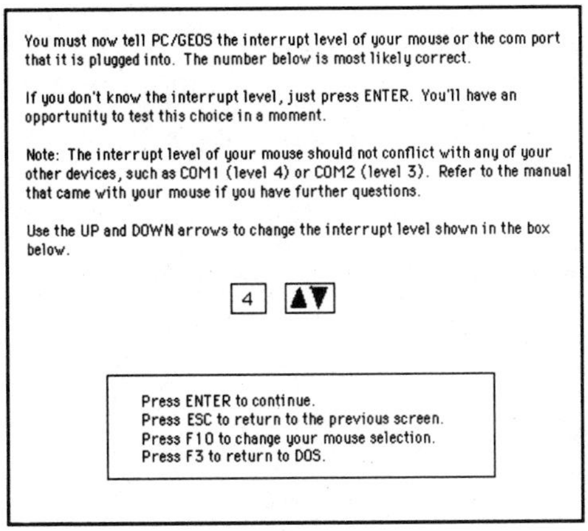

Figure 2-14: Select a mouse interrupt level or press Enter to let the program guess.

> You must now tell PC/GEOS the interrupt level of your mouse or the com port that it is plugged into. The number below is most likely correct.
>
> If you don't know the interrupt level, just press ENTER. You'll have an opportunity to test this choice in a moment.
>
> Note: The interrupt level of your mouse should not conflict with any of your other devices, such as COM1 (level 4) or COM2 (level 3). Refer to the manual that came with your mouse if you have further questions.
>
> Use the UP and DOWN arrows to change the interrupt level shown in the box below.
>
> 4 ▲▼
>
> > Press ENTER to continue.
> > Press ESC to return to the previous screen.
> > Press F10 to change your mouse selection.
> > Press F3 to return to DOS.

👆 The Installer usually guesses correctly at the previous two screens, however, the screen in Figure 2-15 provides a test for the mouse just in case something went wrong.

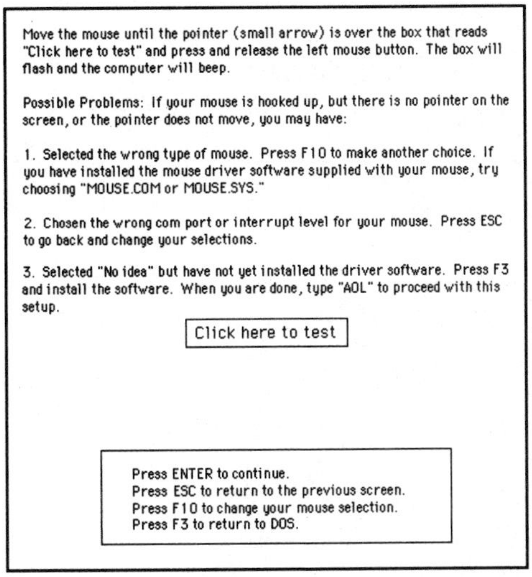

Figure 2-15: This screen includes a test to ensure the mouse is working properly.

> Move the mouse until the pointer (small arrow) is over the box that reads "Click here to test" and press and release the left mouse button. The box will flash and the computer will beep.
>
> Possible Problems: If your mouse is hooked up, but there is no pointer on the screen, or the pointer does not move, you may have:
>
> 1. Selected the wrong type of mouse. Press F10 to make another choice. If you have installed the mouse driver software supplied with your mouse, try choosing "MOUSE.COM or MOUSE.SYS."
>
> 2. Chosen the wrong com port or interrupt level for your mouse. Press ESC to go back and change your selections.
>
> 3. Selected "No idea" but have not yet installed the driver software. Press F3 and install the software. When you are done, type "AOL" to proceed with this setup.
>
> Click here to test
>
> > Press ENTER to continue.
> > Press ESC to return to the previous screen.
> > Press F10 to change your mouse selection.
> > Press F3 to return to DOS.

❀ Click in the box to test the set up of the mouse. You should hear two quick beeps. Then press Enter and wait. It takes a second or two to get to the next screen, which verifies the settings for your modem (see Figure 2-16).

❀ The next screen is a result of the installation program searching for a modem and its connection. If it accurately found the information and is displaying it correctly, press Enter to continue.

Figure 2-16:
This screen
provides the
step for verifying
the modem port
and speed.

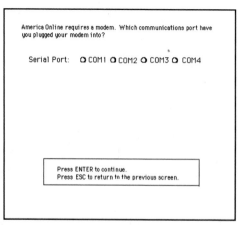

```
SETUP has found a modem on COM1.

America Online will use the baud rate of 2400.

If this is correct, press ENTER to accept these settings.
If you would like to change your modem settings, press the F10 key.




                     Press ENTER to continue.
                     Press ESC to return to the previous screen.
                     Press F3 to return to DOS.
                     Press F10 to override current modem settings.
```

❀ If the installation program cannot identify your modem port, or if you decide to change the current settings, you will see the screen in Figure 2-17.

Figure 2-17: If you
get this screen, se-
lect the appropriate
COM port—the one
your modem is
plugged into. The in-
staller automatically
detects ports and
speeds for COM1
and COM2; but
you'll have to select
COM3 or COM4
yourself if your
modem is using
those ports.

```
America Online requires a modem.  Which communications port have
you plugged your modem into?


    Serial Port:    O COM1 O COM2 O COM3 O COM4




                    Press ENTER to continue.
                    Press ESC to return to the previous screen.
```

▲ If you indicate that you are using COM3 or COM4 for your modem, you're prompted to confirm the interrupt level for your modem at the screen shown in Figure 2-18. The default setting for COM3 is interrupt level 4 and level 3 is the default for COM4. As before, if you aren't sure, pressing Enter will prompt the AOL installer to make a guess.

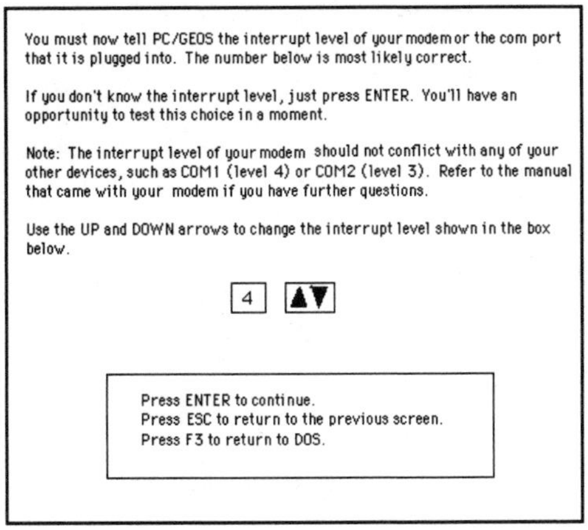

Figure 2-18: If necessary, click on the up and down triangles to change the level. Interrupt levels 2 through 15 may be selected.

> You must now tell PC/GEOS the interrupt level of your modem or the com port that it is plugged into. The number below is most likely correct.
>
> If you don't know the interrupt level, just press ENTER. You'll have an opportunity to test this choice in a moment.
>
> Note: The interrupt level of your modem should not conflict with any of your other devices, such as COM1 (level 4) or COM2 (level 3). Refer to the manual that came with your modem if you have further questions.
>
> Use the UP and DOWN arrows to change the interrupt level shown in the box below.
>
> 4 ▲▼
>
> Press ENTER to continue.
> Press ESC to return to the previous screen.
> Press F3 to return to DOS.

▲ If the installation program cannot identify your modem speed or if you want to change the detected settings, you will have the opportunity to choose a speed at the screen shown in Figure 2-19.

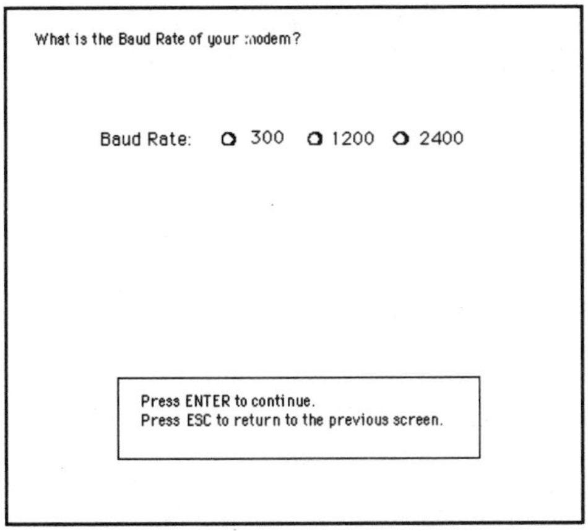

Figure 2-19: Choose either 300, 1200 or 2400 baud at this screen, depending on your modem speed. By the time you read this, America Online may be offering 9600 baud access as well.

> What is the Baud Rate of your modem?
>
> Baud Rate: ○ 300 ○ 1200 ○ 2400
>
> Press ENTER to continue.
> Press ESC to return to the previous screen.

🔺 Now let's select a printer at the next screen (see Figure 2-20). If you have no printer, choose "None."

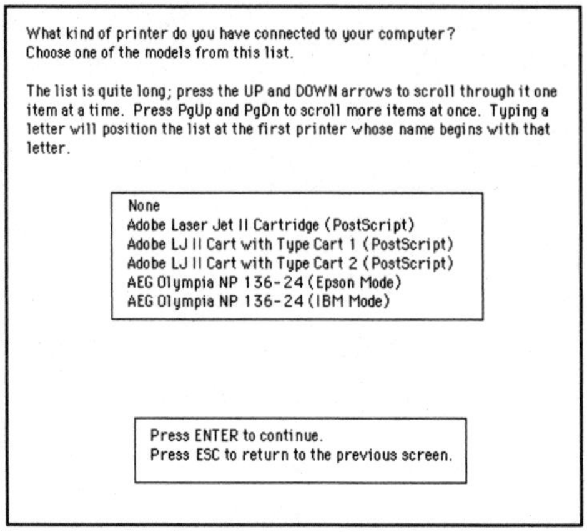

Figure 2-20: There are about 600 printer choices to select from. If you type the first letter of your brand of printer, you'll quickly be taken to the first printer whose name begins with that letter.

What kind of printer do you have connected to your computer? Choose one of the models from this list.

The list is quite long; press the UP and DOWN arrows to scroll through it one item at a time. Press PgUp and PgDn to scroll more items at once. Typing a letter will position the list at the first printer whose name begins with that letter.

```
None
Adobe Laser Jet II Cartridge (PostScript)
Adobe LJ II Cart with Type Cart 1 (PostScript)
Adobe LJ II Cart with Type Cart 2 (PostScript)
AEG Olympia NP 136-24 (Epson Mode)
AEG Olympia NP 136-24 (IBM Mode)
```

Press ENTER to continue.
Press ESC to return to the previous screen.

🔺 The installation program copied all drivers for video, mouse and printers, in addition to the specific ones you selected. At the screen shown in Figure 2-21, you have the opportunity to keep all the extra drivers or delete those you're not using. If you are not an experienced telecommunicator, you probably shouldn't delete any of the optional drivers at this point.

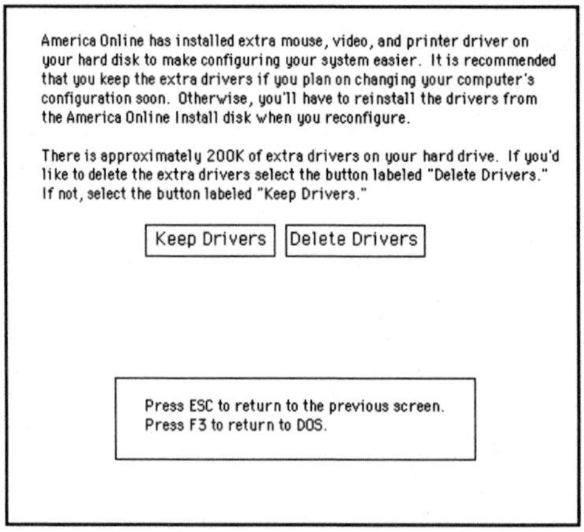

Figure 2-21: The extra drivers take up about 200k on your hard drive. Click on the "Delete Drivers" button if you don't want them or to preserve disk space.

America Online has installed extra mouse, video, and printer driver on your hard disk to make configuring your system easier. It is recommended that you keep the extra drivers if you plan on changing your computer's configuration soon. Otherwise, you'll have to reinstall the drivers from the America Online Install disk when you reconfigure.

There is approximately 200K of extra drivers on your hard drive. If you'd like to delete the extra drivers select the button labeled "Delete Drivers." If not, select the button labeled "Keep Drivers."

```
Keep Drivers    Delete Drivers
```

Press ESC to return to the previous screen.
Press F3 to return to DOS.

There, you've done it! You have installed the software and you're ready to sign on. Eject the floppy disk, put it in a safe place and let's get on with it.

The initial online session

The initial online session takes about 15 minutes. Be sure you have the time and uninterrupted access to the phone before you begin. You needn't worry about money: though you'll be online for quite a while, the setup process is accomplished on AOL's dime, not yours. You needn't worry about indelibility either: plenty of Cancel buttons are offered during the initial session. If you get cold feet, you can always hang up and start over.

Configuring the telephone connection

Before it can successfully make the connection, America Online needs to know a number of things about your telephone and modem: what kind of modem you have and how it's connected to your PC; details about your telephone (e.g., dialing 9 to get an outside line or if you have Call Waiting); and where you're located in the country. It needs to know these things so it can make some suggestions regarding the local access numbers your PC will use to connect to the Stratus. Your modem should be connected to the phone line and to your computer by now, and it should be turned on.

⚠ If you press Enter at the next screen, a setup screen will greet you as soon as the software loads (see Figure 2-22). Otherwise, if you are loading America Online from DOS, simply type "AOL" (without the quotes) at the prompt and press Enter. Carefully read the list of assumptions on this screen. If they describe your situation accurately, click on the OK button. If they don't, click on the Other Options button to change the defaults.

Step 1: Confirm Your Telephone Set Up
America Online will dial a special "800" number so that you can choose local
access numbers. These numbers will be used for all future connections. You
probably...

... live in the continental United States.
... have a 2400 baud modem plugged into COM2.
... do not need to dial a special prefix to reach an outside line.
... require a '1' to make a toll-free call.
... have a touch-tone telephone.

If this is correct, press "OK". If any of the above do not apply or you are not
sure, press "Other Options".

If you decide to cancel the Sign On/Registration process (by clicking on the
'Cancel' button) you will have to re-enter any information typed up to that point.

OK   Other Options   Cancel

It's time to make the first connection. When you click OK, your
software will dial an 800 (toll-free) number to temporarily connect
to the Stratus and search its database of local access phone numbers
for your area. If your modem has a speaker, you should hear a dial
tone within a few seconds. Soon thereafter, the AOL software will
dial the 800 number and you'll connect with America Online.

Isolating connection errors
Though it's rare, things can go wrong during the connect process. The problem could be at your
end (e.g., a problem with the phone lines), or it could be at AOL's end. You can be sure the
problem is at your end if you don't hear a dial tone (again, assuming your modem has a speaker)
before your modem begins dialing. If you hear the dial tone, the dialing sequence and the nerve-
wracking screech that modems make when they attempt to connect, you can be sure that everything is okay all the way to the common carrier (long-distance service) you're using. If your
connection fails on the first try, don't panic. Wait a few minutes and try again. If it fails a second
or third time, call AOL Customer Relations at 800-827-6364. It's a toll-free call, and the people
there will be able to help you.

Selecting access numbers

Now you're connected to the Stratus and it's anxious to say hello. Its initial greeting is friendly, if not a bit laconic. Its singular interest right now is to find some local access numbers for you. To do that, it needs to know where you are. It finds that out by requesting your area code. Enter the area code of the phone number from which you're calling.

Figure 2-23: America Online assigns the primary and secondary access numbers based on the area code of the telephone from which you're calling.

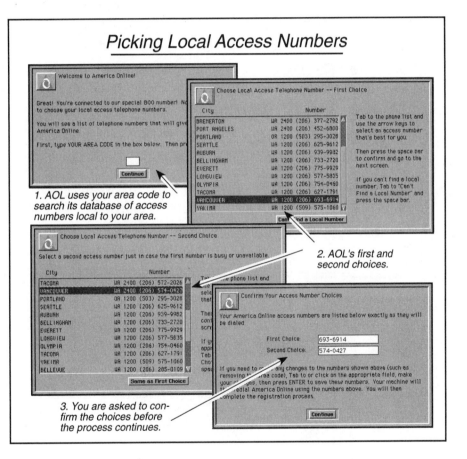

👆 Using your phone number's area code, AOL consults its database of local access numbers and produces a list of those nearest you. Look the list over carefully. The phone number at the top of the list isn't necessarily the one closest to you. Also, note the baud rates listed. Be sure the number you pick represents the baud rate that you intend to use.

👆 It's nice to have a secondary number as well. Secondary numbers (if available) offer your PC another option to dial if your primary number is for some reason unavailable.

👆 Finally, America Online offers a screen confirming your selections. If you're satisfied, click on the button marked Continue. If not, backspace to erase both phone numbers and then re-enter them.

The certificate number & password

Assuming you've clicked on Figure 2-23's Continue button, your computer will disconnect from the 800 number and dial your first local access number. This process is accompanied by the connect window pictured in Figure 2-24.

Figure 2-24:
America Online
now dials your
local access
number.

Notice the different steps that take place during the connection process. You'll see AOL indicate that it is connecting at the proper baud rate and that it is checking a password. Once this initial session concludes, you must provide a password whenever you sign on. The password icon that appears during sign-on is your assurance that

America Online is validating your password. This is comforting. As long as no one else knows your password, no one else can sign on using your AOL account.

Okay, back to the setup. Once the connection is established, AOL presents the screen shown in Figure 2-25. This is where you must enter the identification number and password printed on your certificate. These are the temporary equivalents of the permanent screen name and password you'll soon establish. Enter the words and numbers carefully from the certificate enclosed with your AOL software, and don't waste your time trying to use those pictured in the illustration: they're ancient history and AOL won't accept them again.

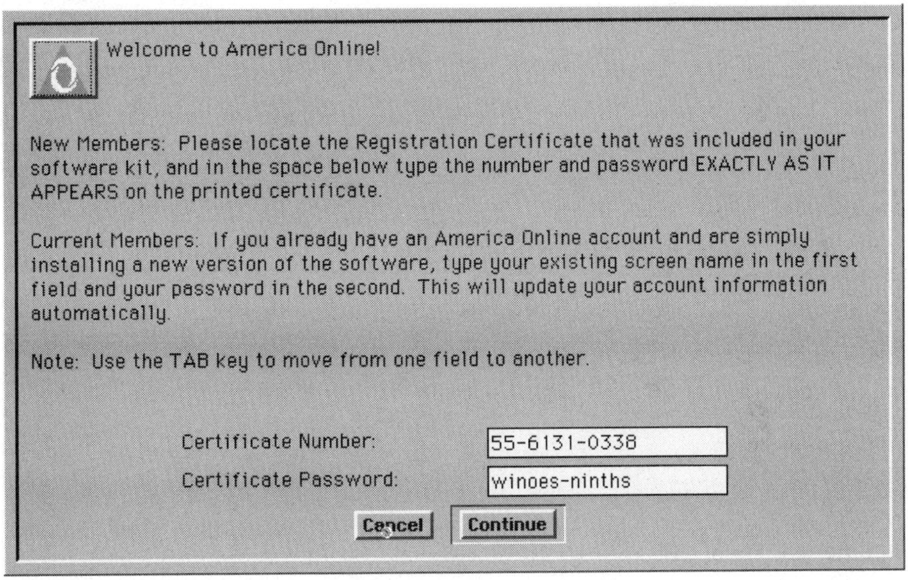

Figure 2-25: Enter the number and password exactly as printed on your America Online certificate, label or card.

Welcome to America Online!

New Members: Please locate the Registration Certificate that was included in your software kit, and in the space below type the number and password EXACTLY AS IT APPEARS on the printed certificate.

Current Members: If you already have an America Online account and are simply installing a new version of the software, type your existing screen name in the first field and your password in the second. This will update your account information automatically.

Note: Use the TAB key to move from one field to another.

Certificate Number: 55-6131-0338

Certificate Password: winoes-ninths

Cancel   Continue

Providing your billing information

Let's be upfront about it: America Online is a business run for profit. In other words, AOL needs to be paid for the service it provides. It offers a number of ways to do this. Your VISA, MasterCard or Discover Card are the preferred method of payment. If you don't have one of these (or if you prefer an alternate method), AOL also accepts American Express cards. AOL can also arrange to automatically debit your checking account. There's a fee for this, so it should be your last choice.

When you click on the Continue button shown in Figure 2-25, AOL provides directions for using an online form like that pictured in Figure 2-26. You'll want to read the directions on this screen carefully. Hint: use the Tab key to move from field to field.

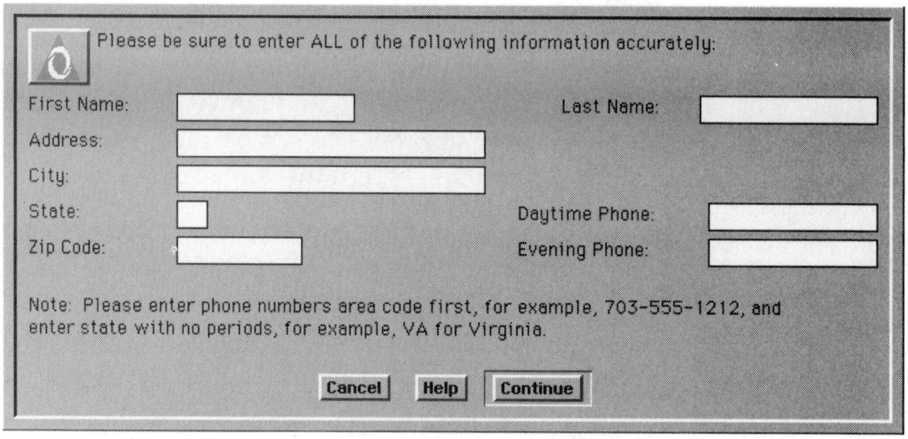

Figure 2-26: AOL needs to know how to contact you off-line. Complete this form in its entirety, using the format described at the bottom of the window.

```
Please be sure to enter ALL of the following information accurately:

First Name: [            ]          Last Name:  [            ]
Address:    [                    ]
City:       [                    ]
State:      [  ]                   Daytime Phone: [            ]
Zip Code:   [        ]             Evening Phone: [            ]

Note:  Please enter phone numbers area code first, for example, 703-555-1212, and
enter state with no periods, for example, VA for Virginia.

          [ Cancel ]  [ Help ]  [ Continue ]
```

America Online primarily uses the mailing information pictured in Figure 2-26 to send you new editions of its software.

The following two screens discuss how your free trial works and what you can expect to be charged after the free trial is up. Read this information thoroughly so you won't encounter any surprises.

Your phone number

Your phone number becomes an important part of your record at America Online, not because they intend to call you, but because AOL's Customer Relations Department uses this number to identify you whenever you call them. Should you ever find the need to call, the first question Customer Relations will ask is, "What's your phone number?" It's unique, after all, so the representative uses it to look up your records. It's an efficient method, but only if you provide the number accurately along with your billing information.

Now we come to the money part. The screens pictured in Figure 2-27 show how to provide MasterCard information. (They're blank of course. Don't get your hopes up.) Similar screens are provided for the input of VISA, Discover Card and American Express card information. Your only other alternative to these forms of payment is automatic deduction from a checking account.

Figure 2-27: The MasterCard data-input screen is similar to those for Visa, Discover Card or American Express information.

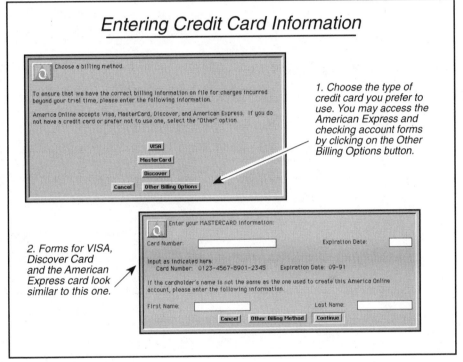

Choosing a screen name & password

When you click on the Continue button shown at the bottom of Figure 2-27, America Online provides a series of screens that address the significance of screen names, concluding with the screen name input form, pictured at the top of Figure 2-28. Do you see the screen name it picked? Don't get stuck with a screen name like that. Be sure to have a few alternate names close at hand in case your first or second choice isn't available.

48

The Official AOL Tour Guide

Figure 2-28: Use
the screens shown
here to pick a
screen name and
password that you
can live with
during all your
time online.

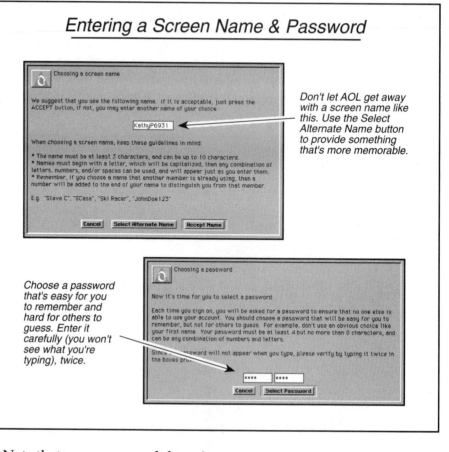

Entering a Screen Name & Password

Don't let AOL get away with a screen name like this. Use the Select Alternate Name button to provide something that's more memorable.

Choose a password that's easy for you to remember and hard for others to guess. Enter it carefully (you won't see what you're typing), twice.

Note that your password doesn't appear on your screen as you type it—instead, an asterisk is substituted for each letter in your password. This is a standard security precaution. You never know who's looking over your shoulder. As you are creating your password, America Online asks you to enter it twice, to be sure you didn't mistype.

There are a few final screens with questions that give you a chance to express your opinion about the sign-on process. Your answers to these queries provide American Online with important information that will help guide decisions about the future of the software and service. It's in your own best interest to provide answers, but don't hesitate to use the "no answer" choice if you'd prefer not to answer the questions.

You will also see a screen with information about a welcome kit that will soon arrive at the address you provided.

Chapter 2: Making the Connection

A letter from the President

Now that you've successfully finished setting up and signing on, you enter the America Online service itself. No doubt, the first thing that will happen is you'll hear a beep and see a letter in the envelope icon notifying you that you have mail. To read the letter, choose Read New Mail from the Mail menu or use your mouse to click on the letter and envelope icon (see Steps 1 and 2 in Figure 2-29). The New Mail window appears, with mail from AOL President Steve Case selected. Double-click on that item and read what he has to say (see the bottom of Figure 2-29).

Figure 2-29: Your first activity online will be to read a letter of welcome from AOL President Steve Case. How many times have you heard directly from the president of the company when you become a customer? How many times have you been invited to respond?

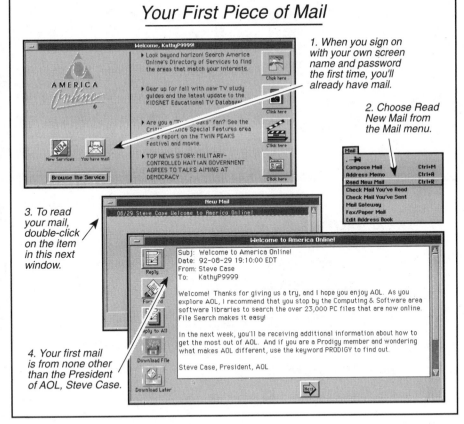

Where to go from here

Once you're online, you have the entire America Online universe to explore. The thought is both enticing and overwhelming. Here's what we suggest: spend a half-hour wandering around right after you read Steve's letter. You have quite a bit of free connect-time coming; don't worry about money. You'll find a button marked "Browse the Service" on the main Welcome screen. Click on that button, then find a department that interests you. Without any particular agenda, explore that department and perhaps one other.

During this initial session, don't try to absorb the contents of America Online. Rather, wander aimlessly, getting a feeling for the nature of the AOL universe. Have fun. Explore.

After a half-hour or so, you may want to sign off by choosing Sign Off from the Go To menu. Once the dust settles, turn to the chapter in this book that describes the department you just visited. Read that chapter, then sign back on and explore that department again. See if you can find the things we described in the chapter. Spend another half-hour at this.

Now you're on your own. Explore another department if you wish, or turn to Chapter 11, "Electronic Mail," and learn how to send mail to somebody. You'll probably get a response in a few days. People at America Online are very friendly. It really is a community.

Moving on

Speaking of the people online, that's one of the subjects covered in the next chapter, "Online Help & the Members." When you next have the time (we know how enticing AOL can be—you may never return to this book now that you're online), turn the page. We have many more things to talk about. [Next]

CHAPTER 3

Online Help & the Members

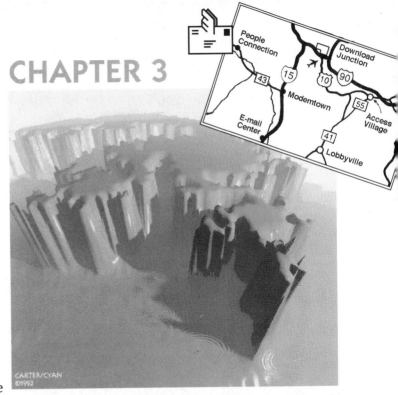

CARTER/CYAN
©1992

T hat sounds like
a heavy-metal band, doesn't it: "Online Help & the Members." Dressed in black leather with chains draped around their waists, Online Help & the Members takes the stage accompanied by waves of cacophony and pandemonium. Spotlights sweep the auditorium like a jailbreak, illuminating a mass of writhing supplicants below. The spotlights converge on Online as he wrests the microphone from its stand. An expectant hush fills the air. In a voice amplified by 2,000 transistors the size of hubcaps, he speaks:

"America Online Customer Relations! May I help you?"

Getting help

Much to our delight, software publishers have recently placed notable emphasis on providing users with help. The version of Microsoft Word we use, for instance, includes a help file measuring 1.8 megabytes—larger than Word itself. The help file is right here on the disk. All we have to do is tap on a couple of keys and there's the help we need: convenient, comprehensive and coherent.

Frontispiece graphic: "Phong Shadows," by Chuck Carter/Cyan. The graphic was created in Infini-D, using Phong shading with shadows. Keywords: File Search; use the criterion "Phong Shadows."

America Online is no different. Like all good software, AOL's help is always a simple keystroke away. AOL, however, has a unique advantage: since a good portion of AOL's help resides on the Stratus, it can be updated any time. This means that AOL's help can be particularly responsive. If members are having frequent trouble with a specific area, AOL can rewrite the help files, tailoring them to address the source of confusion. It's as if Microsoft were to send a representative to our homes with a new help disk every time Word's help files needed to be changed.

Getting help: a methodical approach

If you have a question about AOL and require help, we suggest you use the methods described below, in the order in which they appear. All of the topics mentioned are explained in detail later in this chapter.

1. Look up the topic in the index of this book to see if your question is answered here. We'd like to think that most of your questions can be answered this way.

2. Run the AOL software and choose Help from the menu bar. In this chapter, we refer to this flavor of help as *off-line* help, since it's available when you're off-line. (It's available when you're online as well, but that doesn't help our semantics.) Off-line help offers a list of more than 40 topics and will often answer your question, especially if it involves connecting with America Online.

3. Go online and use the keyword: Help. (Keywords are discussed later in this chapter.) This takes you to AOL's Online Support Center, a particularly comprehensive (and free) resource.

4. Ask Customer Relations for help. If the Online Support Center's files don't have the answer, send your question directly to Customer Relations. Use the keyword: Help, then double-click on any of the topics in the category box. There's an envelope icon at the bottom of every Support Center topic window just for the purpose of sending questions to Customer Relations.

5. Use the keyword: MHM. This takes you to AOL's Members Helping Members bulletin boards. Within a day or so you'll have a response to your question from another member. Peer help is often the best help you can find.

6. Call Customer Relations at 800-827-6364. They're open from Noon to 11:00 PM (Eastern time) Monday through Friday, and noon to 9:00 PM Saturday and Sunday. It's a toll-free call in the continental US, and there's never a charge for support.

There's a flaw in the plan, however. In order to access online help, we have to be online. While this isn't much of a restriction—online is the time we usually need help—there are occasions when we would like to have help without signing on. What if we *couldn't* sign on? What if we were traveling and needed help finding an alternative number?

Altruistically, America Online offers *both* online and off-line help. One set of help files resides on your hard disk and is available at any time regardless of whether you're online. The other set of help files resides on the Stratus. This set is the one that's constantly being updated. It's not just comprehensive, it's downright monumental. It's available whenever you're online, and—incredibly—it's free: whenever you access AOL's online help area, the clock stops and you aren't charged for your time there.

Off-line help

Let's talk about off-line help first. America Online's off-line help is configured to answer the kind of questions you'll encounter when you're disconnected from the service. How do we connect when we're away from our usual location? What's the Customer Relations phone number and when are they on duty? How do we sign up friends?

Choosing help from the menu bar

Off-line help can be accessed in two ways. Perhaps the most obvious one is to choose Help from the menu bar. The list of topics that results is extensive (see Figure 3-1).

Figure 3-1:
Off-line help is
always available:
just choose Help
from the menu.

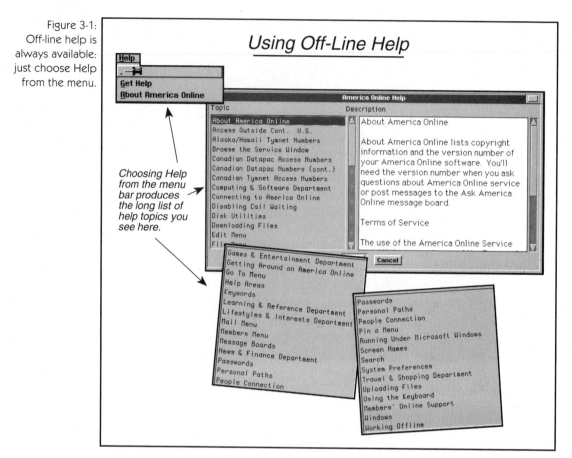

As is the case with all items on the AOL program menu, Help can be chosen at any time, whether you're online or off. These help topics are stored on a file on your hard disk, and as such don't require that you go online in order to access them. You just need to launch the AOL application program.

Look carefully at the list of help topics in Figure 3-1. Some of them are specifically for first-time users. Others are primarily for members on the road: Connecting to America Online, Access Outside the Continental USA and so on. The other help topics are oriented toward America Online's menu bar: the File menu, Help areas, the Go To menu and so on right across the menu at the top of AOL's screen.

Online help

AOL's online help is especially comprehensive. In addition to the online help files proper, both staff and members stand ready to help you as well. This help is world-class, and its breadth is unique to America Online.

Members' Online Support

To access Members' Online Support, choose Members' Online Support from the Go To menu (see Figure 3-2) or use the keyword: Help. You must be signed on for this.

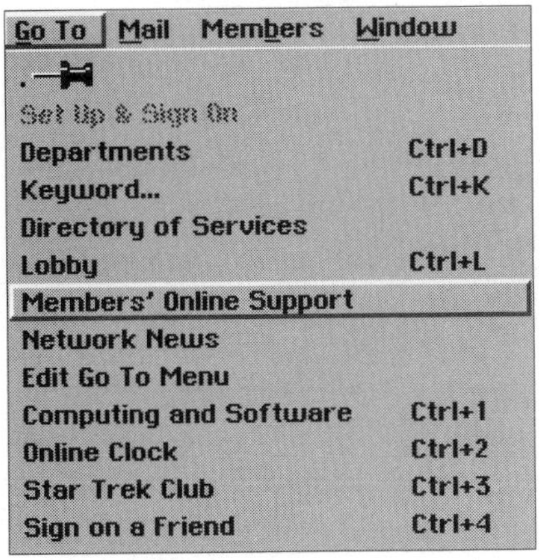

Figure 3-2: Online help is available whenever you're online by choosing Members' Online Support from the Go To menu, or by using the keyword: Help.

Go To	Mail	Members	Window
📌			
Set Up & Sign On			
Departments			Ctrl+D
Keyword...			Ctrl+K
Directory of Services			
Lobby			Ctrl+L
Members' Online Support			
Network News			
Edit Go To Menu			
Computing and Software			Ctrl+1
Online Clock			Ctrl+2
Star Trek Club			Ctrl+3
Sign on a Friend			Ctrl+4

The moment you choose Members' Online Support from the Go To menu, AOL flashes the message pictured in Figure 3-3. Whenever you enter online help, windows for paid activities (things like gateways and chats, which we discuss in Chapters 10 and 12) are closed. Don't let it worry you. Even if your gateway or chat windows *are* closed, you can always reopen them when you leave the free area. The effective message here is that you're about to enter a free area: the clock is about to stop and you'll be free to explore help to your heart's content. It won't cost you a dime.

Closing windows permanently

As the message in Figure 3-3 indicates, gateway and chat windows are closed when you enter Members' Online Support. In fact, no matter how many or how few windows are open at the time, they all close when you enter the free area. The point of the message is that gateway and chat windows will not reopen when you exit help, while all the others will. The contents of gateway and chat windows, in other words, will be lost. Keep this in mind if, for instance, you're in the midst of making an airline reservation (a gateway activity) and don't want to lose your work.

Figure 3-3:
AOL confirms your
command when
you access the free
online help area.

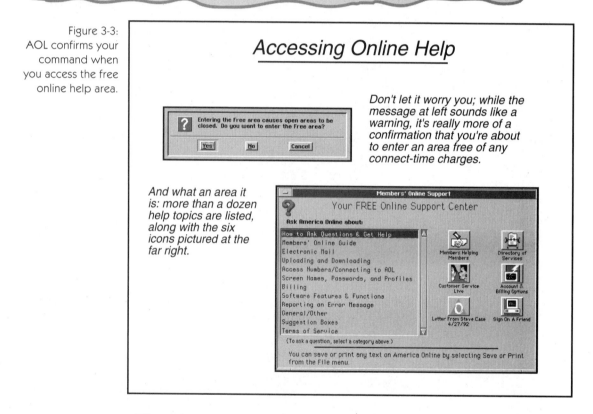

Accessing Online Help

Don't let it worry you; while the message at left sounds like a warning, it's really more of a confirmation that you're about to enter an area free of any connect-time charges.

And what an area it is: more than a dozen help topics are listed, along with the six icons pictured at the far right.

The Ask America Online area (the list box on the left side of the lower window pictured in Figure 3-3) has immediate answers for nearly anything you encounter while online. Each of these help topics may be saved, printed or both. While the list of topics is extensive, the detail offered within each topic is bountiful (see Figure 3-4).

Figure 3-4:
The help topics
available in the
Members' Online
Support area.

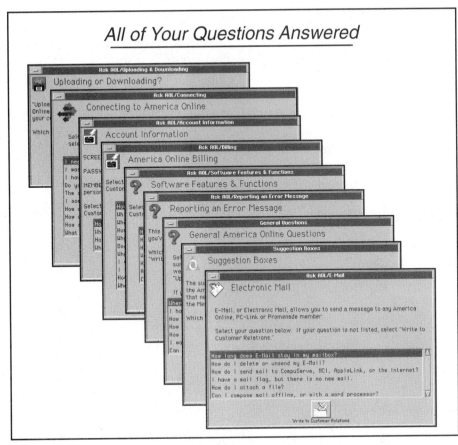

Asking Customer Relations for help

Like the Electronic Mail window pictured at the bottom of Figure 3-4, most of AOL's Help windows offer an icon that lets you send e-mail directly to the people at Customer Relations. Though the help files are comprehensive, they can't address all possible questions members may have. If your question isn't answered there, all you have to do is click on this icon. Another window will open, providing a place for you to type in your question. Questions are answered within 24 to 48 hours via electronic mail.

Saving help   Though AOL's help screens are primarily intended for you to read while you're online (there's no charge for the service, after all, so you can take your time), you may want to save a help topic or two on your disk. Doing so provides you with a text file that can be combined with other help files using a word processor, for instance, to create a comprehensive help manual.

To save a help topic that's currently visible on your screen, simply choose Save from the File menu. America Online asks you what you want to name the file and where you want to save it. Provide the information it needs, and that help topic will be stored on your disk as a text file, ready for any purpose you may have in mind.

Printing help   More likely, you'll want to print a help topic for ready reference. As you might expect, all you have to do is choose Print from the File menu. Printing from AOL is very easy. You'll receive the print dialog box associated with the printers you select during the set-up part of installation. Configure this dialog box as you please and print. By the way, you can print just about any text file you read online, not just the help files. If you run across a file description or news article you want to print, just choose Print from the File menu—AOL will print whatever text is in the front-most (or active) window.

The Directory of Services

Look again at Figure 3-3. In the Members' Online Support window, you'll find a little Rolodex icon representing the Directory of Services, a searchable database of information on all the services offered by America Online. Information for each service includes the following:

- The service's name.

- Any keywords associated with that service (see sidebar).

- A menu path for access to that service.

- A description of that service.

- A button to take you there.

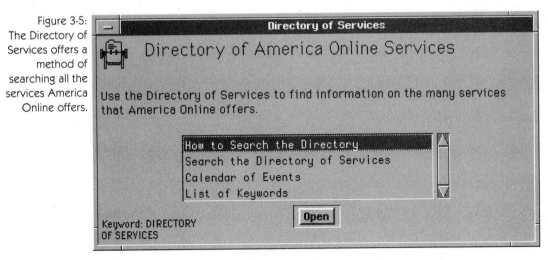

Figure 3-5:
The Directory of
Services offers a
method of
searching all the
services America
Online offers.

Keywords

Keywords are shortcuts to specific destinations within America Online. Without keywords, accessing the Microsoft Knowledge Base via menus and windows, for instance, requires that you choose the Departments item of the Go To menu, click on the Computing & Software Department's button, click on the Industry Connection icon, then click on Microsoft Support, then click on Knowledge Base. *Whew!* There's gotta be a better way.

And there is: keywords. The keyword for the Microsoft Knowledge Base is "Microsoft." Once you know the keyword, all you have to do is choose Keyword from the Go To menu (or type Ctrl-k) and enter "Microsoft" into the area provided. Instantly, AOL takes you directly to the Microsoft Support where you can select Knowledge Base and bypass all other steps in between.

A list of keywords is available in the Directory of Services (see Figure 3-5), or by selecting the Keyword List button from the Keyword menu item on the Go To menu. (A list of the most commonly used keywords is also provided in Appendix A of this book.)

Searching the Directory of Services Last week Tom was having some trouble with his word processor, Microsoft Word. For some reason, whenever he used small caps, Word miscalculated the length of the line containing the small caps and messed up his document. Rather than spend an hour with the manual or calling Microsoft (a long-distance call), he chose to consult the Directory of Services, using the search criterion: Software (see Figure 3-6).

Figure 3-6:
The Directory of
Services provides a
path to the solution
to Tom's word-
processing
problem.

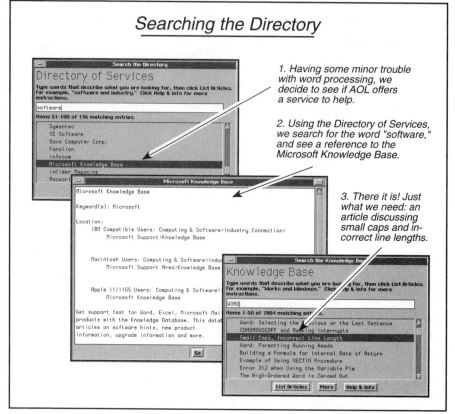

Note that the middle window in Figure 3-6 offers the keyword for the Microsoft Knowledge Base, its location (the menu path that gets you there) and its description. If it isn't what Tom needs, the description saves him the trouble of going there in futility. If it is what he needs, the keyword and location tell him how to get there.

The Directory of Services is America Online's answer to the question: "I wonder if they have anything that addresses my interest in...." Are you interested in model airplanes? Search the Directory of Services. How about music, poetry or fine food? Use the Directory of Services.

The More button

Look again at the Figure 3-6's bottom window. Do you see the button there marked "More"? It's amazing how often this button is overlooked. To tell the truth, Tom's search for the word "Word" was very inefficient. The Microsoft Knowledge Base found over 7,000 entries matching his search criterion. While he thought he was looking for a specific Microsoft product, the Knowledge Base found *every* reference to the criterion, including all the programming-language references. (Search criteria are discussed in Chapter 7, "Computing & Software.")

Rather than spend five or ten minutes listing all 7,000 entries, AOL chose only to display the first 50 (a safe assumption, since we would probably want to narrow our search). Since matching entries remained, AOL activated the More button. If we wanted to see more than the first 50 entries, we'd click on that button and AOL would send another 50; clicking again results in another 50 entries and so on.

Don't overlook this button! It's not unique to the Microsoft Knowledge Base—many AOL windows have one—and if it *is* overlooked, lots of opportunities are missed.

Locating the Directory of Services   There are at least three ways to get to the Directory of Services. As pictured in Figure 3-3, you'll find the directory's icon in the Members' Online Support window. Since you passed through the "free curtain" (the message pictured at the top of Figure 3-3) to get to Members' Online Support, accessing the Directory of Services via Online Support is free.

Alternatively, you can choose Directory of Services from the Go To menu, or use the keyword: DirectoryofServices. If you're not in the free area at the time, accessing the directory this way is on your dime, not AOL's. It's a little faster and more convenient than passing through the curtain, however; so you may wish to use it when you only plan to spend a moment or two there.

Customer Service Live

Let's talk about rooms for a moment. At America Online, a "room" is a place where a number of people gather to talk about a subject of common interest. There are classrooms, for instance, where you'll find a teacher and students (the Online Campus is discussed in Chapter 9, "Learning & Reference"). There's the Lobby (look under the Go To menu) where people go to mingle and meet other people. In fact, AOL offers scores of rooms, and we will explore a number of them in Chapter 10, "People Connection."

Look again at Figure 3-3. Do you see the icon marked "Customer Service Live"? If you click on that icon, you'll find yourself in a room with at least one Customer Service representative and probably a number of other members, all with questions regarding the service. Conversations in the room are real-time: you don't have to wait for replies. This isn't mail and it's not a message board; it is a room, and like real rooms in real buildings, people in rooms can hold real-time conversations.

There's a lot to be learned here. Not only do you receive immediate answers to your questions, you can "eavesdrop" on questions from other members as well—all at AOL's expense (don't forget: you're still in the free area).

Customer Service Live is available evenings. If you need an immediate response, this is the place to find it.

Jay Levitt

As you can imagine, writing this book required hundreds of hours online (such a job!). It seems that every time we started another paragraph, we had a question. Most of the answers were found by just poking around America Online itself. A few, however, eluded our investigation. Remember: there was no manual at the time—this book, after all, *is* the manual, and this book wasn't available while we were writing it. So who do the people who are writing the manual turn to when there is no manual? They turn to Jay Levitt.

Jay is Customer Relations Senior Information Specialist. You can tell he is a Very Important Person at AOL because his screen name is "Jay." Even Steve Case doesn't have a first-name screen name. Jay does. He sits in a little three-sided cubicle just inside the door to Customer Relations, surrounded by computer screens: a Mac, two PCs, a Stratus terminal and a terminal for the ASPECT telephone-answering system that serves as the heart of Customer Relations. He plays these terminals like a keyboard musician at a rock concert, the fingers of his left hand a blur as they tap out a little ditty to a particularly persnickety member, while the right hand tickles the Stratus, coaxing yet another miracle from the omnipotent machine. All the while he carries on a conversation with us, popping witticisms like Victor Borge on a good night.

More

When he's not putting out fires, Jay eternally seeks ways to improve the service. He coordinates beta tests, writes internal documentation for Customer Service representatives, handles technical call-backs, tracks down compatibility problems and manages the Guide program (discussed later in this chapter), among other things. These he does while he helps us (a full-time job in itself) and thousands of other members as well.

The rock-musician analogy isn't far off the mark (though we doubt you'd ever find him in leather and chains), for Jay Levitt is only 21. *Just a kid!* Kid or not, he's a scholar, a prodigy and a gentleman. Most of all, he's one of the finest friends we made at AOL. Few could do as well as Jay.

Figure 3-7:
A glimpse of the Customer Relations Department on a busy night. This is not a picture of confusion and disorder. Things are calm here: the murmur of quiet voices rarely rises above the susurration of the air conditioning.

Members Helping Members

On our IRS 1040 forms, right next to the word *Occupation,* it says "educator." We write books, teach classes and do some consulting. As educators, we attend a number of conferences. Most of these conferences are academic, each featuring speakers and seminar leaders.

Reflecting back on those conferences, we must admit that the greatest value we receive from them is not from the speakers or the seminars, it's from the other people attending the conference. We agree that our education occurs in the hallways and at the lounge tables. People talking to people—peer-to-peer—that's where we find the Good Stuff.

America Online is no different. Some of the best help online is that received from other members. AOL knows that; that's why it provides Members Helping Members—a formalized version of peer support (see Figure 3-8).

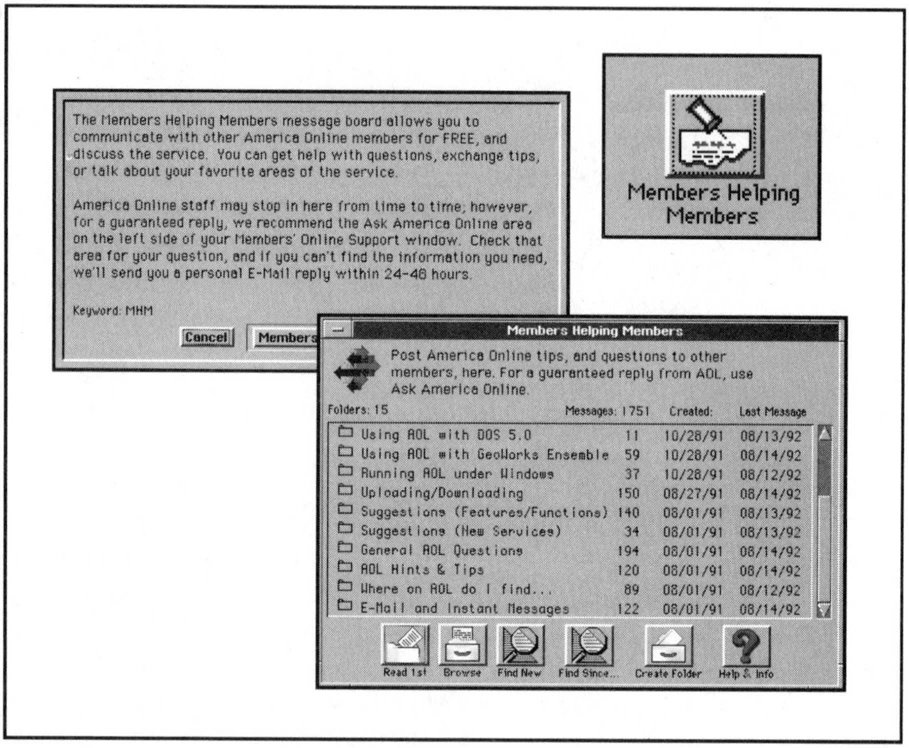

Figure 3-8:
To access Members Helping Members, click on the push-pin icon in the Members' Online Support window, or use the keyword: MHM.

To access Members Helping Members, either click on the push-pin icon in the Members' Online Support window, or use the keyword: MHM. Unlike the Directory of Services, you'll pass through the free curtain regardless of how you choose to access this feature. In other words, it never costs you a dime to use Members Helping Members.

Message boards

Members Helping Members is a *message board*. Though we'll discuss message boards in Chapter 6, "Lifestyles & Interests," the subject is worth a brief mention here as well.

Throughout AOL, you'll see little push-pin icons similar to the one pictured at the top of Figure 3-8. This is AOL's way of identifying message boards. A message board is analogous to the bulletin boards you see hanging in the halls of offices and academic institutions. People post things there for other people to see: postcards, lost mittens, announcements and messages. AOL's message boards are exactly the same (though you may not see many lost mittens on AOL's boards...).

Look again at Figure 3-8. Note how AOL's boards are organized by using folders. The bulletin-board analogy weakens a bit here, but AOL's boards get a *lot* of messages (the Members Helping Members board pictured in Figure 3-8 has 1751). Unless they're organized in some fashion, 1751 messages posted on a single board would be pandemic. The solution is folders.

You can read all the messages in a folder (the left-most icon at the bottom of Figure 3-8); browse through them (viewing only their subjects, rather than the messages themselves); or search a folder, specifying a subject, person or date. This is a very convenient message-reading system and is described in detail in Chapter 6.

For the time being, let's select a folder and read its messages. We picked the "Using Printers & Mice w/AOL" folder and found the messages pictured in Figure 3-9.

Figure 3-9:
BettyS needed help
getting her printer
to fully advance.
Sergio74 was there
to help.

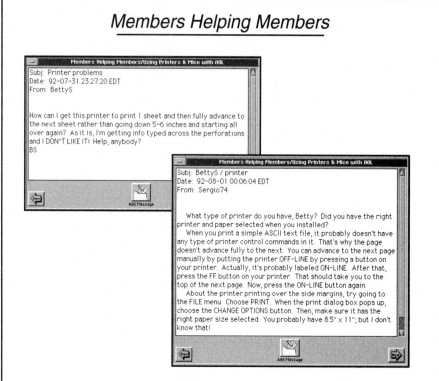

Figure 3-9:
BettyS needed help
getting her printer
to fully advance.
Sergio74 was there
to help.

The value of member help

Look at the message pictured on Figure 3-10. This is a response to someone's inquiry about where to go to find 2400 baud access numbers. The message from CJR3 offers some superb help, and it came from another member (see Figure 3-10).

Figure 3-10: CJR3 offers numbers, a menu path and additional advice.

CJR3's Message

```
Subj:  Re: 2400 baud---How?          92-07-07 19:41:05 EDT
From:  CJR3

The only number in Bartlesville is 1200bps max.  If you're
willing to call outside the immediate area (which,
depending on the type of phone service you have, might not
cost you any extra), here are some numbers to try:

STILLWATER OK 2400   (405)743-1447 Telenet
TULSA   OK 2400   (918)587-2774 Telenet
TULSA   OK 2400   (918)585-2706 Tymnet
ENID   OK 2400   (405)242-0113 Tymnet
[Source: Member Online Support--Access Numbers/Connecting
to AOL--I need a local access number]

Stillwater and Enid will almost certainly result in a
charge on your phone bill, but you might check into the
two numbers in Tulsa.  Note that the 585 number is for the
Tymnet network, so you need to be sure that the proper
setting is made in your configuration (the 'Change Network
Setup' sub-item under the 'Customize' item in the 'Go To'
menu).
     AOL does not levy additional charges for 2400bps
access.  Normal connect rates apply. Hope this helps.
```

Note that CJR3 identifies the menu path he followed to obtain the numbers, and—in the second-to-last paragraph—offers advice on how to reconfigure the software to accommodate an access number. This is exceptional assistance, and it's from a regular member who isn't getting paid for these services.

We're reminded of community again. Visiting a big city a few months ago, Tom was struck by the isolation that seemed to surround everyone he passed on the street. Perhaps it's a defense mechanism for dealing with high population density, but it seemed that everyone was in a cocoon, oblivious to everyone else. No one looked anywhere but straight ahead. Thousands of people jostled together yet none were talking. An incredibly lonely place.

On the other hand, in the little Oregon town where Tom lives, there are no strangers. People stop on the street and say hello, swap some gossip and perhaps offer advice.

AOL is more like Tom's little Oregon community. We've spent years on other services and never felt like we belonged. We never got mail, we never contributed to a message board, and we never knew where to find help. It was like a big city to us, and we were always anxious to leave. At AOL we're walking the street in a small town on a sunny day and everyone is smiling. The first day we arrived at AOL, we each got a letter from Steve Case. People like CJR3 go out of their way to offer assistance. This is our kind of place. We're at home here.

Checking your bill

You can always see the status of your account by using the keyword: Billing. You not only see your account information this way, but you can change your billing method or ask questions about your bill as well. You'll pass through the free curtain, so you're not charged for the time spent checking your account information.

Guides

Guides are members chosen by AOL to serve as real-time assistants. Guides are like Members Helping Members, except there's no waiting. Have a question? Ask a Guide.

We recall the story of an art gallery in Amsterdam where a number of Rembrandts were hanging on the wall just like any other picture. No glass cases or protective Lexan: just those radiant Rembrandts, emancipated and free. A gentleman in uniform stood near. He wasn't a guard: the uniform wasn't that severe. He was a guide. He was a volunteer. He got to spend his days in a room full of the Rembrandts he loved and to share his interest with other people. He explained the Rembrandts to the visitors in a fatherly way, exhibiting a proprietorial regard for his countryman's legacy.

Which is precisely what AOL's Guides are. They're members just like the rest of us—experienced members, with particularly helpful online personalities—but members all the same. They remain politely in the background, leaving us to our own explorations, silent unless spoken to. If we need help, however, Guides are always nearby, ready with friendly advice and information. If you have a question—any question at all—about AOL, its services or its policies, ask a Guide.

Like the guide in Amsterdam, you can identify Guides by their appearance: their screen names have the word "Guide" in them. If Figure 3-10's CJR3 were to be a Guide, he would probably be "Guide CJR," or something like that.

Figure 3-11:
A stop by
the Lobby for
some help from
Guide MO.

A Night in the Lobby

```
7/24/92 3:19:37 PM Opening "Chat Log 7/24/92" for recording.
MajorTom    : Hi all!
Guide MO    : Hey MajorTom :)            ◄──────────────
Lthrneck    : ::::getting out ostrich feather:::::
Guide MO    : Nonononononono!!!
Lthrneck    : ::::TICKLE, TICKLE:::::
Guide MO    : ::giggling::
Guide MO    : Hey Cantoni!! :)
Cantoni     : Hi MO!
Guide MO    : Hiya NyteMaire :)
NyteMaire   : Hiya MO :)
CountStixx  : Maire!!!!   {}{}{}{}{}{}  ◄────
NyteMaire   : {{{{{{Count}}}}}}} **
LovlyVix    : Nyte {}{}{}{}{}{}{}{}{}{}{}
NyteMaire   : {{{Vix}}}}
LovlyVix    : How are you Nyte?
NyteMaire   : Getting crazy, and you? ;)
LovlyVix    : Pretty good Nyte :)
MajorTom    : Anybody know of a utility to convert JPEG to TIFF?
Guide MO    : Let me check the libraries for you, T :) I always use Photoshop :)
PC Kate     : <--trying to type while holding ice pack on face. :)
Lthrneck    : ACK Kate, what happened?
Guide MO    : Kate :( Dentist??
AFC Borg    : Is the ice pack inside or outside the paper bag?
PC Kate     : Lthr, had 3 hours of oral and sinus surgery yesterday.
              They say I should be able to eat again next Friday.
GWRepSteve  : Alchemy would probably be the converter to use, MajorTom...
Lthrneck    : Ouch!  Kate!! {}{}{}{}{}{}{}
Lee123      : awww Kate.    * to make it better.....◄────
LovlyVix    : <--needs to go to dentist for Kates new diet :)
PC Kate     : Vix, works real well... lost just under five pounds  in 2 days. :)
LovlyVix    : Perfect ...that would put me just where I want to be, Kate :)
Guide MO    : MajorTom - I 'm sorry - I don't see what you need offhand,
              though I know we must have it here :/ ◄────
Guide MO    : I'll check later and email you, if that's any help.
MajorTom    : Thanks Guide. Appreciate it. I have a Plus. Can't run PhotoShop.
Guide MO    : Ok - I just wrote a note to myself -
              I'll check for you when I get off shift at 9 and email you :)
MajorTom    : Great! Thanks for the help. G'Night all! ◄
Guide MO    : Night MajorTom :)
```

To help you follow what's going on, my part of the conversation appears in bold.

These are hugs for a new arrival in the Lobby.

The asterisk is a kiss.

Chagrin.

I got an answer the next day.

Figure 3-11 is a little hard to follow if you're not used to AOL's so-called "chat rooms." Though we discuss chat rooms in Chapter 10, "People Connection," a little explanation seems in order. Twenty-one people were in the room when we visited. Many were just watching (lurkers), but others seem to be old friends. The room was full of "smileys" (turn your head counterclockwise 90 degrees and :) becomes a smile) and hugs. Smileys are discussed in Chapters 6, "Lifestyles &

Interests," and 13, "Ten Best." The entire illustration is a "chat log" (see your File menu), discussed in Chapter 5, "News & Finance."

Chat rooms can be intimidating to the first-time visitor. Don't be shy. Jump right in with a Hello, look for the Guide's name and ask your question. More important, note that MajorTom received one immediate answer to his question (from GWRepSteve, a member) and another the next day from Guide MO. He got just what he needed, and it only took ten minutes.

Guides are on duty from noon until 6:00 AM Eastern time during the week, and all day and night Saturday and Sunday. To find a Guide, choose Lobby from the Go To menu, type Ctrl-L, or select the People Connection icon from the Departments screen.

How long have I been online?

Have you lost track of the time? Are you wondering how long it has been since you signed on? AOL anticipates your anxiety with the keyword: Time. Just issue the keyword and AOL tells you how long you've been online, rounded to the nearest minute.

Members

All of this talk about Guides and Members Helping Members might give you the impression that members play a significant part in the operation of America Online. You're right. Members are much more than AOL's source of income: they're contributors (most of the files in the data libraries discussed in Chapter 7—"Computing & Software"— are submitted by members), they're assistants, and, of course, they are the heart of the online community.

Since members play such an important role at AOL, it behooves us to spend a few pages discussing them: how to find them, the member profile and how to be a better member yourself.

The Member Directory

When you first signed on, America Online asked you to complete a voluntary member profile. Though we'll talk about profiles in a few pages, the operative term in the previous sentence is "voluntary." AOL values the individual's privacy, and if you wish to remain secluded in the online community, you may do so. Those members who have completed a profile are listed in the Member Directory (see Figure 3-12).

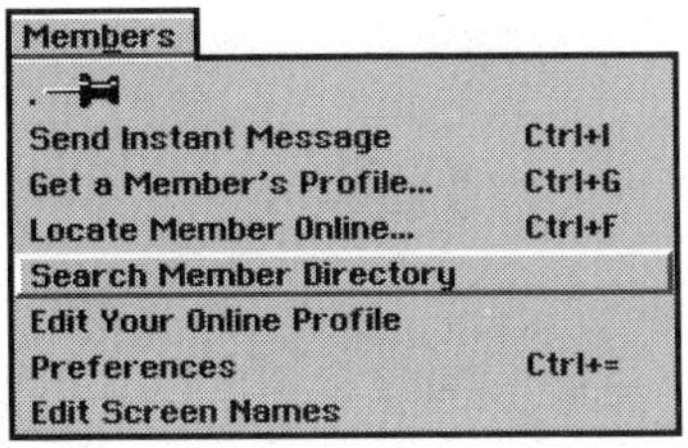

Figure 3-12:
To search the
directory, choose
Search Member
Directory from the
Members menu.

Members
. 📌
Send Instant Message   Ctrl+I
Get a Member's Profile...   Ctrl+G
Locate Member Online...   Ctrl+F
Search Member Directory
Edit Your Online Profile
Preferences   Ctrl+=
Edit Screen Names

You can search for a member by real name, by screen name or by profile. You may see a screen name online and wonder who is behind it: search the directory. You may wonder if a friend is signed up with AOL: search the directory.

What's your sign?

The search mechanism that's used to search the Member Directory ignores numbers. In other words, you cannot search for people by birthdate. Even though the profile asks for your birthdate (and no doubt stores it somewhere), it appears on another member's screen only if you want it to. Instead, your birthdate is converted into an astrological sign (*that's* why you see so many signs in profiles). You may never find the forty-somethings in Philadelphia, but you can find the Tauruses in Toledo.

One of the more interesting things you can do with the directory is to search for people with interests similar to yours. Once you've found them, you can send them mail (we discuss electronic mail in Chapter 11) and perhaps strike up a friendship. It's all part of the electronic community.

One member we know, for instance, enjoys horse-back riding. She's been riding since she was a child, growing up in a rural section of Northern California. Thinking she might find someone to share her interest, she searched the Member Directory for women who have an interest in horse-back riding (see Figure 3-13).

Figure 3-13: Much to our friend's delight, 17 other women share her interests in horses and AOL.

```
┌─────────────────────────────────────────────────────────────┐
│ ─                    Search by Member Profile                 │
│ Search phrase:                                                │
│  ┌──────────────────────────────────────────────────────┐    │
│  │horses and female│                                      │    │
│  └──────────────────────────────────────────────────────┘    │
│ Items 1-17 of 17 matching entries.                            │
│ ┌────────────────────────────────────────────────────┬───┐  │
│ │ ARMSTRONG, VICTORIA              LuvBug1             │ ▲ │  │
│ │  GORDON (VAUGHAN), JEAN ELISE    Jeanelise           │   │  │
│ │ OLSON, KAREN                     Karen05618          │   │  │
│ │ WOLF, ALICE                      K9DOC               │   │  │
│ │ SANDERS, MOLLY                   Lyphard             │   │  │
│ │ , CRYSTAL                        CrystaLily          │   │  │
│ │ OLSON, KAREN                     Hotrider            │   │  │
│ │ AVERY, VICKI                     Shatner            │   │  │
│ │ KRONZ, CANDIE                    CandieK            │   │  │
│ │ ROY, TERRY                       Bic                │ ▼ │  │
│ └────────────────────────────────────────────────────┴───┘  │
│           ┌────────┐ ┌─────────────┐ ┌──────┐                 │
│           │ Search │ │ Display More│ │ Help │                 │
│           └────────┘ └─────────────┘ └──────┘                 │
└─────────────────────────────────────────────────────────────┘
```

Member profiles

As we mentioned a moment ago, member profiles are voluntary. If you elect not to complete a profile, your name won't show up in searches like the one described above. Look again at Figure 3-10. Since we were quoting him (and since we were referring to him as "him," not knowing his gender), we tried to get the profile for CJR3. No luck. CJR3 elected to remain un-profiled.

You may do the same, of course; but you cut yourself out of a number of opportunities to become involved in the online community. If you elect to post a profile (or if you want to edit the profile that is already on file for you), AOL provides a couple of ways for you to do so.

Look again at Figure 3-12. Note that one of the options listed there is Edit Your Online Profile. While this is one way to get the job done, a better way is to go through Members' Online Support. You've got to be signed on in either case, but Members' Online Support is free and the Members menu is not. You may also use the keyword: Profile. Both routes pass through the free curtain.

Once you choose either one of these methods, you'll see the window pictured in Figure 3-14. Click on it and then on the appropriate item(s) in Figure 3-15.

Figure 3-14:
This screen gives
you the options of
creating, modi-
fying, displaying
and asking
America Online
about your profile.

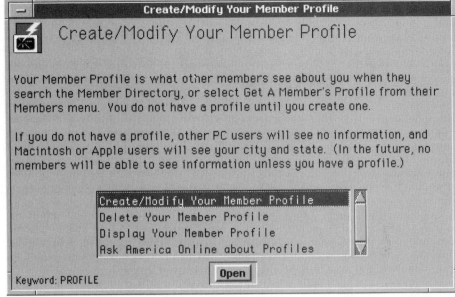

Figure 3-15:
You may create
and modify any
part of your mem-
ber profile by
choosing the de-
sired item from the
list at the right side
of this window.

The profile inquiry consists of several questions about you. Take your time answering these (it's free, after all), and soon you'll have a profile as sterling and poetic as the one shown in Figure 3-16.

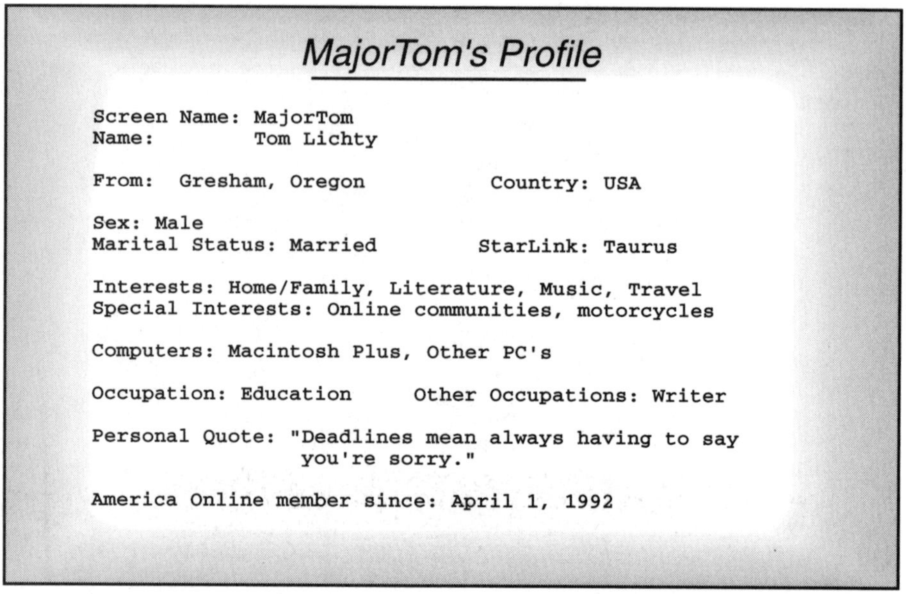

Figure 3-16:
MajorTom's profile
reveals all of his
secrets.

MajorTom's Profile

```
Screen Name: MajorTom
Name:          Tom Lichty

From:  Gresham, Oregon          Country: USA

Sex: Male
Marital Status: Married          StarLink: Taurus

Interests: Home/Family, Literature, Music, Travel
Special Interests: Online communities, motorcycles

Computers: Macintosh Plus, Other PC's

Occupation: Education      Other Occupations: Writer

Personal Quote: "Deadlines mean always having to say
                you're sorry."

America Online member since: April 1, 1992
```

We've come a long way since the heavy-metal band took the stage at the beginning of this chapter. We hope our journey has been confidence building. America Online offers more help—and more *kinds* of help— than any software we know of. It's online, it's off-line, it's Jay Levitt and the Customer Relations Department, it's Members Helping Members and it's Guides. Everyone at AOL—members included—helps someone else sooner or later. That's comforting. Not only is AOL a community, it's a *considerate* community, where no one remains a stranger for long.

Moving on

Now that you're all connected and brimming with confidence, the time has come to visit a department. The one that most people visit first is the Entertainment Department, where sports, comedy, music, TV and the movies reign supreme. We doubt we'll see Online Help & the Members again; but rumor has it the Grateful Dead will make an appearance in the next chapter. Next

Entertainment

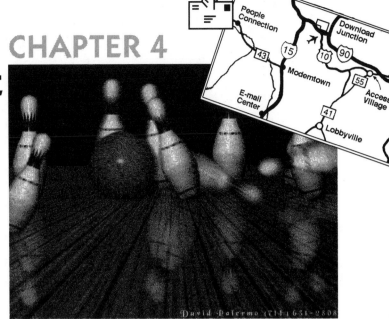

Tom bought a new car the other day. The purchase of a new car happens rarely, especially if you're a starving writer in the boondocks of the Northwest. To exploit the moment, he opted to take a pleasure drive. He drove the car, still on its first tank of gas, to Timberline Lodge near the top of Mount Hood, Oregon's 12,000-foot baronial landmark.

He had no purpose for being there other than it was a sunny day and the mountain was magnificent and he had a new toy and it was a moment to be savored. It was a romp. A frivolous romp. He had a new car and he deserved it.

Welcome to the first stop on our tour, the Entertainment Department. This is our romp. We're here for no legitimate purpose; this is not an academic visit. It's a sunny day and we have a new toy and we're here for the fun of it.

An overview

Take a look at Figure 4-1. The Entertainment Department is America Online's midway. Here's where you read your horoscope (review Figure 1-9), play online games, laugh it up at the Comedy Club and review movies or videos before you rent. Sports fans should head

---

Frontispiece graphic: "Pins!" by David Palermo. File search using the criterion SPACE7.

directly for the Grandstand under Sports & Entertainment Clubs; literati will want to investigate the Book Bestsellers Forum under Entertainment News & Features; and those who enjoy the camaraderie of the corner tavern will appreciate LaPub on Saturday nights.

Figure 4-1: The Entertainment Department: America Online's midway.

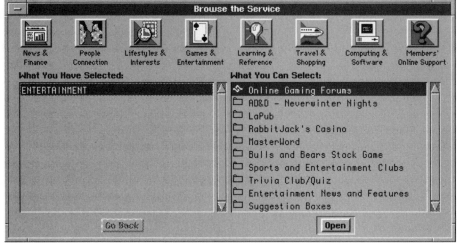

Book Bestsellers

Since you're reading a book at the moment, we can assume you're literate, and as such, you might enjoy a visit to AOL's Book Bestsellers Forum (from the Entertainment Department, select Entertainment News & Features or use the keyword: Books). The top-ten lists you will see here are compiled by *Publishers Weekly* and feature the current week's bestsellers for fiction, nonfiction, mass market and trade (see Figure 4-2).

In addition to *Publishers Weekly* lists, the Book Bestsellers Forum offers a message board where you may post your own reviews or read those of your peers. Reader reviews are the most candid of all.

Figure 4-2: Now you have instant access to the "Publishers Weekly" top-ten book lists. They're all available on AOL in the Book Bestsellers Forum.

Cartoons

Let's take a little survey: what's the first section you read when you pick up the Sunday paper? If you're like us, you read "the funnies" before anything else. Often they're the *only* thing worth reading, depending on how dreary the world has been that week.

America Online is particularly rich in cartoons, and you don't have to wait until Sunday morning to enjoy them. No fewer than four different cartoonists contribute to AOL every week.

- Theresa McCracken is a professional magazine cartoonist who has been cartooning full-time since 1981. Her work appears in more than 300 publications, including the *Saturday Evening Post*, *Compute!*, *Link-Up*, *Popular Electronics*, *ComputerEdge*, the *Baltimore Sun*, *Computer Game Forum* and *Adweek*.

- Mike Keefe is a nationally syndicated cartoonist based in Denver, Colorado. Mike and his cartoons are featured in Chapter 12, "The Download Manager."

- Charles Rodrigues produces cartoons regularly for *MacWEEK* magazine; his work has appeared in *Stereo Review* and *National Lampoon* as well. His "CompuToons" are computer-related and available only on America Online.

- Peter Oakley began drawing pictures on his PC in 1987. He now lives in Seattle, where he's a full-time cartoonist, drawing for a number of publications, including AOL's own "Modern Wonder" cartoon series.

The cartoonist's life

The cartoonist's life seems like an easy one. All you have to do is sketch a funny picture, then send it off to a magazine and wait for a big check to come back in the mail.

Peter Oakley knows better. On the subject of the cartoonist's life, he writes, "The truth is that magazine cartooning is extremely competitive, there are hundreds of remarkably talented cartoonists out there, and few of us are what you would call famous. And because I am doing something new, there was considerable resistance to 'computer-generated' cartoons in the traditional pen-and-ink cartoon market. Of course, the most comfortable home for these cartoons is on the computer, and so it was just a matter of time before they would show up on a telecommunications network. [America Online] is the first national network to host a regular cartoon feature, and I am glad 'Modern Wonder' has found a home here."

Figure 4-3: Three 'toons from the Cartoon Forum: "Heavy Fog," by Theresa McCracken; "Whistle," by Charles Rodrigues; and "Crash and Burn," by Peter Oakley. New cartoons are posted weekly in the Entertainment Department.

As you might assume by looking at the window pictured above, cartoons from members are also available; and the Toon Talk message board offers a lively discussion for those with an interest in cartooning.

The Grandstand

A friend of ours made us smile when she relayed a story regarding her boyfriend. In something of a reversal of stereotypes, she is the computer fanatic of the two; until recently, he had no interest whatsoever in the subject.

He does, however, have a keen interest in sports. Our friend discovered the Grandstand on the first day she signed on to AOL. Grabbing her friend by the hair (we're taking some creative license here, but we kind of like the reverse Cro-Magnon image), she sat him in front of the screen and made him explore the Grandstand with her. In minutes, he was using the mouse, typing messages and downloading files. He had never used a computer before, and now she can't get him away from it.

Ahh, but now who will slay the giant mastodon and protect the cave from the wily saber-toothed tiger?

If you enjoy sports, you'll love the Grandstand (keyword: Grandstand). America Online's homage to the sports enthusiast is current, relevant and vast (see Figure 4-4). In the interest of sports widows everywhere, however, we suggest moderation. The walls of prehistoric caves the world over are riddled with pictographs of smashed keyboards and punctured computers. It's not a pretty sight.

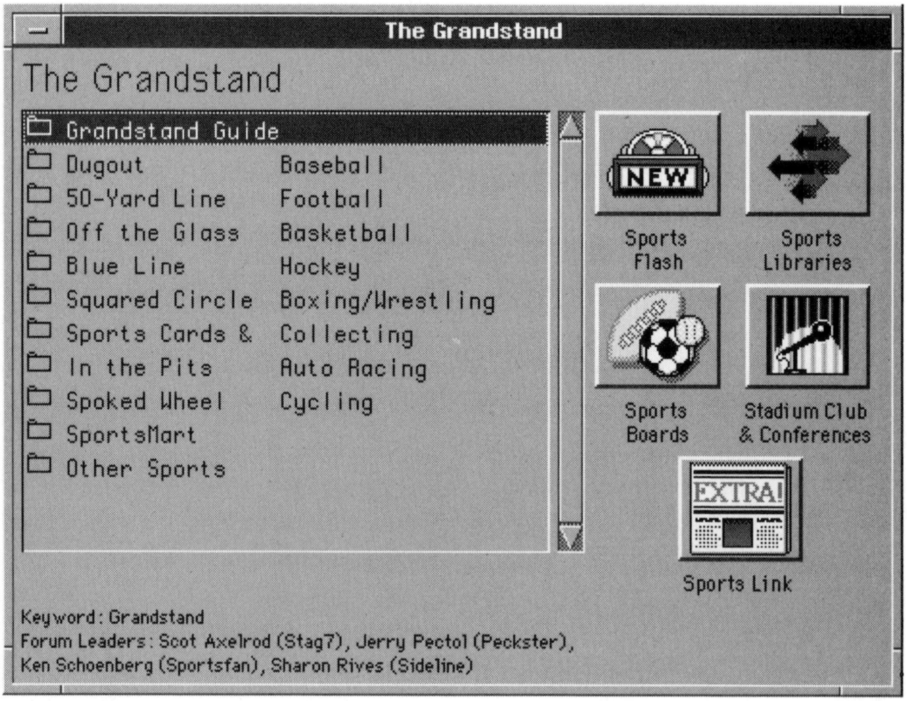

Figure 4-4:
The Grandstand offers something for every sports enthusiast.

While investigating the Grandstand the other day, we downloaded a Microsoft Excel spreadsheet file (we'll explore downloading in Chapter 7, "Computing & Software") that outlined the 1992 NBA draft choices, complete with player notes (see Figure 4-5). We discovered an online club dedicated entirely to baseball cards, providing news, price polls and conferences for collectors throughout the nation. The Pit Stop features articles, messages and files for auto-racing fans; and the Spoked Wheel is a haven for bicycle-racing fans and participants alike. (Online clubs like the Spoked Wheel and the Pit Stop are discussed in Chapter 6, "Lifestyles & Interests.")

Perhaps the most interesting aspect of the Grandstand is its assortment of fantasy teams—make-believe teams (comprising real players in a sport) assembled by AOL members. The Grandstand Fantasy Baseball League (GFBL under Dugout), for example, is modeled after "Rotisserie League Baseball," as described in the book of the same name by Glen Waggoner (published by Bantam Books).

Team owners (that's us—the members of AOL) draft 23 players from the available talent in the American or National Leagues. The players' actual big-league performances are used in computing the standings of the GFBL team. Standings, stats, newsletters and other league information are found in the message and library sections of the GFBL, and members watch them fanatically. The foremost table of player statistics pictured in Figure 4-5 is a fantasy team in the A League of the GFBL.

Anyone can join the Grandstand Fantasy Baseball League. Indeed, if members didn't join, there would *be* no league. Member participation is AOL's foundation: from the GFBL to the "Wheel of Fortune" game in the Center Stage (which we discuss in Chapter 10, "People Connection"), members make the game.

Figure 4-5: The Grandstand offers a club for baseball-card collectors; spreadsheets for sports-minded digit-heads; sports fantasy teams; and dozens of graphics (like that of NHL MVP Jeff Hackett) for downloading.

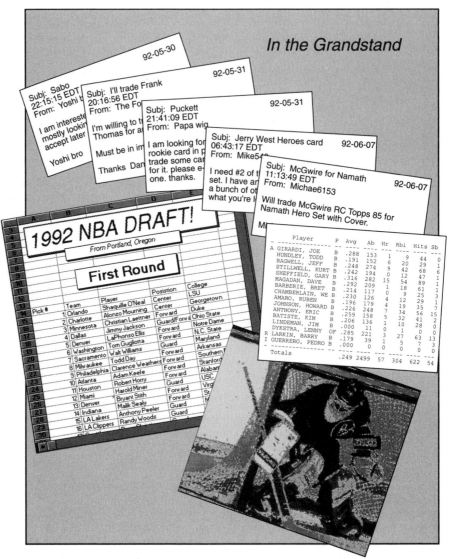

In the Grandstand

92-05-30

Subj: Sabo
22:15:15 EDT
From: Yoshi b

I am intereste
mostly lookin
accept later

Yoshi bro

92-05-31

Subj: I'll trade Frank
20:16:56 EDT
From: The Fo

I'm willing to t
Thomas for a

Must be in im

Thanks Dan

92-05-31

Subj: Puckett
21:41:09 EDT
From: Papa wig

I am looking for
rookie card in p
trade some car
for it. please e-
one. thanks.

92-06-07

Subj: Jerry West Heroes card
06:43:17 EDT
From: Mike54

I need #2 of t
set. I have ar
a bunch of ot
what you're l

92-06-07

Subj: McGwire for Namath
11:13:49 EDT
From: Michae6153

Will trade McGwire RC Topps 85 for
Namath Hero Set with Cover.

1992 NBA DRAFT!

From Portland, Oregon

First Round

Pick #	Team	Player	Position	College
1	Orlando	Shaquille O'Neal	Center	LSU
2	Charlotte	Alonzo Mourning	Center	Georgetown
3	Minnesota	Christian Laettner	Forward	Duke
4	Dallas	Jimmy Jackson	Guard/Forward	Ohio State
5	Denver	LaPhonso Ellis	Forward	Notre Dame
6	Washington	Tom Gugliotta	Forward	N.C. State
7	Sacramento	Walt Williams	Guard	Maryland
8	Milwaukee	Todd Day	Forward	Arkansas
9	Philadelphia	Clarence Weathers	Forward	Southern
10	Atlanta	Adam Keefe	Forward	Stanford
11	Houston	Robert Horry	Forward	Alabama
12	Miami	Harold Miner	Guard	USC
13	Denver	Bryant Stith	Forward	Virg
14	Indiana	Malik Sealy	Forward	S
15	LA Lakers	Anthony Peeler	Guard	M
16	LA Clippers	Randy Woods	Guard	

Player	P	Avg	Ab	Hr	Rbi	Hits	Sb
A GIRARDI, JOE	B	.288	153	1	9	44	0
HUNDLEY, TODD	B	.191	152	6	20	29	1
BAGWELL, JEFF	B	.248	274	9	42	68	6
STILLWELL, KURT	B	.242	194	0	12	47	1
SHEFFIELD, GARY	B	.316	282	15	54	89	1
MAGADAN, DAVE	B	.292	209	1	18	61	1
BARBERIE, BRET	B	.214	117	0	9	25	3
CHAMBERLAIN, WE	B	.230	126	4	12	29	1
AMARO, RUBEN	B	.196	179	4	19	35	7
JOHNSON, HOWARD	B	.226	248	7	34	56	15
ANTHONY, ERIC	B	.259	158	5	32	41	2
BATISTE, KIM	B	.206	136	1	10	28	0
LINDEMAN, JIM	B	.000	11	0	1	0	0
DYKSTRA, LENNY	OF	.285	221	3	27	63	13
R LARKIN, BARRY	B	.179	39	1	5	7	3
I GUERRERO, PEDRO	B	.000	0	0	0	0	0
Totals		.249	2499	57	304	622	54

The Comedy Club

Pursuant to our self-proclaimed romp, let's take a moment to yuk it up. The Comedy Club "…offers relief from the serious, dog-eat-cat world we live in. As they say, laugh and the world laughs with you; cry and

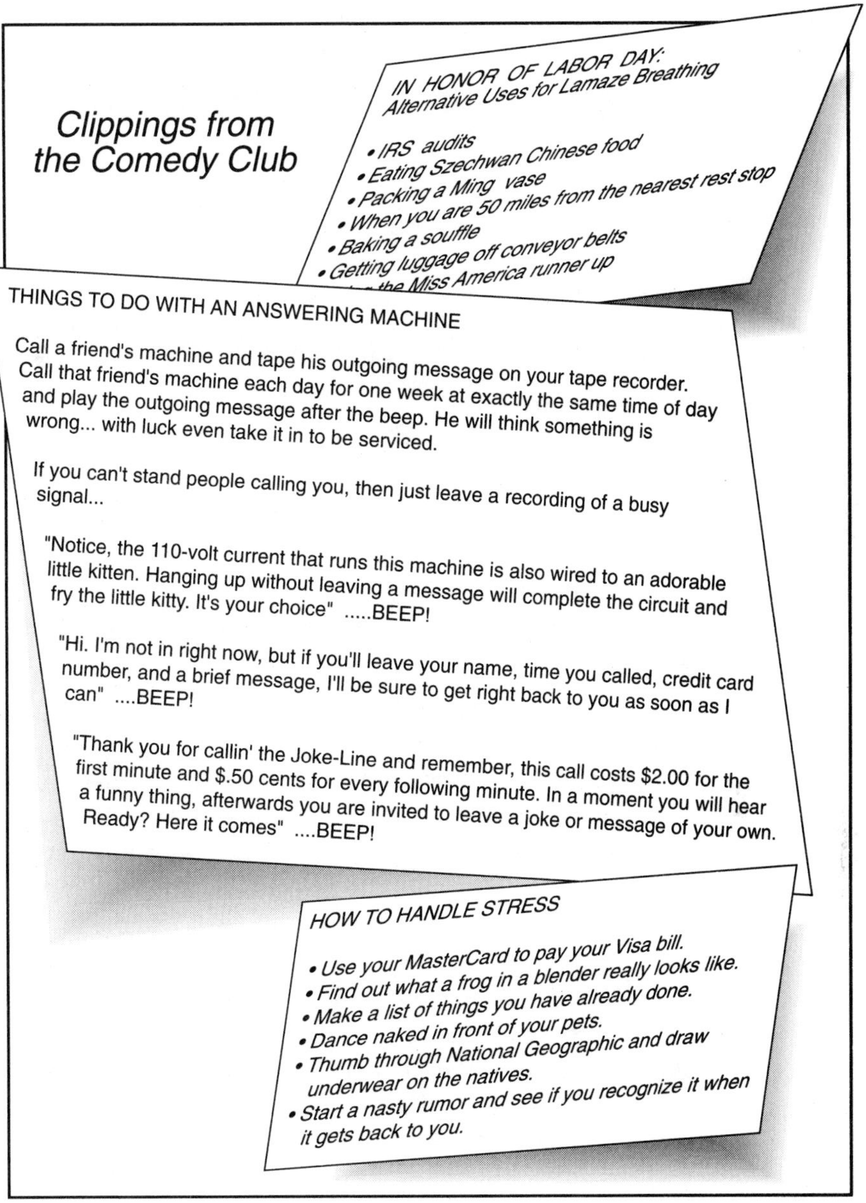

Figure 4-6:
You can spend
hours here: the
Comedy Club
offers a laugh
around every
corner.

Clippings from the Comedy Club

IN HONOR OF LABOR DAY:
Alternative Uses for Lamaze Breathing

- IRS audits
- Eating Szechwan Chinese food
- Packing a Ming vase
- When you are 50 miles from the nearest rest stop
- Baking a souffle
- Getting luggage off conveyor belts
- the Miss America runner up

THINGS TO DO WITH AN ANSWERING MACHINE

Call a friend's machine and tape his outgoing message on your tape recorder. Call that friend's machine each day for one week at exactly the same time of day and play the outgoing message after the beep. He will think something is wrong... with luck even take it in to be serviced.

If you can't stand people calling you, then just leave a recording of a busy signal...

"Notice, the 110-volt current that runs this machine is also wired to an adorable little kitten. Hanging up without leaving a message will complete the circuit and fry the little kitty. It's your choice" .....BEEP!

"Hi. I'm not in right now, but if you'll leave your name, time you called, credit card number, and a brief message, I'll be sure to get right back to you as soon as I can" ....BEEP!

"Thank you for callin' the Joke-Line and remember, this call costs $2.00 for the first minute and $.50 cents for every following minute. In a moment you will hear a funny thing, afterwards you are invited to leave a joke or message of your own. Ready? Here it comes" ....BEEP!

HOW TO HANDLE STRESS

- Use your MasterCard to pay your Visa bill.
- Find out what a frog in a blender really looks like.
- Make a list of things you have already done.
- Dance naked in front of your pets.
- Thumb through National Geographic and draw underwear on the natives.
- Start a nasty rumor and see if you recognize it when it gets back to you.

your eyes leak and get all red and puffy and you look awful." That's the credo of the club, and it's adequate justification for spending a few minutes there whenever you go online.

Figure 4-7:
The punchline
contest is new
each week.
Dozens of
punchlines are
posted; winners
are chosen on
Friday afternoons.

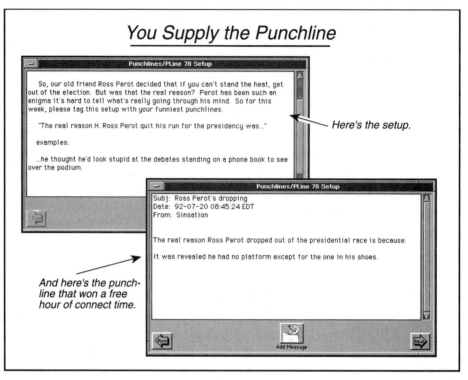

New ideas always crop up around the Comedy Club. One that has remained over the years is the punchline contest (see Figure 4-7). The theory is simple: the forum leader sets up the situation, the members supply the resolution—the punchline. There's ample incentive: each week's winner receives an hour of free connect time. No one really loses: there are plenty of laughs to go around.

When you visit, don't neglect to browse the Comedy Club's library (libraries are discussed in Chapter 7, "Computing & Software"). Dozens of files reside there (including the cartoons mentioned earlier), ready to be downloaded into your computer to read at your leisure. No online session should be concluded without a stop here for a smile.

RockLink Forum

According to Les Tracy, the forum leader for RockLink (keyword: RockLink), the forum is "...committed to delivering the latest, most accurate info in the world of rock and roll." Regular contributors include musicians, record label personnel, reporters at rock radio stations (of which Les is one: he's Operations Manager for Magic 1380 in San Francisco), and—of course—members like us. RockLink features news, reviews, concert dates and a library of files for the music enthusiast (see Figure 4-8).

Figure 4-8: Regular features on RockLink include "The Daily Beat" (top), weekly lists of the Top 30 albums and singles, and reviews.

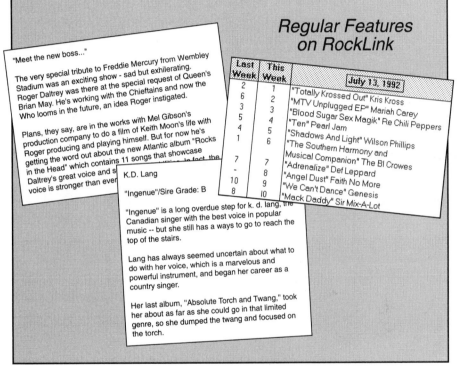

In Chapter 1, we alluded to our preference for classical music. Stephen King may do his writing while rock and roll plays at 120 decibels, but we write to Mozart. However, we must confess to liking the Grateful Dead—Mickey Hart in particular, whose academic pursuit of the art of drumming has taken him literally around the world. The Dead are especially fond of Oregon, and they exhibit that fondness with an annual visit to Eugene, a mecca for Deadheads if there ever was one.

Look at the message board pictured at the top of Figure 4-9. There are 256 messages regarding Stevie Nicks, 150 for the Moody Blues and *450* in the Grateful Dead folder—nearly one-fourth of all the messages in the RockLink Forum!

Figure 4-9:
Unfortunately, the
Dead never played
Oregon in 1992.
Jerry was suffering
from exhaustion
and everybody
stayed home.

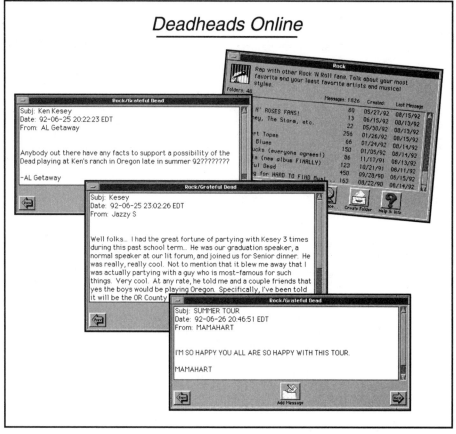

The Trivia Club

One of the Entertainment Department's more popular areas is the
Trivia Club (keyword: Trivia), where members try to better one
another's knowledge of totally useless information. One of the club's
most popular features is the Question of the Day. Each day, the forum
leader posts a question, and members scramble to be the first to post
the correct answer (see Figure 4-10).

Figure 4-10:
You've gotta be
fast to be the first
to post the correct
answer to the
Trivia Club's
Question of the
Day. The first
response (albeit
incorrect) was
published less
than 15 minutes
after the question.

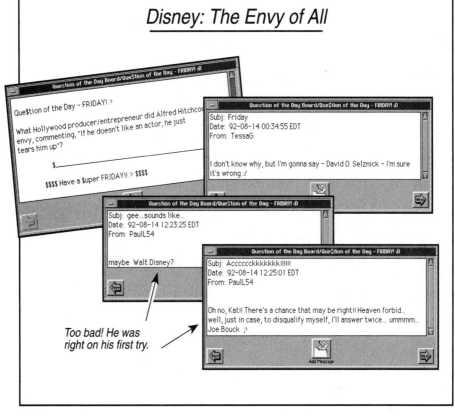

Figure 4-10:
You've gotta be
fast to be the first
to post the correct
answer to the
Trivia Club's
Question of the
Day. The first
response (albeit
incorrect) was
published less
than 15 minutes
after the question.

Movie & video reviews

Videos have become as much a part of the American landscape as the
Fourth of July. Convenience markets, gas stations—everywhere you
turn, someone has a video to rent. No doubt VCRs outnumber computers in American households, even though computers are infinitely
easier to use.

If you're like Tom, you can spend hours in a video store and leave
with nothing to show for it. Unless he knows what he wants before he
walks in the door, he becomes a tremulous enormity of indecision after
ten minutes of browsing. The video store in his town is about the size
of Delaware. One doesn't browse in a place like that. Either you know
what you want or you're swallowed by the immensity of the place,

wandering aimlessly in a labyrinth of racks and little plastic boxes where the exits are known only to pubescent knaves whose imaginations are incapable of grasping the meaning of the question, "May I help you?"

Perhaps one of the most practical services America Online offers is its searchable database of videos. In the solitude of your own home, you can specify any search criteria you wish and AOL complies with a manageable list of prospects (see Figure 4-11). There are no racks and no knaves, and the exits are plainly marked. Use the keyword: Movies.

Figure 4-11: AOL's searchable database of video reviews offers 16 entries matching the "baseball" criterion. If you rent "Field of Dreams," you may become convinced that if you build a baseball diamond in your backyard "he" will come.

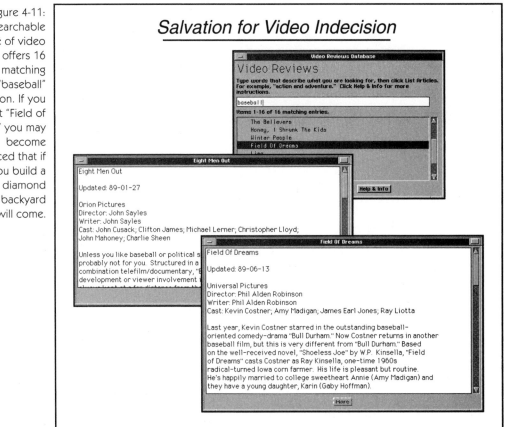

Salvation for Video Indecision

Video Reviews Database

Video Reviews

Type words that describe what you are looking for, then click List Articles. For example, "action and adventure." Click Help & Info for more instructions.

baseball

Items 1-16 of 16 matching entries.

The Believers
Honey, I Shrunk The Kids
Winter People
Field Of Dreams
Lion

Help & Info

Eight Men Out

Eight Men Out

Updated: 89-01-27

Orion Pictures
Director: John Sayles
Writer: John Sayles
Cast: John Cusack; Clifton James; Michael Lerner; Christopher Lloyd; John Mahoney; Charlie Sheen

Unless you like baseball or political s
probably not for you. Structured in a
combination telefilm/documentary, "
development or viewer involvement

Field Of Dreams

Field Of Dreams

Updated: 89-06-13

Universal Pictures
Director: Phil Alden Robinson
Writer: Phil Alden Robinson
Cast: Kevin Costner; Amy Madigan; James Earl Jones; Ray Liotta

Last year, Kevin Costner starred in the outstanding baseball-oriented comedy-drama "Bull Durham." Now Costner returns in another baseball film, but this is very different from "Bull Durham." Based on the well-received novel, "Shoeless Joe" by W.P. Kinsella, "Field of Dreams" casts Costner as Ray Kinsella, one-time 1960s radical-turned Iowa corn farmer. His life is pleasant but routine. He's happily married to college sweetheart Annie (Amy Madigan) and they have a young daughter, Karin (Gaby Hoffman).

More

Kathy Ryan

Airborne at 50 mph, we clenched the armrest and closed our eyes. We were in a parking lot, after all, and there was stationary metal all around us. Immovable, unsuspecting metal that was perfectly capable of ravaging extreme injury to our frail flesh, should we contact it at this speed.

We were in a small red car driven by Kathy Ryan, Product Marketing Director at America Online. A young woman with the metabolism of a bumblebee, Kathy was punctuating her conversation with her right hand while she drove with the left, oblivious to the fact that none of her wheels were in contact with the ground. We were sure we were going to die in a parking lot in Virginia in a red car at the hands of a woman whose idea of a quick lunch is to drive to a neighboring state for kefir and Babaganoush.

Kathy Ryan conducts business the way she drives. Our week with her was like a week with a presidential candidate: inviolable schedules, parades of people and unceasing action. Kathy Ryan is a mover and shaker, and she will propel AOL to eminence if she has to recruit every man, woman and child on the planet into the AOL fold.

Which is to our advantage. The more members the marketing group acquires for America Online, the more bountiful the service. The more bountiful the service, the more that's in it for us. At AOL, bounty is the objective.

If she invites you to lunch, however, offer to drive. That way you'll both live long enough to profit from her labor.

The Online Gaming Forums

There's a world of game players who find the Online Gaming Forums (keyword: OGF) to be their hermitage, the place where games are paramount and challenges are eternal. It is here where knights slay dragons, space voyagers conquer aliens, and residents of the late 20th Century scratch their heads in bewilderment. You owe it to yourself to try an online game if you never have: the challenge of playing with remote competitors—unseen and unknown—isn't quite matched by any other. And if you get hooked, the Online Gaming Forums stand ready to nourish your obsession (see Figure 4-12).

Figure 4-12:
Free-form, play-by-
mail and role-
playing games
abound on the
Online Gaming
Forums.

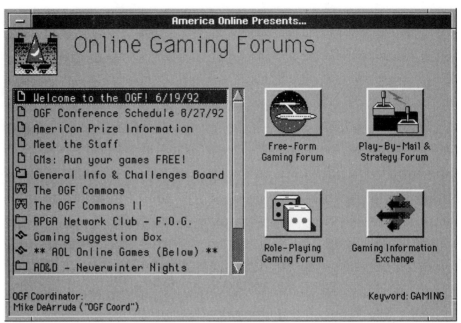

Neverwinter Nights

Neverwinter Nights is an online Advanced Dungeons & Dragons (AD&D) fantasy role-playing game. There's no other online experience quite like it; and there's no better way to play AD&D than with real people in real time, in a medium that combines color, sound, graphics and unbounded intellectual stimulation.

Neverwinter Nights is played using its own software: you sign on, enter the Neverwinter Nights Forum (keyword: AD&D), then start the Neverwinter Nights software that resides on your hard disk (see Figure 4-13). GEOS and AOL disappear, and the land of Lord Nasher, Neverwinter's brave leader, assumes control. Great treasures can be found here. And if you and Nasher succeed in returning peace to the region, bounty can be yours.

Figure 4-13:
Note the topics
that can be
researched before
entering the game.
We advise this; the
more information
you have before
you start, the less
likely your
character will be
killed immediately.

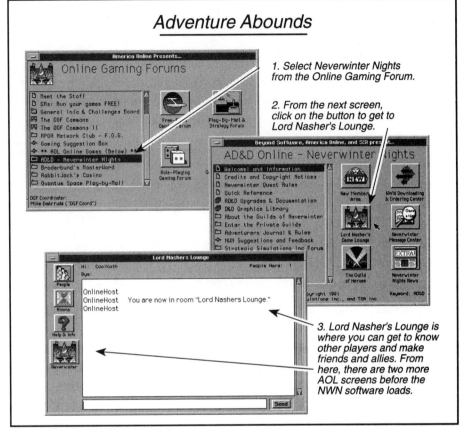

Spectacular sound and 3D graphics are provided by the Neverwinter Nights software on your hard disk (see Figure 4-14). The modest charge of $15 provides everything you need to play the game—a box containing software and documentation arrives on your doorstep a few days after you place your order. Upgrades are free and may be downloaded from AOL.

Figure 4-14:
Even the title
screen you
encounter upon
entering the game
is filled with bright
colors and a
catchy tune, if you
choose to turn the
music on.

Anyone who has played the game can tell you that there's nothing lightweight about Advanced Dungeons & Dragons. America Online is aware of that and graciously provides a number of AD&D experts to help whenever you need it. At the top of the list are the official Neverwinter Nights AD&D staff—easily recognizable by the "NW" in front of their names.

Ordering Neverwinter Nights software

To play Neverwinter Nights, you'll need to buy and install Neverwinter Nights software on your PC. (Use the keyword: Neverwinter, and click on the NWN Downloading & Ordering Center to place your order.) The software package costs $14.95 for AOL members and includes everything you need to play the game; in addition you'll be able to download any upgrades to the Neverwinter software for free on AOL. The program will be shipped via UPS within two weeks of ordering. It's worth the wait.

When we tried out the game, we were a little overwhelmed by its immensity until we happened upon NW Arwen (AD&D Online–NWN Supervisor) and Trollsbane. They kindly showed us some of the ropes (there are a lot of them), let us follow them around, helped us acquire gold, treasures and weapons, cast spells upon our character to make it stronger and less vulnerable to the terrible beasts it met along the way, and saved our character's life on more than one occasion.

In few areas will you find people more helpful and congenial than while playing Neverwinter Nights. There's a Lounge (a "chat room," which we discuss in Chapter 10, "People Connection") where you can relax and get to know other players, and a New Members Area as well.

Neverwinter Nights provides a degree of interactivity and realism that entices the new member and challenges the veteran player. Many people join AOL solely for access to this game—it's that good. While your commitment need not be as fervent, you owe it to yourself to explore the potential of this remarkable realization of the telecommunications medium.

RabbitJack's Casino

If you love the roll-the-dice excitement of Atlantic City and Las Vegas but you don't have the time (or money) to travel to those gambling meccas, you might want to visit RabbitJack's Casino, where you'll find all your favorite casino games, including bingo, poker and blackjack.

Established by RabbitJack, the famous online gambler, the casino is now run by RabbitJill, who promises everyone a good time tempting fate at the wheel of fortune. To play this casino game, use the keyword: Casino, then download RabbitJack's Casino (see Chapter 7, "Computing & Software" for instructions on how to download). The download is free; you'll find complete instructions posted in the casino detailing how to download and install the software.

The casino works much like an America Online chat room, with about two dozen people at a table or in a row at a given time. You receive 250 chips upon entering the casino and 250 more each day you visit. You can transfer some of your chips to a pal or borrow some if you're down on your luck. But don't worry, the chips are only in fun—this is one casino you'll never leave wishing you hadn't bet it all on that last hand.

Play-by-mail games

Also of interest are a number of play-by-mail games. The play-by-mail format allows a group of people from across the country to play a game online, using electronic mail and bulletin boards. Games usually require a short amount of actual playing time each week. The cerebral part of the game—planning moves, figuring strategy, assessing opponents—takes place off-line, while you're driving, falling asleep or staring at bad television. Perhaps best of all, you don't have to find three other people who have an evening free to play.

The superstar of play-by-mail games is Quantum Space, a science-fiction strategy game of galactic exploration and conquest (see Figure 4-15). It's designed to allow a large number of players of different ages and skill levels to compete. Woven through every game is a different mystery story. Some mystery elements can be discovered through exploration, while others must be interpreted through discussion with other players. It's not only a game, it's a terrific way to meet people and become involved with the online community.

Figure 4-15:
The gaming areas
are full of
information, hints
and strategies, and
message boards
for learning more
about their
contents.

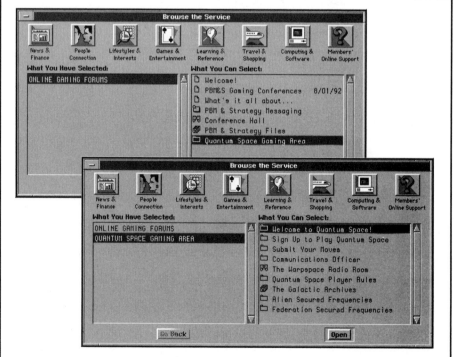

Moving on

As with all romps, this one must conclude. One cannot spend forever on the midway. There's a real world out there, teeming with people and events that promise to change our lives and those of the people around us. There's also the subject of money. Money is a universal elixir: even if you have elected to secede from the real world, you'll still need money wherever you go.

Money and events—obsessions of the '80s, imperatives for the '90s. Naturally, America Online attends to the imperatives, and what better place than the News & Finance Department, coming up next. Next

News & Finance

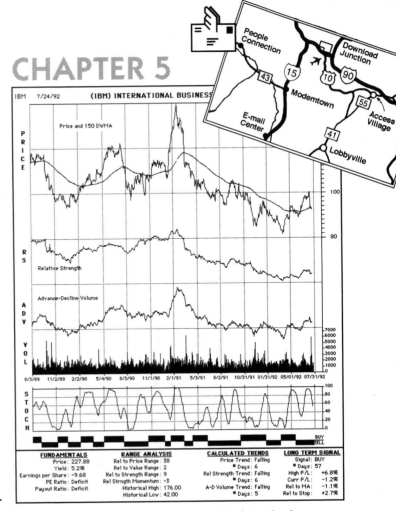

IBM	7/24/92	(IBM) INTERNATIONAL BUSINES...

Price and 150 DWMA

P R I C E

Relative Strength

R S

Advance-Decline Volume

A D V

V O L

| 8/3/89 | 11/2/89 | 2/2/90 | 5/4/90 | 8/3/90 | 11/1/90 | 2/1/91 | 5/3/91 | 8/2/91 | 10/31/91 | 01/31/92 | 05/01/92 | 07/31/92 |

S T O C H

BUY
SELL

FUNDAMENTALS	RANGE ANALYSIS	CALCULATED TRENDS	LONG TERM SIGNAL
Price: 227.88	Rel to Price Range: 38	Price Trend: Falling	Signal: BUY
Yield: 5.2%	Rel to Value Range: 2	# Days: 6	# Days: 57
Earnings per Share: -9.68	Rel to Strength Range: 9	Rel Strength Trend: Falling	High P/L: +6.8%
PE Ratio: Deficit	Rel Strngth Momentum: -3	# Days: 6	Curr P/L: -1.2%
Payout Ratio: Deficit	Historical High: 176.00	A-D Volume Trend: Falling	Rel to MA: -1.1%
	Historical Low: 42.00	# Days: 5	Rel to Stop: +2.7%

Have you ever
seen those little radios that pick up weather reports? A friend of ours
uses one every day. It's tuned to the local NOAA station, which broad-
casts nothing but the weather, 24 hours a day. These gadgets are the
ideal information machine: always current, always available and nearly
free. Now if we could only find a similar source for news and sports....

Aha! What about America Online? If there ever was a machine for
instant news, this is it. Unlike television and radio, AOL's news is
available whenever you want it: there's no waiting for the six o'clock
news, and you don't have to suffer through three stories (and four
commercials) you don't want to hear before you get to the one you do.
Unlike newspapers, AOL is always current. It's not this morning's
news, it's this *minute's* news. It's current, it's always available, and
it's inexpensive.

Frontispiece graphic: A three-year price history of IBM stock. This graphic shows 30
separate indicators or pieces of information, including relative strength, daily volume,
advance/decline volume and 21-day stochastic. File search: IBM.GIF.

Your personal stock portfolio

Let's begin this chapter with a financial exercise. This one is risk-free, but it's nonetheless quite real. A portfolio of investments is a fascinating thing to follow and nourish, even if it's only make-believe. And if you want to add some real punch to it, AOL offers a brokerage service. You can invest real money in real issues and realize real gains (or losses...).

Whether you intend to invest Real Cash or funny money, come along with us as we create a personal portfolio of stocks and securities.

StockLink

Begin the journey by typing Ctrl-K and entering the keyword: News. America Online responds by transporting you to the News & Finance Department (see Figure 5-1).

Figure 5-1:
News, sports and weather: it's all current and it's available 24 hours a day. Just use the keyword: News.

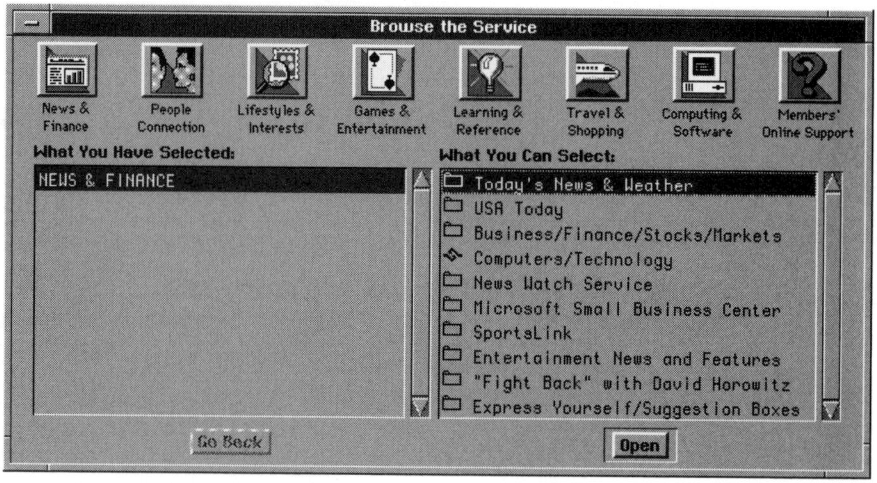

News & Finance is one of AOL's most comprehensive departments. Look at the list of topics in Figure 5-1! AOL may be the perfect information machine: it features news, sports and weather, and an impressive offering of financial information, including the Microsoft Small Business Center and an online game for would-be investors.

Back to our portfolio: click on the topic labeled Business/Finance/ Stocks/Markets, and let's visit StockLink (see Figure 5-2).

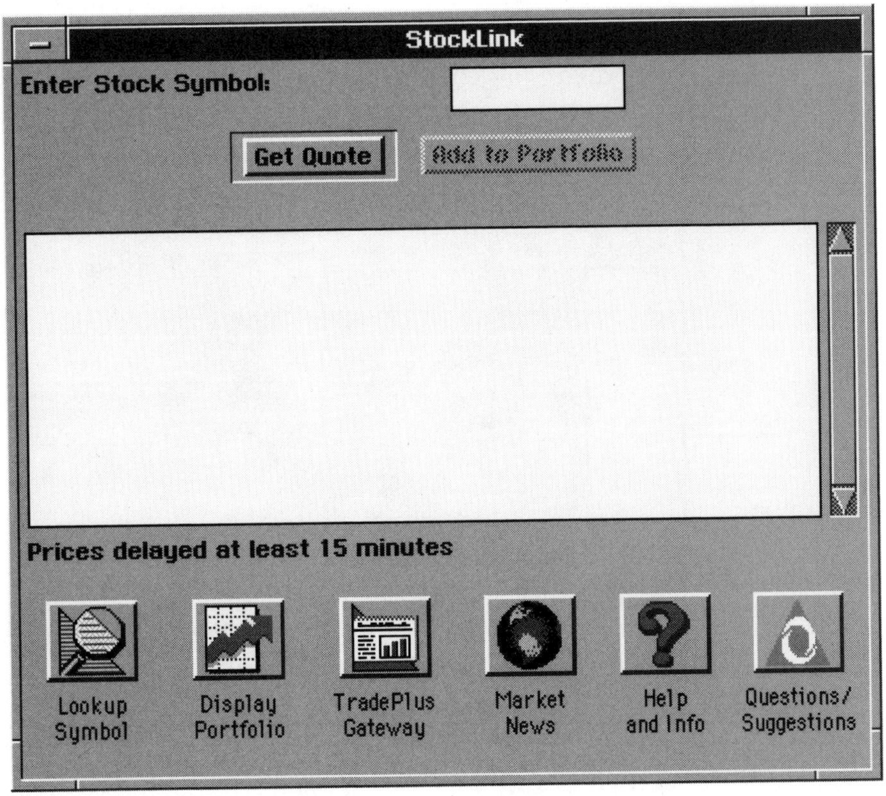

Figure 5-2:
The StockLink
window allows
you to access
market news, look
up a single issue,
build a portfolio,
or buy and sell
issues for real. Use
the keyword:
StockLink.

StockLink

Enter Stock Symbol:

Get Quote   Add to Portfolio

Prices delayed at least 15 minutes

Lookup Symbol   Display Portfolio   TradePlus Gateway   Market News   Help and Info   Questions/ Suggestions

StockLink is a comprehensive financial-information service, equaled by few others in the telecommunications industry and available on AOL without surcharge. The only thing you pay when you're visiting StockLink is your normal connect-time charges. StockLink connects to AOL via high-speed telephone lines, providing financial information updated continuously during market hours on a 20-minute delay basis.

Finding a stock symbol

StockLink is waiting for us to enter a stock symbol. Stock symbols are those abbreviations you see traveling across the Big Board in a stock broker's office. What shall we buy? Since it's something that we all have in common, let's look up America Online itself. AOL is a publicly traded issue, after all, so StockLink should offer a reference to it.

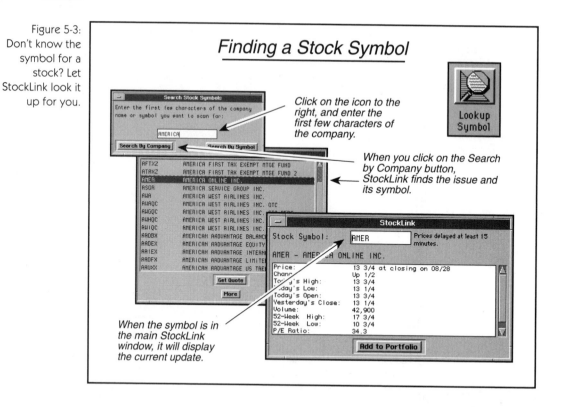

Figure 5-3:
Don't know the
symbol for a
stock? Let
StockLink look it
up for you.

But what's AOL's symbol? Hmmm.... Let's try the Lookup Symbol icon. After we click on that icon, we'll click on the Search by Company button and follow the path pictured in Figure 5-3. Then we discover AMER, the symbol for America Online.

Once we highlight the symbol, all we have to do is click on the Get Quote button. The results are pictured in Figure 5-3's scroll box.

Building the portfolio

Note the current price carefully, then click on the Add to Portfolio button. StockLink responds with the dialog box pictured in Figure 5-4.

Since this is only make-believe, buy as many shares as you'd like. Don't worry: StockLink doesn't share your portfolio with anyone. And you won't be charged any special fees for this exercise; it's a private matter between you and your computer.

Our portfolio consists of the AOL investment we've just described, plus additional investments in IBM, Apple Computer (no favorites

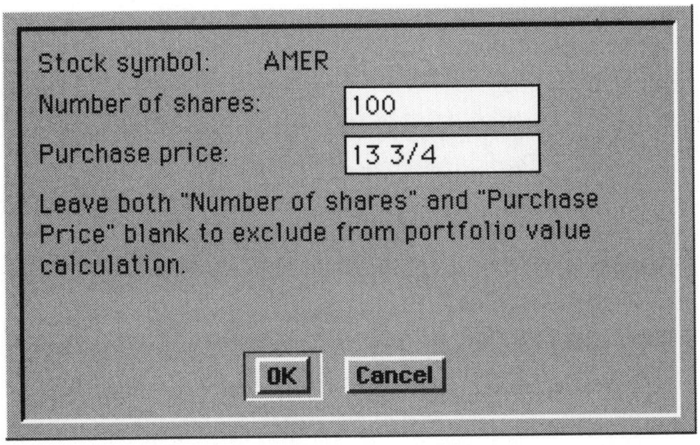

Figure 5-4:
Enter the current
price and the
number of shares,
then click on OK.
The "investment"
will be added to
your portfolio.

Stock symbol: AMER

Number of shares: `100`

Purchase price: `13 3/4`

Leave both "Number of shares" and "Purchase
Price" blank to exclude from portfolio value
calculation.

[OK] [Cancel]

here) and Intel (an Oregon company—it pays to invest locally). Whenever we want to see how it's doing, we use the keyword: Portfolio, and see the window pictured in Figure 5-5.

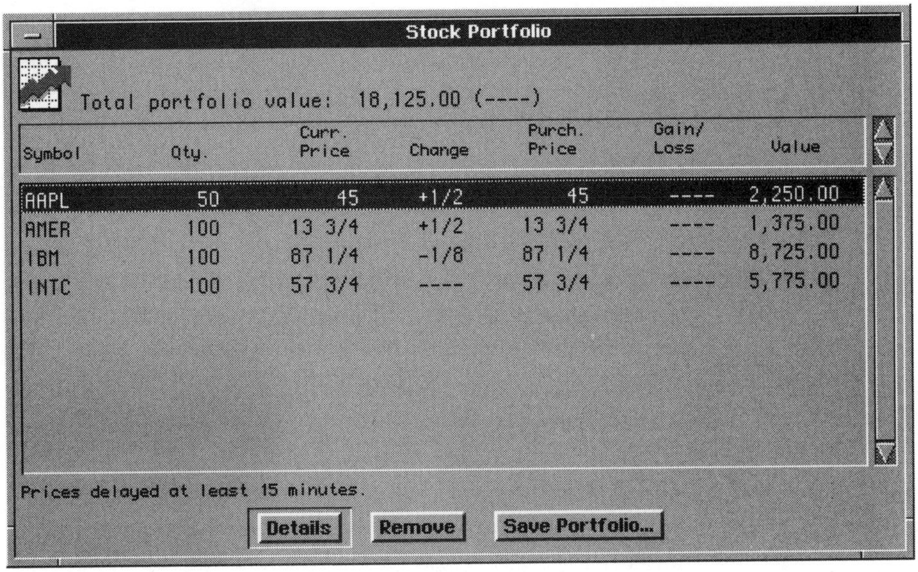

Figure 5-5:
Our portfolio
includes shares in
AOL, IBM, Apple
Computer and
Intel. If only it
were real....

Stock Portfolio

Total portfolio value: 18,125.00 (----)

Symbol	Qty.	Curr. Price	Change	Purch. Price	Gain/ Loss	Value
AAPL	50	45	+1/2	45	----	2,250.00
AMER	100	13 3/4	+1/2	13 3/4	----	1,375.00
IBM	100	87 1/4	-1/8	87 1/4	----	8,725.00
INTC	100	57 3/4	----	57 3/4	----	5,775.00

Prices delayed at least 15 minutes.

[Details] [Remove] [Save Portfolio...]

Charting the portfolio

One of the little-known features offered by America Online is its ability to save portfolios on a disk, providing fuel for electronic spreadsheet programs like Microsoft's Excel (see Figure 5-6).

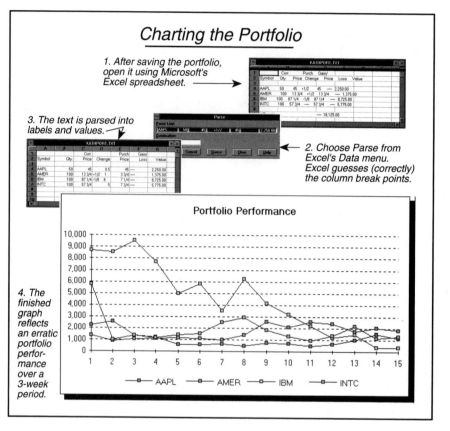

Figure 5-6:
By saving our
portfolio and using
Excel's data-
parsing feature,
we can graph
stock performance
over time.

To save a portfolio, simply choose Save from the File menu. AOL
will provide a file-save dialog box where you can identify the file's
name and destination. The file is saved as standard ASCII text, but
most standard spreadsheet programs like Excel have parsing features
that can convert the ASCII text into spreadsheet cells for easy graphing.

Market News

Look again at Figure 5-2. Do you see the little world-shaped icon
labeled "Market News"? There's a boundless resource of market
information here, ranging from the NYSE to Economic Indexes (see
Figure 5-7).

Note that each of the subjects in Figure 5-7 is preceded by a folder.
The implication is that there's much more here than meets the eye.
Indeed there is. Click on each one and look at the wealth of material
within them.

Figure 5-7:
Subjects covered
in Market News
include all of the
major exchanges
and indexes.

Browse the Service

News & Finance | People Connection | Lifestyles & Interests | Games & Entertainment | Learning & Reference | Travel & Shopping | Computing & Software | Members' Online Support

What You Have Selected:

STOCKLINK

What You Can Select:

- Market Briefs
- New York Stock Exchange
- American Stock Exchange
- Over The Counter
- Dow Jones Average
- General Market Indexes
- Commodities
- Economic Indexes

Go Back   Open

The TradePlus gateway

TradePlus is the home for the market investor. During trading hours, TradePlus tracks NYSE, AMEX, NASDAQ advances, declines and volume; Dow Jones indices (price, change, high, low); Standard & Poor's Index (Put Volume, Call Volume, Ratio); Most Active Issues; and Percentage Gains and Losers. TradePlus also monitors stock, options and commodity prices—all continuously updated on a 20-minute delay basis.

You may buy and sell stocks online via TradePlus as well. The brokerage firm of Quick & Reilly offers discounted commissions and insures accounts up to $2.5 million. You'll be assigned a personal broker and an automated portfolio-management account. The portfolio management system maintains all your personal records and automatically updates your portfolio every time you buy or sell. All brokerage records are available online, 24 hours a day, 7 days a week.

And, except for the commission you pay if you buy and sell real stocks online, all of this is free. You only pay your normal connect-time charges to America Online.

The Bulls & Bears Game

Regardless of whether you choose to invest real money, you're always welcome to participate in AOL's Bulls & Bears Game. Players invest $100,000 in game money in stocks or options of their choice. The game automatically maintains your portfolio, reflecting trading activity and current prices. Each month, contestants who have the top three best-performing portfolios win free online time. There's no better education for the would-be investor, and the rewards are real, even if the investments are not.

Your Money

A local radio station runs a talk show every weekend where people call in to talk about money. They sprinkle their conversations with terms like "Ginny Mae" and "tax-deferred" the way the rest of us might sprinkle pepper on an omelet. They think nothing of it, and they assume everyone knows what they're talking about.

We, however, do not. Until recently, whenever we heard it we wished for some source that would explain all of those terms. We used to browse the business sections of bookstores but found more books on the shelves than terms we didn't understand. Just reading their covers left us in a state of catatonia.

Then we discovered Your Money (keywords: Your Money), a service designed to help you set financial goals for yourself. It then shows you how to effectively manage your money so you can achieve those goals. Along the way, Your Money explains the meaning of all those terms that confound most normal people (see Figure 5-8).

Richard A. Allridge, a certified financial planner and instructor at George Washington University, helps you understand the process of personal financial planning and provides the building blocks you need to realize your financial goals. You can post questions to him on the forum's message board and enter the "Profile of the Month" Contest, where you could win a free analysis of your financial status.

Figure 5-8:
UGMAs and
UTMAs are only
two of the terms
Your Money
defines.

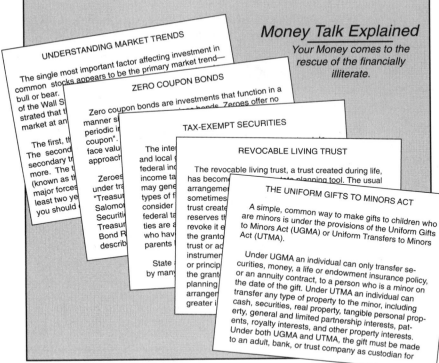

Money Talk Explained

Your Money comes to the rescue of the financially illiterate.

UNDERSTANDING MARKET TRENDS

The single most important factor affecting investment in common stocks appears to be the primary market trend— bull or bear.

ZERO COUPON BONDS

Zero coupon bonds are investments that function in a manner si... bonds. Zeroes offer no periodic i...

TAX-EXEMPT SECURITIES

REVOCABLE LIVING TRUST

The revocable living trust, a trust created during life, has become...

THE UNIFORM GIFTS TO MINORS ACT

A simple, common way to make gifts to children who are minors is under the provisions of the Uniform Gifts to Minors Act (UGMA) or Uniform Transfers to Minors Act (UTMA).

Under UGMA an individual can only transfer securities, money, a life or endowment insurance policy, or an annuity contract, to a person who is a minor on the date of the gift. Under UTMA an individual can transfer any type of property to the minor, including cash, securities, real property, tangible personal property, general and limited partnership interests, patents, royalty interests, and other property interests. Under both UGMA and UTMA, the gift must be made to an adult, bank, or trust company as custodian for

Keeping a log

While articles like those pictured in Figure 5-8 are informative and often fascinating, reading them online is not. We prefer to absorb information like that at our leisure, when the clock isn't running.

One solution is found under the File menu: the Save command, which saves the contents of the current window on a disk of your choosing. Another solution is AOL's Log feature. When a log is turned on, all text that appears on your screen is recorded on your disk. You can zip through an online session without delay, letting articles flash across your screen with the tempo of an MTV video. Then, when you've accessed what you need, sign off and review the log. Any word processor will open a log file, as will your AOL software itself: just choose Open from the File menu.

To start a log, choose Logging from the File menu, and under Session, click on Open. AOL displays a standard file-open dialog box, complete with a suggested file name and location (see Figure 5-9). Change what you want, then click on Save. From then on, everything you see onscreen is saved to your disk.

More

You can always suspend or stop a log by returning to the Logging window and clicking on the Close button. To resume a log later, click on the Append button. If you look carefully at the illustration, you'll note two types of logs: the Conference log captures chat room conversations and instant messages (we'll discuss chats and instant messages in Chapter 10, "People Connection"); the Session log is the one that captures articles such as those discussed elsewhere in this chapter.

Figure 5-9:
Log files capture
on-screen activity
to disk for later
review.

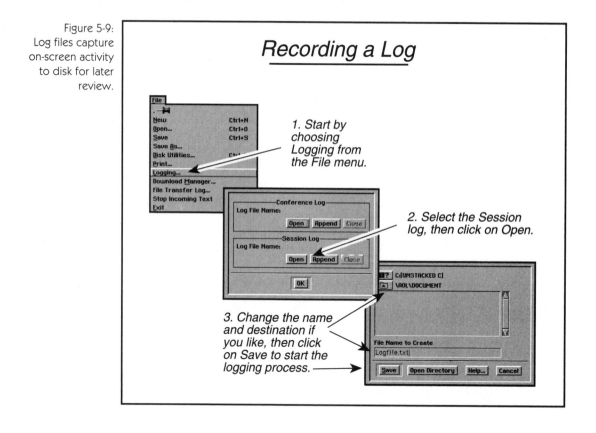

Recording a Log

1. Start by choosing Logging from the File menu.

2. Select the Session log, then click on Open.

3. Change the name and destination if you like, then click on Save to start the logging process.

News Search

Look again at Figure 5-1. There are nine folders in the News & Finance window, and within many of these, there are more folders. Indeed, a minimum of 20 categories of information populate this window on a regular basis, offering more than 200 articles to read (or log) online. If we had to plow through all of these articles every time we wanted to find a story concerning a specific subject, America Online wouldn't be much of an alternative.

As this chapter is being written, the United Nations has enforced a no-fly zone over Southern Iraq, and South Florida has been ravaged by a terrible hurricane. These developments worry us; the situation is changing every minute and we want to stay on top of it. We don't want to watch television and wait for them to get around to the stories we're concerned about; the newspaper was printed early this morning and is old news now; and we don't want to wade through 200 unrelated articles on AOL before we find the one we're after.

The solution is News Search. Anticipating the need, the people at AOL enter all the current news stories into a searchable database. If we're interested in stories about Iraq, all we have to do is enter keyword: News Search, and specify Iraq as the search criterion. America Online responds with all of the stories—from a variety of sources—that meet our criterion (see Figure 5-10). Go ahead, try it. Type in a word or phrase that describes a current topic of interest. Odds are AOL will find a few articles that match what you're looking for.

Figure 5-10:
News Search
offers the capacity
to search the
library of current
news stories for
articles matching
our interests.

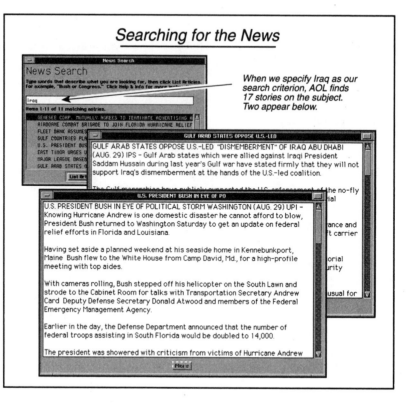

Searching for the News

News Search

Type words that describe what you are looking for, then click List Articles.
For example, "Bush or Congress." Click Help & Info for more info.

iraq

Items 1-11 of 11 matching entries.

GENESEE CORP. MUTUALLY AGREES TO TERMINATE ADVERTISING A
AIRBORNE COMBAT BRIGADE TO JOIN FLORIDA HURRICANE RELIEF
FLEET BANK ASSURES
GULF COUNTRIES PLA
U.S. PRESIDENT BUS
EAST TIMOR URGES U
MAJOR LEAGUE BASE
GULF ARAB STATES O

List Art

*When we specify Iraq as our
search criterion, AOL finds
17 stories on the subject.
Two appear below.*

GULF ARAB STATES OPPOSE U.S.-LED

GULF ARAB STATES OPPOSE U.S.-LED "DISMEMBERMENT" OF IRAQ ABU DHABI
(AUG. 29) IPS - Gulf Arab states which were allied against Iraqi President
Saddam Hussain during last year's Gulf war have stated firmly that they will not
support Iraq's dismemberment at the hands of the U.S.-led coalition.

U.S. PRESIDENT BUSH IN EYE OF PO

U.S. PRESIDENT BUSH IN EYE OF POLITICAL STORM WASHINGTON (AUG. 29) UPI -
Knowing Hurricane Andrew is one domestic disaster he cannot afford to blow,
President Bush returned to Washington Saturday to get an update on federal
relief efforts in Florida and Louisiana.

Having set aside a planned weekend at his seaside home in Kennebunkport,
Maine Bush flew to the White House from Camp David, Md., for a high-profile
meeting with top aides.

With cameras rolling, Bush stepped off his helicopter on the South Lawn and
strode to the Cabinet Room for talks with Transportation Secretary Andrew
Card Deputy Defense Secretary Donald Atwood and members of the Federal
Emergency Management Agency.

Earlier in the day, the Defense Department announced that the number of
federal troops assisting in South Florida would be doubled to 14,000.

The president was showered with criticism from victims of Hurricane Andrew

More

The Microsoft Small Business Center

They say America is the land of opportunity. Our friend started a
business in 1977 that supported him, his partner and their families for
six years. Had he not become involved with computer consulting, it
would probably still be supporting him. (It's still supporting his partner Michael all these years later.)

Our friend recalls approaching the bank for their first big loan. They explained their needs pleasantly, then requested the money. "Where's your business plan?" asked the banker. There was an embarrassing pause. "What's a business plan?" they asked. Have you ever noticed how bankers fail to see the humor in situations like this?

They didn't get the money.

Instead, the bank sent them to its classes, where they learned the wonders of pro forma income statements, cash-flow projections, trend-line analyses and common-ratio comparisons. Had they not learned those business fundamentals, they probably would not have survived the lean years of the early 1980s.

Yes, America is the land of opportunity, but it's also the land of cut-throat competition and a somewhat erratic economy. People who go into business for themselves succumb more often than they succeed. This is not the place for the ill-prepared. Operators of small businesses must be generalists: they often keep the books, write the advertising and sweep the floor. Generalism requires a breadth of knowledge that most people don't have. On top of that, small business operators tend to work in an isolated environment, one which hardly encourages the depth of experience required by a generalist.

That's why Microsoft and America Online, working together with more than 20 companies and associations serving the small business market, have created the Microsoft Small Business Center. The Small Business Center was created as a place where small business owners (or people considering starting a small business) can find information and help on a wide variety of subjects. Our friend is somewhat envious of this resource available to today's entrepreneur when he had to do it all the hard way some 15 years ago.

Figure 5-11:
The Microsoft
Small Business
Center offers
a wealth of
resources for the
small business
owner or manager.

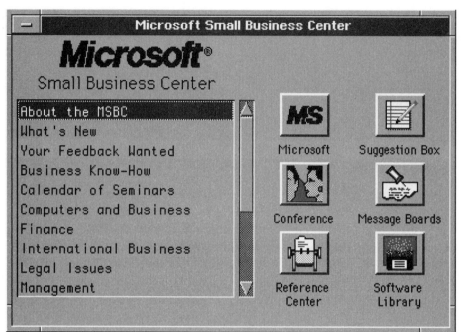

Figure 5-11:
The Microsoft
Small Business
Center offers
a wealth of
resources for the
small business
owner or manager.

What we find interesting about this resource is that, aside from the Microsoft icon pictured in Figure 5-11, Microsoft is rarely mentioned in this forum. The forum seems to be more of a philanthropic donation to the business community than a camouflaged promotion for Microsoft. Perhaps that makes sense: Microsoft started out as a small business, after all; there may remain a sympathy for small business within those marbled halls in Redmond.

The small business owner needs information—information about financing, advertising, human relations and management. Information is what the Microsoft Small Business Center has to offer. The list of resources includes the following:

🚶 The American Institute for Small Business

🚶 American Management Association

- ▲ Attard Communications
- ▲ The Cobb Group
- ▲ Demand Research/Executive Desk Register
- ▲ Dun & Bradstreet
- ▲ Heizer Software
- ▲ *Home-Office Computing*
- ▲ *Inc. Magazine*
- ▲ Information USA
- ▲ International Resource Network on Disabilities
- ▲ Management Advisory Services
- ▲ Microsoft Corporation
- ▲ *Nation's Business*
- ▲ New American Business System
- ▲ National Federation of Independent Business
- ▲ Nolo Press
- ▲ Overseas Market Development Institute
- ▲ Service Corps of Retired Executives
- ▲ Small Business Administration
- ▲ The Travelers Insurance Companies
- ▲ US Chamber of Commerce

Indeed, there's so much information in the Microsoft Small Business Center that we can't possibly begin to relate it here. Just look at the lists of topics pictured in Figure 5-12.

Figure 5-12:
Six of the ten lists
of articles available
from the Microsoft
Small Business
Center. Not
pictured:
Computers and
Business, Penny
Wise Office
Products,
Personnel, Sales,
Starting a Business
and Women in
Business.

$Business Know-How$ Online

SBA Veteran Loans
SBA Microloans
Getting Paid
Technology Tidbits
Writing Correspondence Schools
Venture Capita
Leases; Joint V
Getting Grants
Trade Show B
Renting Lists/E
Errand Service
Getting the Fir
What Price Go
Cancellation C
Tough Decision
ISBN, Print Co
Can I Get a Pa
Copyrights & P
Pricing Writing
Tips on Market
Business and
News Worth N
Evaluating Bu
Facts, Figures
Special Report
Look Before Yo
Malpractice an
Contractors' St
Interstate & Int
Marketing Soft
Are You a Slav
Avoiding Legal
Before You Us
Don't Get Caug
Get Good Res
Get It In Writin
Moonlighters a
Reaching Your
The Home Offi
The Road to R
Sell What Cust
Should You Inc
Should You Ta
What's in a Na

Finance

Alternative Ways to Find Capital
Audio Book -- Capitalism and Freedom
Audio Book -- The New Industrial State
Audio Book -- The Theory of the Leisure...
Banking: Courting Candidates
Borrowing Bas
A Buyer's Mark
Cash Flow Ana
Choosing A Ba
Credit and Coll
Do You Need a
The Economic
Facts About C
Five Simple St
Helping Small
How to Price Y
Keeping Pace
Key Pointers W
Make Smarter
Managing Risk
Managing Your
Money and He
Monthly Small-
More of the Sa
Preparing to S
Pricing Your Pr
Progress -- Bu
Raising The Fir
SBA's Busines
SBA's Financia
SBA Loan Prim
Services Watch
Shield Against
Simplified Emp
Taxes for Busin
Ten Smart Tax
Ten Basics abo
Video -- Free t
Video -- Money

International Business

Beyond Exporting
Business Travel Abroad
Export Hotline
Export Information System
Export Regulations and Product Standards
Exporters Offered Free Legal Advice
The Export of
Export Strateg
Exporting: Bu
Free Trade Ad
Gulf Reconstr
Information on
International T
International T
Learn Exportin
Learn Foreign
Going it Alon
Kuwait 900 So
Making Overs
Money For Se
Mosbacher Le
Opportunities
Organizations
Overseas Trav
Selling Overse
Selling Overse
Small Busines
Special Progra
State Governm
State Internati
Trade Fairs an
U.S. Internatio
Video -- Wall S
Why Export?

Legal Issues

Avoiding Legal Problems
Companies Go To Court
Complying w
Consumer W
Copyright Ba
Copyright Qu
Copyright Re
How to Moni
The Law and
Negotiating A
Obtaining Go
Publications
Selecting Yo
Sexual Hara
Sexual Hara
Sexual Hara
Law...
Sexual Hara
Sexual Hara
Company...
Small Busine
The Prompt
Tracking Sta

Management

Americans with Disabilities Act
Audio Book -- The Concept of Corporate...
Audio Book -- Corporate Cultures...
Audio Book -- Greed & Glory on Wall...
Audio Book -- Leadership in Administration
Buying A Computer For A Small...
The Challe
Credit and
Criticism w
Customers
Customer
Expanding
Know The
Making the
Manageme
Managing A
Manageme
Meetings: F
New Uses
On Being S
Organizing
Planning...
Setting Go
Succeeding
Waste Not,
When Fam
Worker on

Marketing/Advertising

Audio Book -- Confessions of an...
Advertising...A Must For Your...
Be Your Own Publicist
Customer Relations: Pushing the...
Developing A Market Plan
DRC Company Information Directories
Five Ways to Get Instant Business
Forecasting Sales
Knowing Your Market
Marketing...Key To Business Success
Marketing to the 'New Majority'
Media Power: Authority Figures
Media Power: Bettering the Odds
Persuasive Speaking Video
Sales: Customer Teachers
Selling Your Product or Service
Telephone Strategies That Work
Video -- Creating a Winner: The Real...
Why Market Research?
Writing Your First Press Release

Ctrl-X

Some of the articles offered in the Small Business Center are lengthy. The center doesn't have a monopoly on long articles; in fact, long articles are found throughout AOL. Sometimes, after reading the first few sentences of an article, you will find it's not what you're after. What do you do? Wait while the hourglass cursor commandeers your screen, mocking your impatience?

Indeed not. You use, Ctrl-X, the AOL command that means *STOP!* It works nearly everywhere on AOL; and it's especially useful when long articles or lists threaten to make morning molasses out of your quicksilver 486.

Whenever you want to interrupt something, press Ctrl-X. It works for long articles, ponderous downloads, dreary mail and ceaseless searches. It's particularly valuable when a sluggish sign-on sequence portends a noisy line and a need for redialing. It inspires a feeling of omnipotent power and will become your best online friend. Keep it in mind.

As you can see from Figure 5-12's caption, the list of articles offered by the Microsoft Small Business Center is prodigious. Articles aren't all that's offered, however. There's a message board where you can ask questions and share thoughts of experts and fellow businesspeople; and there's a library of downloadable files.

Free of extra charges

Most commercial online services offer some of the news and finance features found on America Online. None offer them all, however; and none offer them at the price AOL charges: nothing beyond the normal connect-time charges. This is unique to America Online. In an industry where the word "premium" invariably indicates an extra charge, "premium" services on AOL are rare. Aside from sending the occasional fax or piece of mail via the US Post Office (which we discuss in Chapter 11, "Electronic Mail"), you'll rarely find an extra charge for any of the services America Online offers. With all the money you save, perhaps you can invest in the stock market or buy a small business. If you do, AOL stands ready to help—at no extra charge, of course.

Moving on

We have only scratched the surface of the News & Finance Department. Be sure to check out the *USA Today*, Ernst & Young, job listings, classified ads, Weather and "Fight Back" folders. Look for discussions of the Mike Keefe folder in Chapter 12 ("The Download Manager"), the Sports Report folder in Chapter 3 ("Online Help & the Members") and the Newsbytes folder in Chapter 7 ("Computing & Software").

Too much time in the News & Finance Department can lead to information overload. By now you probably need a break. How about a respite: a sip of wine perhaps, or a journey to a land where no one has gone before. In Chapter 6, we'll do just that, and it's coming up next.

CHAPTER 6

Lifestyles & Interests

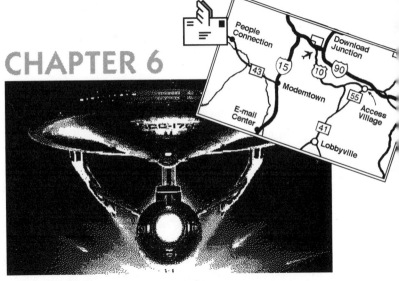

Probably no
department is broader in scope than Lifestyles & Interests (keyword: Lifestyles). As we write this, four screens are required to display a complete listing of the 40 forums in the department, and that number is growing exponentially (see Figure 6-1).

Figure 6-1:
In alphabetical
order, the 40
clubs and forums
that comprise
Lifestyles &
Interests. This
number grows
daily.

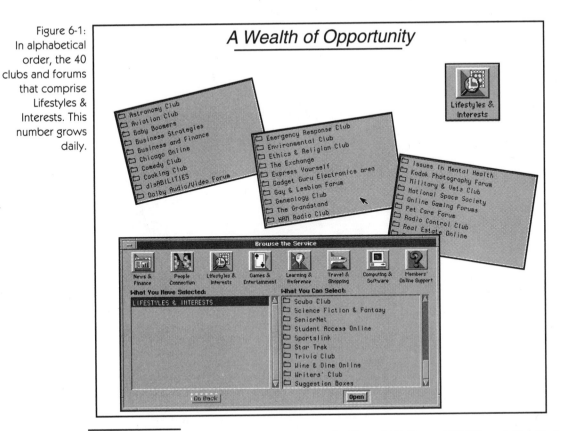

Frontispiece graphic: "USS Enterprise 1701a," by Kasey K.S. Chang (PCC Kasey), Star Trek Forum, keyword: Trek.

Forums defined

Of course, it helps to know exactly what a forum is, and what better place to find out than Lifestyles & Interests. We need an example, one that's familiar to all and resplendent with people, goodies and activity.

The perfect candidate is Wine & Dine Online Forum (keyword: Wine). This is a particularly refined forum, one that every epicure should visit. To quote from the forum's credo: "We owe it to ourselves to learn more about smell, taste and touch.... Wining & Dining is the best way to train our senses of smell and taste (the touch part will follow naturally). Wine & Dine Online's goal is to help us all grow as sensual, sensory beings by offering a feast of information."

Sounds hedonistic enough. Which, if for no other reason, is a good excuse to click on the icon and see what this forum has to offer (see Figure 6-2).

Figure 6-2: The Wine & Dine Online Forum offers articles, folders, message boards and a library of files.

🗁 ABOUT WINE & DINE AND YOUR HOSTS
🗁 News, Announcements, Calendar
🗁 Reading Room, References
🗁 Wine Ratings, Reviews, Database
🗁 Restaurant, Winery, Merchant Guide
🗁 Travel Guide
🗁 Message Center & WineLocator
🗁 Beer & Brewing Message Center
🗇 Library of Files to Download

We picked this forum because its composition is fairly representative of most forums on America Online. It offers six articles and folders of reference materials (perhaps a few more than normal), two message boards (we will describe message boards later in this chapter) and a library of files for downloading (most forums do).

Reference materials

Look carefully at the icons in Figure 6-2. The little page icon with a turned-down corner represents an article. Double-click on these icons to read them. The folder icon holds a collection of articles, grouped by subject. Icons with push-pins are message boards, and the disk icons represent libraries.

Articles & folders

Let's begin our exploration of this forum by double-clicking on the folder labeled "News, Announcements, Calendar" (see Figure 6-3).

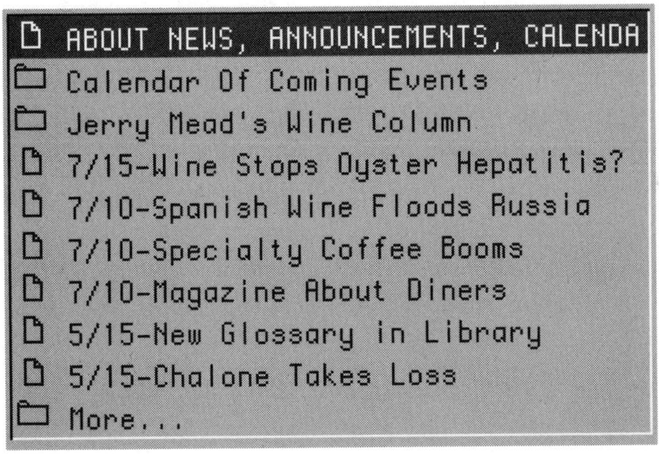

Figure 6-3: News and calendar items may appear as either articles or folders.

```
🗋  ABOUT NEWS, ANNOUNCEMENTS, CALENDA
📁  Calendar Of Coming Events
📁  Jerry Mead's Wine Column
🗋  7/15-Wine Stops Oyster Hepatitis?
🗋  7/10-Spanish Wine Floods Russia
🗋  7/10-Specialty Coffee Booms
🗋  7/10-Magazine About Diners
🗋  5/15-New Glossary in Library
🗋  5/15-Chalone Takes Loss
📁  More...
```

The articles/folders metaphor is repeated here. Six articles and three folders appear in this window. Double-click on any one of them to open it. The article entitled "The Night Margaritas Died" piques our interest (we found it in the "More" folder at the bottom of the screen). Let's look it over (see Figure 6-4).

Figure 6-4:
The world will be
a more temperate
place now that
Danny Herrera is
no longer around.

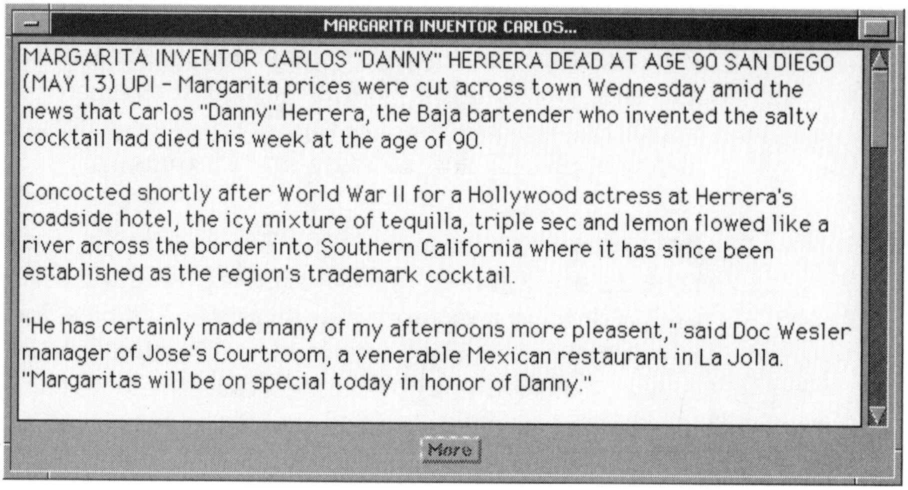

MARGARITA INVENTOR CARLOS...

MARGARITA INVENTOR CARLOS "DANNY" HERRERA DEAD AT AGE 90 SAN DIEGO (MAY 13) UPI - Margarita prices were cut across town Wednesday amid the news that Carlos "Danny" Herrera, the Baja bartender who invented the salty cocktail had died this week at the age of 90.

Concocted shortly after World War II for a Hollywood actress at Herrera's roadside hotel, the icy mixture of tequila, triple sec and lemon flowed like a river across the border into Southern California where it has since been established as the region's trademark cocktail.

"He has certainly made many of my afternoons more pleasant," said Doc Wesler manager of Jose's Courtroom, a venerable Mexican restaurant in La Jolla. "Margaritas will be on special today in honor of Danny."

More

Notice the byline in Figure 6-4: UPI (United Press International). Someone has been bird-dogging the UPI wire, watching for stories that might be of interest to forum visitors. When they spotted the margarita story, they posted it. This is not only an example of an online reference, it also illustrates the value America Online offers those of us with special interests. While this story was glossed over by traditional media, the Wine & Dine Online Forum found it and posted it for us.

When finished with the article, you can double-click on the Close box to return to the Browse the Service window for more.

No fruit flavors, please

The UPI story illustrated in Figure 6-4 continues: "It was sometime in 1947 or 1948 that Danny Herrera began experimenting with a cocktail that had a tequila base but was smooth enough for the palate of a visitor known as Marjorie King, an actress who enjoyed a drink but had an allergic aversion to whiskey. The original recipe was three parts white tequila, two parts Cointreau and one part lemon juice. The mixture was shaken by hand with shaved ice and poured into a glass with the trademark salted rim...."

Triple Sec may be used in place of Cointreau, or a packaged Margarita mix used in place of both the Cointreau and lemon; but if you really want to do justice to Danny's memory, mix your Margaritas as Danny preferred them.

Online databases

The online searchable database is unique to the telecommunications industry. It's a benefit that simply can't be matched anywhere else. Searchable databases are perpetually maintained, with not only the latest information, but archives of past information as well. They can be searched without having to leave your keyboard. They arrive in the form of plain text, ready to be included in other documents or printed out. They're fast, immediate and usually extensive. America Online offers nearly 50 of these databases; when you see one, take a few minutes to explore it. It's always worth the time.

Let's explore an eloquent example. The database of wines offered in the Wine & Dine Online Forum is probably the largest of its kind available to the public. Thousands of wines are listed here, along with prices and ratings from the Beverage Testing Institute. This is an excellent tool for cutting through a mystique that prospers in the obscurity of unfamiliar names and the bewilderment of heterogeneous prices.

We need a wine for tonight's dinner. Always the parochial Oregonians, we would like an Oregon wine if one's available. Before we go shopping, however, we consult Wine & Dine Online's wine database (see Figure 6-5).

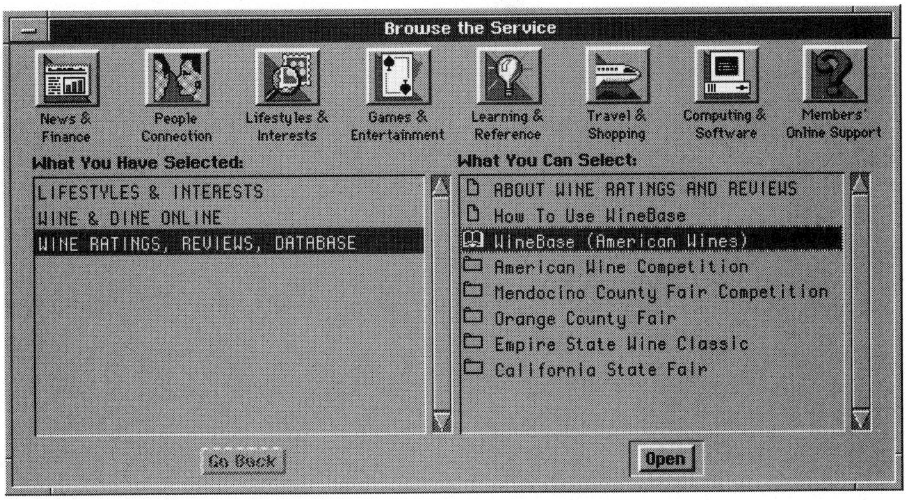

Figure 6-5:
Become an instant enologist. Impress your friends with your wisdom and frugality. Look it up in WineBase.

Browse the Service

News & Finance | People Connection | Lifestyles & Interests | Games & Entertainment | Learning & Reference | Travel & Shopping | Computing & Software | Members' Online Support

What You Have Selected:
LIFESTYLES & INTERESTS
WINE & DINE ONLINE
WINE RATINGS, REVIEWS, DATABASE

What You Can Select:
ABOUT WINE RATINGS AND REVIEWS
How To Use WineBase
WineBase (American Wines)
American Wine Competition
Mendocino County Fair Competition
Orange County Fair
Empire State Wine Classic
California State Fair

Go Back | Open

To get here on your own computer, double-click on the folder Wine Ratings, Reviews, Database under the Wine & Dine Online Forum. Note the open-book icon next to WineBase (American Wines) on the right side of the window (see Figure 6-5). That's AOL's way of identifying a searchable database. Significant riches are available here almost instantly. That's a good thing: your dinner guests will be arriving shortly. Double-click on that item and type in the word "Oregon" as a search criterion (see Figure 6-6).

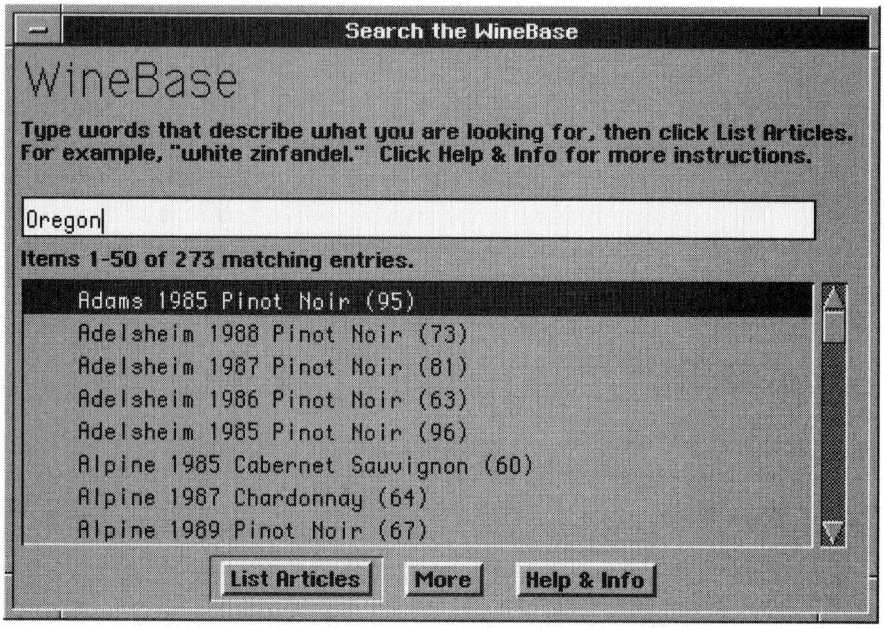

Figure 6-6: A search of the criterion "Oregon" produces 273 wines, far too many from which to make this night's decision.

Looking at Figure 6-6, we can see that WineBase contains 273 references to the word "Oregon." Note that only eight references appear in the window pictured in Figure 6-6 and we could use the vertical scroll bar to see the rest of the first 50 choices. Note that a button marked "More" appears at the bottom of the window. If you wanted to view more choices, you would use this button to see the next 50 wines, eight visible at a time. By the time you read through that many listings, your guests would have departed in a pique, unfed and without libation, muttering disparagements about America Online and your preoccupation with the computer.

You need to refine your criteria. It's summer, after all, and you're in the mood for a cool white wine. A Chardonnay would be nice (see Figure 6-7).

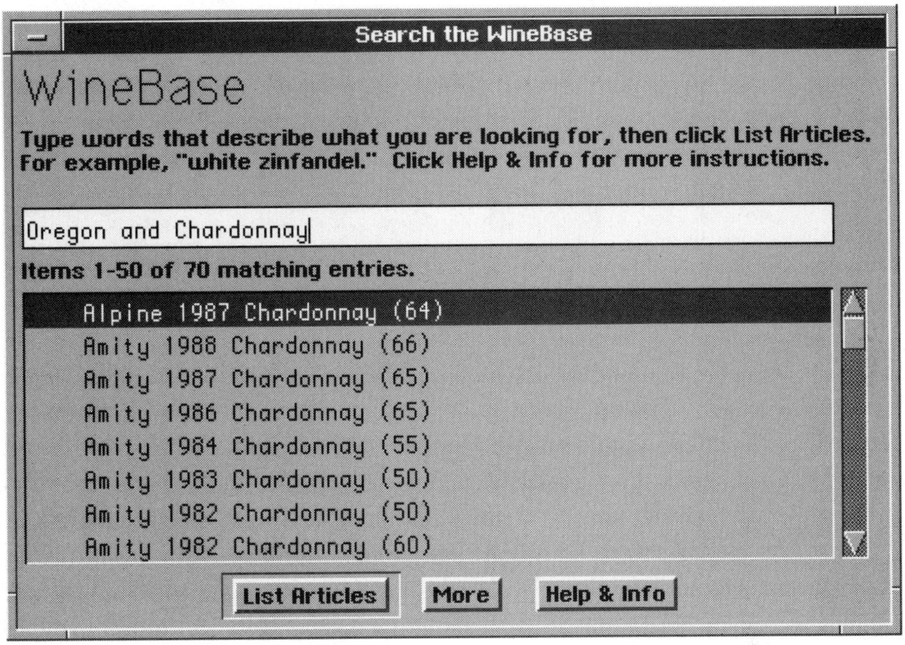

Figure 6-7: By using the word "and," the search criteria can be refined.

Search the WineBase

WineBase

Type words that describe what you are looking for, then click List Articles. For example, "white zinfandel." Click Help & Info for more instructions.

Oregon and Chardonnay|

Items 1-50 of 70 matching entries.

Alpine 1987 Chardonnay (64)
Amity 1988 Chardonnay (66)
Amity 1987 Chardonnay (65)
Amity 1986 Chardonnay (65)
Amity 1984 Chardonnay (55)
Amity 1983 Chardonnay (50)
Amity 1982 Chardonnay (50)
Amity 1982 Chardonnay (60)

| List Articles | More | Help & Info |

Notice the criteria used in Figure 6-7. By saying "Oregon *and* Chardonnay," you're able to exclude all wines that don't meet *both* criteria. You've narrowed it down to 70 wines, but that's still too many to read before your guests arrive.

And these are important guests. People you want to please. Only the best will do. WineBase includes references to medals each wine may have won: bronze, silver, gold or platinum. You can exclude the no-medal wines as well as the bronze-medal wines with some *or* criteria (see Figure 6-8).

Figure 6-8:
Improper use of
"or" criteria is
worse than no
criteria at all.

*Incorrect use of search
criteria produces
unexpected results.*

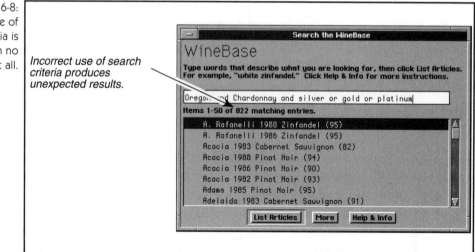

Uh-oh. Over *800* matches! A mistake has been made. This is a problem similar to an algebraic statement, such as "x = 5 plus 2 times 7." What's the answer: 49 or 19? Do you add the 5 and the 2, then multiply; or do you multiply first, then add? WineBase has the same problem. It seems to be interpreting the criteria as "Oregon and Chardonnay and silver—or gold, or platinum."

The solution is the same as the solution for mathematical expressions: parentheses. There's only one proper answer to the statement "x = 5 plus (2 times 7)." That statement is specific. So is the criteria in Figure 6-9.

Figure 6-9:
That's more like it.
Eight wines is just
the right number
from which to
make a choice.
You can take the
list to the store
and be back by
the time your
guests arrive.

*Attention to the
syntax of your
criteria will
produce the
results you want.*

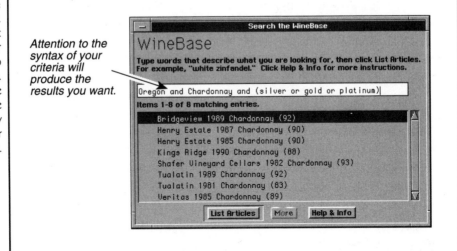

Because the selection of wines at the shop you frequent is especially comprehensive, you suspect it will have all eight of the wines pictured in Figure 6-9. Rather than pick one at random, let's poll the database further. A double-click on the Bridgeview 1989, for instance, produces the description pictured in Figure 6-10.

Figure 6-10:
The database
record for a single
wine reveals its
price, awards
and ranking.

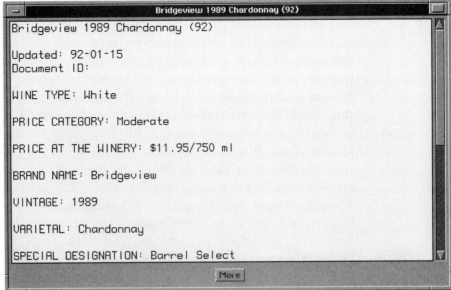

Reviewing all eight listings takes about ten minutes. Indeed, the whole process only required about 15 minutes from sign on to sign off. Your dinner guests will be astounded with your enological expertise and entranced by your conversation. You can take all the credit, though WineBase properly deserves it.

An angel in heaven

Nancy Gralow is a producer. Before joining AOL, she worked at the Mutual Broadcasting Company and, later, at ABC. She certainly looks the part. Indeed, pictures of Nancy posed with celebrities are strategically placed around her office, and it's difficult to distinguish her from the stars.

Her producer's background becomes apparent when she demonstrates the forums she oversees. During her first year at AOL, Nancy recruited Orson Scott Card, Craig Goldwyn and Peter G. Miller, who host the Science Fiction, Wine & Dine Online and Real Estate forums, respectively. Each is a leader in his field: Card has received both the Nebula and Hugo awards; Goldwyn was recently recognized as one of the 12 most influential wine writers in the US; and Miller has written six prestigious books on real estate and marketing.

Unlike show business, online productions are on-going. They're a producer's heaven; and in AOL, Nancy Gralow has certainly found hers. We, the members, are the richer for it.

Bulletin boards

Not all forums feature databases, and not all members require access to one. Fortunately, there's much more to America Online's forums than databases. Forums, after all, are more like clubs than anything else (indeed, many of them are referred to online as clubs). People gather in forums to discuss subjects of mutual interest and to learn more about their field. They may conduct some database research while they're online as well; but *people* make a club, and people make America Online's forums.

America Online's *message boards* are the electronic analog of the old familiar cork board and push-pins (look for the icons with a push-pin). Message boards (call them "boards") are especially appropriate to online clubs. One of the unique advantages forums offer is convenience: you can drop in any time, not just during regular meetings. While there, you'll want to read and reply to messages posted on the club's boards—at your convenience, at any time, day or night. Most of us visit our favorite clubs every time we sign on, and anxiously read all the messages posted since the last time we visited. The feeling is remarkably immediate, and withdrawal sets in after about three days' absence. In other words, boards are addictive—but that's part of the fun.

Editing the Go To menu

Once you've found a club to your liking, you will want to visit it every time you sign on. Rather than navigate a stack of menus or type a keyword, give the club a place on your Go To menu. Items at the bottom of the Go To menu are under your control, you can add or delete any one you please. Let's say you've become an active participant in the Star Trek Club. To add it to your Edit menu, follow the procedure illustrated in Figure 6-11.

Figure 6-11: Adding menu items is accommodated via the Edit Go To Menu command.

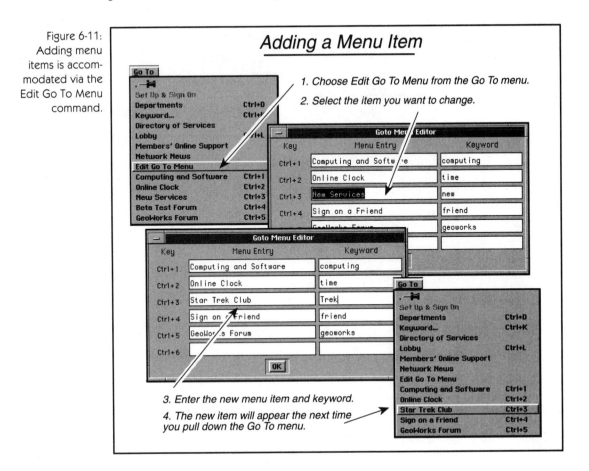

The Lifestyles & Interests Department offers a number of forums, most of which are club-like in atmosphere. An especially imaginative forum is the Star Trek Club (keyword: Trek). It not only offers articles and folders of information, but simulations as well. The club's role-playing "Starfleet Academy" meets every evening except Saturdays and boldly goes where no one has gone before.

Reading messages

But we're getting ahead of ourselves. Before we don our Starfleet communicator pins, let's nose around a message board and see what people are talking about.

Figure 6-12:
Type the keyword
"Trek" to open the
Star Trek Club's
main window;
then double-click
on the Star Trek
folder to see
what's happening.

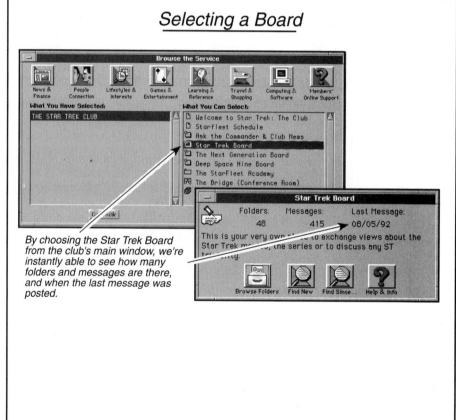

By choosing the Star Trek Board
from the club's main window, we're
instantly able to see how many
folders and messages are there,
and when the last message was
posted.

Four icons appear across the bottom of the board's window: Browse Folders, Find New, Find Since... and Help & Info. Let's browse (see Figure 6-13). Click on the Browse Folders button.

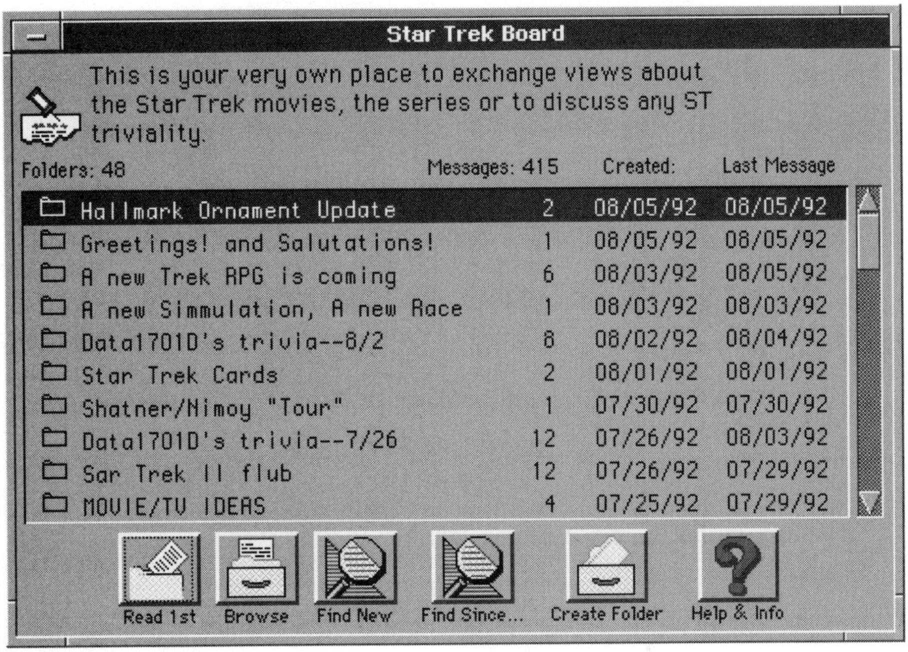

Figure 6-13: Ten of the 48 folders posted on the Star Trek Board.

Star Trek Board			
This is your very own place to exchange views about the Star Trek movies, the series or to discuss any ST triviality.			

Folders: 48   Messages: 415   Created: Last Message

Folder			
Hallmark Ornament Update	2	08/05/92	08/05/92
Greetings! and Salutations!	1	08/05/92	08/05/92
A new Trek RPG is coming	6	08/03/92	08/05/92
A new Simmulation, A new Race	1	08/03/92	08/03/92
Data1701D's trivia--8/2	8	08/02/92	08/04/92
Star Trek Cards	2	08/01/92	08/01/92
Shatner/Nimoy "Tour"	1	07/30/92	07/30/92
Data1701D's trivia--7/26	12	07/26/92	08/03/92
Sar Trek II flub	12	07/26/92	07/29/92
MOVIE/TV IDEAS	4	07/25/92	07/29/92

Read 1st   Browse   Find New   Find Since...   Create Folder   Help & Info

The bulletin-board metaphor is warped (forgive the pun: it *is* the Star Trek Board, after all) a bit here. Individual messages aren't normally posted on boards; folders are posted on boards; the messages themselves are inside the folders. Look again at Figure 6-13: this board is currently holding 420 messages. If all the messages were posted independently, the board would be a mess. You would never find a thing. The folders are merely organizational tools placed on the board to help you locate topics of interest to you.

Notice the Create Folder icon at the bottom of Figure 6-13. Folder subjects are not America Online's responsibility; new folders and new folder topics are members' prerogative. (This is the reason when you look at the Star Trek Forum, the numbers on your screen may differ from ours.) While this is a little anarchistic, it's also democratic; and that's the way message boards should be. If you feel like making a comment that's off the subject, make a new folder for it.

To read the messages placed in a folder, simply double-click on the folder. As you will see in Figure 6-14, the first message in that folder appears on your screen.

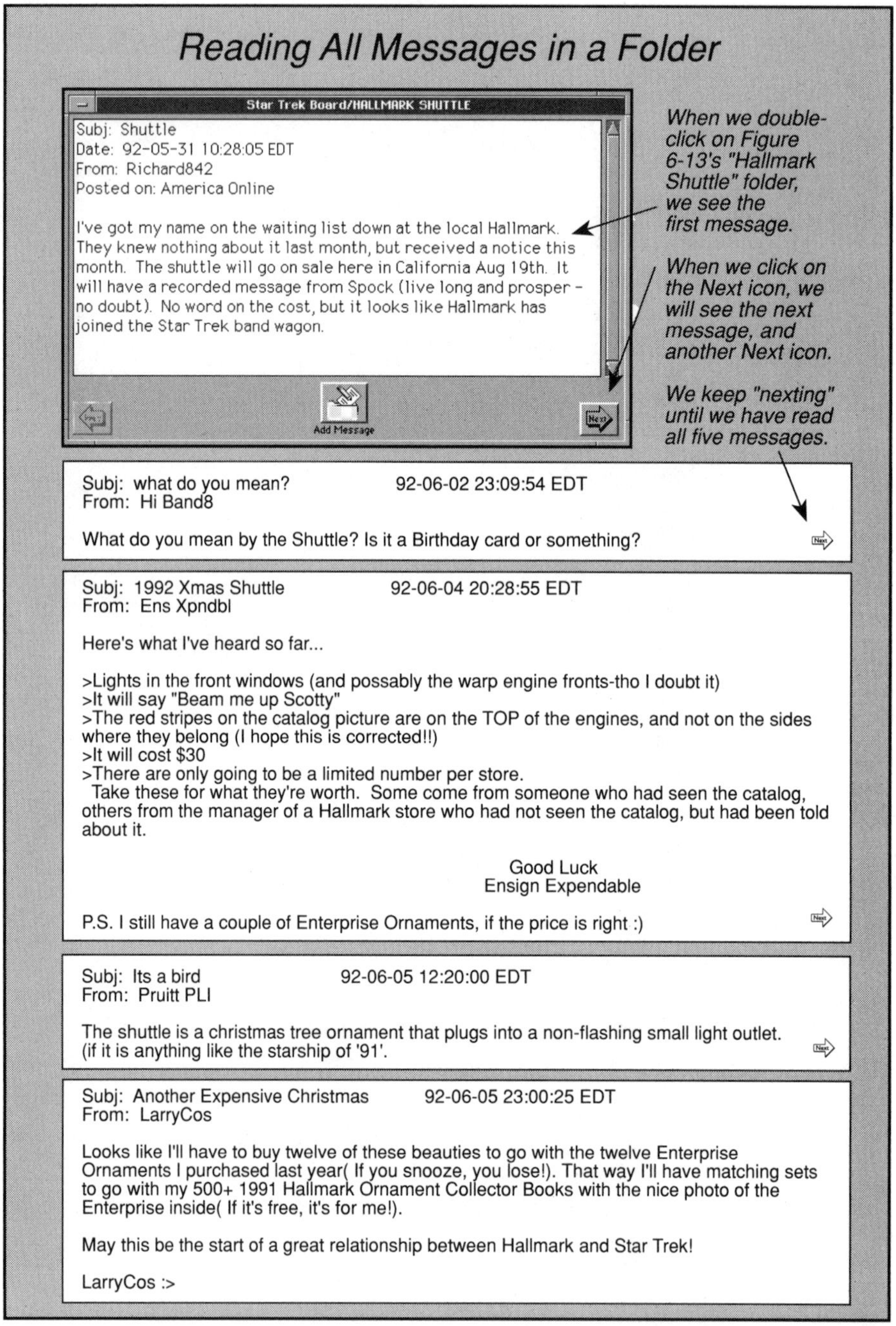

Figure 6-14:
Once you've read the first message in a folder, click on the Next icon to read the rest in the order in which they were posted.

Reading All Messages in a Folder

Star Trek Board/HALLMARK SHUTTLE

Subj: Shuttle
Date: 92-05-31 10:28:05 EDT
From: Richard842
Posted on: America Online

I've got my name on the waiting list down at the local Hallmark. They knew nothing about it last month, but received a notice this month. The shuttle will go on sale here in California Aug 19th. It will have a recorded message from Spock (live long and prosper - no doubt). No word on the cost, but it looks like Hallmark has joined the Star Trek band wagon.

Add Message

When we double-click on Figure 6-13's "Hallmark Shuttle" folder, we see the first message.

When we click on the Next icon, we will see the next message, and another Next icon.

We keep "nexting" until we have read all five messages.

Subj: what do you mean?   92-06-02 23:09:54 EDT
From: Hi Band8

What do you mean by the Shuttle? Is it a Birthday card or something?

Subj: 1992 Xmas Shuttle   92-06-04 20:28:55 EDT
From: Ens Xpndbl

Here's what I've heard so far...

>Lights in the front windows (and possably the warp engine fronts-tho I doubt it)
>It will say "Beam me up Scotty"
>The red stripes on the catalog picture are on the TOP of the engines, and not on the sides where they belong (I hope this is corrected!!)
>It will cost $30
>There are only going to be a limited number per store.
  Take these for what they're worth. Some come from someone who had seen the catalog, others from the manager of a Hallmark store who had not seen the catalog, but had been told about it.

                    Good Luck
                 Ensign Expendable

P.S. I still have a couple of Enterprise Ornaments, if the price is right :)

Subj: Its a bird   92-06-05 12:20:00 EDT
From: Pruitt PLI

The shuttle is a christmas tree ornament that plugs into a non-flashing small light outlet. (if it is anything like the starship of '91'.

Subj: Another Expensive Christmas   92-06-05 23:00:25 EDT
From: LarryCos

Looks like I'll have to buy twelve of these beauties to go with the twelve Enterprise Ornaments I purchased last year(If you snooze, you lose!). That way I'll have matching sets to go with my 500+ 1991 Hallmark Ornament Collector Books with the nice photo of the Enterprise inside(If it's free, it's for me!).

May this be the start of a great relationship between Hallmark and Star Trek!

LarryCos :>

Log those messages

Reading messages is one of the most time-consuming activities America Online has to offer. Rather than read messages online, save a log of them (we discuss logs in Chapter 10, "People Connection") as they download to your computer. Let them scroll off your screen as fast as they can; don't try to read them while you're online. When you have finished the session, sign off, open the log and read it at your leisure. You can always add messages to boards by signing back on again.

Browsing, finding & reading messages

We need to take a side trip here. We'll get back to our interstellar journey in a moment. The verbs *browse*, *find* and *read* have particular meanings when it comes to message boards, and require your unequivocal understanding. Think of a public library. On some days, you might go to the library simply to pass the time. You would walk in and *browse*, picking up a book here and there as different titles strike your fancy. On other days, you may visit the library with a specific title already in mind, in which case you would go to the card files and *find* that particular book, without dawdling. Regardless of how you come across a book, you eventually want to sit down and *read* it, page by page.

America Online uses these verbs similarly. Look again at Figure 6-13. Six icons parade across the bottom of the window, representing variations on the three verbs we're discussing.

The Read First icon produces a window displaying the first message in the folder (see Figure 6-15). This icon is the default: if you double-click on a folder, you will read the first message there regardless of whether you've read it before.

Figure 6-15:
The Read First icon
jumps right to a
display of the first
message in the
folder. After
you've read the
message, click on
the Next arrow (in
the lower-right
corner of the
window) to
display the next
message in that
folder.

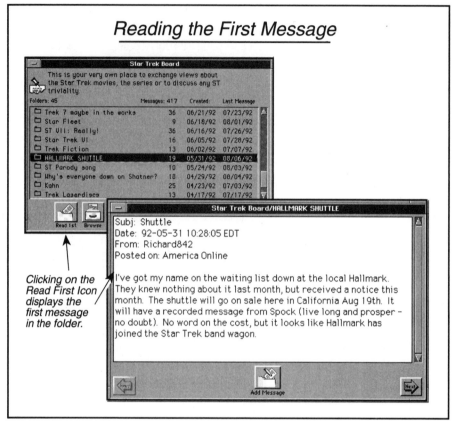

On the other hand, you may not want to read every message in the folder. There may be some subjects that don't interest you, or perhaps you're looking for messages posted by a specific member. Whatever the reason, the Browse icon displays the folder's message subjects and authors, not the messages themselves (see Figure 6-16). AOL automatically adds your screen name to any message you compose, and it won't let you post a message without filling out the Subject field. This way, every message has a subject and an author—no anonymous, unlabeled messages are allowed.

Figure 6-16:
The Browse icon
allows you to
select messages
for reading.

Browsing a Folder

```
┌─────────────────── Star Trek Board ───────────────────┐
│ ─                                                       │
│        This is your very own place to exchange views about│
│        the Star Trek movies, the series or to discuss any ST│
│        triviality.                                      │
│ Folders: 45              Messages: 417   Created:  Last Message│
│  📁 Star Fleet                    9    06/18/92  08/01/92│
│  📁 ST VII: Really!              36    06/16/92  07/26/92│
│  📁 Star Trek VI                 16    06/05/92  07/28/92│
│  📁 Trek Fiction                 13    06/02/92  07/07/92│
│  📁 HALLMARK SHUTTLE             19    05/31/92  08/06/92│
│  📁 ST Parody song               10    05/24/92  08/03/92│
│  📁 Why's everyone down on Shatner? 18  04/29/92  08/04/92│
│  📁 Kahn                         25    04/23/92  07/03/92│
│  📁 Trek Laserdiscs              13    04/17/92  07/17/92│
│  📁 STAR TREK GAMES WANTED       20    12/09/91  07/21/92│
└─────────────────────────────────────────────────────────┘
      [Read 1st] [Browse] [Find New] [Find Since...]
```

Clicking on the
Browse icon
produces a list
of messages in
the folder.
Subject and
author listings
enable you to
read only those
messages which
interest you.

```
┌─────────────────── HALLMARK SHUTTLE ───────────────────┐
│ ─                                                       │
│        NEW CHRISTMAS ORNAMENT                           │
│                                                         │
│ Messages: 19                      Author        Date    │
│  Shuttle                          Richard842    05/31/92│
│  what do you mean?                Hi Band8       06/02/92│
│  1992 Xmas Shuttle                Ens Xpndbl     06/04/92│
│  Its a bird                       Pruitt PLI     06/05/92│
│  Another Expensive Christmas      LarryCos       06/05/92│
│  The word is out!                 T Lichty       06/09/92│
│  1992 Hallmark Shuttle Specs..... LarryCos       06/10/92│
│  Shuttle                          Sailorr        06/28/92│
│  Update on what I know            LarryCos       07/12/92│
│  Snow Flake Ball                  GregBan        07/14/92│
└─────────────────────────────────────────────────────────┘
                    [Read] [Add Message]
```

The subject line

As you read through this section, note the role played by the messages' subject lines. A subject line like the one in Figure 6-16—"It's a bird"—bears little relationship to the actual message (look again at the message text in Figure 6-14). Alternatively, the subject line "What do you mean?" clearly summarizes the content of the message and intrigues the reader. Spend a moment thinking about subject lines when you post your own messages; they're significant.

This may be a board you read often. You may visit it every time you sign on. If so, all you're really interested in are messages posted since your last visit. The Find New icon produces a display of only those messages posted since you last visited, with the option of reading all messages on the board, should you wish to do so (see Figure 6-17).

Figure 6-17:
Only new
messages appear
in the Browse
window when you
click on the Find
New icon.

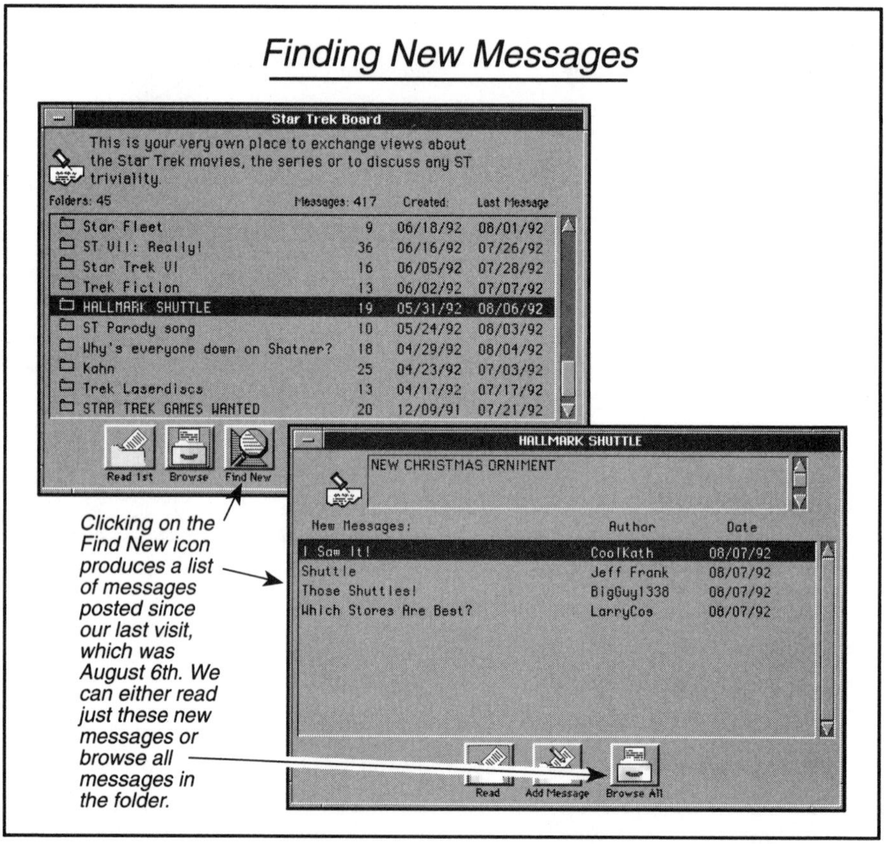

Finding New Messages

Star Trek Board

This is your very own place to exchange views about the Star Trek movies, the series or to discuss any ST triviality.

Folders: 45	Messages: 417	Created	Last Message
Star Fleet	9	06/18/92	08/01/92
ST VII: Really!	36	06/16/92	07/26/92
Star Trek VI	16	06/05/92	07/28/92
Trek Fiction	13	06/02/92	07/07/92
HALLMARK SHUTTLE	19	05/31/92	08/06/92
ST Parody song	10	05/24/92	08/03/92
Why's everyone down on Shatner?	18	04/29/92	08/04/92
Kahn	25	04/23/92	07/03/92
Trek Laserdiscs	13	04/17/92	07/17/92
STAR TREK GAMES WANTED	20	12/09/91	07/21/92

Read 1st   Browse   Find New

Clicking on the Find New icon produces a list of messages posted since our last visit, which was August 6th. We can either read just these new messages or browse all messages in the folder.

HALLMARK SHUTTLE

NEW CHRISTMAS ORNIMENT

New Messages:	Author	Date
I Saw It!	CoolKath	08/07/92
Shuttle	Jeff Frank	08/07/92
Those Shuttles!	BigGuy1338	08/07/92
Which Stores Are Best?	LarryCoe	08/07/92

Read   Add Message   Browse All

Note the Add Message icon at the bottom of Figure 6-17. This is how you add messages to the folder. All you need to do is click on the icon, enter a subject and text of your message, then OK your effort. Your message will be added to the folder immediately. We'll discuss this further in a moment.

Your personal date of last visit

Your personal "date of last visit" is marked the instant you visit a board. This implies two things: 1) no matter how many (or how few) messages you read while visiting a board, none of the messages posted prior to that visit show up when you next click on the Find New icon; 2) if anyone (including you) posts a message on a board while you're reading, that message *will* appear when you next click on the Find New icon.

Note that we're talking about *boards* here, not folders. If a board contains 600 messages in 24 folders and you read one message in one folder, *none* of the remaining messages will show up the next time you click on the Find New icon, in *any* folder on the board. This is a significant subtlety. Don't let it trip you up.

Most boards contain hundreds of messages. No matter how interested in the subject you might be, it's doubtful you will want to read every message the first time you visit a board. Or maybe you have been away from the board for a few months and don't want to be deluged with all the messages posted since your last visit. These are two of the reasons why America Online provides the Find Since icon (see Figure 6-18).

Figure 6-18:
The Find Since
icon lets you
specify the extent
of a message list.

Finding Messages Posted Since a Specific Date

Star Trek Board

This is your very own place to exchange views about the Star Trek movies, the series or to discuss any ST triviality.

Folders: 45   Messages: 417   Created   Last Message

🗁 Trek 7 maybe in the works	36	06/21/92	07/23/92
🗁 Star Fleet	9	06/18/92	08/01/92
🗁 ST VII: Really!	36	06/16/92	07/26/92
🗁 Star Trek VI	16	06/05/92	07/28/92
🗁 Trek Fiction	13	06/02/92	07/07/92
🗁 HALLMARK SHUTTLE	19	05/31/92	08/06/92
🗁 ST Parody song	10	05/24/92	08/03/92
🗁 Why's everyone down on Shatner?	18	04/29/92	08
🗁 Kahn	25	04/23/92	07
🗁 Trek Laserdiscs	13	04/17/92	07

Read 1st   Browse   Find New   Find Since...   Create Folder   Help &

HALLMARK SHUTTLE

Find Only the Messages Posted:

In Last ⬚3⬚ Day(s)

Date of last visit: 92-08-07 10:58:35 EDT

Search   Help & Info

Clicking on the
Find Since
icon displays
this window.
Since today is
August 8th, we
see all of the
messages
posted since
August 7th.

HALLMARK SHUTTLE

NEW CHRISTMAS ORNIMENT

New Messages: Author   Date

Star Trek Christmas hangup	nERT1	08/05/92
Greed	Redlion	08/05/92
10 down and two to go	LarryCos	08/05/92
Where are you?	Linda57	08/06/92

Read   Add Message   Browse All

It took us a while to figure out the Browse, Find and Read icons. We hope this little discussion saves you the trouble. Regardless, find a board that interests you and start reading its messages. Start with just one or two folders, read the last seven or ten days' worth of messages, and become familiar with the subject and the people. When you feel confident, post your own messages. It's at that moment—when you have joined the fray—that message boards start to get really interesting. This is part of the fun; don't deny yourself the opportunity.

Posting messages

A moment ago we suggested you post your own messages. It might help if we review that process. There's not much to it: take a look at Figure 6-19.

Figure 6-19:
Posting your own
message is as
simple as clicking
on an icon.

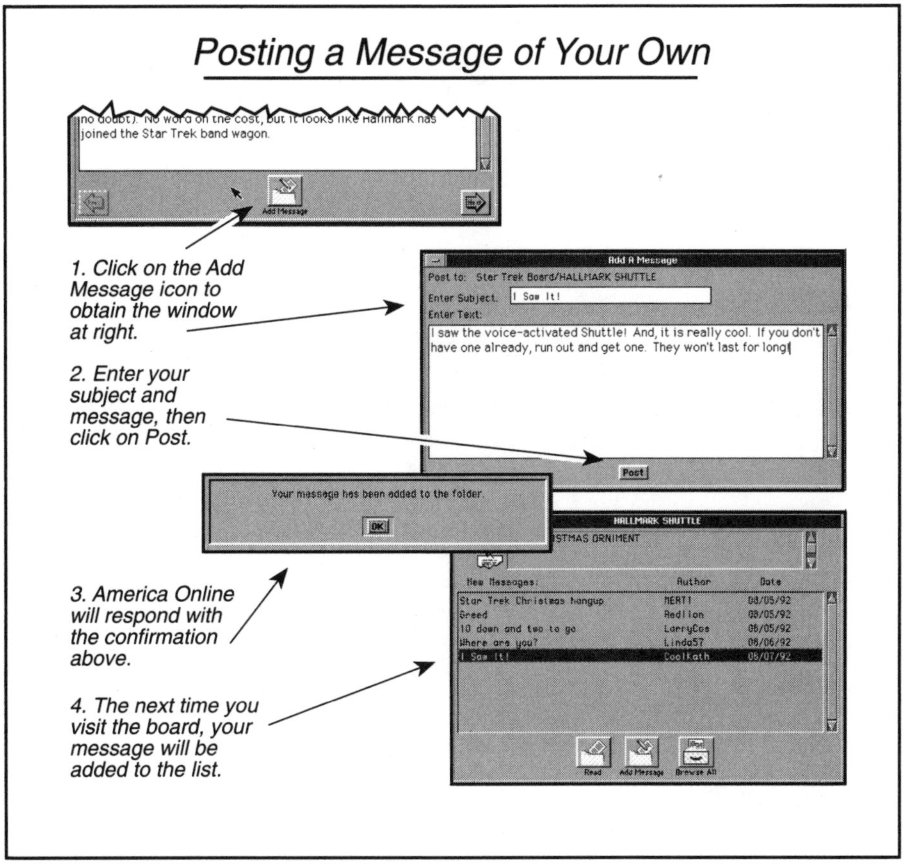

Posting a Message of Your Own

(no doubt.) No word on the cost, but it looks like Hallmark has joined the Star Trek band wagon.

Add Message

1. Click on the Add
Message icon to
obtain the window
at right.

Add A Message

Post to: Star Trek Board/HALLMARK SHUTTLE
Enter Subject: I Saw It!
Enter Text:

I saw the voice-activated Shuttle! And, it is really cool. If you don't have one already, run out and get one. They won't last for long!

Post

2. Enter your
subject and
message, then
click on Post.

Your message has been added to the folder.

OK

3. America Online
will respond with
the confirmation
above.

HALLMARK SHUTTLE
...STMAS ORNIMENT

New Messages: Author   Date

Star Trek Christmas hangup	MERTI	08/05/92
Greed	RedIion	08/05/92
10 down and two to go	LarryCos	08/05/92
Where are you?	Linda57	08/06/92
I Saw It!	CoolKath	08/07/92

4. The next time you
visit the board, your
message will be
added to the list.

Read   Add Message   Browse All

Posting effective messages is something of an art. Messages like "Me too" or "I don't think so" don't really contribute to a board. Before you post a message, be sure you have something to say, take the time to phrase it effectively and give it a proper subject header.

Online etiquette

If you want to be heard, if you want replies to your messages, and if you want to be a responsible online citizen, you will want to acknowledge those few rules of telecommunications etiquette. Since Emily Post and Miss Manners haven't yet offered a treatise on the subject, we'd best discuss it here.

- Post messages only when you have something to say, phrase the subject header effectively and be succinct. The best messages are those with provocative headers and laconic prose. If your message requires more than a screen of text—if it requires a trip to the scroll bar to read—edit it.

- Stick to the subject. If the folder you're participating in is entitled "Amphibians in Wyoming," don't discuss the new-car purchase you're considering.

- If your message wanders, summarize before responding. You might quote a previous posting (do so in carets: "When you said <<I really prefer Versailles>> were you talking about the font or the city in France?"). This will help others stick to the topic.

- Don't post chain letters, advertisements or business offers unless the board was created for it. And *never* send junk mail to unsuspecting recipients.

- HEY YOU! CAN YOU HEAR ME??!! (Did we get your attention? Did you like the way we did it?) Using all caps is dissonant, hard to read and arrogant. Use all caps only when you really want to shout, and those occasions are rare. For emphasis, set off your text with asterisks: "I *told* you he was a geek!"

- Do not issue personal attacks, use profanity or abuse a privilege. If criticism is specifically invited, remember that there is no vocal inflection or body language to soothe the potential for misinterpretation. Be gentle.

- For the same reason, subtleties, double-entendres and sarcasm are rarely effective. Be forthright.

- Avoid emotional responses. Think before you write. Once you've posted a message, you can't take it back.

- Remember your options. Some replies are better sent as personal e-mail than as messages. If you're feeling particularly vitriolic, send mail to the perpetrator. This saves face for both of you.

Libraries

Libraries are collections of computer files. The Star Trek library, for instance, contains text files, graphic files, sound files and even a few animations. Text and graphics files are usually generic and may be viewed with the appropriate software on any type of computer. Sound and animation are more computer specific. If you're not sure whether you have the appropriate hardware or software needed to use a file, double-click on the file's name to get a description of it. There you will see headings for "Needs" and "Equipment" that clearly describe what's needed to take advantage of that particular file.

Files are *downloaded* from the Stratus to your computer. They're transferred over the telephone lines using elaborate protocols that guarantee their integrity. Technically, the downloading process is quite complex, but America Online manages all the technical necessities for you. All you really have to do is select the file and the destination (on your hard disk), and AOL takes care of the rest. Though we examine the subject of downloading in the next chapter (and we discuss the Download Manager in Chapter 12), you may be interested in seeing how we got the graphic that appears on the cover page of this chapter. Figure 6-20 identifies that process.

Figure 6-20: A
quick glimpse
of the file-
downloading
process. (We
discuss it in
detail in the
next chapter,
"Computing &
Software.")

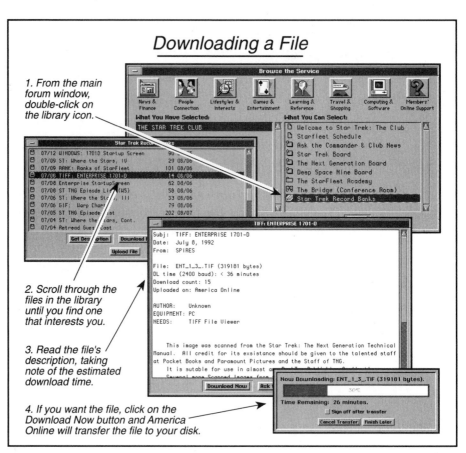

Figure 6-20: A quick glimpse of the file-downloading process. (We discuss it in detail in the next chapter, "Computing & Software.")

Note the Cancel Transfer and Finish Later buttons in the "thermometer" shown at the bottom of Figure 6-20. There's a certain comfort in
that button. If you start a download and change your mind, America
Online accommodates your ambivalence. All you have to do is click on
Cancel and the process stops dead in its tracks. If you click on Finish
Later and later decide that you want to finish downloading the file, you
don't have to start all over again—AOL will pick up where it left off.

The forums at Lifestyles & Interests

With 40-plus forums overall, Lifestyles & Interests is far too large to describe in detail here. Nonetheless, we want to give you a perspective for this bountiful and diverse department, one that merits the exploration of all who advocate the variety and delight life has to offer.

The Environmental Club

It only makes sense that America Online should become a leader in the environmental movement. There's no better forum for the discussion and debate of environmental issues than an online telecommunications service, and America Online exhibits a particularly plentiful capacity for the subject with its Environmental Forum. Hosting the forum is Don Rittner, president of the American Pine Barrens Society and recipient of the prestigious Oak Leaf Award from the Nature Conservancy. Don's book *EcoLinking* is the environmentalist's guidebook to networking with other environmentalists, scientists and concerned citizens throughout the world. Environmental salvation, in the opinion of many, is a grassroots movement, and facilities like America Online stand ready to serve that goal.

Don's forum (keyword: Earth) reflects his fervor and affection for the environment. The forum's boards include the Biosphere, Mother Earth and the Water Cooler (a board for debate). The forum has been chosen by the Environmental News Service—an international news service of substantial esteem—for dissemination of its material. The "Litter Free Library" is substantial and diverse. If you're a responsible citizen of the planet, this forum more than entertains, it serves.

Figure 6-21: A browse through the Environmental Club produced a clip from the Environmental News Service, a recycling logo, a series of messages regarding composting and a satellite photograph of North America.

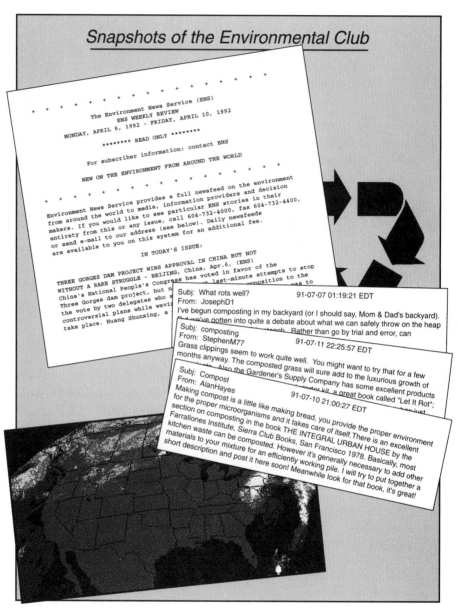

Snapshots of the Environmental Club

+ + + + + + + + + + + + + +
The Environment News Service (ENS)
ENS WEEKLY REVIEW
MONDAY, APRIL 6, 1992 - FRIDAY, APRIL 10, 1992

******** READ ONLY ********

For subscriber information: contact ENS

NEW ON THE ENVIRONMENT FROM AROUND THE WORLD

+ + + + + + + + + + + + + + + +

Environment News Service provides a full newsfeed on the environment from around the world to media, information providers and decision makers. If you would like to see particular ENS stories in their entirety from this or any issue, call 604-732-4000, fax 604-732-4400, or send e-mail to our address (see below). Daily newsfeeds are available to you on this system for an additional fee.

IN TODAY'S ISSUE:

THREE GORGES DAM PROJECT WINS APPROVAL IN CHINA BUT NOT WITHOUT A RARE STRUGGLE - BEIJING, China, Apr.6, (ENS) China's National People's Congress has voted in favor of the Three Gorges dam project, but ... last-minute attempts to stop the vote by two delegates who ... opposition to the controversial plans while wavi... ...was to take place. Huang Shunxing, a ...

Subj: What rots well?   91-07-07 01:19:21 EDT
From: JosephD1
I've begun composting in my backyard (or I should say, Mom & Dad's backyard).
...we've gotten into quite a debate about what we can safely throw on the heap
...ch. Rather than go by trial and error, can

Subj: composting
From: StephenM77   91-07-11 22:25:57 EDT
Grass clippings seem to work quite well. You might want to try that for a few
months anyway. The composted grass will sure add to the luxurious growth of
... Also the Gardener's Supply Company has some excellent products
...der kit a great book called "Let It Rot";

Subj: Compost
From: AlanHayes   91-07-10 21:00:27 EDT
Making compost is a little like making bread, you provide the proper environment
for the proper microorganisms and it takes care of itself. There is an excellent
section on composting in the book THE INTEGRAL URBAN HOUSE by the
Farrallones Institute, Sierra Club Books, San Francisco 1978. Basically, most
kitchen waste can be composted. However it's generally necessary to add other
materials to your mixture for an efficiently working pile. I will try to put together a
short description and post it here soon! Meanwhile look for that book, it's great!

An earth-shaking lesson

In *EcoLinking*, Don Rittner tells a story of the grassroots movement guaranteed to bring a smile to the lips of any environmentalist: "Teaching longitude and latitude to nine and ten year olds is not an easy task," he writes. "Fourth-grade schoolteacher Linda Smith taught her students a lesson in real-life geology—and telecommunications—that they won't soon forget. She used a worldwide earthquake-tracking network provided by the US Geological Service.

"As part of a science fair project, Linda connected a personal computer in her Terre Haute, Indiana, classroom to a phone line. After a basic telecommunications lesson, she linked her students to the network.

"Each day, she would allow two students to access the earthquake-tracking network, and they would gather information on earthquakes that had happened in the past 24 hours. Those two students would then go to a very large map of the world, and using the longitude and latitude information given on the earthquake printout, they would use pins with colored heads to pinpoint each earthquake.... Using a searchable encyclopedia on America Online, Linda's students looked up information about the population, the land formations, the climate, the soil type and the known faults of each continent under study. By downloading the information into a word processor, the youngsters were able to prepare reports on...major recorded earthquakes."

Don goes on to say that by pinpointing the earthquake sites on the map, the students easily grasped the concepts of latitude and longitude. "Perhaps equally as important," he writes, "the students developed the skills and self-confidence to use the vast electronic resources available for learning about the world."

EcoLinking—Everyone's Guide to Online Environmental Information, published by Peachpit Press, is available in bookstores or by contacting Don Rittner (screen name "Host Earth") on America Online.

Real Estate Online

If you're ever again in the market for real estate, this is the first place you should go for information. Real Estate Online, AOL's real estate forum, offers tips on buying a home, information on mortgage loans, property listings in all 50 states and an especially comprehensive "reading room" (see Figure 6-22).

Figure 6-22:
The Real Estate
Forum offers
everything a home
buyer (or seller) will
ever need. In a
15-minute visit, we
found a listing for a
home in Carmel and
a library of articles
that would make a
broker blush.

The person responsible for this wealth of information is Peter G. Miller, author of six real-estate books, two of which were in the top ten best-selling nonfiction book list recently. Miller's forum features weekly commentaries, home prices and trends in all 50 states, current mortgage rate listings and a board featuring properties for sale. You'll find handy financial programs in the library, and an "Ask Our Broker" board where you can obtain answers to those sticky real-estate questions that simply can't be asked of brokers or agents who are involved in a transaction. Few personal transactions equal the monetary significance of buying or selling a home, and the real estate forum is one of the few unbiased sources of information available. It's as near as your computer (keyword: Real Estate).

The Bicycling Forum

In Chapter 11 ("Electronic Mail"), we'll discuss the Internet, a network of nearly 15 million computer users around the world.

A few years ago, a forum for the recreational bicyclist appeared on the Internet named "rec.bicycles." Though the Internet has millions of subscribers, most are from governmental and educational institutions and the forum was not readily accessible to the general public. In 1992, the enthusiasts from rec.bicycles began a search for a more accessible medium. They found it in America Online and the result is BikeNet (keyword: BikeNet).

Figure 6-23: Four of the leading bicycling organizations accompany articles, message boards and a library in the BikeNet Forum.

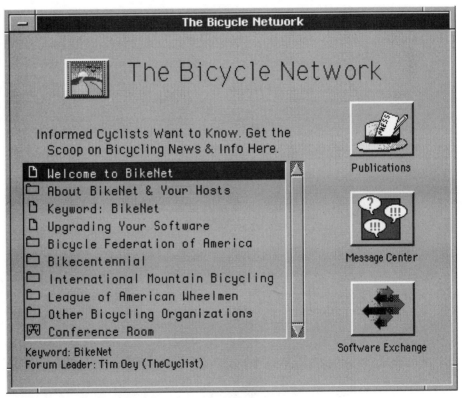

BikeNet is sponsored by four of the leading bicycle organizations in the United States: BikeCentennial, Bicycle Federation of America (BFA), International Mountain Bicycling Association (IMBA) and the League of American Wheelmen (LAW). Each of these organizations has its own sub-area that contains a description of the organization, an electronic membership application, selected articles from its periodicals and an entry point into its library of files.

If you're a bicyclist, you'll want to visit this forum regularly. Like many others in Lifestyles & Interests, BikeNet is a forum that's produced with quality, proficiency and élan. With all four of the leading bicycling organizations represented, it's the undeniable voice of authority, and with the thousands of riders it brought from the Internet, it's also the voice of the people.

Figure 6-24:
A haven for
bicyclists: BikeNet
offers advice,
articles and
graphics.

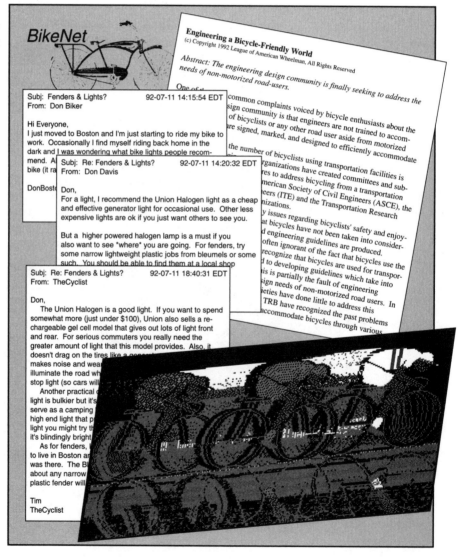

Moving on

The time has come to move on, but not because we've run out of material. We could devote an entire book to this department and still leave some areas unexplored. Lifestyles & Interests is the Athens of AOL—diverse, sublime and forever appealing.

While few departments exceed Lifestyles & Interests' diversity, one does exceed its volume: Computing & Software. While Lifestyles & Interests is the Athens of AOL's Departments, Computing and Software is its colossus.

The Colossus of Memnon were erected in the 14th Century B.C. by the Egyptian king Amenhotep III. The Colossus are two seated stone figures each measuring 38 feet high. If they ever stood up, they would tower over every structure in Washington, DC, including AOL's four-story office building a few miles away. While King Kong was satisfied with only one Faye Ray in the palm of his hand, it would take six Faye Rays to fill a Colossus hand, and there are four of those.

By volume, the colossus of departments at AOL is Computing & Software. All other departments pale by comparison—mere King Kongs: pebbles in the sandals of a colossus like Computing & Software. Exploring a colossus takes a while, but that's what we're about to do. Fortify yourself: here we go.... Next

CHAPTER 7
Computing & Software

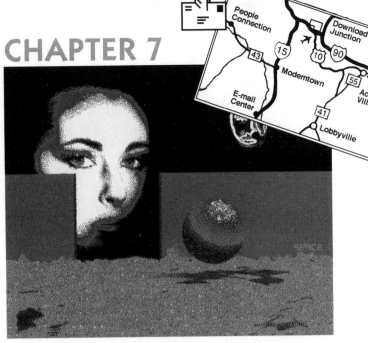

If you love your PC, if it beckons with an alluring radiance whenever it's in the same room, and if you needlessly optimize your hard disk and reorganize your subdirectories and files, you're going to love this department. Computing & Software is the consummate carnival for PC maniacs. It's an opiate, a tabernacle, a jubilation. You'll spend a lot of time here.

In fact, even if you're *not* a computer fanatic, Computing & Software may still become one of your mainstays. There are thousands of files here—fonts and graphics in particular—that will appeal to even the casual PC user. If you need help with either your PC or the software you run on it, Computing & Software is ready to oblige. And there are some invigorating forums here, ranging from the fundamental to the existential. This place is as rife with opportunity as a sunny Saturday in August, and you can enjoy it any day of the year.

Frontispiece graphic: "Jane," by David Palermo (Space7), miscellaneous library: Graphic Arts & CAD Forum.

Computing & Software

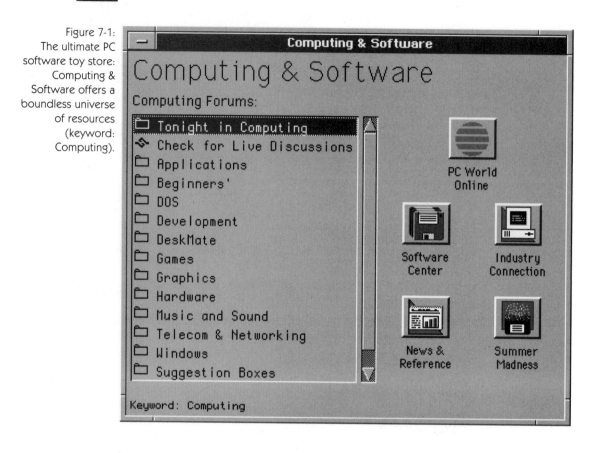

Figure 7-1:
The ultimate PC
software toy store:
Computing &
Software offers a
boundless universe
of resources
(keyword:
Computing).

PC World Online

There's so much great stuff here, it's hard to know where to begin. Starting at the top is probably appropriate, and at the top of Figure 7-1 is PC World Online (keywords: PC World). Many devoted PC users subscribe to *PC World*, but if you're like us, you've given up filing past issues. After a few months, the magazine goes into the trash. Naturally, you regret trashing it soon thereafter: only then do you need to look up a specification or review of software you have decided to buy.

We have good news: you can trash those magazines without guilt, because *PC World* is available on America Online (see Figure 7-2). You can read current or past issues, preview next month's issue, save articles, download files and working models of newly released software and even talk to the editors.

Figure 7-2:
Everything but the
ads: nearly all the
latest issues of "PC
World" are online,
plus past issues and
software libraries.

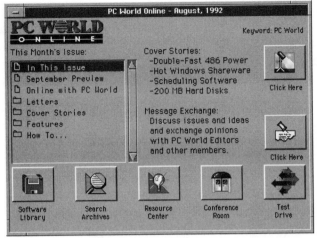

We both visit this area once a month without fail, and every time
we contemplate a purchase—hardware or software—we consult the
reviews. A recent search for much-needed information on scanners
yields 28 announcements and reviews (see Figure 7-3).

Figure 7-3:
Searching past
issues of "PC
World" produced
28 references to
scanners.

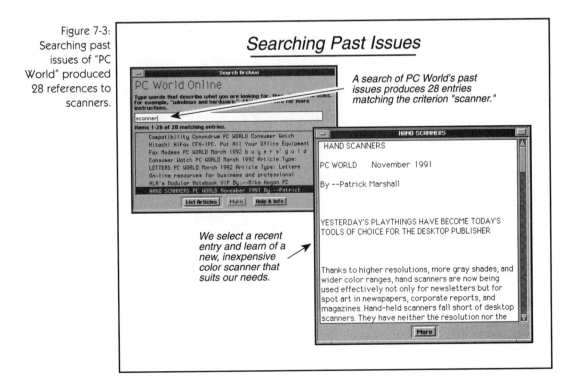

While the ability to search archives is a primary feature of PC World Online, hundreds of news stories, reviews and files are also available—all searchable, and all in a form you can use for inclusion in documents of your own. In addition, a special section called "Message Exchange" features message boards that put you in touch with *PC World's* editorial staff and readers, and a library of files offers indices to past issues, macros and other goodies (see Figure 7-4).

Figure 7-4: Current issue cover stories, test drives, a library of software and a one-on-one forum with the editors round out PC World Online.

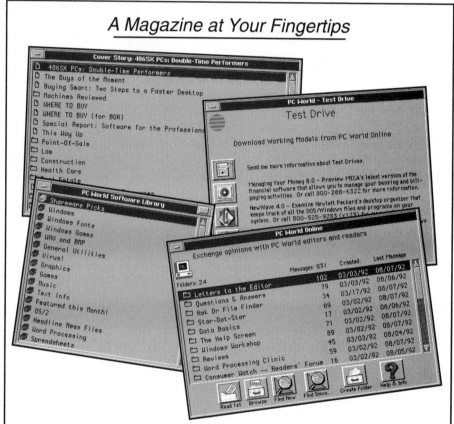

Computer news & reference sources

All *true* computer nerds are myopic, struggle with carpal tunnel syndrome and suffer a misanthropic social life. They are unaware of the environment and society that surrounds them and have no concept of either past or future.

So what's wrong with that?

Perhaps just one thing: we must make room in our awareness for knowledge of our industry. We may not need to know about society, the environment, the past and the future; but we must be aware of the society, the environment, the past and the future *of computing*. How else will we know when to upgrade, how to strip the least significant bit off v.32bis data packets, and whether Ross Perot will buy Microsoft?

We need news. And we don't want to leave our computers to get it.

We've got Good News, bit blitters: all the industry enlightenment you'll ever need is right here on America Online in the Computing & Software Department. It's current, it's accurate, it's interactive, and it's really great stuff. All you have to do is click on the News & Reference icon (see Figure 7-5).

Figure 7-5: News, opinion, background—even a dictionary. It's all in News & Reference.

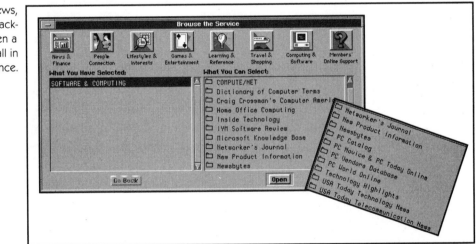

You should get to know each of these areas. There's a rainbow of information here, always current and comprehensive. Some highlights:

🔺 Craig Crossman is a nationally syndicated computer columnist with the *Miami Herald*. His weekly column, "Techno-File," in which he writes Q&A articles, commentaries and product reviews, currently appears in hundreds of newspapers. Additionally, Craig is the creator and host of a live, nationally syndicated two-hour radio talk show called "Craig Crossman's Computer America." His forum on AOL reflects that show—sort of the "Dear Abby" of computerdom.

Home-Office Computing, the magazine, offers up-to-date reviews of the latest computer hardware, peripherals, office equipment, software and accessories for your home office. It also features tips from experts in all areas of business—who give you the basic information you need to run your home-based enterprise—and profiles of successful home-based businesspeople who provide the inspiration you need to embark on your new lifestyle. *Home-Office Computing*, the forum, offers all of that, plus a buyer's guide and a set of message boards where you have an opportunity to offer feedback to the magazine's editors. *PC Today* and *PC Novice* are here, too, for your reference needs.

IYM Software Review is your online guide to being a smart PC software consumer. IYMSR began publication in 1989 and concentrates on practical information regarding software, offering you an analysis of important concerns like how much memory and disk space you need for performing specialized tasks, and whether a particular program runs well under Microsoft Windows, for example. If you're tired of hearing a software company tell you that you only need 2 Mb of RAM to run its newest program, only to find that once you buy and install it, you actually need 4 Mb, then a visit here is in order before you shop. You can browse through IYM's magazine archives; and as an AOL member, you can even order their print magazine at a reduced rate (keyword: IYM).

Microsoft Knowledge Base is a searchable database of articles on Microsoft products. A search of its files using the keywords *Excel* and *trend* yielded 17 references to Excel's statistical functions.

We really didn't expect a single one. This is one source you'll want to use when experiencing compatibility problems between Microsoft products and other software, or when you need to examine possible pitfalls before you upgrade. Say you're about to buy a commercial memory management package. Will it work with Microsoft Windows or MS-DOS Version 5.0? Check it out here first and you may save yourself from lots of trouble later on.

In *New Product Information* you'll find the latest information on software, hardware, books and general industry news. This information is gathered from manufacturers' press releases, industry trade publications and newsletters, plus personal contacts throughout the industry. A library of text and program files provides everything from catalogs to product documentation. Look here before you buy anything for your PC.

The *Networker's Journal* offers an aggregate of pertinent articles of interest to the networking and telecommunications industries.

Newsbytes News Network is the largest independent computer industry news service in the world and has been published continuously since 1983. Newsbytes has eight domestic and eight international bureaus in cities such as London, Toronto, Tokyo, Hong Kong and Moscow. Newsbytes articles are stored as a searchable database. Whenever you want to know more about any kind of computer-related (not just PC-related) subject, use the keyword: Newsbytes, then click on the icon representing the Newsbytes database. Or browse the Newsbytes folders if you wish: the folder marked "Trends" is particularly contemporary and insightful. If you're interested in staying abreast of the non-stop developments in our industry, we suggest adding Newsbytes to your Go To menu.

Figure 7-6: A snapshot of News & Resources. As this chapter is being written, these are some of the stories of the day.

Glimpses of News & Resources

DISNEY SOFTWARE INTRODUCES NEW ENTERTAINMENT SOFTWARE
Burbank, Calif. — May 28, 1992

Walt Disney Computer Software today announced sound support for Microsoft Windows version 3.1 for The Sound Source and previewed new software at the Summer '92 Consumer Electronics Show in Chicago. Disney Software is now showing pre-release versions of Stunt Island: The Flying and Filming Simulation and Coaster.

"Disney Software has become well known for producing high quality software primarily designed for children," said Ralph Giuffre, director of marketing for Disney Software. "Now with Stunt Island and Coaster we have high quality software that will appeal to adult computer game players, and through the Windo...

FEDS RAID MASS. "DAVY JONES LOCKER" BBS ON COPYRIGHT WARRANT
Networker's Journal — June 12, 1992

The FBI this week raided a Millbury, Mass., bulletin board system called the "Davy Jones Locker," accusing it of illegally distributing copyright software to subscribers in 36 states and 11 foreign countries. No arrests were made, but several computers and various telecommunications equipment were seized, along with business records.

The Software Publishers Association obtained the search warrant that authorized the raid.

Ilene Rosenthal, SPA's director of litigation, told Jack Lesar of United Press International, "We do a lot of investigation and this one looked like it was serious enough...

REACH OUT AND SEE SOMEONE
By Dan Gutman — Technology Highlights

The Jetsons had one. Dick Tracy had one. And now you can have one on your desktop or your computer screen--a video telephone. Perhaps the most anticipated invention of the last 30 years, telephones that transmit images as well as sound are finally technologically feasible, affordable, and yes...available. Recently, AT&T introduced their standalone Videophone 2500 and San Jose-based Compression Labs introduced the Cameo Personal Video System, an on-screen computer videophone. Both products make it possible to conduct a telephone conversation in which both parties can see each other as well as hear...

GLOBAL TELECOM IS HOT AND HAPPENING
By Denise Caruso — Inside Technology

Sometimes in the electronics business, all of a sudden a lot of people are talking about the same thing at the same time, and they all say that Something Real Big is going to happen right away.

Such talk is often a consensual hallucination, a domino effect caused by people with wild imaginations bouncing off each other's brain cells. For example, it's been "The Year of the LAN (local-area network)" at least since 1983. And I remember InfoWorld publishing a cover story on optical disk storage in 1984. Both those technologies are just now beginning to gain popularity.

Altho...

AMERICA ONLINE OFFERS SOVIET SECRETS EXHIBIT
Vienna, Virginia — June 16, 1992

The America Online network has launched an on-line exhibit, held in conjunction with the Library of Congress. The US library, in conjunction with the Committee of Archival Affairs of the Russian Federation, will display highlights of previously secret Soviet records on the America Online system called "Revelations from the Russian Archives." The "exhibit" will run concurrently with the opening of a more extensive exhibit of the documents which opens June 17 at the Madison Building of the Library of Congress. The exhibit features approximately 300 historically significant documents, photographs and films which have been previously inaccessible from the Russian archives, including those of the Central Committee of the Communist Party and the Foreign Ministry. This collection...

In the face of disaster

As this book is being written, residents of Florida and Louisiana are still cleaning up in the aftermath of Hurricane Andrew, which caused record damage and has been declared the worst natural disaster in American history. Meanwhile, Hurricane Iniki has battered the Hawaiian Islands.

While the regular news networks focused on the relief effort to provide shelter and food to those hardest hit, Newsbytes was hot on the trail of locating assistance for the vast number of computer systems damaged by the storms. Though the loss of data pales in comparison to the loss of life and the needs of daily survival, the problem of important computer records being lost forever is no small issue. American commerce is more computerized today than ever before, and the records of many small businesses are likely to exist exclusively on computer, making the recovery of that data critical in restoring operations and getting companies rolling again.

Newsbytes was perhaps more aware of the dilemma of storm-wrecked computer systems than any other news service. The following article was added to its news database following the last of the storms.

"'If Hurricane Andrew, or any other disaster, damaged your computer hard drive, all may not be lost,' says a Minneapolis-based company.

"Ontrack Data Recovery says it is possible for experts to recover computer hard disks which have sustained water or physical damage, even if the drive was severely damaged, according to Ontrack's engineering manager, Stuart Hanley.

"Hanley offers some tips to computer users with storm-damaged computers. First, don't attempt to operate visibly damaged drives. 'In this state, the drive and the data are extremely vulnerable,' he says. The drive shouldn't be operated without the supervision of an engineer who can recognize symptoms of drive distress.

"Hanley also recommends that you not attempt to recover data with commonly available utility software programs, claiming 'even minor manipulations may collapse any hope for a successful data recovery.'

"Also, don't shake the drive, or remove its cover. Once the drive has been opened, your warranty may be voided. 'The drive casing should only be opened in the controlled environment of a clean room,' says Hanley. A 'clean room' is a room specially constructed to keep out any kind of contamination.

"Ontrack says it has successfully recovered data from disk drives that went through floods in Chicago, Texas, and the Ohio River Valley, as well as hurricanes in the southeast United States. The cost of data recovery depends on the complexity of the problem, but according to Hanley, 'For businesses that are stalled until accounting records, customer information or engineering data can be restored, the costs of a recovery operation are almost always less than the cost of downtime and of re-keying lost data.'

More

"Ontrack claims it can typically return usable data from DOS, Novell, Macintosh, OS/2, Unix/Xenix, Sun, DEC, Wang or Banyan Vines systems to customers in two to five days. It is an authorized repair facility for several hard drive manufacturers, providing warranty service for those companies.

"The company says it plans to offer discounted and expedited service for hurricane victims, and has established a toll-free hotline number."

Industry connection

Even die-hard PC users need help with their software or hardware now and again. There are a number of methods:

- Worry about the problem, trying solutions as they come to mind. This usually solves problems within a month, or maybe a week if you're lucky.

- Look up the solution in the manual (if you remember where you put it). This usually takes a half-day.

- Call the customer support line that's offered by the publisher or manufacturer. This usually involves 20 minutes on hold (listening to a bad radio station playing commercials for stores in a city 3,000 miles away), then wait for a call back, which usually comes within a couple of days.

- Post your question on America Online. Within 24 hours, you will receive a response from the vendor you're trying to reach (see Figure 7-7), plus two or three others from fellow users who have had the same experience.

Figure 7-7: Patti had a problem at 7:38. Less than an hour later, she had a response.

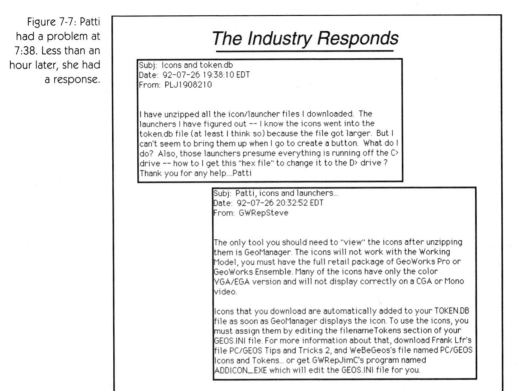

The Industry Responds

Subj: Icons and token.db
Date: 92-07-26 19:38:10 EDT
From: PLJ1908210

I have unzipped all the icon/launcher files I downloaded. The launchers I have figured out -- I know the icons went into the token.db file (at least I think so) because the file got larger. But I can't seem to bring them up when I go to create a button. What do I do? Also, those launchers presume everything is running off the C> drive -- how to I get this "hex file" to change it to the D> drive ? Thank you for any help....Patti

Subj: Patti, icons and launchers...
Date: 92-07-26 20:32:52 EDT
From: GWRepSteve

The only tool you should need to "view" the icons after unzipping them is GeoManager. The icons will not work with the Working Model, you must have the full retail package of GeoWorks Pro or GeoWorks Ensemble. Many of the icons have only the color VGA/EGA version and will not display correctly on a CGA or Mono video.

Icons that you download are automatically added to your TOKEN.DB file as soon as GeoManager displays the icon. To use the icons, you must assign them by editing the filenameTokens section of your GEOS.INI file. For more information about that, download Frank Lfr's file PC/GEOS Tips and Tricks 2, and WeBeGeos's file named PC/GEOS Icons and Tokens... or get GWRepJimC's program named ADDICON_EXE which will edit the GEOS.INI file for you.

Online hardware & software help for the asking

There are some things to keep in mind when posting a technical question. You should always be very specific, include any necessary information and be concise. Give the version number of the software you have a question about, as well as any relevant information about your system and how it's configured (including RAM, hard drive space, cards, monitors, etc.).

If we all communicated problems—no matter how frustrating and agonizing—this effectively, we might always receive prompt, courteous responses like the one posted for Patti's question in Figure 7-7. Requests for industry support are not the place to demonstrate theory or try to prove expertise; nor are they opportunities for vilification.

It's helpful to prepare your question in advance, before you sign on. Spend a few moments scrutinizing it for brevity and courtesy. Sign on and post your message only after you're sure you've included everything needed for a prompt and complete response. You can prepare a message off-line, away from a message board, by choosing New Memo from the File menu (or pressing Ctrl-N). Then, after signing on and finding the message board you want, just copy the text of your new memo and paste it into the form used for posting messages on the board.

The service that provides this solution is AOL's Industry Connection (see Figure 7-8). More than 100 vendors currently maintain message boards on America Online; and each board is checked every day—often more frequently than that—by the appropriate vendor. Not only is excellent vendor support found here, so is peer support, libraries of accessories and updates, announcements from the industry and tips from other users.

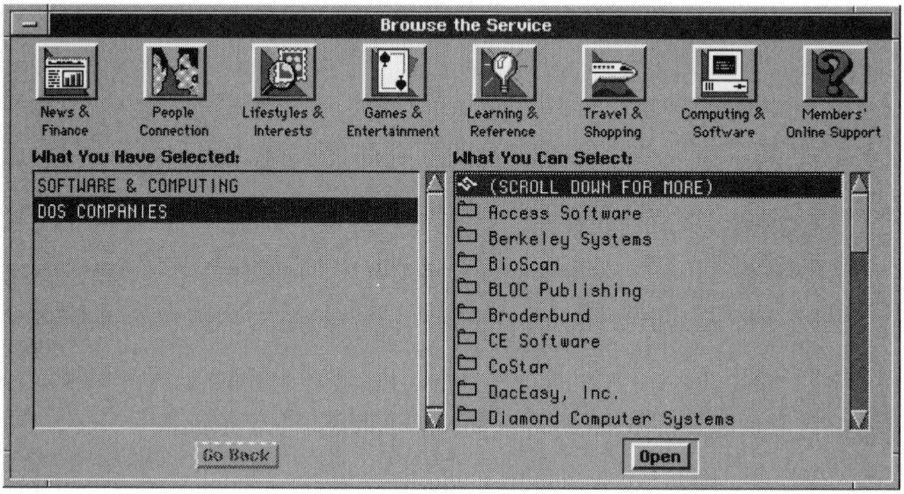

Figure 7-8: More than 100 companies offer support via America Online. You're only seeing a few of the DOS companies here.

Software libraries also usually help round out a company support area online. These libraries boast a wide variety of programs for downloading, including patches, demo versions, diagnostic tools or hardware/software drivers that would otherwise only be available directly from software manufacturers.

Take, for example, Diamond Computer Systems. Many computer users own Diamond SpeedSTAR graphics boards or accelerated Windows video boards. If you owned such a board and then upgraded to Windows 3.1, you might have found that your old video driver no longer worked properly. Instead of calling Diamond Computer Systems in Sunnyvale, California, and asking them to mail you the new video drivers—which could take a week or more if you happen to live on the East Coast—you can enter the Industry Connection, select DOS Companies from the menu, then click on Diamond Computer Systems. There you'll find the necessary driver file online with complete instructions on its installation. Download a copy (more instructions on that later in this chapter and in Chapter 12), install it, and you're back in business again.

The GeoWorks Support Center has been an active player in AOL's Industry Connection for a few years now, supporting Ensemble, its graphical user interface designed for XT and 286 computers. Support staff (readily identified by the GWRep prefix on their screen names) provide help on all matters related to running Ensemble with MS-DOS, PC-DOS or DR DOS operating systems. Lots of GeoWorks special utilities and help can be found in the libraries there. And the message boards see heavy traffic as new Ensemble users seek help and veteran users share their tips and tricks.

Microsoft offers support for MS Works (both Windows and DOS versions), MS Money and MS Publisher. Other neat features include the Microsoft Suggestion Box, which allows you to send your feedback to Microsoft on how you view their products and service. You can also access the Microsoft Small Business Center: a must for up-and-coming entrepreneurs looking for assistance on everything from financial planning to marketing ideas. There are no extra charges for these services. They're yours for the cost of the connect time (keywords: MS Support). And don't be surprised if you bump into a Microsoft representative (they sport the MSFT prefix in their screen names) as you check out the many forum conference rooms online. Microsoft reps can often be found sitting at their keyboards late into the night, munching a snack while sharing a tip in the Windows, PC Development and DOS forums online.

Check out Gateway 2000's support area as well. Gateway has made a name for itself both for its custom-assembled computers and its distinctive cow theme advertising (every Gateway computer is shipped in a white box with black spots). Since its debut in the industry in 1985, Gateway has racked up an impressive number of Editor's Choice, Best Buy and Service Excellence awards from various computer periodicals. It sells more computers through the direct market channel than any other PC manufacturer in the country. Online, you'll find Gateway's support area packed with data on products, prices and problem-solving. You can access Gateway's area with the keywords: Gateway 2000, or with its more popular variation, the keyword: MOO.

This is just a *sampling* of the dozens of companies online that support complete computer systems, peripherals, PC software and operating systems. Other companies with an online presence in Industry connection include Broderbund, MicroProse, Origin, TimeWorks, ZSoft, Strategic Simulations and Sierra Online.

Figure 7-9: Here are three of the vendors offering online support for their products.

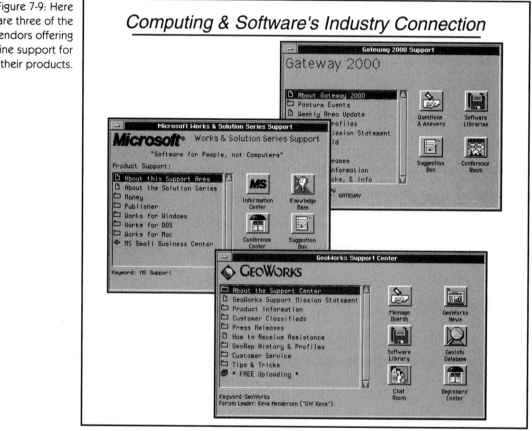

We know several folks who used to be computer consultants and now work in other capacities, but they always told us that online support was the best kind of support money can buy (perhaps that's why they're no longer consultants). Humbling as it may seem, no matter how complex or peculiar your problem, someone else has probably experienced it before. Chances are, just the right person will read the boards, see your posting and reply. This is peer support—people helping people—almost the definition of the online community.

Contribute to that community: post questions when you've got them, and post replies when you know them. Also, don't be afraid to post your response and then e-mail a copy of it directly to the member who posted the message. That's a courtesy that members will appreciate and perhaps repeat for you should you someday run into a vexing problem.

The forums

Perhaps the busiest forums on America Online can be found in Computing & Software. This industry is a moving target, and those who try to keep it in their sights seek information with eagerness that borders on the fanatic. Computing & Software offers forums for every level of computer enthusiast, from beginners to developers, and those forums are as popular as ice cream in July.

It's appropriate, then, that we steal a peek at a few. We want you to see the breadth of this department, to expand your horizons. Perhaps you'll discover something that interests you in the process.

The DOS Forum

DOS is the software everyone loves to hate, yet it's the system in place on tens of millions of computers worldwide and is without a doubt the most widely used software on earth. The DOS Forum (keyword: DOS) serves to mediate this dichotomy. Twenty-seven libraries house thousands of files, message boards allow users and staff to help one another, and five live conference sessions meet each week to address the needs of both novice and veteran DOS users. Click on the Forum Update icon from the main DOS Forum menu to see the complete meeting schedule, which is continuously updated and covers events up to a month in advance.

Figure 7-10: The
DOS Forum
conference room,
where Kate and
the Prompters
appear every
Wednesday
evening.

```
                                        DOS
   ___|_____|___
       |  Hi:  PCC Joe, TIMEREPAIR, MarkT14848, AFC Doug      People Here:  17
       |  Bye: FeinDavid
People |       be changed for use in QB.
       | PCC Aud     But Lou.... Kate will be getting VB4DOS, so :)
       | PC Kate     Thank you, Aud. ;)
       | PCC Chuck   to knock off those 6-line one-time specials to massage
       |             files and so on...
 Rooms | PCC Aud     hi Timerepair :)
       | PC Kate     Hi TimeRepair, welcome to the DOS Forum. :D
       | PCC Lou     Aud  ;D  I have her now!  heh heh heh }:>
       | TIMEREPAIR  Hi. Thanks for the warm welcome
Help & | PC Kate     The DOS Forum: where one good prompt deserves another.
 Info  |             ::ducking::
       | PCC Aud     True Chuck. There's always a need for that! :D
       | TRS80       $p$g
       | Sue         (Isn't Kate still using version 2 of DOS? :D)
       | PC Kate     Hee hee, TRS! :o
       | PCC Chuck   VM/CMS and OS/2 people have REXX....   Many DOS/VSE
   _____ Send
```

The DOS Forum's message boards offer a haven for the perplexed
DOS user. Want to know how to configure EMM386, increase your
PATH limit or unstick your Shift key? You'll find the answers on the
DOS Forum's message boards.

Perhaps the DOS Forum's greatest asset is its fast emergency assistance to members who install a new piece of hardware or a software
program, only to find their computers suddenly don't function as they
should. It's not uncommon to find a DOS staffer online well after
midnight, helping to rescue a damaged CONFIG.SYS file, long after
most company support hotlines have closed for the day.

Certainly of equal value to beginning and advanced users alike is the
DOS Forum's extensive library of files, ranging from command enhanc-
ers to full scale disk managers. During a browse the other day, we
discovered utilities to fix the aforementioned sticky Shift key problem,
optimize a hard disk and align DR DOS with Windows (see Chapter 13,
"Ten Best," for a listing of the ten best downloads). There are so many
files that a single library would be ineffective. Instead, 27 libraries are
offered, each housing hundreds of individual files (see Figure 7-11).

Figure 7-11: Only four of the DOS Forum's 27 libraries appear here.

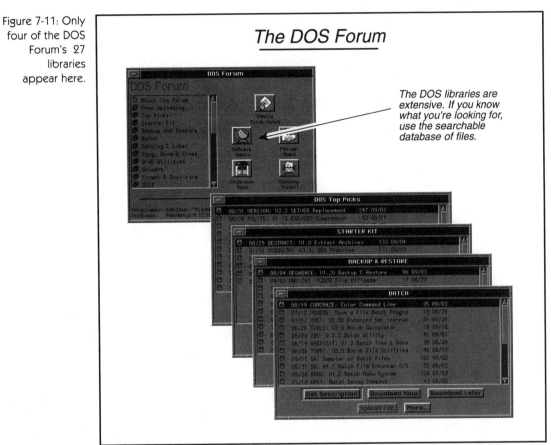

The DOS Forum isn't limited to MS-DOS, either. DR DOS is supported here. Novell Desktop Systems Group—formerly known as Digital Research and current publisher of DR DOS—has an Industry Connection area featuring a user tip file library, message boards and more. Even OS/2—IBM's answer to Microsoft's dominance in the operating system market—is thoroughly covered here. Moreover, the DOS Forum's conference room has featured a variety of prestigious guests, including Microsoft DOS support personnel, DR DOS support personnel, 386Max and QEMM support teams, Kay Yarborough Nelson (author of *Voodoo DOS*), and *Windows Magazine* Editorial Director Fred Langa.

In many of the computing forums online, visits from industry guests—like Microsoft VP Steven Ballmer, Symantec's Norton Group and representatives from premier gaming companies like Sierra Online and LucasArts—are often accompanied by software giveaways doled out to certain lucky forum participants. Dozens of special prizes—like MS-DOS 5.0, Microsoft Windows 3.1, 386Max, GeoWorks Ensemble, DESQview 386, Microsoft C/C++ 7.0, Norton Desktop for Windows and popular game and network software packages—have been given away to members, as have dozens of free hours of online time. Although the DOS Forum is just one of many forums that feature these special events, if you're a DOS user (aren't we all?), this forum should be a regular visit.

Finding leadership online

If you've ever wondered who's in charge of running the forums, you've probably run into the answer to your question if you spend much time online: the forum leader. Forum leaders are responsible for the day-to-day management of the forums in their charge, so forum life online is busy. Thus, each forum leader selects a staff of forum assistants and consultants, usually selected from the general membership on the basis of their expertise and help skills in a given area. Each forum leader, consultant and assistant then works as a team to provide technical support, answer member inquiries, process file uploads and help direct forum conferences. You can identify forum personnel quickly by looking for one of these three prefixes on a screen name: PC (forum leader), PCA (forum assistant) or PCC (forum consultant). (AFL prefixes denote forum leaders for the Mac.) Look for these folks when you have a question, and you'll likely find the forum staffer will bend over backward to help you.

The PC Animation & Graphics Forum

Imagine having access to almost 8,000 graphics files, with more being added every day. Imagine a database of these files, searchable by keywords, author names and file names. Imagine reviews of graphics software, tips from graphics experts and a comprehensive manual describing the ins and outs of online graphics. This, of course, is the PC Animation & Graphics Forum (keyword: Graphics).

The PC Animation & Graphics Forum's libraries are even more prodigious than those of the DOS Forum. At this writing, 52 different topical libraries populate the forum, and like the DOS Forum, a searchable database allows you to search the thousands of files for subject matter that meets your needs. There's a Start Up Library for the novice, a Graphics Reference Guide for the inquisitive, scores of message

Figure 7-12: Three of our favorite graphics from the PC Animation & Graphics Forum. At left, "Sphere," by Gwydian; top right, "Portland," by DiGino; and below that, "City," posted by PC John. Use the keywords: File Search, and specify the title or the artist to locate these graphics.

Images from the Graphics Forum

boards, and a Graphics Meeting Room where public conferences are held every weeknight at 9:30 Eastern time. To attend, use the keyword: Graphics, then click on the Graphics Meeting Room.

- Mondays feature the *Graphics Conference* with a new topic or guest each week.

- Tuesdays offer the *Multimedia Conference*.

- Wednesday evenings bring us the *CAD Conference* for engineers, architects and all other users of computer-aided design systems.

- Thursdays offer the *Artists' Studio*.

- The *Animation Conference* meets every Friday evening at 9:30.

No place for chauvinism

Only half the graphics available online reside in the PC Animation & Graphics Forum. An equal number await the adventurous in the—dare we say it?—*Macintosh* Graphics Forum (keyword: MGR). This sister forum is just as plentiful as the PC forum, and many of the graphics there are in GIF format, meaning they can be easily viewed and used by nearly every PC. Even those graphics in the Mac Graphics Forum that are saved in Macintosh-specific formats are accessible with the proper software (see Chapter 13, "Ten Best," for a list of graphic conversion programs). So go ahead, slip into the Mac Graphics Forum by using the keyword: MGR, and check out the files that reside there—no one will ever know, and we promise we won't tell anyone we sent you there.

The Windows Forum

Here's one to watch. With AOL's ability to run as a DOS application under Windows, this forum is attracting more interest than ever. And there's plenty of opportunity for interest: the Windows environment offers sound, animation and color as standard equipment—no accessories required. Perhaps more significant, a fertile programming environment—Visual Basic—offers the opportunity for custom applications without the need for extensive programming experience. Windows Version 3.x has only been around for a few years, yet it's already taken hold in a number of key markets and is one of the fastest growing operating systems around today. It's an incredibly complex system, yet its complexity is more enticing than daunting. It's rife with challenge, opportunity and reward, and its custodian is the Windows Forum (see Figure 7-13).

Figure 7-13: The Windows Forum is your one-stop Windows community.

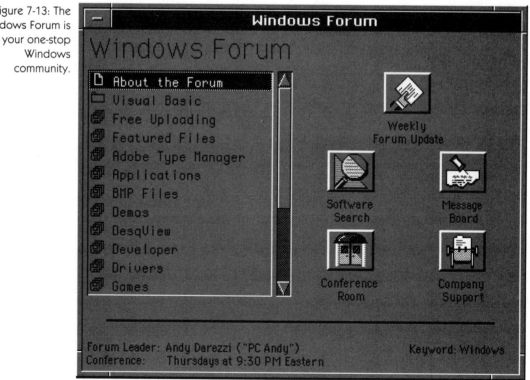

Once again a treasure of resources awaits the forum visitor. A lively collection of message boards serves Windows professionals and newcomers alike, conferences are held here every Tuesday and Thursday evening at 9:30 Eastern time (use the keyword: Windows, and click on the Conference Room icon), and a searchable database of files puts thousands of Windows applications and resources at your fingertips.

Many Windows users get so inspired with ideas for new Windows programs, they decide they want to try to write their own. Enter Microsoft's *Visual Basic*, a relatively new programming environment providing both amateur and professional software creators with access to all of Windows's features (like pull-down menus, dialog boxes and graphics). It's an exciting, easy new way to dabble with inventing Windows-based programs, and it's a concept that has generated a lot of interest in a short time. Ideas for possible new programs often surface in a Windows Forum chat and then travel over to the PC Development Forum (keyword: PDV), where the staff specializes in helping people use *Visual Basic* (or one of several other programming languages, including C, C++ and Pascal) to implement their ideas. *Visual Basic* help and samples are found in both a library and a message board shared by both forums.

In fact, the Windows Forum's libraries abound with programs ranging from the trivial to the profound, offering a wealth of graphics, sound files, games, utilities and text help to assist you in customizing your Windows environment.

Figure 7-14: Two shareware programs available in the Windows Forum. On the outside, "Paint Shop Pro," by Robert Voit and JASC, Inc. Within the Paint Shop window, "BioWin," a biorhythm charting program by Steven L. Dodds, written in Visual Basic.

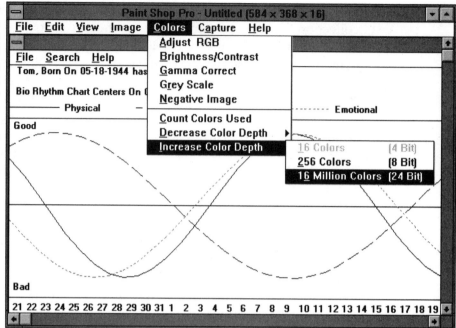

No discussion of this forum would be complete without mention of fonts. Unlike the DOS environment, Windows fonts are a system-level adjunct. Once installed, a font becomes available to all programs running under the system: word processing, spreadsheet and desktop publishing alike. One can never have enough fonts (as long as you don't try to use them all at once), and there are certainly plenty of them available in the Windows Forum. When we ventured into the Forum's font libraries to count the number available, we were overwhelmed by their abundance, in both PostScript and TrueType format. Best of all, these fonts are shareware, and most are available for less than $20.

What is shareware?

The traditional commercial channel for distributing software involves software publishers (or developers), distributors and retailers. Each must make a living, thus each adds a bit to the cost of the product. By the time a piece of software reaches an end user, it has traveled a considerable distance since it left the hands of the people who actually created it.

More▷

An alternative software distribution method is referred to as *shareware*. The shareware method is usually a direct connection between the user and the person who created the program. Shareware programs and data are posted on telecommunications services like AOL, where they may be freely downloaded whenever a user pleases. Shareware can also be distributed among individuals or through user groups, without restriction. Every piece of shareware we've seen avidly encourages this kind of distribution.

Shareware is usually complete. If you download a shareware program, you get the complete program—not a "crippled" version—and you usually get some form of documentation as well. You can try out a piece of shareware for a while—usually at least a few days, sometimes a few weeks—before you decide to buy. If you elect to keep it, the author usually requests that you send money. Since the money is sent directly to the author—no publishers, distributors or retailers are involved—shareware is usually much less expensive than commercially distributed software. The author's share is all you pay for shareware (that same share is a small portion of the total cost of traditional software distributed through commercial channels).

The shareware model also provides a direct channel for communication between user and author. If you have a complaint or a suggestion for improvement, send e-mail to the author. Chances are you'll get a reply. This is a significant feature: to whom do you send mail if you think your car or your refrigerator can be improved? And do you really think they will reply?

While most shareware authors request financial remuneration, a few others simply give their material away (freeware), or request a postcard from your city or town (postcardware), or a donation to a favored charity.

But the shareware concept only works if users pay. And since payment is voluntary, less than 10 percent of the people who use shareware programs actually pay for them. This is undoubtedly the biggest fault in the shareware concept. The potential that shareware offers is especially rewarding for end users, but only if we honor the honor system that's implicit in the shareware concept. In other words, if you use shareware, pay for it and encourage others to do the same.

The PC Games Forum

If all this talk of operating systems, Windows interfaces and GIF conversions is starting to sound like more work than fun, then a foray to the PC Games Forum—a place that takes fun seriously—is in order (keywords: PC Games).

Be prepared for temptation, because this forum's libraries are better stocked with glorious graphics adventure, arcade, board, gambling, simulation and role-playing gameware than most software stores could ever hope for. Don't let the "shareware" tag on most of these files fool you: though the games online usually cost much less than their commercial counterparts, many of them sport better visual and adventure effects than even some of the top-rated mainstream games. That temptation continues in the forum's nightly conferences and message boards, where participants exchange clues and reviews of the hottest new game releases. You'll come away from one night's session determined to spend the week's grocery budget on the latest game packages from the Games Top Picks' library.

There are no age restrictions here, as you'll discover when you see pre-teens raving over sedate chess and Mahjongg selections while more mature types race to grab the latest high-octane arcade battle.

Click on the Company Support icon from PC Games' main menu, and discover special areas resplendent with gaming jewels. Apogee's support area is a favorite, offering supreme graphics and challenges at unbeatable shareware prices. Apogee has a game here for every taste: *WordRescue* is charming fun for very young players while *Castle Wolfenstein 3-D* is rated PC for "profound carnage." Interplay, another noted game producer, also has a support area here offering demo versions of its most popular PC titles, including *BattleChess*, *Star Trek: 25th Anniversary* and *Bard's Tale*. In fact, you will find demo versions of many popular games from a host of different companies online.

For more on games, you may want to review Chapter 4, "Entertainment," where several popular games are featured.

While we have highlighted some of our favorite PC forums, don't fail to check out the other great forums online, including PC Development, Music & Sound, Hardware, Applications, Telecom & Networking, Beginners and even DeskMate. Also stop by the Software Center—which features The Help Desk—where personnel will answer your questions and help you find what you're looking for in this ever-growing computing department. The keyword: TITF is an invaluable tool to forum regulars and beginners alike. TITF stands for "Tonight in The Forums"; it gives you a comprehensive list of computer conferences held online each night. You can even click on Check for Active Rooms to see which conference rooms have sessions in progress and then enter one right from where the keyword TITF takes you.

Computing & Software is a feast for the PC appetite. If you ever get the hunger, there's a forum here waiting to sustain.

Big Brother need not apply

Tim Barwick gazes at the woods outside his window, just a few minutes from downtown Washington, DC. Red squirrels scamper up deciduous trees, reveling in the springtime sun. The forest's contrast to the rush hour chaos on Route 7 a half-mile away somehow reflects Tim's contrast to the hubbub at AOL. Originally a member, then a forum leader, Tim now oversees AOL's most active department—Computing & Software. The contrast is heard rather than seen: a native of England, Tim speaks with an Old World elegance that hardly conforms to the fast-paced, cutting-edge department he runs.

Tim's Old World heritage is reflected in his management philosophy: he is strictly hands-off. "I treat my forum leaders like adults," says Tim. "Each has a vision; each has a vested interest; each is left alone." It's precisely this kind of attitude that has closed the door on Big Brother at AOL. This is the home of the individual and the community, and Tim is here to see that it stays that way.

Tim is a *Department Head* at America Online. As such, he is a full-time employee with an office at AOL headquarters. Forum leaders, on the other hand, work in the field—usually from their homes—and are usually independent contractors. In the telecommunications industry, Department Heads can be dictatorial—even tyrannical—but never at AOL. Tim expresses his philosophy with unusual eloquence, but at AOL, the philosophy is standard operating procedure.

Downloading files

The most popular aspect of the Computing & Software Department is its extensive collection of software. All it takes is a browse through the libraries: the number of times a file has been downloaded is shown beside each file's name, and most of those numbers exceed 100. One hundred downloads for each of 25,000 files equals 2,500,000 downloads. *Two million, five hundred thousand!* But that's just the Computing & Software Department. Thousands of other files reside within America Online, spread across the service like flowers in a meadow. Members graze this meadow, downloading bouquets of files and smiling. People must be on to something here.

It might be appropriate, then, to spend a few pages discussing down-loads: what they are, where they are and how do you get one for yourself?

What is downloading?

Simply put, downloading is the process of transferring a file from America Online's Stratus to a disk on your computer. Files can be programs, fonts, graphics (all of the graphics in this book have been downloaded), sound, animation or, of course, text. In fact, this whole book has been downloaded: using AOL's electronic mail capabilities, we uploaded the manuscript to America Online (more about uploading later), and the publisher downloaded it.

A downloading session

Perhaps the best way to explain downloading is to download a file for you and explain the process as it's happening. Later in this chapter, we'll discuss a file format for graphics called GIF (Graphics Interchange Format). It's a popular format for online graphics: it accommodates monochrome or color graphics of any size and complexity, and it's efficient—it doesn't take much time to download a GIF file compared to most other formats.

The GIF format is independent of any type of computer. PC users download GIFs (you can tell a GIF file by its ".GIF" file-name extension), but it's also a file format used by Macintosh owners, Amiga users and Apple II users. Each user requires some form of a conversion program to convert GIFs into a form that's visible on the receiving computer, and that's what we're about to download.

There are dozens of these programs, but our favorite general-purpose DOS GIF converter is Graphics Workshop, by Alchemy Mindworks. (Paint Shop Pro, by Robert Voit, mentioned earlier in this chapter, would be an excellent choice as a Windows program GIF converter.) Graphics Workshop reads and displays GIF files, then converts them into any PC format you want. Converted to the TIFF format, for example, a GIF file can be loaded into most word processing, graphics and desktop publishing applications.

There's another reason why we prefer Graphics Workshop. It's shareware, and shareware is usually inexpensive. A program of Graphics Workshop's quality and complexity could easily command a handsome price via commercial channels; instead, it's distributed through shareware channels and sells for next to nothing.

Before you can download a file, you've got to find it. This could be a horrendous task were it not for America Online's searchable database of online files. The database is only a keyword away.

⚠ Begin by typing Ctrl-K (for keyword) and entering the keywords: File Search (see Figure 7-15).

Figure 7-15: The keywords: File Search take you directly to a database of files stored on AOL. There, you can enter specific criteria to help you find exactly the file you want.

Using File Search

Go to Keyword

Enter keyword: file search

OK   Keyword List

The keyword "file search" takes you directly to the searchable database of files stored on America Online.

File Search

List files made available during: (Click one)

◆ All dates   ✓ Past month   ✓ Past week

List files only in these categories: (Click on one or more)

☐ All Categories

☐ Applications   ☐ Games   ☐ Programming
☐ Deskmate   ☐ Graphics   ☐ Basic Programs
☐ DOS   ☐ Hardware   ☐ Telecom
☐ Education   ☐ Music

List files with these words reflecting my interest: (Optional)

Graphics Workshop

List Matching Files   Get Help & Info

🔥 Two references emerge here once the search has been completed (see Figure 7-16). As a matter of convenience, files are sometimes posted in more than one location online, especially if a particular file defies easy categorization or could be used for a number of different purposes. Graphics Workshop could also be found under other forums.

Figure 7-16: Before downloading a file, you can read a detailed description of it that outlines what the file is, what it does, and what you will need in the way of software and hardware to be able to use that file.

The File's Description

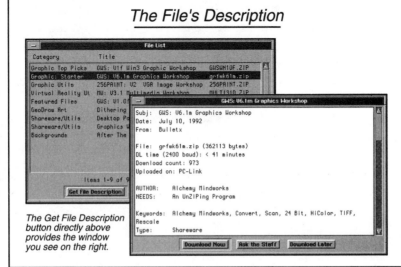

File List

Category	Title	
Graphic Top Picks	GWS: V1f Win3 Graphic Workshop	GWSWN10F.ZIP
Graphic: Starter	GWS: V6.1m Graphics Workshop	grfwk61m.zip
Graphic Utils	256PRINT: V2 VGA Image Workshop	256PRINT.ZIP
Virtual Reality Ut	MW: V3.1 Multimedia Workshop	MULTI310.ZIP
Featured Files	GWS: V1.0f	
GeoDraw Art	Dithering	
Shareware/Utils	Desktop Pa	
Shareware/Utils	Graphics W	
Backgrounds	After The	

Items 1-9 of 9

Get File Description

The Get File Description button directly above provides the window you see on the right.

GWS: V6.1m Graphics Workshop

Subj: GWS: V6.1m Graphics Workshop
Date: July 10, 1992
From: Bulletx

File: grfwk61m.zip (362113 bytes)
DL time (2400 baud): < 41 minutes
Download count: 973
Uploaded on: PC-Link

AUTHOR: Alchemy Mindworks
NEEDS: An UnZIPing Program

Keywords: Alchemy Mindworks, Convert, Scan, 24 Bit, HiColor, TIFF, Rescale
Type: Shareware

Download Now   Ask the Staff   Download Later

▲ When you click on the Get File Description button, America Online provides a complete description of the file (again, see Figure 7-16). This intermediary step is critical. There are lots of things we need to know about this file before we choose to download it. Download-ing takes time, and time is money on AOL. There's no point in downloading a file unless you're fairly sure it's what you want.

The online file database

Using the keywords: File Search to browse the file listings is a conven-ient way to search all of AOL's libraries with one command. The keyword cuts across forums and departments to provide access to all the files currently available online. This method also assigns the file-searching task to the Stratus rather than to your PC, and the Stratus searches quickly—rarely taking more than a couple of seconds to search the tens of thousands of files available.

Look again at the File Search dialog box pictured in Figure 7-15. Two categories of check boxes are provided, allowing you to specify only those files that have recently been uploaded (the "past week" option is great for finding new files), or only those files that fit certain criteria.

More important, a text box is also available within the File Search dialog box. This is where you specify your own criteria. Staff members at AOL are in charge of reviewing every file before it is posted in the software libraries. They assign each file a set of key search words. These words include the screen name of the person who uploaded the file (so that you can search for all the files uploaded by MajorTom, for instance); the name of the file; the software category into which the file falls (font, utility, game, etc.); and other words that might describe the file or otherwise be associated with it. You can enter any words you wish in the File Search dialog, and any files that match the criteria you specify are then listed.

There are three special words you can use in a search phrase: "and," "or" and "not." Each of these words modifies how the next word in the phrase is used. We may receive dozens of matches to the search phrase "Versailles," most of which would be references to the city, not the font. The search phrase "Versailles *and* font," on the other hand, narrows the search. (The *and* modifier is the default, by the way: whenever more than one word appears in a search phrase, AOL assumes there's an *and* between them. Thus the phrase "Versailles and font" is the same as the phrase "Versailles font.")

Perhaps we want the Utopia font as well as the Versailles font. Here is where the *or* modifier comes in. The phrase "Versailles *or* Utopia" finds either one.

The *not* modifier excludes material matching the criterion that follows it and narrows the search. The phrase "Versailles *not* France" would provide a listing of all references to Versailles that aren't associated with the city in France.

Combining modifiers can be unclear. The phrase "Versailles or Utopia and font" is ambiguous. Do we mean "Versailles, or Utopia and font," or do we mean "Versailles or Utopia, and font"? (Do you remember this discussion from the previous chapter, when we were searching for wines? It's not as subtle as it seems.) The solution is found in the use of parentheses. The phrase "(Versailles or Utopia) and font" says "look for Versailles or Utopia, excluding everything but fonts from either category." It pays to be specific.

🍎 When the File Search dialog box opens, we can enter our criterion: Graphics Workshop (again, refer to Figure 7-15). In this case, we know the name of the file we want to find. That's not always the case, and America Online can accomodate myriad search strategies to deal with the alternatives.

Reading a file description
Let's look at part of the file description posted online for Graphics Workshop (see Figure 7-17).

Figure 7-17: A wealth of information is found in file descriptions.

Subj: GWS: V6.1m Graphics Workshop
Date: July 10, 1992
From: Bulletx

File: grfwk61m.zip (362113 bytes)
DL time (2400 baud): < 41 minutes
Download count: 973
Uploaded on: PC-Link

AUTHOR: Alchemy Mindworks
NEEDS: An UnZIPing Program

Keywords: Alchemy Mindworks, Convert, Scan, 24 Bit, HiColor, TIFF, Rescale
Type: Shareware

Macpaint, GEM/IMG, PCX, GIF, TIFF, WPG, IFF/LBM, Pictor PIC, Targa, BMP, MSP, EPS,
Self-displaying EXE pictures, Text, Halo CUT

Note that there is a WINDOWS version of GWS online in this forum.

Graphic workshop is a simple, menu driven environment which will let you perform the
following operations on the aforementioned files.
- View them.
- Convert between any two formats (with a few restrictions).
- Print them to any LaserJet Plus compatible or PostScript laser and many dot matrix printers.
Graphic Workshop can print colour pictures to colour PostScript and inkjet printers.
- Dither the colour ones to black and white.
- Reverse, Rotate and flip them.
- Scale or Crop them.
- Reduce the number of colours in them and do colour dithering.
- Sharpen, soften and otherwise wreak special effects on them.
- Scan in completely new files, assuming that you have a supported scanner.
- Adjust the brightness and colour balance of the colour ones.

▲ The Subject, From and File lines that appear in Figure 7-17 are all searchable criteria, and not just for Graphics Workshop, but for any file entered into AOL's searchable database. If we wanted to see all the files submitted by BulletX—the screen name of the person who uploaded this file—we could specify "BulletX" in the search phrase pictured in Figure 7-15. This is particularly valuable when you want to find all the files submitted by your favorite graphic artist, or if you find that a particular member always seems to upload only the best files. Note that the File line not only includes the file's name, but its version number and size as well.

▲ The file date is used when you specify Past Month or Past Week in the File Search dialog box.

▲ The download time is America Online's best guess as to how long it will take to download the file. This time is estimated based on the baud rate at which you're currently connected. If you're connected at 1200 baud, the estimate is based on that baud rate. *This number is only an estimate.* If you sign on during a peak usage period (evenings around 9:00 Eastern time is a peak usage period), it might take you a little longer than the estimated download time to retrieve the file. If you're signed on at four in the morning, you will probably download the file in a little less than the estimated time. For example, we downloaded *Graphics Workshop*, which AOL estimates as a 41-minute download, in less than 33 minutes during a Thursday evening session.

- The download count is a rough indication of the file's popularity. While this may not be too significant for new postings, which haven't been uploaded long enough to have gained a following, it's an indication of the popularity of files that have been around for a while. If you're looking for a graphic of a cat, for instance, and 40 files match your search criteria, you might let the number of downloads (review Figure 7-16) direct you. Often, however, the number of downloads is more reflective of the catchiness of a file's name or description than of its content.

- The Needs line is critical: if your PC isn't up to the task, or if you need special software, it's nice to know *before* you download the file. For instance, you'll need an unzipping program, and the Needs line informs you of this.

- Keywords are those that provide matches when you enter your own search criteria. Read these. They offer valuable insight as to how to word your search phrases. *Note:* In this context, a keyword—a word assigned to a shareware file—is used to help categorize and describe a file for easy search and retrieval. These are separate from and can't be substituted for AOL's navigational keyword function (accessed by typing Ctrl-K or choosing "Keyword" from the Go To menu), which lets you move quickly from one place on AOL to another.

- The description itself is provided by the person who uploaded the file. Graphics Workshop's description lists its GIF conversion capabilities, as well as some we didn't expect.

- Before being posted, each file uploaded to America Online is checked for viruses by one of the forum's personnel. Occasionally, the file descriptions also tell you what virus detection software was used to check the file and which version of that software was used.

🔺 File descriptions can be saved for later reference. Simply choose Save from the File menu before you close the description window. America Online asks where you want to store the description, which it will store in ASCII text format. All the text you read on your PC's screen is formatted this way, and it can be read off-line (after you've saved it to a separate file) on any word processor or with the America Online software itself (just choose Open from AOL's File menu).

Choosing a local access number

As we mentioned in Chapter 1, America Online employs long-distance services—or *common carriers*—to provide you with the best possible connection to the Stratus. When you first sign on to AOL, the Stratus consults its database of local access numbers in your area and assigns one of them as your primary America Online calling number. The other becomes the alternate.

The quality of these numbers may differ from time to time, and there are occasions when one is simply faster or more reliable than the other. Whatever the reason, if downloading always takes longer than the file description's estimate, even during off-peak times, try the alternate number (see below for details on how to do this).

The most effective way to judge downloading efficiency is to use a modem with indicator lights. One of them should be marked "receive data" or "RD." This light usually stays continuously lit during an efficient download. Inefficient downloads are indicated when this light flashes on and off like a digital clock that needs to be set. Usually, this condition is caused by a heavy load on the Stratus. Calling back at a different time often solves the problem.

If calling back later doesn't help, try the alternate number. Here's how:

🔺 Sign off if you're online (choose Exit from the File menu).

🔺 If the sign-on screen isn't showing, choose Set Up & Sign On from the Go To menu.

🔺 Click on the button marked Setup.

🔺 Two major segments dominate the Setup screen, marked First Choice and Second Choice. Try reversing the numbers you see here. You do this simply by clicking on the Swap Phone Numbers button. The phone number, common carrier and baud rate will all be switched with this single button. Be sure to save the changes as you exit the dialog.

🔺 Sign on again and try out your new number.

More➤

Remember: the file description's downloading time is an estimate. However, if your downloads always exceed this estimate, you may have a problem. If neither calling back at a different time nor swapping access numbers improves your downloading time, you can go to Members' Online Support, choose Ask America Online message board and read the Access Numbers/Connecting information. Or send an e-mail message (we discuss e-mail in Chapter 11) to Customer Relations (the screen name is CS Manager). Sometimes they're aware of a service problem in your area and can set your mind at ease.

The downloading process

Once you've read the file's description, you may decide to download it. This is the easy part: all you have to do is click on the Download Now button. (The Download Later button is discussed in Chapter 12, "The Download Manager.")

Remember that downloading is the process of transferring a file from America Online to a disk in your computer. In other words, you're going to have to decide where to put the file. The destination can be either a hard disk or a floppy, and that's the next decision you'll be asked to make (see Figure 7-18). Pick a drive and a subdirectory, then click on the button marked Save.

Figure 7-18: The
download process
is automatic once
you've specified a
file name and
destination.

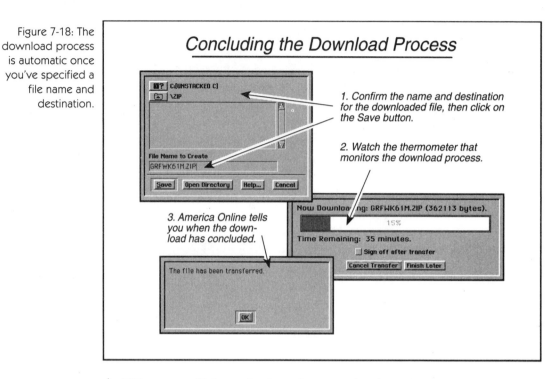

Concluding the Download Process

1. Confirm the name and destination
for the downloaded file, then click on
the Save button.

2. Watch the thermometer that
monitors the download process.

3. America Online tells
you when the down-
load has concluded.

When you click on the Save button, the downloading process
progresses predictably, monitored by the on-screen thermometer
pictured in Figure 7-18. When the download is completed, you'll be
notified on screen (see the message at the bottom of Figure 7-18).

File names & destinations

Look again at Figure 7-18. A file name is suggested for you by AOL. If you want to use a file name
other than the one proposed, all you have to do is start typing. We don't recommend this, unless
the proposed file name conflicts with one already on your disk. The name given is usually
descriptive and purposeful; and the file's documentation, for instance, may refer to the file by
name. If you change the name, the reference might be unclear. Forum discussions may refer to the
file's original name; and if you go searching later for an update to the file, you'll need to refer to
it by its original name. Some programs require that their names not be changed for any reason.
So, use the original name unless you have a good reason not to.

File formats

The number of potential file formats for downloaded files is staggering. Fortunately, some standards and conventions relieve the situation.

All downloadable files for the PC follow DOS naming conventions. DOS file names consist of up to eight characters, a period and a three-character file-name extension, such as GRFWK61M.ZIP. Though this is stifling (eight characters are hardly enough for a descriptive file name), the three-character extension is particularly useful. All you have to do is look at a DOS file's name to see what kind of file it is. DOS file names ending in .PM4 are PageMaker files, for instance; those ending in .TXT are text files and are readable by most any word processor or text editor, including the AOL software on your hard drive; those ending in .ZIP are files compressed using the PKZip utility (more on PKZip later in this chapter); and those ending in .TIF are TIFF graphic files.

The chart pictured in Figure 7-19 identifies some of the common file-name extensions and their meanings. File format compatibility differs from program to program. PageMaker, for instance, reads all these formats except the compressed ones, GIF and JPEG. Excel, on the other hand, can only read TXT and Excel formats. Read your software documentation to determine which formats you should use.

Figure 7-19: File-
name extensions
for some of the
most common file
formats you'll
find online.

Filename Extensions

Textual formats

TXT	Unformatted ASCII text
RTF	Rich Text Format
DOC	Microsoft Word, WordPerfect

Graphic formats

TIF	Tagged-image file format
GIF	Graphic interchange format
PCX	PC Paintbrush (also Windows)
WMF	Windows metafile
EPS	Encapsulated PostScript

Compressed formats

SIT	StuffIt (Macintosh)
JPG	Joint Photographic Experts Group
SEA	Self-Extracting Archive
ZIP	PKZip (AOL unzips automatically)

Macintosh formats

PIC	Macintosh PICT (also MAC)
MW	MacWrite (common text editor)
PNT	MacPaint
QT	Macintosh QuickTime (multimedia)

File compression & decompression

Look again at Figure 7-19. Four compressed formats are identified there, and they require further explanation.

Why compress files? There are three good reasons: 1) compressed files are much smaller than their uncompressed counterparts, and thus take significantly less time to download; 2) compressed files require less space on your hard drive; 3) compressed files are often stored in an "archive," a collection of several files all compressed into a single file (the archive). Archives are a convenient way of grouping multiple files for storage and downloading.

Amazingly, compressed files may be as small as 20 percent of the original—sometimes even smaller than that—yet when they're decompressed, absolutely no data is lost. We don't know how they do that. Smoke and mirrors, maybe.

Figure 7-20: The original image on the left measures 21,394 bytes. The image on the right was compressed to 9,111 bytes (43 percent of the original), then decompressed for printing. No data was lost; both pictures are identical. (Drawing by David Palermo using Adobe Photoshop.)

Figure 7-20 indirectly identifies a problem common to all compressed images: they're useless until you decompress them. The compressed image in Figure 7-20 couldn't be included in the illustration until it was decompressed. In other words, you must have decompression software before you can use compressed images. That's the bad news. The good news is that you already do: it's part of the America Online software in your PC.

PKZip

A shareware program called *PKZip* is responsible for a great deal of the file compression encountered in the PC environment. PKZip can compress (or "zip," as it's called) a single file or a multitude of files into a single file—the archive. PKZip archives are identified by the .ZIP file-name extension.

Like all archives, PKZip archives must be decompressed ("unzipped") before use, and incredibly, that happens automatically when you use America Online. If compression is done with smoke and mirrors, automatic decompression must be done with smoke and mirrors and the eyes of a newt. Whatever the technique, it works, and we're the beneficiaries.

When your America Online software downloads a file with .ZIP in its file name, it makes a note to itself to unzip the file immediately after you sign off. (You must have this option chosen under Preferences from the Members menu. Notice that you can also have the original .ZIP file automatically deleted after its files are decompressed.) An *unzipped* copy of the file appears on your disk, ready for use. Your AOL software also automatically decompresses any files with the .ARC file-name extension.

America Online only gives you the *un*zipping part of PKZip. While you can use your AOL software to unzip any file with the .ZIP file-name extension (just choose Open from AOL's File menu), if you want to *zip* your own files, you'll need your own copy of PKZip. Fortunately, PKZip is available online: use the keywords: File Search, then search for PKZip. You'll find a number of files meeting the criteria; the one you want is named *PKZ110.EXE*. PKZip is shareware: if you like the program, pay the person who wrote it and you can use it indefinitely with a clear conscience.

StuffIt

While PKZip is the file-compression standard for PCs, a program called *StuffIt* is the standard for the Macintosh platform. Instead of being zipped and unzipped, StuffIt files (followed by the .SIT extension) are "stuffed" and "unstuffed." A number of files suitable for use on either platform—graphics, mostly—were originally constructed on a Mac and are stuffed rather than zipped. (This is beginning to sound like a recipe for baked turkey: "First stuff, then zip the carcass, then bake at 350 degrees for four hours....")

Stuffed files won't decompress themselves automatically on a PC, nor are they self-extracting archives. To use them, you have to acquire unstuffing software. That, too, is shareware available on America Online. Use the keywords: File Search, then search for "StuffIt." You'll get two files: one is a program to unstuff Mac files under Windows, and the other is a program that runs under DOS.

Self-extracting archives

You now know all about .ZIPs, but there is another type of archive you'll find online: the self-extracting archive. Just as the name implies, these are archives, or multiple files all squeezed into one smaller format, that will decompress themselves when you type the name of the file at your DOS prompt, much like you would type a DOS command. Self-extracting archives even look like DOS programs because they usually end with the .EXE program-name extension, but so do many uncompressed files, so check the example here.

For example, let's say you find a file online called WIDGIT.EXE, and you see this line in the file description:

This File is Self-Extracting, Requiring 112,500 bytes.

That tells you WIDGIT.EXE is a self-extracting archive, and clues you in to how much room (or bytes) it will take up on your disk when you download it. You would download it just like any other file; but, because it's self-extracting, AOL's automatic decompression feature won't work here. That's not a worry. You need simply get to the DOS prompt in the directory or subdirectory in which you downloaded WIDGIT.EXE and type: WIDGIT (like DOS programs, you do not type the .EXE extension). The files contained within WIDGET.EXE will decompress themselves (or, it may be a single file), and you're ready to run the program according to the instructions contained in the online file description.

Uploading files

With all this talk about downloading, it's easy to forget that before a file can be *down*loaded, it first must be *up*loaded. Pursuant to its community spirit, America Online depends on its members for most of its files. Uploading isn't the exclusive realm of AOL employees and forum staff, nor is it that of the supernerds. Most of the files you can download from America Online—we'd guess more than 90 percent—have been uploaded from members, using PCs just like yours.

Earlier, we defined downloading as "the process of transferring a file from America Online's Stratus to a disk on your computer." Uploading is just the reverse: the process of transferring a file from a disk on your computer to America Online's Stratus. Once received, it's checked for viruses and the quality of its content, and if it passes AOL's inspection, it's posted in the appropriate library where any member can download it. The process rarely takes more than a day: upload a file on Monday and you'll probably see it available for downloading Tuesday morning.

The uploading process

Begin the uploading process by visiting the forum where your file seems to fit. If it's a graphic, post it in the PC Animation & Graphics Forum. If it's poetry, post it in the Writers Club. Once you're in the forum, select the appropriate library for your file (if there's more than one library in the forum) and click on the Upload File button. Some forums have an icon marked Submit a File; use this icon if it's available.

Recently, we uploaded a magazine article to the Writers Club. When we clicked on the Upload button, we received the Upload File Information form pictured in Figure 7-21. You'll encounter this form every time you upload a file to America Online.

Figure 7-21: You'll
be asked to fill out
the Upload File
Information form
for every file you
upload to AOL.

Uploading a File

*To submit a file to the Writers
Club, we clicked on the Upload
File button in the club's library,
then filled in the form on the right.*

	Upload File Information
Subject:	Reminiscence & renaissance
Author:	Tom Lichty
Equipment:	Any computer
Needs:	ASCII text reader

Description:

Excerpts from an article regarding five acres in the country and
life therein. I've been writing this in my spare time and intend
to submit it, unsolicited, to some unsuspecting magazine
someday. Meanwhile, I solicit comments from would-be and
real-life contributing authors alike.

[Send]

Writers Club Lib

- 09/03 Cyberpunk story Chapter 14
- 08/30 TWIN SIMPSON
- 08/30 ViewPOINTS 2.0 Newspaper #1
- 08/30 Fourth Realm Chap. 2
- 08/30 Mylo
- 08/30 commuting – alaska style
- 08/30 Fourth Realm: Chap. 1
- 08/19 Novel Workshop 11-92
- 08/17 Chapter 13 of Cyberpunk story
- 08/10 Chapter 12 of Cyberpunk story
- 08/07 Twisted poems.

20 09/04
26 09/04
31 09/05

[Get Description] [Download Now] [Download Later]

[Upload File] [More...]

The Upload File Information form

All too often, uploaders fail to complete the Upload File Information
form adequately. After all, this form "sells" your file to other members,
and what you have to say about it determines whether a member will
take the time to download it. Here are some hints for creating accurate,
useful and compelling descriptions of files you upload:

- The Subject field should be 1) descriptive and 2) catchy, in that
  order. Look at the window in the background of Figure 7-21. Do
  you see how the subjects are listed there? The Subject line is your
  headline: if you want members to read your story, hook 'em with a
  really great Subject line.

- The Equipment line should identify any special hardware required
  to access the file. For instance, a VGA graphic requires a VGA or
  better display system: CGA won't do. Be sure to be accurate and
  thorough in your evaluation of necessary hardware, since no one
  wants to download a file only to find out they don't have the
  necessary equipment to use it.

⚠ The Needs line is where you specify the particular software application or program required to access your file. A GIF file, for instance, requires some kind of GIF conversion program. An amortization template for Microsoft Excel obviously requires a copy of Excel, but don't assume other members know that.

⚠ The Description field is where you get specific. Here you differentiate your file from others that may be similar. If you're submitting an application, include the version number. Be specific and persuasive: you're selling your file here. Think about what you would want to read if you were considering downloading the file. Make it sound irresistible.

If you're submitting a number of related files, or if your file's size exceeds about 20k, zip it using PKZip. This saves downloading time and is thus the polite way to offer your material. If possible, archives should generally be smaller than 720k, so they'll fit on a single 3.5" floppy disk.

Concluding the uploading process

America Online's thermometer keeps you entertained while the upload is underway.

The time spent uploading your files to the Stratus will be credited back to you. Though you may not see the credit before you sign off, it will appear soon thereafter. To check your billing information, click on the Departments button in the sign-on window, click on Members Online Support, click on Billing Information, then click on Check Current Bill (or simply type the keyword: Billing). There you should see a note crediting your account with any time you have spent uploading files. The billing area is free, so you won't be charged for the time you spend online checking your account.

Tips from Tim

Earlier in this chapter, we mentioned Tim Barwick, the AOL staffer charged with the responsibility of managing the Computing & Software Department. We asked Tim if he had any tips for uploaders. His response appears below. He's quoting our questions, surrounded by chevrons (<< >>), ahead of his replies.

> Date: 92-06-15 16:58:01 EDT
> From: Tim Barwick
> Subj: Uploading
> To: MajorTom

Tom, in answer to your uploading questions.

<<Any hints? Specifically, any hints about keywords, descriptions, titles, etc.? Any hints about file size?>>

In general, keywords, descriptions and titles will be adjusted by the online staff. They'll bring them into line with the forum's look and feel. Any tips about functionality or especially neat features are very helpful.

<<The member zips, right?>>

Yes, the member zips the file before uploading. We accept both .ZIP and self-extracting archives.

<<Once the file is sent, does the Forum Leader look it over before it's added to the library? Is this process standardized? How do you check for viruses? Do you always check for them?>>

Every file is checked for viruses before being released. The program that was used to check the file is listed at the bottom of the file description.

<<What does the uploader get out of the deal?>>

Credit time is given for uploading, and the screen name of the uploader appears in the file's description. We also feature the best uploads in the Software Center so the member gets recognition from peers for having contributed a "top" file.

<<When are files removed? Under what conditions?>>

Files are removed when an update is issued. We'll also remove files if the uploader requests we do so. Let me know if you have any other questions on uploading, Tom.

:D - Tim

Moving on

This has been a long chapter, steeped in technicalities. We've explored the largest department on the service and peeked at a few of its forums; we've downloaded files, unzipped files and uploaded files. We've even explored how to search the online database for exactly the file we need. For making it this far, you deserve a gold star.

You also deserve a break from technicalities. The next chapter offers that break as we explore the Travel & Shopping Department, and there's no better place to have fun. You can travel around the world, stopping in exotic places to buy foolish things—and never leave your PC or spend a dime.

Pin your gold star to your pocket, fasten your seat belt and prepare for takeoff. We're about to embark on some serious fantasizing.

Travel & Shopping

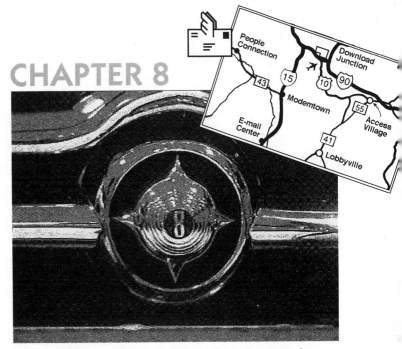

Who hasn't indulged in the "If I had a million dollars..." fantasy? At the top of both of our lists is travel: the British Isles, a blue-water cruise, the Orient Express, Australia....

Heck, we'd be happy if someone just gave us a ticket to Tucumcari.

Of course, fantasies require money. That's why they're fantasies. If you want money-optional indulgences, try America Online's Travel & Shopping Department. Not only can you indulge your fantasies here, you can actually commit them: you can book airline, car and hotel reservations; you can buy toys for yourself or your computer; you can even shop for a car. Either click on the Travel & Shopping icon in the Departments window, or use the keyword: Shopping & Travel (see Figure 8-1).

As is so often the case, the list of topics in Figure 8-1 is incomplete. Many more options are available by pressing the Down Arrow key or using the scroll bars. You can buy music (and a system to play it on), flowers, laser printing, office products, magazines, software and hardware. As we said earlier, you can book travel or buy a car in the Travel & Shopping Department. This place can really get expensive if you give it a chance. You'd better hide your credit card before you read any further.

Frontispiece graphic: "50 Ford," by Andy Baird (AFC Andy) from an 8mm video camera image. Keywords: File Search; criterion 50 Ford.

Figure 8-1:
Everything from
automobiles to
accommodations
in Zanzibar is
available in the
Travel & Shopping
Department.

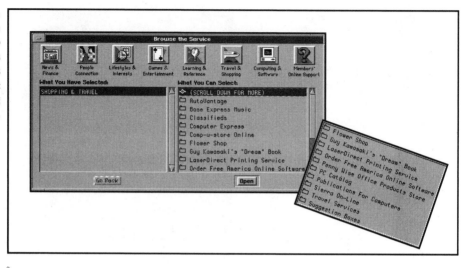

The EAASY SABRE gateway

Though we'll discuss other gateways later in this chapter and in Chapter 11 ("Electronic Mail"), the term requires a definition before we go any further. A *gateway* is a path to another computer system—one that's independent of the Stratus. American Airlines's *SABRE* reservations system is a good example. As one of the few centralized travel reservations systems, it's used by travel agents and airline-reservation counters as well as AOL members. When you enter the EAASY SABRE gateway, you actually log on to the Sabre computer itself. AOL's Stratus remains relatively passive until you exit the gateway.

Few telecommunication services are as easy to use as AOL. Most are purely textual: no windows, no pull-down menus, no dialog boxes. Like most other telecommunications systems, Sabre is textual. In the rough, it's almost intimidating. It's designed to serve travel agents, after all, and they attend schools for this kind of thing. The moment you enter the service, everything you're used to in AOL changes. Even the mouse becomes essentially inactive. A text-filled window appears instead. Yet, it's still menu-driven and easy to use.

When travel agents find out that AOL members are using Sabre, they tend to be incredulous: they attend school for weeks to become proficient at it. America Online members, on the other hand, can use it with no training whatsoever.

Travel agents also can't believe AOL members use their standard telephone line to access it and pay nothing but the normal America Online connect-time charges to use it. Not only is EAASY SABRE easy to use, it's a bargain as well.

Being a professional system, Sabre is in no way abbreviated. Not only can you make airline reservations (on *any* airline, not just American), you can also reserve automobiles and hotels (see Figure 8-2). Indeed, EAASY SABRE allows you to make reservations on more than 350 airlines, reserve rooms at over 27,000 hotels, or rent a car from nearly 60 car rental companies worldwide.

Figure 8-2: EAASY SABRE's menu includes a full range of travel necessities.

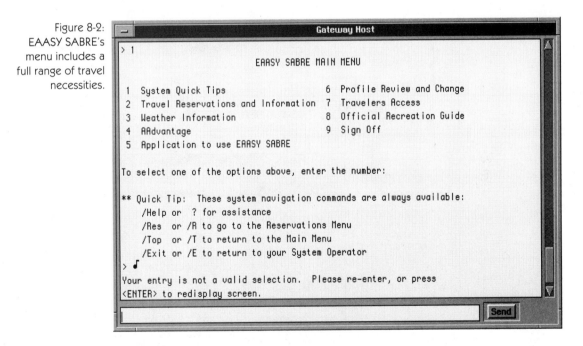

Don't let Figure 8-2 fool you: you don't have to be a Sabre member to poke around the EAASY SABRE system, but becoming a member is easy. You don't have to be Someone Important, and membership doesn't cost a dime. To get to EAASY SABRE, click on Travel Services and then EAASY SABRE, or just use the keyword: Sabre.

Finding a flight

A favorite jaunt is a trip to North Carolina in the spring. They have some delectable cuisine there (to say nothing of the mint juleps), it's a comely place, and the natives talk with a lilt that could melt even Jack Palance's heart. (Did we mention that our publisher is there, too? And that they usually pay for the trip? It's amazing how a travel allowance can make a place seem suddenly endearing.) Let's use EAASY SABRE to see what flights can get us there (see Figure 8-3).

Figure 8-3:
All you have to
do is identify
where and when
you want to travel;
EAASY SABRE
supplies the how.

Finding a Flight

```
                          Gateway Host
  /Top  or /T to return to the Main Menu
  /Exit or /E to return to your System Operator
> 2
                    RESERVATIONS MENU

1  Flight Reservations and Availability   5  Airline Fares
2  Flight Arrival/Departure Information    6  Itinerary Review and Change
3  Hotels                                  7  Sign On another User
4  Rental Cars                             8  Flight Schedules

To select one of the options above, ent

Quick Tip:  The following system naviga
   /Help or  ? for assistance, or
   /Res  or /R to return to this menu
   /Top  or /T to return to the MAIN M
   /Exit or /E to return to the System
> 1
```

From the main menu, you choose to view flights and schedules, and then specify the cities and dates involved.

```
                          Gateway Host
Quick Tip:  The following system navigation commands are always available:
   /Help or  ? for assistance, or
   /Res  or /R to return to this menu or
   /Top  or /T to return to the MAIN MENU or
   /Exit or /E to return to the System Operator
> 1
From what city will you be departing?

Example:  LOS ANGELES or LAX

Quick path examples for flight AVAILABILITY:
```

The result lists several flights meeting your criteria and allows you to book a flight or continue looking.

```
                          Gateway Host
                    FLIGHT AVAILABILITY

From:  (PDX) PORTLAND, OR
  To:  (RDU) RALEIGH/DURHAM, NC              MONDAY    MAR-01-93
-----------------------------------------------------------------
   Flight  Leave      Arrive   Meal Stop Aircraft OnTime  Classes of Service**
1  AA1800  PDX  620A  DFW 1204P  B   0    S80      9      F  Y  M  B  H  K  Q  U
   AA 810       1247P RDU  413P  L   0    S80      8      F  Y  M  H  B  K  Q  U
2  AA2042  PDX  641A  ORD 1238P  B   0    S80      8      F  Y  M  B  H  K  Q  U
   AA1270       120P  RDU  417P      0    100      6      F  Y  M  H  K  B  Q  U
3  DL 902  PDX  700A  ATL  229P  B   0    767      N      F  Y  B  M  Q  H  K  L
   DL 779       339P  RDU  440P      0    73S      N      F  Y  B  M  Q  H  K  L
-----------------------------------------------------------------
To SELECT a flight, enter the line number, or

8   View MORE flights        11   View all FARES
9   CHANGE flight request    12   Translate CODES
10  View FIRST flight display 13  View LOWest one-way fares
```
                                                        [Send]

There are three points we should make about Figure 8-3. One, we didn't have to use the airport abbreviations (PDX, RDU) that you see in the middle window. We could have specified Portland, Oregon, and Raleigh, North Carolina, and the system would have supplied the same information. Two, EAASY SABRE found something like nine flights

that met that criteria, though only three appear in Figure 8-3's lower window (the First and More choices reveal the others). And three, we could see how reliable each flight has been recently by looking in the arrival/departure information.

Finding the cost

Another ten minutes on the system reveal the cost of not only the airline tickets, but the car rental and hotel as well (see Figure 8-4). These rates differ drastically (especially for car rentals, all of which offer essentially the same service), and Sabre practically begs you to do some comparison shopping.

Figure 8-4:
Let's see: $440 for the flight, $120 for the car and $89 a night for the hotel—that's about $1,000 for the trip.

Tallying the Charges

Gateway Host

```
> 11
     From:  (PDX) PORTLAND, OR                              MAR-01-93
     To:    (RDU) RALEIGH/DURHAM, NC
All airlines - Regular and discount far

              Round
     One Way  Trip   Fare Code  Airli
     -------  -----  ---------  -----
1             440.00  QE14NR    UA
2             440.00  KE14N     TW
3             440.00  KE14NR    AA,DL
4             470.00  QE14NR    UA
5             490.00  KE14NR    AA
6             500.00  ME7NR     UA
7             500.00  ME7NR     DL

To view fare RULES, enter the line numbe
```

Gateway Host

```
> 3
ALAMO      rentals in RALEIGH/DURHAM, NC
Pick up-Drop off Dates: MAR 01, 1993 - MAR 06, 1993
          Location: In Terminal    RALEIGH DURHAM AIRPO
          Rate Type: Standard                              Rates in USD

  Vehicle Type       Weekly Rate  Free Miles  Mileage Charge  Status
  ------------       -----------  ----------  --------------  ------
Car
1 Economy            119.99       UNL  mi     .00 /mile       Available
Four Door Car
2 Economy            129.99       UNL  mi     .00 /mile       Request
Special
3 Economy            86.99        UNL  mi     .00 /mile       Request
Car
4 Compact            127.99       UNL  mi     .00 /mile       Available
```

Send

Gateway Host

```
Hotel availability in RALEIGH/DURHAM, NC
  Check in: 01MAR MONDAY    Check out: 06MAR SATURDAY
Preferences: Chain:                          Name:
             Location:                        Zip:
             Bed type:                        Area:
             Special rate:                    Trans:

  Chain code  Name        Miles from RDU   Lowest rate
  ----------  ----        --------------   -----------
1  DI  -  DI RALEIGH N RALHB    16E        $31.00
           RALEIGH NC
2  RD  -  RD GOVERNORS INN       6W        $89.00
           RTP NC
3  HH  -  NORTH RALEIGH HILTON  11NE       $99.00
           RALEIGH NC

For details or reservations enter the line number, or

4  View MORE hotels              7  Translate CODES
```

Send

Booking the reservations

Before you can book reservations, you need to sign up for a "member-ship" in EAASY SABRE. Though it sounds formal, membership amounts to little more than providing your credit card number and mailing address. As we mentioned before, membership in EAASY SABRE is free. Once you're a member, you simply enter the number by the line of the item you want to book. EAASY SABRE establishes an itinerary for that trip (which you can review and print at any time—look again at the top of Figure 8-3), and within a few days provides confirmation numbers and (in the case of airline reservations) mails the tickets to you.

Not only is membership free, so is browsing the system. You pay only your normal AOL connect charges. Even if you don't plan to go anywhere, no one will tattle if you indulge in a little fantasy traveling. It's a great cure for the wintertime blues; and who knows, maybe you too will visit the beautiful Raleigh-Durham area of North Carolina. Sip a mint julep while you're there: there are none better in the South.

The Independent Traveler

As long as we're in a traveling mood, let's check out the Independent Traveler. Articles, message boards and a library offer a wealth of information and tips for the domestic or world traveler (see Figure 8-5). The Independent Traveler area is located under Travel Services of the Travel & Shopping Department.

Are you looking for a romantic hideaway for your getaway week-end? Check the US Travel message board. If you're looking for the best itinerary for your train trip through Europe, check the World Traveler message board. In-depth articles cover topics such as "How to choose the right guide book" and "Should I buy trip cancellation insurance?" Back issues are housed in the Travel Library.

Figure 8-5:
The Independent
Traveler offers
articles on
European rail
travel and packing
tips, a list of all the
toll-free telephone
numbers for hotels
and airlines
around the
country, and a
little program that
calculated the
automotive route
between Oregon
and North
Carolina—just in
case Ventana
won't pay airfare.

The Independent Traveler

PACKING TIPS FOR THE INDEPENDENT TRAVELER

In this modern day of worldwide independent travel, steamer trunks are long gone and carry-on luggage has become the preferred baggage of the frequent traveler. Good quality, softsided carry-on bags are lightweight, durable, washable and absorb shock better than hardsided luggage. By carrying your luggage with you on the plane, you save valuable travel time, and you never need to worry about the airline losing your luggage or have it miss the plane. Just have this happen to you once when you're in a hurry and you'll be a carry-on traveler for life.

Choose the Right Bag
When looking for carry-on luggage, make sure you get something that will fit under the seat in front of you. FAA regulations state that carry-on bags be

EUROPEAN RAIL PASSES 1991

If you're headed to Europe, trains are a great way to travel around. European trains still retain the romance and convenience long ago lost in American trains. They're fun, romantic, fast, efficient and reasonably priced. A train can take you to the center of town in just about any city or village you might want to visit in Europe. Trains are also considerably less expensive than flying or driving if you're covering any distance.

Train travel is even more cost effective and convenient if you purchase one of the many rail passes available. Rail passes are very easy to use. The first time you use the pass you'll need to validate it at the train station. After that, simply hop on a train and you're f to go wherever and whenever you want to. With a r pass there is no waiting in lines to buy tickets, and have complete flexibility to change your plans and itinerary.

If you plan to tour several countries, then a Eurailpass is the way to go. There are several different types of Eurailpasses available, all of which are good for unlimited travel in 17 countries: Austria, Belgium, Denmark, Finland, France, Germany, Greece, Hunga (new this year!), Italy, Ireland, Luxembourg, The Nethe Portugal, Spain, Sweden and

HOTEL 800 NUMBERS

A T Reef Ventures	(800)-327-7333
Adam's Mark Hotels	(800)-231-5858
Admiral Benbow Inns	(800)-451-1986
Affordable Inns	(800)-851-8888
All American Room Reservations	(800)-634-3466
All Seasons Resorts	(800)-424-2403
American Intl. Vacation Club	(800)-634-6163
American Leisure Hotels	(800)-231-5804
American West Motor Hotels	(800)-547-4262
Americana Hotels	(800)-228-3278
Amex Hotels Ltd.	(800)-854-2026
AMFAC Hotels	(800)-227-1117
	)-621-6909
	)-854-2608
	)-327-0787
	)-238-2552
	)-528-1234
	)-525-2257

PENDLETON			
BOISE	Interstate 84	211 Miles	**PORTLAND OR**
OGDEN	Interstate 84	217 Miles	
CHEYENNE	Interstate 84	323 Miles	**DURHAM**
DENVER	Interstate 80	444 Miles	
SALINA	Interstate 25	98 Miles	**2939 Miles**
TOPEKA	Interstate 70	429 Miles	
KANSAS CITY	Interstate 70	114 Miles	
ST. LOUIS	Interstate 70	60 Miles	
MT VERNON	Interstate 70	254 Miles	
LOUISVILLE	Interstate 64	72 Miles	
LEXINGTON	Interstate 64	190 Miles	
HUNTINGTON	Interstate 64	78 Miles	
CHARLESTON WV	Interstate 64	112 Miles	
WYTHEVILLE VA	Interstate 77	47 Miles	
WINSTON-SALEM	US Route# 52	123 Miles	
GREENSBORO	Interstate 40	83 Miles	
DURHAM	Interstate 85	30 Miles	
		54 Miles	

[Another]
[Quit]
[Info]

Travel plans, perhaps above all else, benefit from peer support. The Independent Traveler is where you can solicit the advice of peers and pros alike. No travel plans are complete until you talk to those who have been there.

Online Safari Help

Part of the excitement of travel is visiting new and exotic places. But planning a trip to somewhere remote and primitive, like the heart of East Africa, can be complicated and frightening. What about the local customs, the weather and the uncertainties of schedules and budgets? It's enough to frighten even the most adventurous traveler into staying home and watching Marlin Perkins on TV.

But with America Online, you can probe the murky depths of the Dark Continent risk-free. Below are excerpts from the Africa folder of the World Travel message board, located in the Independent Traveler section. There are dozens of messages posted in the Africa folder—too many to show here—but they range from tips on finding cheap airfare and hotel rooms to securing reservations for a dramatic hot air balloon ride across Kenya and Tanzania.

Subj: Safari—without advance plans? From: Audrey

I am planning a trip to East Africa in August, and would like some advice. I plan to fly in and out of Nairobi, and can only stay for about nine days. I would like to see the Masai Mara, Serengeti and Ngorongoro Crater. Is it realistic/possible to do all three in nine days? Is it possible to arrange a guide when we arrive in Africa, rather than book in advance? Should we do this in Nairobi or go out to the Masai Mara? Any suggestions on good guides or safari outfits? Thanks, Audrey.

Subj: Reply to Audrey   From: TomT50

I am a very frequent traveler to East Africa. Kenya is a wonderful place to visit. In your nine days (short stay!), try to go to one of the tent camps in Masai Mara for two or three days; take the train to Mombasa for two or three days; take a day trip from Mombasa to Tsavo East (Voi Safari Club area), where you'll see lots of elephants; take a couple of hours and go into the Nairobi game park just outside of town. It may sound unbelievable, but you'll find a lot of animals right there (but no elephants). Treetops (at Nyeri) is very nice and close to Nairobi. The soda lakes ,with all their flamingos, are a sight, and are also close to the city. August is a high tourist month, so I would not advise going without some prior arrangements. We use an American friend for Kenyan arrangements. His name is Mike O'Neille. He is the CEO of Prestiege Safaris in Nairobi. His

More >

company can provide anything you need from a private driver to a plane flight into the bush. I'll be in Kenya all of August. If you get in a pinch, I'll be teaching at KTTC University just outside Nairobi and available at 502-029 in the evenings. Have a great trip! Tom Trone

Subj: Gorilla viewing   From: Paresh
Has anyone been to either of the two places to experience the gorillas? How easy is it to organize a trip? What are the approximate costs for permits, land or air travel, hotels, etc.?

Subj: Response to Paresh   From: L Illes
Going to Rwanda to see the gorillas is an experience not to be missed. It is important to remember that you are a visitor to their habitat, and to behave accordingly. No littering or loud noises—common sense things. Also, expect a strenuous workout. Sometimes, you can hike for eight hours before you find the troupe, and sometimes they can be found in less than half an hour. Regardless of the time or effort put into finding the troupe, you will only be allowed to spend one hour with them. It will be the shortest but most rewarding hour of your life.

Subj: Gorilla Viewing in Zaire   From: Wadahuhu
Zaire is a great place to view gorillas. I was there in September of 1989 and found it to be just fantastic. Unfortunately, the last thing I heard was that there has been considerable civil disorder in Kinshasa (the capital of Zaire) and some problems in other towns.
If you decide to do it, whether in Rwanda or Zaire, get your visas in Nairobi and fly to Kigali, Rwanda. From there, you can book a gorilla visit into the Parc de Volcans or get transport to Goma, Zaire (one day), and book a trip to visit the gorillas in Zaire. Either way, expect to pay a park fee of at least $100 per person. This is the basic fee. In addition, you will have to pay for transport and lodging and food. It's expensive by African safari standards, but well worth it. I have seen all the major game parks and hiked all the mountains in East Africa, but nothing was as impressive as the gorillas.

Computer Express

One thing we all have in common is computers. Computers are a little like children: they provide simple rewards in exchange for exorbitant expenditures. They're never satisfied with what they have; they promise to be much better if you'll just spend some money on them; and in the end, they're replaced by new models (grandchildren, if you're still trying to follow the analogy).

Nonetheless, there comes a time in both parenthood or computer ownership when we lower our defenses and spend a few bucks on the little rascals. When that time arrives, the Travel & Shopping

Department stands ready to assist in your expenditures. For a sample, let's explore Computer Express, an online retail outlet for computer hardware, software and accessories (see Figure 8-6).

Figure 8-6:
Six partial lists of the products available online via Computer Express.

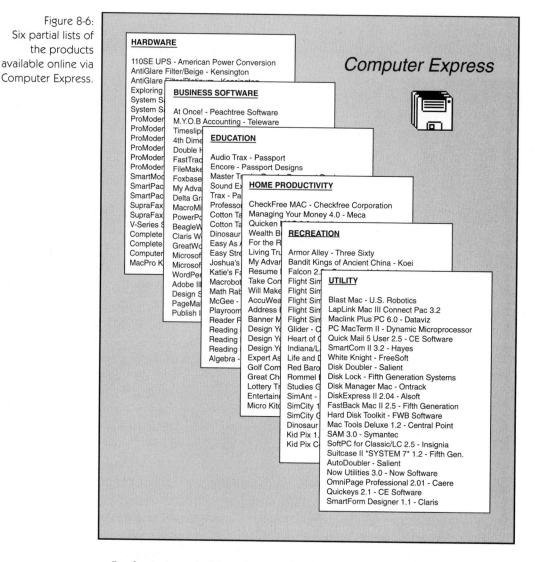

In the interest of brevity, each of the lists in Figure 8-6 is abbreviated. They're all at least twice as long as they appear. In other words, the spectrum of products available from Computer Express is expansive. The entire warehouse is available for browsing online, complete with product descriptions and prices.

AutoVantage

A few pages back we mentioned that most telecommunications services are textual in nature and much more difficult to use than AOL. Like EAASY SABRE, AutoVantage, too, is textual. While these areas are not as pretty as the rest of AOL, they are made up of menus and clear instructions and don't require you to memorize a lot of code words. AOL has made these areas easy to use, textual interface and all (see Figure 8-7).

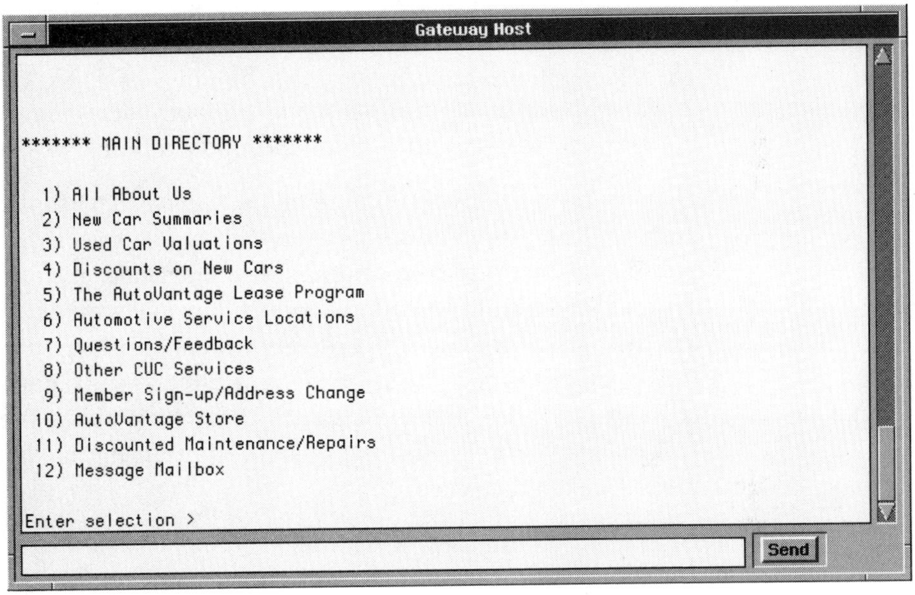

Figure 8-7: Like EAASY SABRE, AutoVantage offers shoppers a very valuable resource.

```
                                    Gateway Host
 ‾‾

  ******* MAIN DIRECTORY *******

   1) All About Us
   2) New Car Summaries
   3) Used Car Valuations
   4) Discounts on New Cars
   5) The AutoVantage Lease Program
   6) Automotive Service Locations
   7) Questions/Feedback
   8) Other CUC Services
   9) Member Sign-up/Address Change
  10) AutoVantage Store
  11) Discounted Maintenance/Repairs
  12) Message Mailbox

 Enter selection >

                                                              Send
```

AutoVantage is one of the few premium services (one for which an extra fee is charged) available to AOL members: its annual fee of $49 entitles you to the following:

- *New car summaries* that detail a model's features, the pros and cons of buying the model, specifications, available options, sticker and dealer prices and road test highlights.

- *Used car pricing on-screen*, instantly from the vast nationwide used car AutoVantage database. This service gives you the estimated selling and trade-in prices, an overview of the model, bargaining tips and recall history for any car up to 20 years old (see Figure 8-8).

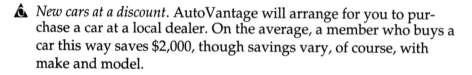

- *New cars at a discount.* AutoVantage will arrange for you to purchase a car at a local dealer. On the average, a member who buys a car this way saves $2,000, though savings vary, of course, with make and model.

- *Locate nearby service centers online.* AutoVantage members are able to access a list of all participating service centers within a 50-mile radius. Each listing highlights the address, phone number, contact name and discount offer made by the servicing agency. You may search by type of service, type of car needing service or the service center name.

- *Pre-negotiated national discounts.* Savings of 10 to 20 percent off the local price on virtually everything from oil changes, tune-ups and transmissions to auto glass and body repair.

Premium services are scarce on AOL. So are textual interfaces. Nonetheless, AutoVantage may well pay for itself through the money you'll save on regular maintenance and service, and it certainly pays for itself the first time you buy or sell a car. We all do it at one time or another; when we do, it's probably the second-largest financial transaction of our lives (for the largest—real estate—see Chapter 6, "Lifestyles & Interests"); and most of us know very little about the business. If all this makes you nervous (and it should), investigate AutoVantage. It helps to even the score.

Figure 8-8: "Psst: Hey Buddy! Wanna buy a used Camaro?" Before you do, check out AutoVantage.

AutoVantage

CHEVROLET CAMARO, 1982-1992 MODELS

SUMMARY:
Third-generation, rear-drive sporty coupe is tight in back for grown ups, though lift-up hatch and fold-down rear seatback add cargo space. Base engine through 1986 was Pontiac's 2.5-liter four, but most Camaros carry a 2.8-liter V-6 or 5.0 V-8. Standard in the plush Berlinetta, the V-6 gained port fuel injection for 1985. Hooked to 5-speed manual shift, it offers the best performance/economy balance. Four 5.0-liter V-8 versions have been sold: a base 4-barrel; Cross-Fire with twin injectors in 1982-83; high-output carbureted, starting late-1983 (fuel inj___ed for '88); ___ 7-liter Corvette V-8 (automatic Starting in 1987, the top-rung IROC-Z ___ dropped for '88, IROC-Z became a model on its own rather th___ ___ed some Z28 styling touches. For 1991, the Z28 ___ only), while the 4-cylinder engine de___ Convertibles have been available s___ base engine for 1990, and Camar___ marks Camaro's 25th season. Av___ performance. Other V-8s perform___ suspension gives Camaro some ___ traction bad on wet roads. Snu___ models and expect squeaks a___ nor similar Pontiac Firebird is ___ insurance rates are high, tho___ keep thieves at bay.

DIMENSIONS

	Wheel-Base In.	Avg. Length In.	Cargo Height In.	Width In.	Weight Lbs.	Volume Cu. Ft.	Tank Gal.
2d cpe	108.4	53.0		74.1	3262	17.7	17.5

ENGINES	L/CID	BHP	MPG	Avail.
ohv I-4 FI	2.5/151			
ohv V-6 2 bbl.	2.8/173	88-92	19-23	82-86
ohv V-6 FI	2.8/173	107-112	17-21	82-84
ohv V-6 FI	3.1/191	135	17-21	85-89
ohv V-8 4 bbl.	5.0/305	140	17-21	90-92
ohv V-8 FI	5.0/305	150-190	13-16	82-87
ohv V-8 FI (TPI)	5.0/305	165-175	12-15	82-83
ohv V-8 FI	5.0/305	195-230	15-19	85-92
ohv V-8 FI	5.7/350	170	15-19	88-92
		225-245	14-18	87-92

KEY: L/CID = liters/cubic inch displacement; BHP = brake horsepower; MPG = estimated average miles per gallon; OHC = overhead cam; DOHC = double overhead cam; OHV = overhead valve; I = in-line engine; V = V engine; flat = horizontally opposed engine; D = diesel; T = turbocharged; BBL. = barrel (carburetor); FI = fuel injection

YEARLY COSTS

Listed below are e___
you requested. Wh___
results.

We have include___

* GASOLINE & ___
15,000 miles pe___
$1.26 per gallon.

* AVERAGE INSURANCE - Estimating insurance costs is diffic___ ___
on where you live, your age, your driving record, and the type of car you drive. We have ___
over 200,000 participating drivers to determine their Average Yearly Insurance. Use these
estimates to compare between models. Your actual insurance must be quoted by a licensed
insurance provider to give you a fair estimate.

SAMPLE THREE YEAR ESTIMATED COSTS FOR CHEVROLET CAMARO

Yearly Costs Shown for Year*:	'92	'93	'94	'92	'93	'94	'92	'93	'94
Gasoline & Oil:	$970	$970	$970	$979	$970	$970	$970	$970	$970
Maintenance, Tires & Repairs:	460	480	490	450	480	500	420	490	520
Projected Trade-In Value:	4030	3270	2590	4430	3680	2990	5570	4700	3910

Your wallet is safe at AOL

All of this talk about premium services, buying cars and booking airline tickets may make you a little squeamish: "Does my AOL membership obligate me for anything beyond the standard connect charges?" No, not at all. All of the additional-expense items we've discussed in this chapter are voluntary—not at all requisite to membership in America Online. This is the Travel & Shopping Department, after all, and most travel and nearly all shopping is discretionary...and an additional expense.

Moving on

We've only scratched the surface of the Travel & Shopping Depart-ment. You can order flowers online via the Flower Shop, or have your documents printed on high-resolution imagesetters at the LaserDirect Printing Service. You can sell your old adding machine in the Classifieds and buy a new one at the Penny Wise Office Products Store. If you're fond of department stores where everything from refrigera-tors to camcorders is under a single roof, investigate the Comp-u-Store, AOL's members-only shopping club. They not only offer the conven-ience of online shopping, they guarantee the lowest prices anywhere, or they'll refund the difference.

The pursuit of materialism, however, is no longer our concern. There are personal matters to which we must attend. There are friends to be made and fellowships to discover. The virtual community of Lobbies, rooms and instant messages awaits us in the People Connection, and it's coming up next.

Learning & Reference

CHAPTER 9

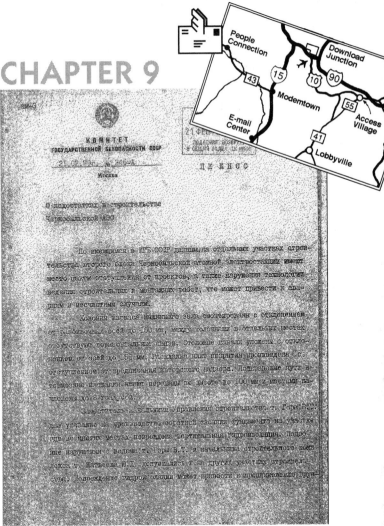

T his department could be ineffectually redundant. It could duplicate reference material that's readily available in printed form, offering little or no advantage over books and public libraries. Frankly, that's the way the reference departments are on most telecommunications services.

But not America Online. While it is important, the word "reference" receives second billing at AOL, not only in the department's title, but in its emphasis as well. This is the *Learning* & Reference Department, and the emphasis here is on learning. Students, teachers and parents of students (or students-to-be) are especially well served by this department. If you fall into any of those categories, you must investigate

---

Frontispiece graphic: February 21, 1979, Chernobyl report from the Soviet KGB, courtesy of Library of Congress. Use the keyword: Library.

Learning & Reference (keyword: Learning). But before you do, read this chapter. It's a big department; this chapter will refine your investigation and offer some tips as well.

Figure 9-1: A wide array of folders offers a wealth of learning opportunities in the Learning & Reference Department.

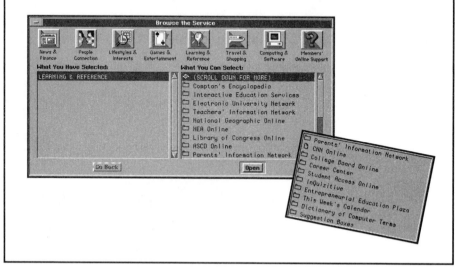

Learning & Reference for everyone

While teachers and students are exceptionally well served by this department, the rest of us are not overlooked. There's a Career Center, *National Geographic* magazine and the Electronic University. Imagine access to these resources without paying for magazine subscriptions or private tutoring fees!

Compton's Encyclopedia

Second billing or not, there's one reference that lends itself well to the telecommunications medium: the encyclopedia. Printed encyclopedias are expensive and difficult to maintain. They go out of date quickly, they take up a lot of shelf space, they're usually neglected, and few people are adept at searching them properly (quick: find all of the references to "mammal" in your encyclopedia).

Compton's Encyclopedia is published by Britannica Software, Inc., a division of Encyclopaedia Britannica, Inc. It features 8,784,000 words;

5,200 full-length articles; 26,023 capsule articles; and 63,503 index entries. The multimedia version of this encyclopedia took top honors at the 1991 Software Publisher's Association Awards Ceremony, taking the annual prize awarded for the best stand-alone educational product, and a Critic's Choice award as Best Education Program. The online version (keyword: Encyclopedia) is perpetually updated and effortlessly searchable. Finding all the references to the word "mammal" takes only moments, and nothing is inadvertently omitted.

Tom loves trains. He loves the sound and smell of trains; he escapes to the romance of trains, he rides a light rail system to work (Metropolitan Area Express [MAX] in Portland, Oregon, voted "America's Best" in 1989), and Amtrak's most popular route—the Coast Starlight—passes within a few miles of Tom's house. To demonstrate Compton's Encyclopedia, we searched for the word "train" and were more than gratified with the results (see Figure 9-2).

Figure 9-2: Seventeen references to railroads: Elysian Fields for the enthusiast.

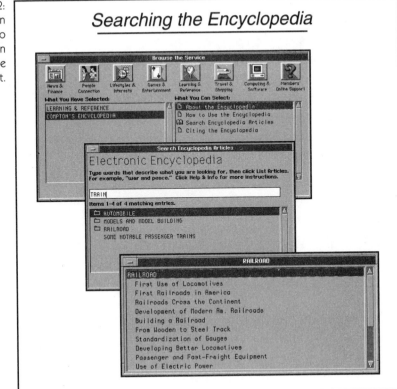

Notable passenger trains

These are the trains you may want to travel in someday. The text below is extracted from Compton's Encyclopedia, Online Edition, and downloaded from America Online.

- **The Blue Train, South Africa.**
  Said to be the most luxurious train in the world, the Blue Train makes a leisurely 1,000-mile, 26-hour trip once or twice a week between Pretoria and Cape Town.

- **The Coast Starlight, United States.**
  Though we've already indicated that this is Amtrak's most popular train, it warrants a second mention here. The Coast Starlight crosses the Cascade Mountains and follows the coastline of California in a 1,400-mile, 33-hour trip between Seattle and Los Angeles. Save your pennies and get a sleeper.

- **The Indian Pacific, Australia.**
  Another luxury train, the Indian Pacific crosses the Australian continent, from Sydney to Perth, in 2 3/4 days.

- **The Orient Express, Europe.**
  Europe's first transcontinental express, for years unmatched in luxury and comfort. From 1883-1977 (with interruptions during the world wars), it ran from Paris, France, to Constantinople (now Istanbul), Turkey. Short runs are still made over portions of the original route.

- **The Rheingold, West Germany.**
  One of Europe's finest trains, the Rheingold runs between Amsterdam, The Netherlands, and Basel, Switzerland, following the Rhine River and stopping at such cities as Cologne, Mainz and Munich.

- **Rossiya, Trans-Siberian Railway.**
  The Rossiya runs daily between Moscow and Vladivostok. The trip takes a week.

- **TGV, France.**
  This is the fastest train in the world, cruising at 180 miles per hour and covering the 267 miles between Paris and Lyon in two hours.

Whoa! One hundred and eighty miles an hour! Few cars can reach that speed—in fact, few private aircraft can reach that speed. Let's hope no cows wander onto the tracks....

Even at that speed, the TGV is rock-steady. Forget about the cows. Recline your seat back a bit and turn your attention to a good magazine. Can we interest you in a copy of the *National Geographic*? Read on.

National Geographic Online

Here you will find selections from *National Geographic* magazine and National Geographic's *Traveler* and *World* magazines, as well as a variety of news stories and press releases (keyword: Geographic). The television program is also featured in the Geographic TV Forum (see Figure 9-3).

Figure 9-3: "National Geographic," "Traveler" and "World" magazines are all included in National Geographic Online.

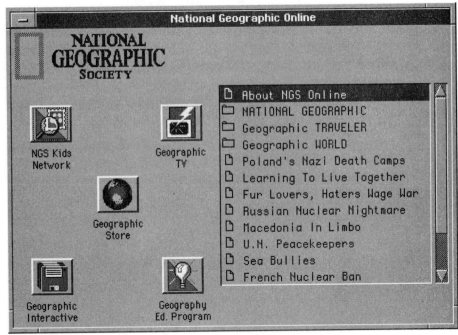

National Geographic's *Earth Almanac* tracks events on earth of particular interest to the Geographic reader. Written in the traditional Geographic style, the stories are always intriguing and often a little unusual. On the afternoon that we looked in, two stories struck us as particularly interesting—especially one recounting the adventures of ten-foot serpents intent on decimating the US territories in the South Pacific (see Figure 9-4).

Figure 9-4:
National Geographic's "Earth Almanac" regales the reader with reports of rapacious reptiles and recycled rubber.

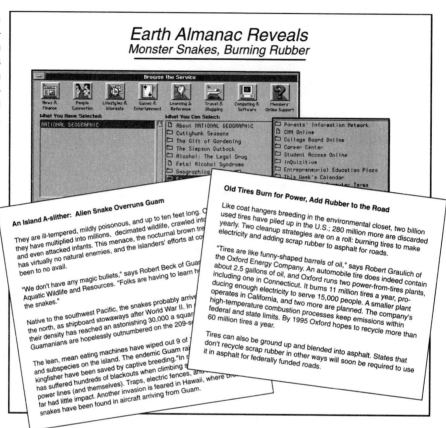

The Online Russian Archives

The Online Russian Archives are a temporary "exhibit" in the Learning & Reference Department, not unlike the exhibit upon which they are based in the Library of Congress (keyword: Library). In the museum business, temporary (or traveling) exhibits don't stay in any one museum permanently; after an appropriate stay, they move on to other museums where others may see them. Indeed, the Library of Congress returned the Russian Archives exhibit to Moscow in July of 1992.

We include the Online Russian Archives as an example of the topical material endemic to this department and to impress you with the quality and opulence of its "traveling" exhibits. It also represents the world's first online version of a major national exhibit, and it appeared on America Online.

The Online Russian Archives (more properly, *Revelations from the Russian Archives*) is a collection of documents culled from several declassified secret archives of the former Soviet Union. The full exhibit of some 300 Soviet documents, photographs and films—which were on display in the Library of Congress in the spring of 1992—is the first such exhibition in the West. It shed new light on some of the major events of the 20th Century, from the Russian Revolution to recent times. Included in the exhibit are materials relating to such topics as Stalin's reign of terror, the Gulag system, censorship, the workings of the secret police, substandard construction practices at the Chernobyl nuclear plant and the 1962 Cuban Missile Crisis.

The online exhibit consisted of excerpts from 25 of the 250 documents in the museum exhibit. When the exhibit appeared on AOL, scans of the original documents were posted in GIF format (GIF is a graphics format, discussed in Chapter 12, "The Download Manager").

Each scanned original was accompanied by an English translation, which you could read online or save to your hard drive for further study, and a piece providing the appropriate historical background. Reading these documents was an experience never to be forgotten, a John Le Carre novel come to life—an event best illuminated by the Russian originals, downloaded and displayed on your screen, in heirloom color and Cyrillic mystery (see Figure 9-5 and Frontispiece).

Figure 9-5: The Chernobyl report exceeded 1,000 words and occupied nearly six pages. The page shown here, which documents early construction flaws, was written in early 1979. The plant exploded at 1:21 AM on April 26, 1986, a little over seven years later.

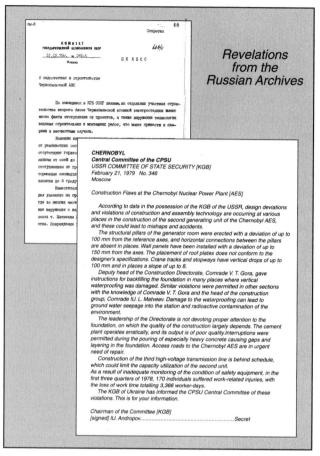

Revelations from the Russian Archives

CHERNOBYL
Central Committee of the CPSU
USSR COMMITTEE OF STATE SECURITY [KGB]
February 21, 1979 No. 346
Moscow

Construction Flaws at the Chernobyl Nuclear Power Plant [AES]

According to data in the possession of the KGB of the USSR, design deviations and violations of construction and assembly technology are occurring at various places in the construction of the second generating unit of the Chernobyl AES, and these could lead to mishaps and accidents.

The structural pillars of the generator room were erected with a deviation of up to 100 mm from the reference axes, and horizontal connections between the pillars are absent in places. Wall panels have been installed with a deviation of up to 150 mm from the axes. The placement of roof plates does not conform to the designer's specifications. Crane tracks and stopways have vertical drops of up to 100 mm and in places a slope of up to 8.

Deputy head of the Construction Directorate, Comrade V. T. Gora, gave instructions for backfilling the foundation in many places where vertical waterproofing was damaged. Similar violations were permitted in other sections with the knowledge of Comrade V. T. Gora and the head of the construction group, Comrade IU. L. Matveev. Damage to the waterproofing can lead to ground water seepage into the station and radioactive contamination of the environment.

The leadership of the Directorate is not devoting proper attention to the foundation, on which the quality of the construction largely depends. The cement plant operates erratically, and its output is of poor quality. Interruptions were permitted during the pouring of especially heavy concrete causing gaps and layering in the foundation. Access roads to the Chernobyl AES are in urgent need of repair.

Construction of the third high-voltage transmission line is behind schedule, which could limit the capacity utilization of the second unit.

As a result of inadequate monitoring of the condition of safety equipment, in the first three quarters of 1978, 170 individuals suffered work-related injuries, with the loss of work time totalling 3,366 worker-days.

The KGB of Ukraine has informed the CPSU Central Committee of these violations. This is for your information.

Chairman of the Committee [KGB]
[signed] IU. Andropov...Secret

The Electronic University Network

The word "University" in academic circles implies accreditation: real baccalaureate degrees recognized across the nation. The word also implies an accredited program of graduate studies leading to post-baccalaureate degrees. The Electronic University Network (keyword: EUN) offers both, each available without leaving your computer.

The university is based on the belief that quality education can be made available to people where they are—the home, the workplace, the barracks, the hotel room, the hospital; the belief that it's the quality of

Figure 9-6: The Electronic University Network offers accredited learning, ranging from Associate to Master's degrees.

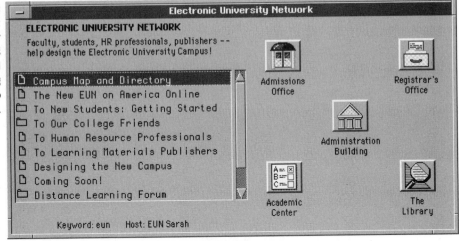

the dialog between teacher and student that determines the quality of education, not the distance between them; the belief that reading, writing and thinking are at the heart of the educational process.

The university offers nearly 100 undergraduate courses that earn college credit and enable students to receive an Associate or Bachelor's degree. You can also earn a Master of Business Administration (MBA) through the university. The MBA is offered in association with Saginaw Valley State University; the program is comprehensive and nationally recognized.

The Career Center

The Career Center (keyword: Career) is a professional guidance and counseling service designed to help you advance and enrich your personal, social and career development. This is the place to visit if you want to take on a new challenge in the job market.

Figure 9-7: The Career Center offers counseling services, databases, articles and a library of resources.

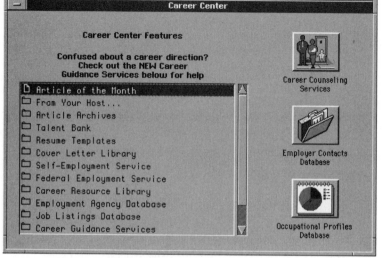

The Career Center is a surprisingly relevant and comprehensive resource. It offers four searchable databases (employment agencies, job listings, employer contacts and occupational profiles) and four libraries (articles, resources, cover letters and résumés). If you are in the market for a job or are thinking about a change in careers, consider the possibilities offered by the Career Center. Here, you can do the following:

🔥 Read articles on issues important to your personal and career development.

🔥 Schedule a private session with a counselor to get the personalized attention you need to sort out your personal, social and career needs.

🔥 Leave questions for a counselor on the message board or send a note through e-mail.

🔥 Create your own résumé from a variety of résumé styles (templates) available to view on-screen and/or download.

🔥 View on-screen and/or download sample employment letters you can edit and use in your own job search.

🔥 Turn your personal computer into a successful business by downloading profiles of home computing business opportunities.

- Gather information on thousands of American employers to help find potential employment opportunities.

- Complete a series of career guidance exercises to determine a career direction.

- Identify sources of financial aid to pay for your college education.

- Obtain information on over 700 occupations, including job descriptions, entrance qualifications, salary, future employment demand and working conditions.

- Access information about thousands of job openings across the country.

- Peruse listings of thousands of employment agencies that can help you find employment nationwide.

- Learn how to seek and secure employment with any one of 162 federal departments and agencies.

- Get information on dozens of degree and diploma programs you can complete at home to enhance your current skills or develop new ones.

- Locate career resources (books, tapes, etc.) useful in satisfying personal/social, educational, career, employment and self-employment needs.

- List your professional skills in the center's talent database to enable other AOL members to easily find you if they're looking for someone with your qualifications.

- Buy complete, ready-to-go business opportunities directly from the Career Center for use in starting your own business with your personal computer.

Selecting only one feature from this forum is a challenge, though one did strike us as useful for nearly everyone: the database of résumé templates. The templates are provided by the author of the *Damn Good Résumé Guide* and *The Résumé Catalog* (both published by Ten Speed Press). Each template walks you through what needs to be done to make you look like a "hot candidate," with snappy, ready-to-go designs in easy-to-modify formats (see Figure 9-8).

Figure 9-8: One of
the many résumé
formats available
in the Career
Center.

YOUR NAME
Your street and number
City, State, and Zip
(415) xxx-xxxx

OBJECTIVE

A position as Coordinator of Whatever, focusing on this and that areas.

HIGHLIGHTS

- o Number of years experience in work** at all <u>relevant</u> to the objective above.
- o Credentials or education or training, relevant to this objective.
- o A key accomplishment* that shows you're a "hot candidate" for this job.
- o A strength* or characteristic* of yours, that's important to you and relevant to this job.
- o Something else the employer should know ... a skill*, a trait*, an accomplishment*.

 * reflected in the details below, of course **including unpaid work

RELEVANT SKILLS & EXPERIENCE

ONE MAJOR SKILL *(that is directly relevant to the job objective stated above)*
- o An accomplishment that illustrates this skill (<u>including</u> where/when this occurred).
- o An accomplishment that illustrates this skill (<u>including</u> where/when this occurred):
  - A substatement that elaborates on one step in the process of the accomplishment above.
  - A substatement elaborating on another step in the process of the accomplishment above.

ANOTHER MAJOR SKILL *(that is directly relevant to the job objective stated above)*
- o An accomplishment/compound one-liner that illustrates this skill (<u>as above</u>):
  - A substatement that elaborates on one step in the process of the accomplishment above.
  - A substatement elaborating on another step in the process of the accomplishment above.
- o An accomplishment that illustrates this skill (<u>including</u> where/when this occurred).
- o An accomplishment that illustrates this skill (linking it to the work history below).

ANOTHER MAJOR SKILL *(that is directly relevant to the job objective stated above)*
- o An accomplishment that illustrates this skill (<u>including</u> where/when this occurred).
- o An accomplishment that illustrates this skill (linking it to the work history below).

A SPECIAL KNOWLEDGE-AREA (essential to the objective named above)
- o An accomplishment illustrating/documenting this special knowledge (+ where/when).
- o A list of equipment or processes you're familiar with, consistent w/ expertise in this area.
- o A list of courses or trainings you took, that shows your expertise in this area.

WORK HISTORY

1990-present	*Job Title*	**COMPANY NAME** and city (+*another line of explanation if needed*)
198x-xx	*Job Title*	**COMPANY NAME** and city
198x-xx	*Job Title*	**COMPANY NAME** and city
197x-xx	*Job Title*	**COMPANY NAME** and city

EDUCATION

University of So-and So, Podunk City
B.A., Basket Weaving, 1989

Snappy Functional Resume format o © Damn Good Resume Writer newsletter, 1991

Learning & Reference for the student

As we mentioned earlier, the emphasis in this department is education: learning more about it, getting more of it and exploring new avenues. For the student, perhaps that last opportunity is the most valuable. Of all the online opportunities AOL provides for the student, three deserve specific mention here: Student Access, the Academic Assistance Center and College Board Online.

Student Access

A number of resources are available to help students get more out of college, expand graduate school and career options and network with students nationwide. The Princeton Review, the nation's most effective test-prep company, has brought these resources together as an AOL service called Student Access Online (keywords: Student Access).

Figure 9-9: Student Access offers a number of exclusive educational, financial and career services.

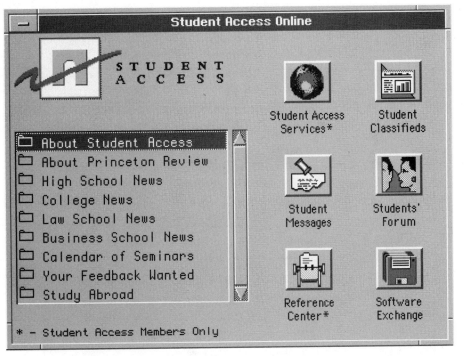

Membership in Student Access enables the student to take advantage of a variety of exclusive educational, financial and career services, including the following:

- Financial planning.

- Internship opportunities.

- Admissions counseling.

- Job-placement services.

- Group buying power offering hundreds of products and services at discounted rates.

- The service's greatest asset—the Student Access members themselves. Student Access forums and trips connect thousands of college students nationwide.

Student Access represents an almost unfair advantage to the student, yet membership is open to anyone. At this writing, the annual fee for this wealth of opportunity is $49.

Tom de Boor

Tom de Boor's office is a windowless cube, devoid of ornamentation. The only break in the monotonous white sheetrock is a lone corkboard, suspended by a single nail at the upper-left corner. The other nail—the one intended to hold the upper-right corner—pulled out of the wall some time ago. The corkboard dangles at a 45-degree angle above Tom's Macintosh SE. Two other computers are present in the room, a Stratus terminal and an IBM-PS1. Neither is turned on; both are shrouded in opaque layers of dust. The Stratus terminal has been recently used: the dust has been wiped away from the area on screen that Tom wanted to see.

Tom frequently brushes unruly hair from his eyes as he talks. And talking is something he's good at: animated, enthusiastic talk. In contrast to the disarray in Tom's office, his thinking is organized and methodical, and his conversation is compelling and ardent. As Manager/Senior Producer of the Learning & Reference Department, Tom oversees AOL's most ambitious and scholarly effort, and he doesn't take this work lightly.

Tom's attitude is reflected in his department. All the unique and remarkable offerings discussed in this chapter are Tom's doing, and he has many more up his sleeve. Few can equal his ambition, and that ambition is outwardly directed: Tom couldn't care less about the charm of his office or the pedigree of his coiffeur. He's singularly devoted to his department. Students, teachers, parents and administrators would have to search far and wide for a service as comprehensive, convenient and affordable as the Learning & Reference Department, and Tom de Boor is the man to thank for it.

The Academic Assistance Center

The Academic Assistance Center (keyword: Homework) is designed for students who need additional reinforcement of the concepts they're learning, help with their homework or help with skills that have become rusty. In particular, this is the place to find teachers—teachers online and dedicated to the pursuit of academic goals.

Figure 9-10: The Academic Assistance Center is where students find teachers and professionals who can help with academic issues.

```
┌─────────────────── Browse the Service ───────────────────┐
│  News &   People   Lifestyles &  Games &    Learning &   Travel &   Computing &  Members'  │
│  Finance  Connection  Interests  Entertainment Reference  Shopping   Software   Online Support │
│  What You Have Selected:              What You Can Select:                                   │
│  ACADEMIC ASSISTANCE CENTER           About Academic Assistance                             │
│                                       Monthly Schedule                                      │
│                                       Homework Help Drop-In                                 │
│                                       Subject-specific Sessions                             │
│                                       The Study Skills Service                              │
│                                       The Teacher Pager                                     │
│                                       Exam Prep Center                                      │
│                                       Online Research Service                               │
│                                       Homework Helper Survey                                │
│            Go Back                                            Open                          │
└─────────────────────────────────────────────────────────────────────────────────────────┘
```

The Academic Assistance Center is dedicated to providing the student with academic assistance—online, without surcharge and guaranteed: all the message boards mentioned below are closely monitored—if a student posts a message on any of them and doesn't receive a response within 48 hours, AOL credits the student with an hour of free time.

🔥 The Homework Help area is designed to help students who have a need for general help in several different areas.

🔥 Live, real-time help with a specific subject area can be obtained in the "Subject-Specific Instruction" area, where students can post questions, attend one of many regularly scheduled sessions in a variety of subjects, or sign up for a special individual instruction session with one of AOL's instructors.

🔥 During the evening, a new service called the "Teacher Pager" is ready to connect a student with a teacher online and live; all a student needs to do is use the keywords: Teacher Pager.

▲ Help with research or term papers can be obtained through the Academic Research Service.

▲ Special help with end-of-term exams is available through the Exam Prep Center.

▲ Help in preparing for a standardized exam—like the GED and SAT exams—is available in the Study Skills Instruction area.

Homework is one area that's often foremost on the student's mind, and it's the subject that provokes most students to discover the Academic Assistance Center in the first place. Figure 9-11 identifies a few of the subject areas that were active when we visited—and we visited at the end of the summer, when activity on these boards is slow in comparison to that of the middle of the school year.

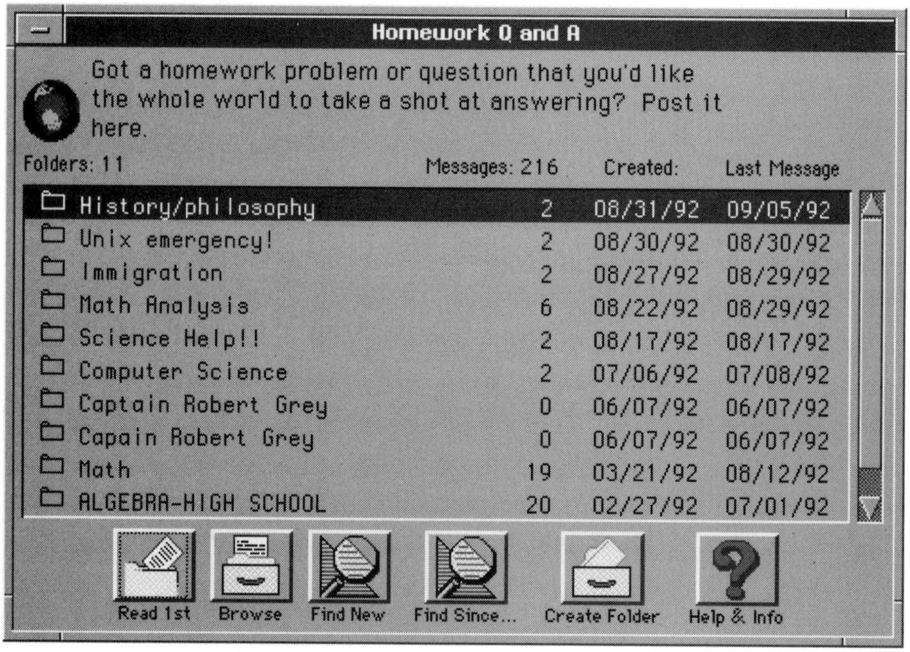

Figure 9-11: Even at the end of the summer, over 200 questions and answers appeared on the Homework Q and A message board.

Homework Q and A			
Got a homework problem or question that you'd like the whole world to take a shot at answering? Post it here.			
Folders: 11	**Messages: 216**	**Created:**	**Last Message**
📁 History/philosophy	2	08/31/92	09/05/92
📁 Unix emergency!	2	08/30/92	08/30/92
📁 Immigration	2	08/27/92	08/29/92
📁 Math Analysis	6	08/22/92	08/29/92
📁 Science Help!!	2	08/17/92	08/17/92
📁 Computer Science	2	07/06/92	07/08/92
📁 Captain Robert Grey	0	06/07/92	06/07/92
📁 Capain Robert Grey	0	06/07/92	06/07/92
📁 Math	19	03/21/92	08/12/92
📁 ALGEBRA-HIGH SCHOOL	20	02/27/92	07/01/92

Read 1st   Browse   Find New   Find Since...   Create Folder   Help & Info

Silly Putty

Sometimes you find the most interesting material in the least likely place. This most certainly was the case when we explored the Student-Teacher Exchange in the Academic Assistance Center. Andy Baird, an AOL forum consultant in the graphics library whose graphic graces the title page in Chapter 8, responded to a New Hampshire high school student's request for information about the now-famous synthetic rubber with the following piece:

"Silly Putty was indeed invented more or less by accident in the 1940s. A Scottish engineer named James Wright was working in the laboratories of General Electric in an attempt to create a superior synthetic rubber. (The battles in the Pacific had cut off the supplies of natural rubber from the Far East, so synthetic rubber was a hot priority during WWII.)

"Wright combined boric acid and silicone oil in a beaker, which resulted in a gooey mass. When he dropped a blob of the stuff, Wright was surprised to find that it bounced back and hit him in the face! Yet it could be stretched like putty, and if left to itself, would flow like a liquid. GE sent samples of the strange substance to engineers and researchers, hoping someone would find a use for it...but no one could.

"Six years later, an unemployed advertising executive named Peter Hodgson found out about the putty and tried selling it as a novelty gift item through a book catalog. To everyone's surprise, the putty outsold almost everything else in the catalog. Deeply in debt, Hodgson borrowed $147 and bought a big batch of the glop from GE; then he packaged it in plastic eggs, added the name 'Silly Putty' and took some samples to the annual Toy Fair in New York. That led to an article in *The New Yorker* magazine, which in turn set off an avalanche of sales—250,000 orders came in in three days!

"The rest is history. Blinney and Smith, the product's owners, say that over 200,000,000 eggs—that's 3,000 tons of Silly Putty!—have been sold over the years. (They're currently produced at the rate of 12,000 eggs a day at a putty plant in Pennsylvania.) Peter Hodgson died in 1975, leaving an estate of $140,000,000—and many happy Silly Putty owners!"

College Board Online

Founded in 1900, the College Board is a national, nonprofit association of more than 2,500 institutions and schools, systems, associations and agencies serving both higher and secondary education. The College Board assists students who are making the transition from high school to college through services that include guidance, admissions, placement, credit by examination and financial aid. In addition, the board is chartered to sponsor research, provide a forum to discuss common problems of secondary and higher education, and address questions of educational standards.

Which is a mouthful. This means that the College Board Online (keywords: College Board) is an invaluable service to the student faced with all the college-related questions: Where should I go? What will it cost? What are the admission requirements? What are my chances of getting in?

Figure 9-12: The College Board Online is invaluable for the student contemplating a college education.

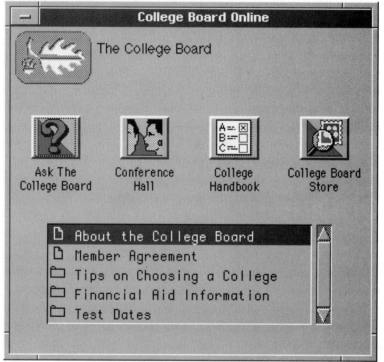

Perhaps the best way to introduce the College Board is to play the part of a prospective student and query the College Board Handbook. The handbook contains descriptions of over 3,100 colleges and universities. Information about each school includes majors offered, academic programs, freshman admissions, student life and athletics. The handbook can be searched either by topic or college name.

Let's say you're interested in journalism and black history, and you've decided to pursue the combination of the two as a career. For this, you need an education. Perhaps the College Handbook has the answer (see Figure 9-13).

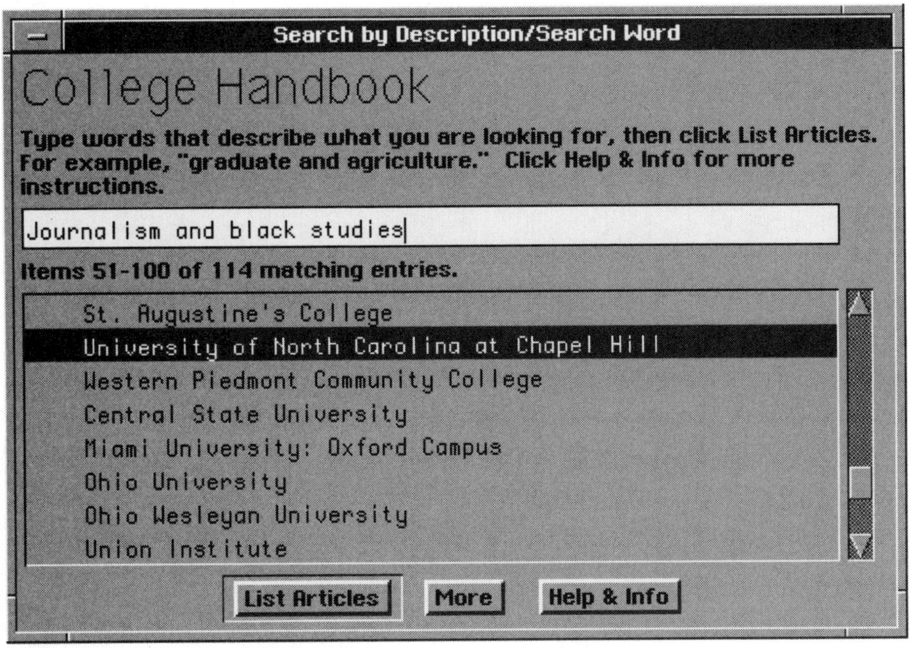

Figure 9-13: A
query of the
College Handbook
identifies the
University of North
Carolina at Chapel
Hill as a possible
candidate for your
interests in
journalism and
black studies.

Search by Description/Search Word

College Handbook

Type words that describe what you are looking for, then click List Articles. For example, "graduate and agriculture." Click Help & Info for more instructions.

Journalism and black studies|

Items 51-100 of 114 matching entries.

St. Augustine's College
University of North Carolina at Chapel Hill
Western Piedmont Community College
Central State University
Miami University: Oxford Campus
Ohio University
Ohio Wesleyan University
Union Institute

[**List Articles**] [**More**] [**Help & Info**]

Note the criteria at the top of Figure 9-13: journalism and black studies. Directly below that, the College Handbook found 114 colleges that matched that criteria, one of which is the University of North Carolina at Chapel Hill. By double-clicking on the UNC listing, we receive a long list of pithy articles about UNC. This is profuse information, and it's available for each of the other 113 candidates as well.

One thing we notice as we read the UNC admission requirements is that this is one tough school to get into. Your application is going to have to be sterling. For this you may need help, and for help you can turn to the College Board Store (see Figure 9-14).

Figure 9-14:
Shopping the
College Board
Store, we discover
the perfect book
for honing
application-writing
skills and a book/
tape offer to boot.

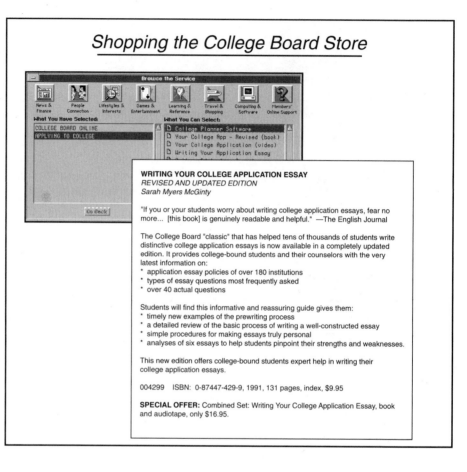

Learning & Reference for the teacher

Education is not an isolated activity. Education involves the transfer of knowledge, and the transfer of knowledge typically begins with a teacher. The people at America Online know that, and that's why the Learning & Reference Department features a number of areas specifically intended for teachers. Here we will take a look at three of the service areas.

Teachers' Information Network

The Teachers' Information Network (keyword: TIN) not only provides information pertaining to education, but also provides a gathering

place where teachers can come to exchange information, ideas and experience (see Figure 9-15).

The Teachers' Information Network includes many more features than those pictured in Figure 9-15. Some of the sources include the following:

- *The Newsstand*, containing educational news items hot off the wires, regular feature articles from prestigious magazines such as Scholastic's Electronic Learning and the NSBA's American School Board Journal, articles of interest to educators from smaller presses, software reviews and a searchable database of information about more than 300 magazines.

- *The Resource Pavilion*, where experts and educational organizations with particular specialties wait to answer teachers' questions.

- *The Idea Exchange*, the TIN message board center, used for the creative exchange of information and ideas on a variety of topics.

- *The Multimedia Exchange*, for the development of joint multimedia projects and the exchange of software, building the education of tomorrow today.

- *The Electronic Schoolhouse*, dedicated to the creative use of telecommunications in education, where a variety of innovative projects are posted or unfolding, and where teachers can arrange for joint connects with other schools or with home-schooling students.

- *Teachers' Libraries*, containing a rich array of public domain educational software programs, files, graphics, sounds, lesson plans and exams.

Figure 9-15:
Clockwise from
the top: the TIN
forum; a search of
the TIN radio and
television
database for
recommended
music programs;
the Electronic
Schoolhouse; the
Resource Pavilion;
and a math exam
from the Exam
Exchange. See the
text for
descriptions of
these services.

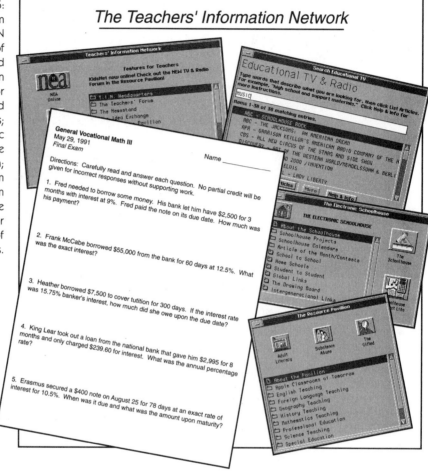

- *Teachers' University*, teachers teaching teachers in live seminar-style classes, an opportunity to learn new skills from old pros and to contribute to the education of the next generation of educators.

- *The Convention Center*, where teachers can learn about education conferences and events scheduled by various educational boards, associations and organizations across the country, and receive live reports from major conventions.

Figure 9-16: NEA Online offers a number of services for the teacher.

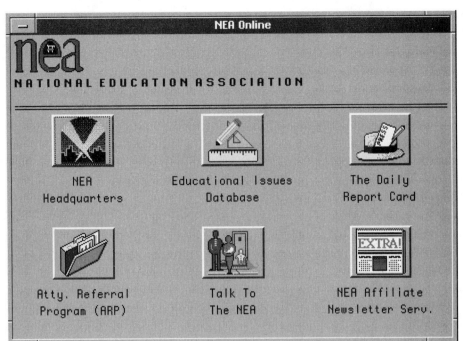

NEA Online

The National Education Association (keyword: NEA) is a teachers' union providing benefits, support, networking and—through related associations—accreditation for teachers and institutions. NEA Online is an ideal communications vehicle for the association: most teachers have access to a computer, and communication of this sort is best handled quickly, efficiently and bilaterally. AOL excels at this.

Most of the services pictured in Figure 9-16 are available to anyone (including parents and students), not just NEA members.

Perhaps the resource of greatest significance is the Educational Issues Database, a compilation of current education issues and NEA positions. The program is a pilot study developed by NEA and AOL as part of ongoing research in technology and telecommunications. The database includes information, articles and listings about the following:

🔥 Competency testing for teachers.

🔥 At-risk children.

🔥 Intern and mentor programs for new teachers.

- Business/education partnerships.

- Certification and licensure.

- States' actions on parental choice.

- Child-care coordinators and advocates.

- Paraprofessional licensing in early childhood education.

- More than 100 educational associations.

- National enrollment in educational institutions.

- Pre-K–12 teacher/pupil enrollment and school expenditures for all 50 states.

The list above is just a sample. Hundreds of entries are posted in the database. The "Talk to the NEA" message board (pictured in Figure 9-16) can be used to communicate with NEA's division of Education Policy and Professional Practice, which is responsible for the database.

NEA Online also includes The Daily Report Card, an eight-page daily update on America's progress in the educational arena; the Attorney Referral Program, providing access to attorneys for help in the resolution of personal legal problems; and the "Talk to the NEA" message board, where teachers and NEA officials exchange opinions and information.

ASCD Online

The Association for Supervision and Curriculum Development (keyword: ASCD) is a nonprofit, nonpartisan international education association. ASCD's strategic plan for the '90s focuses on:

- Improving student achievement.

- Developing better methods of assessing student learning.

- Restructuring school organizations.

- Strengthening and expanding early childhood education.

- Supporting international and global education.

ASCD's online area brings the resources of the association to members and the general public. Featured are articles from *Educational*

Leadership (ASCD's flagship publication), catalogs of information about new ASCD products and services, an Ask ASCD research service, articles from *ASCD Update* and the *CTRC Quarterly*, and an opportunity to discuss curriculum issues on the area's "Talk About Curriculum" message board.

Figure 9-17: ASCD Online offers numerous resources for the educational administrator.

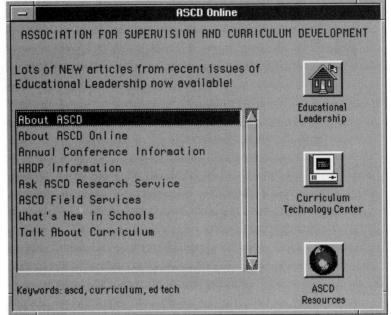

Learning & Reference for the parent

The Parents' Information Network (keyword: PIN) is an integrated full-service set of online services for parents, offering interactive forums on issues of importance to parents, articles from educational periodicals, databases of useful information, real-time conferencing opportunities and parent-oriented guides to other parts of America Online.

Figure 9-18: The
Parents'
Information
Network gathers
features from
throughout the
service and
incorporates them
into one easy-to-
use service.

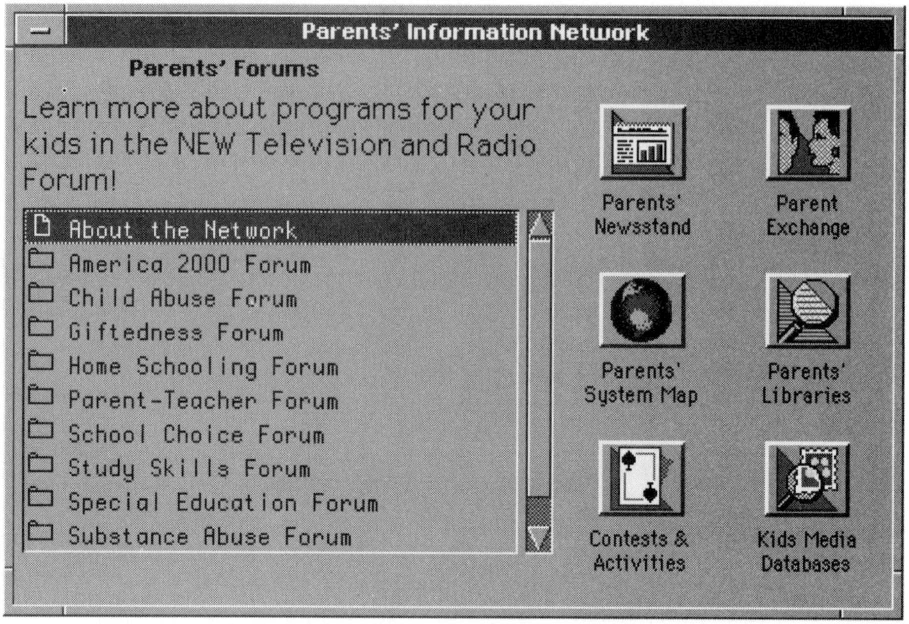

Parents' Information Network

Parents' Forums

Learn more about programs for your
kids in the NEW Television and Radio
Forum!

- About the Network
- America 2000 Forum
- Child Abuse Forum
- Giftedness Forum
- Home Schooling Forum
- Parent-Teacher Forum
- School Choice Forum
- Study Skills Forum
- Special Education Forum
- Substance Abuse Forum

Parents' Newsstand

Parent Exchange

Parents' System Map

Parents' Libraries

Contests & Activities

Kids Media Databases

Of particular interest is the Parents' System Map—a guide to AOL from the parent's perspective. This is an innovative service, and a necessary one: AOL—as you have no doubt discovered—is huge. Learning the locations of forums, databases and libraries is a challenge, one that's well met by the Parents' System Map. If it is useful to a parent, it's no doubt on the map, including its title, brief description and location.

Look again at the forums in Figure 9-18: child abuse, giftedness, home schooling—here's where you can meet other parents who share the same interests as you and exchange concerns, techniques, successes and failures. When you need an empathetic friend, the Parents' Forum is the place to look.

Moving on

Learning & Reference is a mature, competent and vast department populated by professionals, parents and students alike. Coupled with America Online's ease of use and graphical interface, it's not only one of the most comprehensive online resources available, it's really fun. Educators will tell you that learning is most effective when it's enjoyable—an experience that encourages students. Learning & Reference is that kind of experience.

There's a lot to be learned from spontaneous experiences as well, especially those involving a lively exchange of attitude and experience among a variety of people. People Connection is the real-time headquarters of America Online, and it's an outstanding educational benefit in and of itself. Whether you visit People Connection for its educational benefits or just for the fun of it, you'll want to read the next chapter.

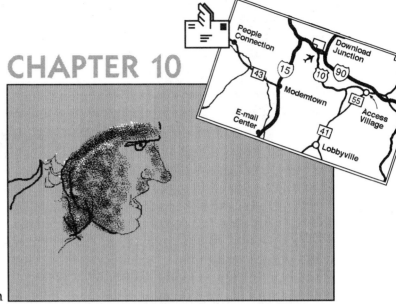

CHAPTER 10

People Connection

People Connection is the real-time headquarters of America Online. This is not the home of message boards and electronic mail: communication here is as immediate as a telephone conversation. Unlike telephone conversations, however, People Connection can involve any number of people, there's never a long-distance fee (unless your access number is long distance), and half the people you talk to are strangers—but not for long.

People Connection is the heart of the America Online community. Here you make the enduring friendships that keep you coming back, day after day. People Connection offers "diners," where you can order a short stack and a cup of coffee, and talk over the weekend ahead. It offers "pubs," where you can sip a brew after a long day on the job. It features events, where you can interview eminent guests and hobnob with luminaries.

Doesn't that sound like a community to you? Not only is it community, it's interactive. This is not couch-potato entertainment—this is two-way telecommunications, where imagination and participation are contagious, and the concept of community reaches its most eloquent expression.

It sure beats reruns.

Frontispiece graphic: "Leonardo da Vinci," by Clinton Fox, courtesy of BrentDent. Graphic Arts & CAD Forum.

A haven for shy people

America Online is a haven for shy people. Shy people usually like other people, and they're usually quite likable themselves; they just don't do well with strangers. This doesn't mean they don't *like* strangers: most shy people want to make friends—and all friends were once strangers—they just aren't very adept at doing it.

Which is why shy people like AOL. Nobody can see you online, nobody seems to notice if you don't talk much, and no situation is inescapable: you can always sign off. Perhaps best of all, you can use a *nom de plume* and no one will even know who you are. There's a bit of a masquerade ball in People Connection: you can wear the mask of a different screen name and be whatever or whomever you want. There's something comforting yet exciting about those possibilities.

Shy people usually begin their AOL journey in some "safe" place like a forum. No one's the wiser when a shy person reads a few forum messages or downloads a file or two. Later, a shy person may make an online friend and exchange some mail. Regardless of the path taken, it takes a shy person a long time to work up the courage to venture into People Connection. Whenever you visit there you invariably end up in a room full of strangers. This is not where shy people feel their most comfortable.

The irony is that shy folks *love* People Connection once they become acquainted with it. It's the perfect outlet for years of pent-up sociability. We know a shy person who joined AOL. It took him weeks to work up to People Connection. Yet now it's one of his greatest rewards. He goes there whenever he has time. You will too, once you get the hang of it.

The Lobby

Unlike the other departments we've explored, a visit to People Connection requires that you first pass through the *Lobby*, one of AOL's so-called "chat rooms." Chat rooms are rooms populated with real people, communicating in real time. No messages are left here. There are no files to download. AOL's Lobby is similar to the lobby of a hotel: it's an area people pass through, often on their way to some other destination. Every so often, people bump into an acquaintance, or sit there a moment to rest.

Entering the Lobby

To begin our People Connection adventure, choose People Connection from the Department screen, choose Lobby from the Go To menu, use the keyword: Lobby, or press Ctrl-L. No matter how you do it, you will soon find yourself in the Lobby (see Figure 10-1).

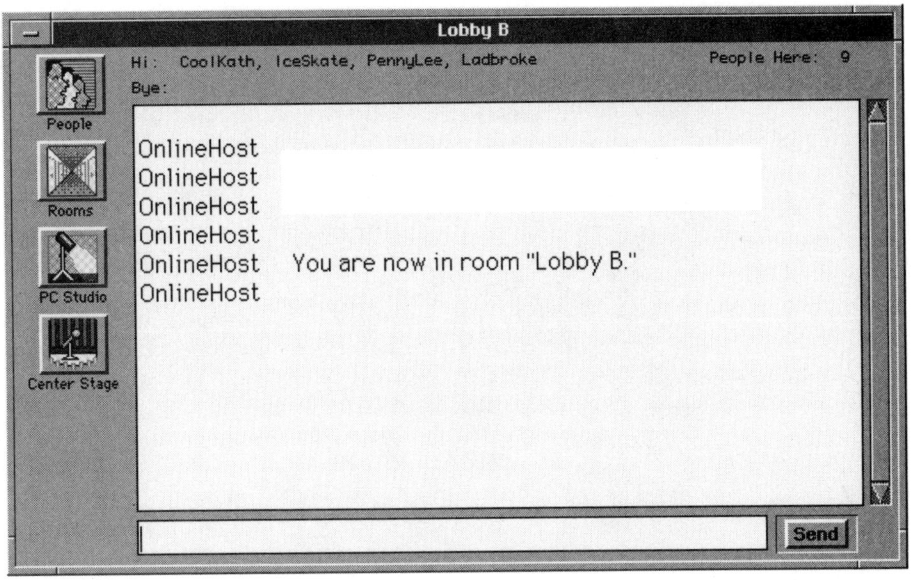

Figure 10-1: The Lobby screen seems empty just after you enter.

```
 ___                           Lobby B
|___|
       Hi:  CoolKath, IceSkate, PennyLee, Ladbroke        People Here:  9
       Bye:
 [People]
       OnlineHost
 [Rooms]   OnlineHost
       OnlineHost
       OnlineHost
 [PC Studio]  OnlineHost    You are now in room "Lobby B."
       OnlineHost
 [Center Stage]

                                                            [Send]
```

Note that the title bar of the window pictured in Figure 10-1 says "Lobby B." When Kathy entered the Lobby, AOL routed her to Lobby B. This happens whenever traffic is heavy on the system. When the main Lobby reaches capacity (rooms are considered filled when they contain 23 members), AOL places people in the secondary lobby—Lobby A. It too must have been filled by the time Kathy arrived, so she got placed in Lobby B. Note that it too didn't have far to go before approaching capacity, in which case new arrivals would be routed into yet another lobby.

People in a room can see when others enter it by watching the text at the top of the window, following the word "Hi." Since CoolKath is the first name on the list, she was the most recent arrival. Departing members' names appear after the word "Bye." CoolKath just got here; no one has left since she arrived.

Finally, note that the only text in the main (conversation) portion of the window is the online host telling her where she is. The only conversation that will appear is that which occurs *after* your arrival. That situation changes the moment someone speaks (see Figure 10-2).

Figure 10-2: No matter how shy you're feeling, say hello when you enter a room.

```
┌─────────────────────────────────────────────────────────────┐
│ ─                          Lobby B                            │
├─────────────────────────────────────────────────────────────┤
│  ┌────┐  Hi: Rorqual, ManuelL923, VMc1762522      People Here:  9 │
│  │    │  Bye: BrucieK, Trisha A, BILL14U, Airdale912, Jdm50, BobF907544, WRW 2ND │
│  │People│ ┌──────────────────────────────────────────────────┐▲│
│  ├────┤  │OnlineHost                                          │ │
│  │    │  │OnlineHost    You are now in room "Lobby B."        │ │
│  │ ✕  │  │OnlineHost                                          │ │
│  │Rooms│  │Mic11560      Hi y'all!                             │ │
│  ├────┤  │CoolKath      Hi everyone.                          │ │
│  │ ┬  │  │CoolKath      Hi Cheryl, MrMaster, Tsikes, CarlHub  │ │
│  │ │  │  │CarlHub       Hi                                    │ │
│  │PC Studio│MicI1560     Hi Carl                               │ │
│  ├────┤  │CoolKath      Looks like everyone's lobby-hopping today. │ │
│  │ ▊▊ │  │CoolKath      Any place exciting today?             │ │
│  │Center Stage│CoolKath  Hi PennyLee, Attendant, VMc, Jdm, MLisa, │ │
│  └────┘  │                 CocoKitty                          │ │
│          │CoolKath      Hi IceSkate.                          │▼│
│          │IceSkate      Hey Collkath!                         │ │
│          └──────────────────────────────────────────────────┘ │
│          ┌────────────────────────────────────────┐  ┌──────┐ │
│          │                                        │  │ Send │ │
│          └────────────────────────────────────────┘  └──────┘ │
└─────────────────────────────────────────────────────────────┘
```

Look again at Figure 10-2. This Lobby is active today. People are rushing through it with hardly a pause. By the time CoolKath said hello, three more people have arrived and seven have left. This occurred in a matter of seconds. Lobbies are something like a hotel lobby just after a large meeting has let out: people are scurrying everywhere.

Don't feel obligated to immediately become involved in a conversation. It's perfectly all right to say hello, then just watch for a while. In fact, we recommend it: it gives you a chance to adapt to the pace of the conversation—to get to know who is in the room and what they're like. Lobbies are good for this. They're lobbies, after all. People sit in lobbies and watch other people all the time.

Guides

If we may carry the hotel-lobby analogy a bit further, you may find a "concierge" there—a Guide—someone to answer your questions. Like a hotel concierge, AOL's Guides are chosen on the basis of their knowledge of the territory and their neighborly personalities. Watch the conversation for a while. No doubt you'll soon see someone with the word "Guide" in his or her screen name. More likely, a Guide will welcome you to the room.

Take a moment to look back at Figure 3-12. Do you see the Guide there? She welcomed Tom the moment he walked into the room and went out of her way to be of assistance. This is the way all Guides tend to be.

Guides are on duty from 12:00 noon to 6:00 AM Eastern time during the week, and all day Saturday and Sunday. Since we already discussed them in Chapter 3 ("Online Help & the Members"), we won't go over their function again. But if you would like to review that section, turn back to that chapter.

Exploring other public rooms

As is the case with hotel lobbies, you won't want to stay in AOL's lobbies indefinitely. Lots of other rooms await you, where the conversations are more focused and the residents less transitory. These rooms can be great fun; all you have to do is find the one that suits you best.

The Event Rooms Guide

Room exploration is best not done randomly. The method we recommend is to become familiar with the Event Rooms before you enter them. To do this, click on the PC Studio icon, pictured in Figure 10-2. The PC Studio window opens with its selection of options. Double-click on What's Happening This Week, then double-click on Event Rooms Guide (see Figure 10-3).

Figure 10-3:
Become familiar
with the Event
Rooms before you
spend time there.

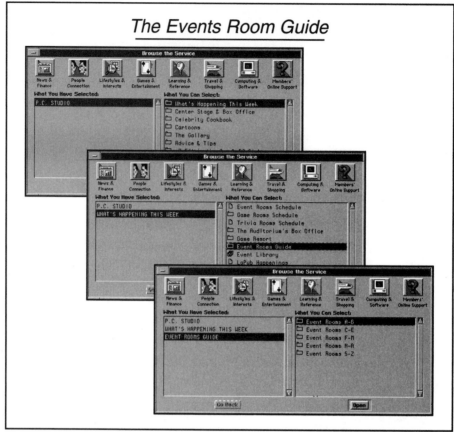

Many of the rooms available on AOL at any particular moment are
spontaneous. While spontaneous rooms can sometimes be entertaining
and fun, they lack the tradition found in the regularly scheduled Event
Rooms. Event Rooms are populated by "regulars," people who have
developed an online camaraderie and whose patter is familiar and
neighborly. They're not cliquish, however: you're never made to feel
unwelcome in one of AOL's Event Rooms. At this writing, 36 Event
Rooms are listed (a number that's sure to change), ranging from the
Best Lil' Chathouse to Parents R Us (see Figure 10-4).

Figure 10-4: Thirty-six Event Rooms are scheduled this week. Double-click on any one for a full description.

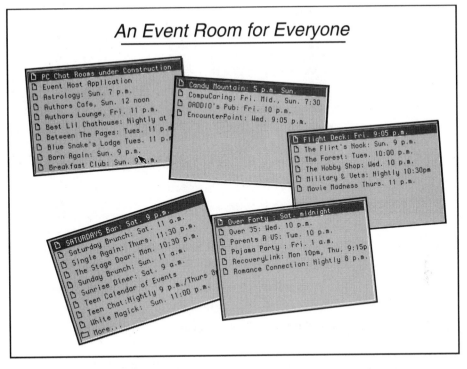

An Event Room for Everyone

One of our favorites is the Authors' Cafe, which meets every Sunday at noon. You never know who'll turn up, though a number of familiar writers visit it regularly. America Online is a favorite haunt for writers, partly because of the Writers' Club (discussed in Chapter 6, "Lifestyles & Interests") and partly because of its unique chat rooms like the Authors' Cafe. One morning when we visited, best-selling author Tom Clancy dropped by, unscheduled and unannounced. The log of his appearance appears below. Typical of a chat room, smileys and shorthand abound. (Refer to Chapter 11, "Electronic Mail" to review their meanings.)

D P Gumby: Hi Tom!! :)

Tom Clancy: Good morning, Gumby

Tom Clancy: and Rosey

D P Gumby: Hey Tom..... you should think about joining us at the Allentown Bash!

Tom Clancy: when's the party?

D P Gumby:	We've got about 100 onliners coming to the Bash.... it's gonna be a blast! :)
D P Gumby:	August 21-23.... in Allentown PA!
Tom Clancy:	busy then—doing something with Johns Hopkins
Tom Clancy:	their summer camp for kids with cancer
ROSEY DAWN:	Got any new books close to being released, Tom???
Data Dump3:	<—showing a prospective customer the service :D
Tom Clancy:	sorry, Rosey, no. I just came to terms with Putnam for #7, which I now have to write :(
Gleeful:	Hiya Prospective Customer..;D
Data Dump3:	Mornin' Tom :D
D P Gumby:	I'll be first in line for it, Tom! :)
ROSEY DAWN:	Oh well, anticipation makes it even better!
Tom Clancy:	hello, Dump
Gleeful:	lol Tom...you sold it and you haven't written it yet?? :D
Tom Clancy:	that's normal
ROSEY DAWN:	Heck, Glee — I'd *buy* it too —- just knowing Tom is going to write it
Tom Clancy:	the advance money is the literary equivalent of a gun to the head
Gleeful:	Tom...doesn't that put a lot of pressure on you tho???
D P Gumby:	I think, based on past performance...we can assume it'll be a good investment on behalf of the publisher
Tom Clancy:	pressure....what do you think?
Tom Clancy:	they pay you $XM, and you have to deliver a product, from inside your head, that's worth $XM
ROSEY DAWN:	What's in your head, Tom, is worth at least $XXXXX
D P Gumby:	Or more! :)
Tom Clancy:	thanks, ma'am, I'd like to think so
Gleeful:	awww Tom...You'll be just fine....just ask us..we know.. :D
Data Dump3:	Sheesh Tom, I would hate to run around w/ a price on my head....let alone in it!!! ;D
Tom Clancy:	don't worry, all writers are scared at this stage
Tom Clancy:	we're SUPPOSED to be insecure, but not as badly as actors are

D P Gumby: That's a good point, Tom... i do a lot of theater... and it's awfully frightening sometimes!!

Tom Clancy: I speak a lot, and I always get stage fright

D P Gumby: they say the best of them do, Tom...

Tom Clancy: there's no dishonor in it, it happened to Olivier, too

Tom Clancy: it's a thoroughly crummy way to earn a living, but you do it because you love it, and because you have to do it

Gleeful: Have to Tom??

Tom Clancy: yeah, it's my mission in life, it's what I do

Rich OO: Money is a great motivator. :)

Gleeful: Tom...do you give a lot of talks??

Tom Clancy: quite a few, yes

Rich OO: Tom...I always draw a blank til the speech is over,,,I have no idea what I've said. :)

Gleeful: Are books usually the subject or something else, Tom?

Tom Clancy: me, too, Rich

Tom Clancy: Glee, I just get up there and ramble

Tom Clancy: I just got an invite to talk to a big IBM gathering

Tom Clancy: and all my speaking money goes to my kids' school.

ROSEY DAWN: Will you run for President, Tom????

GATEWAY: You have my vote, Tom!

Tom Clancy: Rosey, do I LOOK that STUPID?????

Gleeful: See ya'll later!! I have an appt to keep..;D

Gleeful: Tom...it was nice to meet you...:D

AFC Doug: <— off to jump out of an airplane. :D

Tom Clancy: don't forget the chute, pal

D P Gumby: Time for me to run... see y'all later! Take care, Tom!

Tom Clancy: see ya

ROSEY DAWN: well — time for me to be productive!

ROSEY DAWN: take care all!!!!! nice seeing you again, Tom

Tom Clancy: Bye, all

The Event Rooms Schedule

The Event Rooms Schedule is posted in the PC Studio along with the Event Rooms Guide. Look again at the center window in Figure 10-4: see the schedule there? Double-click on it to view it. It lists times, events and hosts for each day of the week. See Figure 10-5 for an example of Friday's schedule.

Figure 10-5: The Event Rooms Schedule for a Friday. Use this article along with the Event Rooms Guide to plan your event room visits.

```
Fri.    8:00 pm  Romance Connection   RCWitchDr/RC Softie
                                      RCdeLune/RC Amore
                                      RC Sheena/RC Dreamer
        9:00 pm  LaPub Happy Hour     PubTend Mo
        9:00 pm  Teen Chat            Vaprok,Orca13, or
                                      Monopoly8,Bearzy
        9:05 pm  Flight Deck          MileHigh
        9:00 pm  New Member Lounge    NML Lisa
       10:00 pm  LaPub                PubTend LS
       10:00 pm  Daddios Pub          Daddio
       11:00 pm  Authors Lounge       SteveGlasr
       12:00 mid LaPub Late Night     PubTend Aeo
       12:00 mid Best Lil Chathouse   MastrVGogh,MastrSkeev
       12:00 mid CompuCaring          Heels lovr
        1:00 am  Pajama Party         PJ Johnny
```

It's important to note that the Event Rooms Schedule lists only those events in the People Connection Department and not those scheduled by individual forums or clubs. The Ten Forward Lounge, for instance, is the Star Trek Club's chat room, and it isn't mentioned in the Event Rooms Schedule. Consult individual clubs (see Chapter 6, "Lifestyles & Interests," for a discussion of clubs) for their chat rooms and schedules.

Finding other rooms

You can always tell which other rooms are available at any particular moment by clicking on the Rooms icon at the left of any chat window (review Figure 10-2 for Lobby B's window). When you click on that icon, you'll see the window pictured in Figure 10-6.

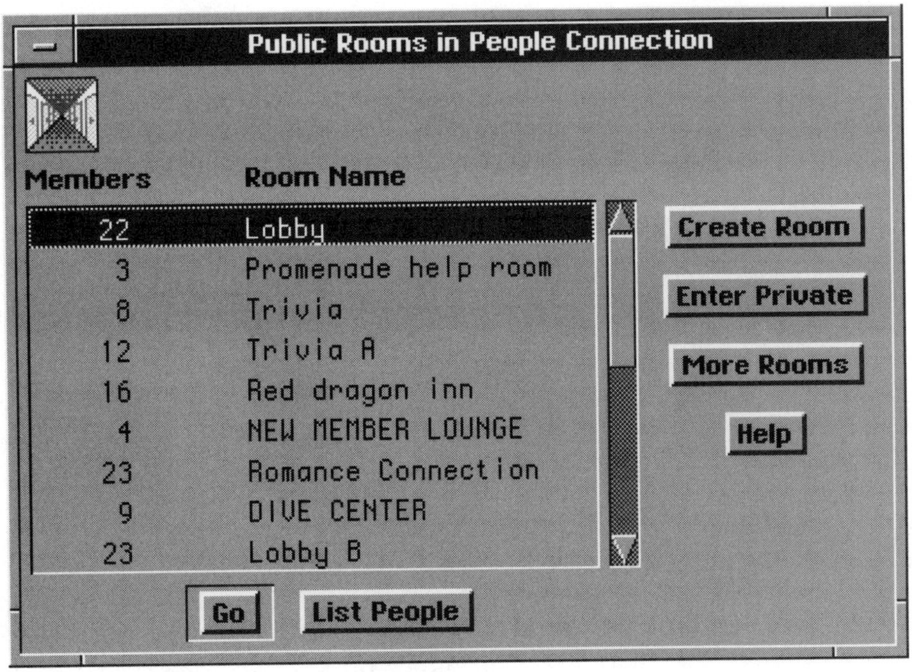

Figure 10-6: A list of available public rooms appears whenever you click on the Rooms icon in a chat window.

Public Rooms in People Connection

Members	Room Name
22	Lobby
3	Promenade help room
8	Trivia
12	Trivia A
16	Red dragon inn
4	NEW MEMBER LOUNGE
23	Romance Connection
9	DIVE CENTER
23	Lobby B

Create Room

Enter Private

More Rooms

Help

Go   List People

You can go into any room by double-clicking on it in the Public Rooms window, or you can get a list of all the people in a room (without going in) by clicking on the List People button at the bottom.

Note also that Figure 10-6 contains a Create Room button. Rooms, in other words, are up to members. Anyone who wishes may create a room, to talk about any topic, or no particular topic at all. These are the spontaneous rooms we mentioned earlier. If one appeals to you, click on the List People button first: you can tell a lot about a room by seeing who's there.

The New Member Lounge
If you're a shy person and new to chat rooms, you may want to start at the New Member Lounge. It meets every evening (except Monday and Wednesday) at 9:00 Eastern time.

If you *are* new to chat rooms, here are a few hints:

⚠ If you intend to stay in a room for a while, say hello when you enter.

⚠ Don't type in uppercase. That's shouting.

⚠ Speak when spoken to, even if you say nothing but "I don't know."

⚠ Use a screen name containing your first name or a nickname. Talking to "TLic7563" is like talking to a license plate. "MajorTom" allows people to call Tom "Major," "Tom" or "T."

⚠ Keep a log of your first few chat room visits by choosing Log from the File menu (logs are discussed in Chapter 5, "News & Finance"). Review the log off-line when your session has concluded. You learn a lot about chats this way.

⚠ Learn your shorthands and smileys, if for no other reason than to figure out what people are doing when they type something like "{{{{{{{{{{{{**}}}}}}}}}}}}}" or "ROFLWTIME." To find shorthands online, choose Online Shorthands from the What's Happening This Week window, pictured in Figure 10-4. Smileys are discussed in Chapter 11, "Electronic Mail" and again in Chapter 13, "Ten Best."

⚠ There are no stupid questions. Guides and members love to help.

Private rooms

Private rooms are the same as public rooms except that they don't appear in the rooms window, pictured in Figure 10-6. Private rooms may hold as many as 23 people and are established by members. There's no way to see a list of private rooms. You'll never know about a private room unless you create one of your own or someone invites you into his or her room.

Look again at Figure 10-6. The Enter Private button pictured there allows you to create a private room. When you click on this button, AOL asks you for a room name. If the room already exists, AOL takes you into that room. If it doesn't exist, AOL creates it and takes you there. If you create a room, the only people who can enter it are those who know its name, or who might be able to guess your room's name, which is about as likely as someone guessing your password if you're the least bit creative in naming your room.

> ### Online conference calls
>
> Consider the private room as an alternative to the conference call. We don't tend to think of them that way, but private rooms are, essentially, mechanisms whereby people from around the country can hold real-time conferences. AOL's private rooms are much less expensive than the phone company's conference calls, and participants can keep logs of the conversation for review once the conference has concluded (see Chapter 5, "News & Finance," for a discussion of logs). Conferences are often more productive when participants write what they say (makes 'em think before they speak) and vocal inflections don't cloud the issue.
>
> To hold a private-room conference call (or to simply meet some friends for a chat in a private room), tell the participants the name of the room and the time you want to meet beforehand, then arrive a few minutes early and create the room. Instruct the participants to enter the Lobby (Ctrl-L) when they sign on, click on the Rooms icon, click on the Enter Private button, then type in the name of your room. Try it: it's in many ways superior to a conference call, and cheaper to boot.

Chat-room technique

It's easy to participate in an online chat. All you need to do is read other members' comments and type your responses. When you are ready to send what you've typed, press the Enter key. But if you plan to spend a lot of time chatting online, here are a few techniques that might come in handy while you're visiting a chat room.

Cut & paste

Remember that most of America Online's windows may be resized and relocated anywhere on the screen. If the chat window fills most of your screen when it opens, size it down to leave a small open area on your screen. Now choose New Memo from the File menu and size the resulting Untitled window to fit the open area (see Figure 10-7). Use the Untitled window as a scratch pad. Make notes and jot responses there. If you want to send one as a chat comment, copy it from the Untitled window, paste it into the comment box and click on Send.

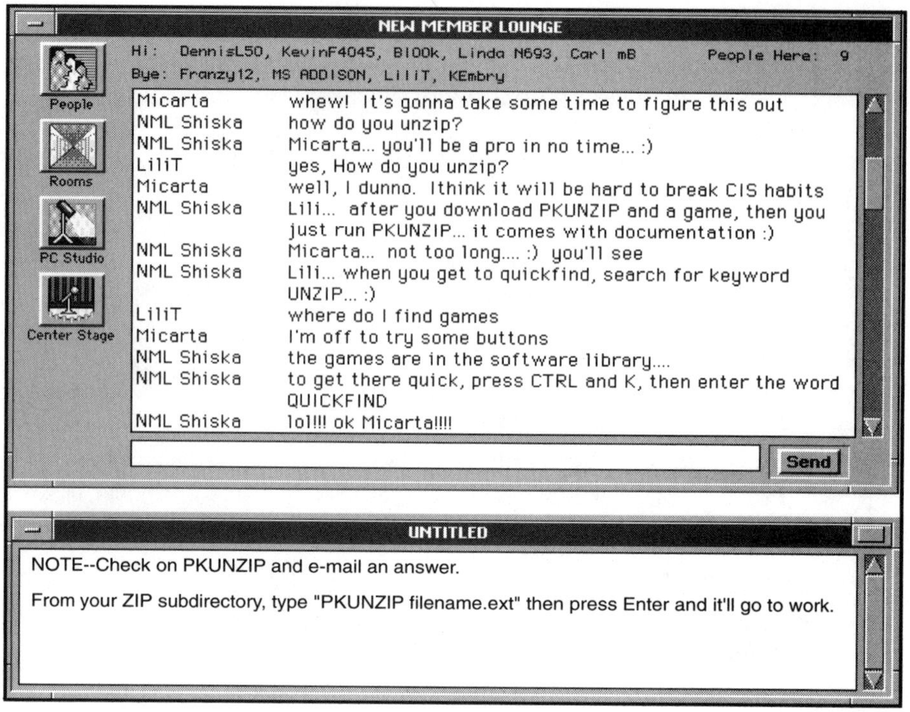

Figure 10-7: Two windows on the screen: at top, a the New Member's Lounge; below, an Untitled window where we can scribble notes. The notes may later be copied into the top window.

NEW MEMBER LOUNGE

Hi: DennisL50, KevinF4045, Bl00k, Linda N693, Carl mB   People Here: 9
Bye: Franzy12, MS ADDISON, LiliT, KEmbry

Micarta	whew! It's gonna take some time to figure this out
NML Shiska	how do you unzip?
NML Shiska	Micarta... you'll be a pro in no time... :)
LiliT	yes, How do you unzip?
Micarta	well, I dunno. I think it will be hard to break CIS habits
NML Shiska	Lili... after you download PKUNZIP and a game, then you just run PKUNZIP... it comes with documentation :)
NML Shiska	Micarta... not too long.... :) you'll see
NML Shiska	Lili... when you get to quickfind, search for keyword UNZIP... :)
LiliT	where do I find games
Micarta	I'm off to try some buttons
NML Shiska	the games are in the software library....
NML Shiska	to get there quick, press CTRL and K, then enter the word QUICKFIND
NML Shiska	lol!!! ok Micarta!!!!

People **Rooms** **PC Studio** **Center Stage**

Send

UNTITLED

NOTE--Check on PKUNZIP and e-mail an answer.

From your ZIP subdirectory, type "PKUNZIP filename.ext" then press Enter and it'll go to work.

Getting information about people in a room

You can find out about anyone in a chat room by clicking on the People icon in the room's window (review Figure 10-2). The People in this Room window will open to list—you guessed it—all of the people in the room (see Figure 10-8).

Figure 10-8: Want
to know who's
in your room?
Click on the
People icon.

List People in Room

Screen Names:

GordonE373
Humngbird
PopALot
RickL51531
Chi Mike
Bish22
RXMAN2B
SGTPEPPER3
Jo Ann Ts
NYCe Guy1

Message

Get Info

Highlight

Ignore

If you want to know more about a specific person, click on the Get Info button pictured in Figure 10-8. If that person has completed a profile (profiles are discussed in Chapter 3, "Online Help & the Members"), everything they want you to know about them will appear on your screen.

The Gallery

If you want to know even more about a person, check out the Gallery (keyword: Gallery). Members may send their photographs to a scanning service and the electronic result will be posted in the Gallery. Printed gallery photos make great trading cards: "I'll trade you one Steve Case for one MajorTom and one CoolKath...."

Locating a Member Online

Every so often, you'll know (or suspect) that a member is online, but not know where they are within the system. Fortunately, America Online has anticipated this need and provides a command—Locate a Member Online—under the Members menu. This feature not only tells you if a member is online; if he or she is in a public room, it also tells you which one.

Highlighting & excluding members

Investigate the Highlight and Ignore buttons pictured in Figure 10-8. When rooms become full and everyone is talking, it can be difficult to follow what's going on. Often, three or four conversations are going on at the same time. If you wish to exclude a member's comments (or those of all the members in a conversation in which you're not interested), select the member's name in the People in This Room window and click on the Ignore button. From then on, that member's text will not appear on your screen.

Conversely, if you want to emphasize a specific member's comments, select the member's name in the People in This Room window and click on the Hilite button. If you have a color monitor, each person's comments can appear in a unique color. If you have a monochrome monitor, you can underline someone's name. These two buttons are a real boon when chats get busy, yet not every member is aware of them.

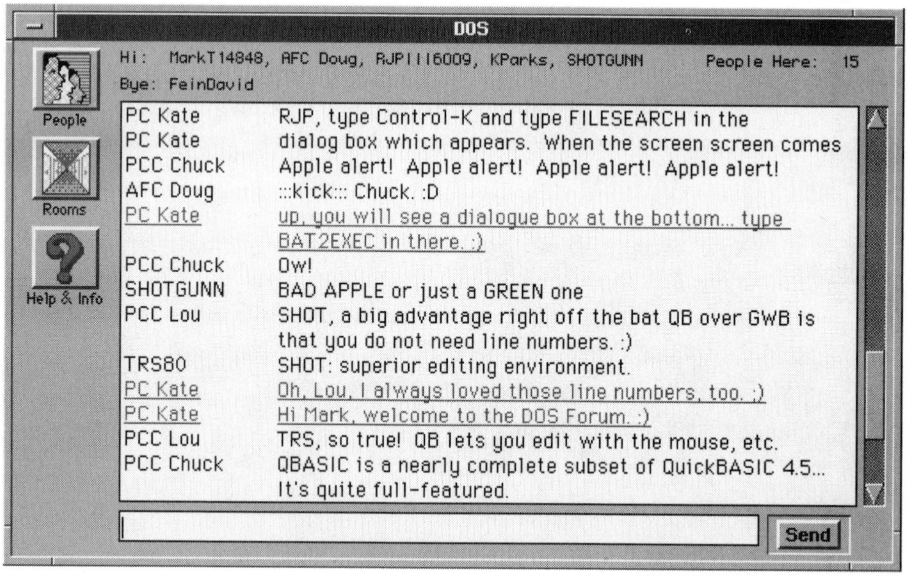

Figure 10-9: You can highlight or ignore the comments of any member in a chat room. This is a helpful tip for following complicated online conversations.

```
DOS

Hi:  MarkT14848, AFC Doug, RJPI116009, KParks, SHOTGUNN      People Here:   15
Bye: FeinDavid

PC Kate        RJP, type Control-K and type FILESEARCH in the
PC Kate        dialog box which appears. When the screen screen comes
PCC Chuck      Apple alert! Apple alert! Apple alert! Apple alert!
AFC Doug       :::kick::: Chuck. :D
PC Kate        up, you will see a dialogue box at the bottom... type
               BAT2EXEC in there. :)
PCC Chuck      Ow!
SHOTGUNN       BAD APPLE or just a GREEN one
PCC Lou        SHOT, a big advantage right off the bat QB over GWB is
               that you do not need line numbers. :)
TRS80          SHOT: superior editing environment.
PC Kate        Oh, Lou, I always loved those line numbers, too. :)
PC Kate        Hi Mark, welcome to the DOS Forum. :)
PCC Lou        TRS, so true!  QB lets you edit with the mouse, etc.
PCC Chuck      QBASIC is a nearly complete subset of QuickBASIC 4.5...
               It's quite full-featured.

                                                              Send
```

Instant Messages

An Instant Message is a message sent to someone else online. Don't confuse Instant Messages with e-mail; unlike e-mail, Instant Messages work only when both the sender and the recipient are online at the same time.

An Instant Message sent to someone else in a chat room is something like whispering in class, though you'll never get in trouble for it. You'll probably encounter Instant Messages most often when you're in a room. It's then, after all, that other people know you're online. Instant Messages aren't limited to chat rooms, however: they work whenever you're online, wherever you may be.

A moment ago, we suggested a private room as an alternative to conference calls. You might also consider Instant Messages as alternatives to long-distance phone calls. Kathy and Tom live in different states from one another, and Ventana Press, our publisher, is located on the East Coast, across the country. While working on this book together, our phone bills were getting out of hand. Then we hit upon the idea of using Instant Messages for our conversations. We agreed on a mutual time to go online, and now we "talk" without worrying about the cost: all we pay for is our normal connect-time charge. One of our messages appears in Figure 10-10.

Figure 10-10: An Instant Message window contains one message at a time. You'll see a window when you initiate an Instant Message. You'll see another when you receive one. To respond, click on the Respond button and start typing in the new box that appears.

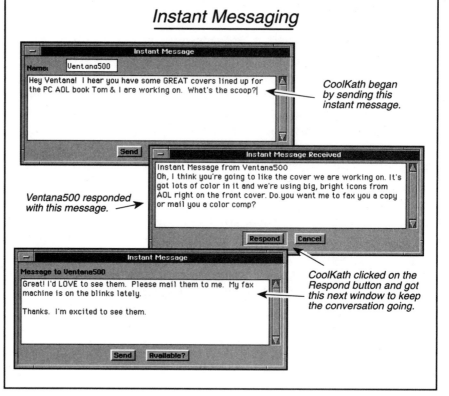

To send an Instant Message, choose Instant Message from the Members menu or type Ctrl-I. Enter the recipient's screen name and press Tab to move to the message area. Start typing and when ready to send, click on the Send button. If the recipient is available, you may see a response in a few minutes.

⚠ Before you send an Instant Message, use the Available button, pictured in Figure 10-10, or the Locate a Member Online command under the Members menu. If the recipient isn't online when you send an Instant Message, AOL tells you and you'll have to wait for another opportunity. (If a member is not available online, consider sending electronic mail, which is discussed in the next chapter.)

⚠ You cannot receive or send Instant Messages while in a free area such as the Members' Online Guide. AOL closes any open Instant Message windows when you enter a free area.

⚠ Determine where the intended recipient is before sending an Instant Message by choosing Locate a Member Online from the Members menu. This feature tells you if a member is in a chat room, in which case you may want to go to the room rather than send an Instant Message.

⚠ If the recipient is online but in a free area, is downloading or in some other way is unable to receive an Instant Message, AOL tells you, but only after it tries to deliver the message.

⚠ Instant Messages are accompanied by a double beep and they become the foremost window on your screen when they're received.

⚠ Since you only see one Instant Message at a time, you may want to copy and paste Instant Messages (handy for "phone call"-style Instant Messages such as those we as co-authors exchange) into a separate text file for later review.

⚠ If you don't wish to be disturbed by Instant Messages, you may turn them off at any time by sending an Instant Message to "$im_off" (without the quotation marks, but with the dollar sign and lowercase letters). To turn them back on, send an Instant Message to "$im_on."

Virtual romance

Robin Williams writes wonderful little books for computer users. Her book *The PC Is Not a Typewriter* (published by Peachpit Press) should be on every desktop publisher's shelf. Robin is the penultimate romantic: she's charmed by the Byronic, the poetic, the courtly. She writes:

"There was a letter in my mailbox. I didn't recognize the name of the sender. The letter quoted Hamlet, 'Tomorrow and tomorrow and tomorrow creeps in this petty pace from day to day, to the last syllable of recorded time....' The writer complained of a gloomy evening in Atlanta, wet and dark and lonely. I realized this person had probably done a search for users who listed Shakespeare as an interest in their bios. So I sent a letter back, which included, 'Hey, lighten up. Hamlet's dysfunctional. I know a bank where the wild thyme blows, where oxlips and the nodding violet grows.'

"We exchanged several other short letters. He was a 24-year-old son of a minister. I was a 37-year-old single mother of three, pure heathen. It was easy to be friends because neither of us expected anything from the other.

"One late night I was hanging around in the Lobby. I had only been connected to America Online for about a month, so I was still learning the etiquette and the conventions of online socializing. I heard a tinkling sound, as if someone threw fairy dust at me. [The sound a Macintosh makes when it receives an Instant Message.] On the screen was my first Instant Message, and it was from my friend. We sent a few messages back and forth, then he suggested we go to a private room. I had no idea what a private room was at that time, nor was I aware of what private rooms are generally used for. So I innocently tripped along with him to a room.

"I remember the feeling that night so clearly because it gave me a brief glimpse into the power of virtual reality. Meeting him in the Lobby that night was as if I saw him across the floor of a crowded room. He winked at me, nodded his head toward the hallway, and we snuck out and met in the corridor. We tiptoed down the hall and slipped into an empty room. It was very innocent; we chatted about our lives, history, philosophy, religion. I was so involved in this conversation that took place in the computer's nether world of digital bits and analog streams that when my neighbor walked into my room I jumped. I felt like she had intruded on a very personal moment, as if I had been caught in a dimly lit room, holding hands.

"Somehow, over the months, this unlikely relationship took an unexpected romantic turn. When I received a letter telling me how he had reached up with his left hand, reached into his fantasy, and pulled me down beside him, when he said, 'I would trade my loneliness for the warmth of her laughter; she would trade her nightgown for the cloak of a young man's affection,' when I found emotions raging in me that fought between my brain and my heart, I realized there were facets to human nature that this new medium of communication was going to expose in new and different ways. It was going to be an interesting summer."

Center Stage

America Online offers a special form of chat room called the Center Stage. This is the format AOL uses to present special guests or conferences or to offer "game shows" for members to play.

Typically, members attending a Center Stage event sit in "rows" of seats in the audience. Each row has up to eight seats. Your Center Stage window contains the text of everything that's happening on stage, along with comments from other members in your row. You won't see the comments from other rows. You can change rows if you like, as long as there's an empty seat in that row, and you can turn off the comments of members in your row if they're distracting.

Provision is usually made to submit questions or comments to the people on stage. The event's host receives your message and (optionally) delivers it to the guest for a response.

Center Stage schedules are posted in the Box Office. To get to the Box Office, click on the Center Stage icon in a chat room window (review Figure 10-2), or use the keyword: Center Stage (see Figure 10-11).

Figure 10-11: The Box Office lists all upcoming Center Stage events. Double-click on any one for details.

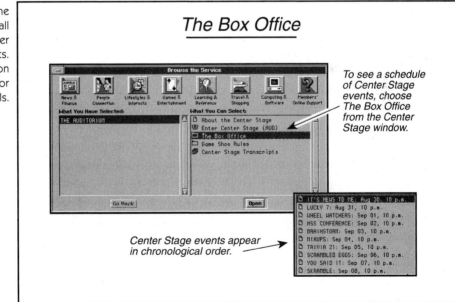

To see a schedule of Center Stage events, choose The Box Office from the Center Stage window.

Center Stage events appear in chronological order.

Rules for the Center Stage game shows are available by opening the Game Show Rules folder pictured in Figure 10-11. Read them before you take part in a game. Game shows are often profitable: winning contestants are awarded free connect time.

As we mentioned a moment ago, the Center Stage feature is often used to present conferences to members. One of those recently featured was the GeoWorks Ensemble Conference:

OnlineHost: Good evening! Welcome to the GeoWorks Ensemble Conference with your hosts, "GW Folks" and "GeoRepJohn." Tonight's topic is PC/GEOS and DOS versions. Bring your questions directly to the experts for quick and accurate answers. Remember that questions are received in the order shown so there may be a brief delay until your hosts get to yours. Welcome, GW Folks and John!

MegK: Hi everyone!

GW Folks: Hello everyone. I see some familiar names out there.

GWRepJohn: Hello everyone!!

MegK: We are anxious to hear what you have for us tonight.

GW Folks: We are talking on PC/GEOS and DOS tonight. Did everyone bring their DOS questions and ideas tonight?

OnlineHost: If you have a question or comment regarding the current event, please use the "Ask A Question" feature; for comments, the "Comment" feature. Input sent via those queues is received by your hosts in the order sent: first-come, first-served.

MegK: OK. Here is the first question:

Question: My computer will not go to geos when i turn it on...it is supposed to...and i don't know what i did...it says system error:cannot load proper file system driver

GW Folks: What is the person's name Meg? Are you using version 1.0 or 1.2?

MegK: MoShowman asked that question. Please answer GW Folks by the comment queue.

GWRepJohn: You need to edit your Autoexec.bat file and enter cd\geoworks and geos (v1.0) or Kernel (v1.2) as the last two lines.

GW Folks: When you state your question, please include which software version you are using, 1.0 or 1.2. Thanks.

MegK: We will go on, while we are waiting.

Question: Is it recommended to use FASTOPEN with 1.2?

GW Folks: Version 1.2 automatically removes Fastopen. It is recommended not to use it.

GWRepJohn: No it is not. If you want to improve performance, use a cache instead.

Question: I have problems formatting after one disk format on drive a:. I get error, unable to read disk.

GWRepJohn: Try to access the drive before you launch PC/GEOS. Can you format reliably from DOS?

GW Folks: That sounds like one we have heard before. Can you send specifics to the GW Generic mail box with your hardware setup? It would be good to know what system this is happening on to track this down better. Can you format in DOS?

Question: Is there any interest in incorporating sound (i.e. Sound Blaster VOC files) in to GWE?

GWRepJohn: No immediate plans for sound support, but that could change in the future.

Question: When will geos be network compatible?

GW Folks: It is network printing compatible now. For some networks, Novell, Lantastic, PCNFS, and a few others, we already recognize network disks.

Question: My geos.exe file locks up if I have sqplus.sys in my config.sys file. This program gives me a d: drv by my giving 20meg of my c: drv I can have a 40meg d: drv. What seems to be the problem?

GWRepJohn: Place REM at the beginning of the line with the sqplus.sys command. If your problems are solved then the driver must be the culprit.

GW Folks: This may be fixed in 1.2. Send information on who makes SQPlus.

MegK: We have a clear slate, everyone—so send in any PC or DOS questions to us. This is from Pos1:

Question: I would like to set up 2.0 on a network at work. What do I need to do? I know it's a big question but would help me a great deal.

GWRepJohn: V1.2 is the current version and it is network aware. You will need to install.

GW Folks:	You will be able to do that with 2.0 when it is released. We are working for 1992.
GWRepJohn:	a copy of GWE on each workstation.
GW Folks:	Pos1 you are the proud owner of a new GeoWorks Mouse Pad. Please send you full name and address to the GW Keva mail box and she will mail it to you.
MegK:	Nice going, Pos!
OnlineHost:	Our thanks to the folks from GeoWorks for a look at the Ensemble package. Remember, even though the "live" conference has ended, there's a wealth of information available online in the GeoWorks area of the service. Using keyword: "Geoworks" you can learn tips for using Ensemble that other member have taken the time to share. You might have some tips to share too!

Moving on

Many of those who are new to America Online sidestep People Connection at first. Perhaps it's too intimidating. Perhaps they're shy. Whatever the reason, it's a shame. People Connection is the heart of the AOL community. It is there that you finally stop thinking of AOL as an electronic service and begin thinking of it as people. In the search for community, People Connection is where you find the bounty.

One important aspect of interpersonal communications remains to be discussed, however: electronic mail. Perhaps nothing is as much a part of the electronic community as electronic mail, and AOL's version is especially comprehensive. It's so comprehensive it deserves its own chapter, and that chapter is coming up next.

Electronic Mail

CHAPTER 11

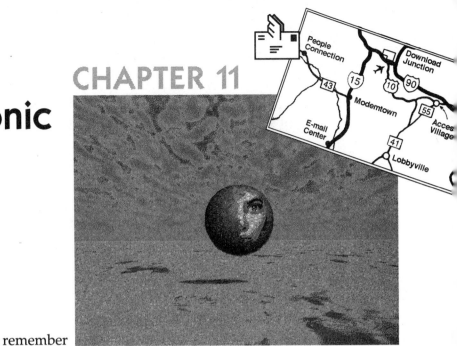

We remember days when the phrase "the mail" meant only one thing. If you wanted to mail something, you gave it to the postman or you left it in a mailbox. You put it in the mail. There was no UPS, no fax, no e-mail, no Internet and no FedEx. There was only "the mail" and it was the Post Office, and a stamp was three cents and that was that.

The information age has provoked alternatives: package delivery, overnight letters, facsimile, voice mail and e-mail. Each has its place. Each offers something the others do not. Electronic mail offers immediacy, convenience, multiple addressing and the ability to enclose computer data. Moreover, it's cheap—perhaps the least expensive of the bunch—and ecologically responsible. It has all the makings of a darling, and e-mail is just now entering its prime.

America Online's e-mail service is especially eminent. It does all the things e-mail should do, of course, and adds to that a magnificence of features that's enough to make a mail carrier resign. You can compose mail both online and off-line, address it to multiple recipients, send carbon copies (and blind carbon copies), attach (and receive) text files, receive and read mail online, reply to mail received and forward mail

---

Frontispiece graphic: "Alien," by Kai Krause. File search: Kai.

to another member. Mail can be sent to and received from anyone who subscribes to nearly any telecommunications service (not just AOL). It may be faxed, or—if the recipient is *really* in the dark ages—even sent via the US Mail.

What exactly is electronic mail?

Electronic mail (e-mail for short) is simply mail prepared on a computer and sent to someone else who has a computer. There are lots of private e-mail networks—computers wired together and configured to send and receive mail—and lots of public e-mail networks, like America Online.

A number of characteristics are common to most e-mail systems:

- Messages are composed of pure ASCII text. Fancy formatting, graphics and special characters aren't accommodated within messages.

- Because they're pure text, messages may be sent between dissimilar computers. You can communicate with people using Macs, Amigas, mainframes—even terminals, which aren't really computers at all.

- The addressee must be known to the mail system.

There are additional features offered by some e-mail systems, including America Online:

- Files may be attached to messages. In most cases, files are specific to a particular computer or operating system, so the receiving computer must be compatible with the sending computer in order to open the file. On the other hand, files may contain anything: graphics, formatted text, even sound and animation.

- Messages may be replied to or forwarded to other members.

- Messages may be addressed to multiple recipients. "Carbon copies" may be sent to people other than the addressee, and "blind" carbon copies (copies sent without the other addressees' knowledge) may be specified as well.

- Received messages need not be read when they're received. Any incoming message may be filed and saved as a text file for later retrieval and read at your convenience.

Why use e-mail?

Nothing matches the convenience, immediacy and ecology of electronic mail. Composing a message amounts to nothing more than typing it; mailing a message is accomplished with a single click of the mouse; and AOL files a copy for you automatically. There is no long-distance calling. Archaic inconveniences such as envelopes and stamps are never required, and fax funny paper—an ecological disaster if there ever was one—never enters the picture. Indeed, paper of any kind is not necessary when mail is sent electronically.

America Online obediently holds your mail until you're ready to read it, announces its availability every time you sign on and never sends you junk mail. Not ever.

Perhaps best of all, about all you'll ever pay for this service is a nickel—maybe a dime if you're really pedantic. It's not exactly a return to the three-cent stamp, but it's close.

A circular exercise

Before we get to the details, here's an exercise in futility that might clarify the role of electronic mail.

△ With America Online up and running, sign on. Leave the Welcome screen showing and choose Compose Mail from the Mail menu. The Compose Mail window will appear (see Figure 11-1).

△ The insertion point is now flashing in the To text box—where you insert the screen name of the person to whom you wish to send e-mail. For practice, type in your own screen name. This is the futile part of the exercise: sending mail to yourself is a little like narcissism—a little less vainglorious perhaps, but no less futile. Nevertheless, do it just this once. Nobody's looking.

Figure 11-1:
This window
appears whenever
you choose
Compose Mail from
the Mail menu. AOL
has already
identified you as
the sender; it's now
waiting for you to
identify the
recipient.

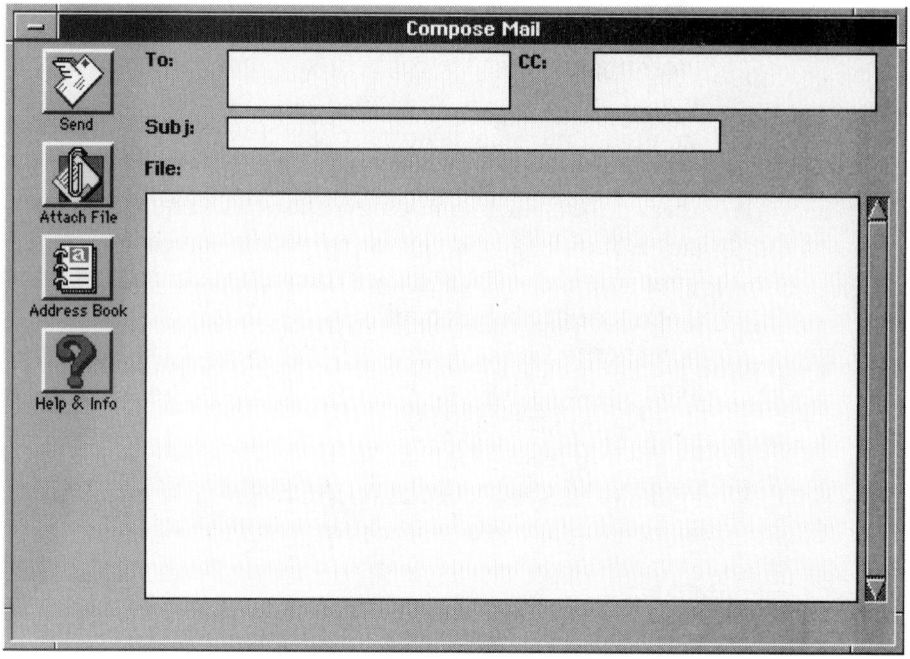

Compose Mail
To: **CC:**
Send   **Subj:**
Attach File   **File:**
Address Book
Help & Info

Screen names made easy

Few people—even those who know America Online well—know that screen names are not case sensitive. *Major Tom* works no better than *majortom*. Moreover, screen names function independent of spaces. Even if a screen name contains a space, it doesn't need it. *Cool Kath* is the same person as *CoolKath*. This is really comforting: we had a tendency to fret these kind of details with a mania approaching obsession, worrying that imperfectly addressed mail would end up in electronic limbo somewhere at AOL headquarters in Virginia and that no one would be the wiser. It was a futile mania (as most are). If you fail to capitalize a screen name or you leave out a space, AOL won't mind. (It does reject any substitution of a 0 [zero] for an O and vice versa.)

If you misspell a screen name, America Online immediately notifies you that there's no match for the screen name you've typed. In other words, you can't misaddress mail to another member, unless of course you just happen to correctly spell another member's screen name in your error. However, there's no "dead mail" room at AOL.

<ul>
<li>▲ Tap the Tab key once to move the cursor to the subject text box and enter the word "Test."</li>

<li>▲ Move the cursor to the message text box and type a message. This is the pretentious part when you're writing to yourself—don't overdo it. People will talk.</li>

<li>▲ Click on the Send icon.</li>
</ul>

As long as you don't already have unread mail, a double beep instantly announces you have mail. There's a particular comfort in that. Mail moves around the AOL circuit quite literally at the speed of light. You'll never wonder again if your mail will get to its destination by next Thursday. It gets there the instant you send it.

Note also that two more things have happened: 1) the mail icon on the Welcome screen has a letter stuffed into its envelope, and 2) a tiny mailbox appears (see Figure 11-2).

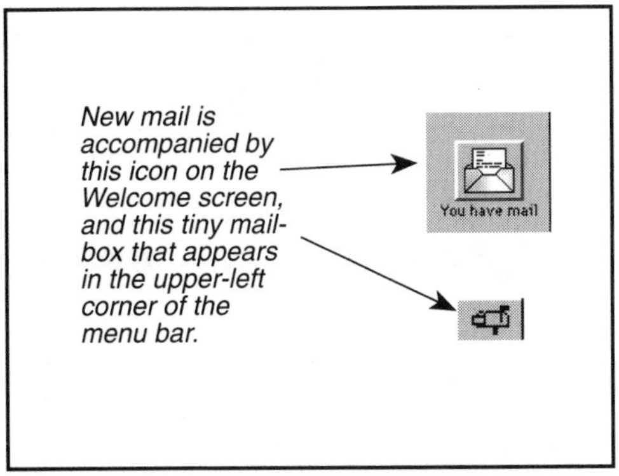

Figure 11-2:
America Online
wants you to
know when you
have mail.

New mail is accompanied by this icon on the Welcome screen, and this tiny mailbox that appears in the upper-left corner of the menu bar.

You have mail

<ul>
<li>▲ By now, the untitled window has closed and you receive a prompt indicating your mail has been sent. Click on the OK box and you'll be back at the Welcome screen.</li>

<li>▲ Click once on the envelope icon. The New Mail window appears (see Figure 11-3). This window is a little redundant when you only have one piece of mail waiting, but soon you'll be a Popular Person and dozens of entries will appear here every time you sign on.</li>

<li>▲ Double-click on the entry, which represents the mail you sent a moment ago.</li>
</ul>

Figure 11-3: The
New Mail window
appears whenever
you elect to read
incoming mail.

```
┌─────────────────────────────────────────────────────────────┐
│  ─                        New Mail                         ▲  │
│  ┌──────────────────────────────────────────────────────┐ ▲ │
│  │ 07/26 CoolKath Test                                  │ │ │
│  │                                                      │   │
│  │                                                      │   │
│  │                                                      │   │
│  │                                                      │   │
│  │                                                      │   │
│  │                                                      │   │
│  │                                                      │   │
│  │                                                      │ ▼ │
│  └──────────────────────────────────────────────────────┘   │
│                        [ More... ]                           │
└─────────────────────────────────────────────────────────────┘
```

🔺 The message window appears, identifying the subject, the date and
time sent, who sent the message, the service the mail originated
from, when they sent it, and what they had to say (see Figure 11-4).

Figure 11-4:
The mail as it's
received. Note
that replying,
forwarding and
downloading an
attached file are all
accomplished with
a single mouse
click on one of the
icons at the left of
this window.
(We'll discuss
attaching files later
in this chapter and
downloading files
in Chapter 12.)

```
┌─────────────────────────────────────────────────────────────┐
│  ─                          Test                           ▲  │
│  ┌───────┐ ┌──────────────────────────────────────────┐ ▲   │
│  │ [🖉]  │ │ Subj: Test                               │ │   │
│  │ Reply │ │ Date: 92-07-26 17:17:44 EDT              │ │   │
│  ├───────┤ │ From: CoolKath                           │     │
│  │ [📄]  │ │ To:   CoolKath                           │     │
│  │Forward│ │ Posted on: America Online                │     │
│  ├───────┤ │                                          │     │
│  │ [🗒]  │ │ Hi Kathy!                                │     │
│  │Reply to All│                                        │     │
│  ├───────┤ │                                          │     │
│  │ [⬇]   │ │                                          │     │
│  │Download File│                                       │     │
│  ├───────┤ │                                          │     │
│  │ [🕐]  │ │                                          │     │
│  │Download Later│                                      │ ▼   │
│  └───────┘ └──────────────────────────────────────────┘     │
│                        [ Next→ ]                             │
└─────────────────────────────────────────────────────────────┘
```

It's probably best for you to put this mail away now, before anyone sees what you've done. To close the Mail window, double-click on its Close box. You can also double-click on the Close box of the New Mail window to close it now. We just wanted you to see how simple, fast and easy the process really is. That's the whole idea—above all, e-mail should be convenient, and America Online certainly makes it so.

 Mail menu

All day-to-day mail activities can be performed using the Mail menu. You'll notice several key combinations next to items on the menu that can also be used to execute those specific activities (see Figure 11-5).

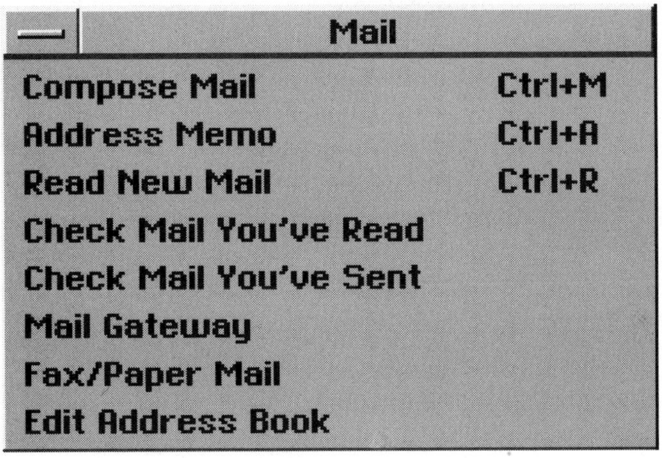

Figure 11-5:
The Mail menu
handles all your
daily e-mail
activities.

Mail	
Compose Mail	**Ctrl+M**
Address Memo	**Ctrl+A**
Read New Mail	**Ctrl+R**
Check Mail You've Read	
Check Mail You've Sent	
Mail Gateway	
Fax/Paper Mail	
Edit Address Book	

Composing your mail

The first option on the Mail menu is Compose Mail, which you choose whenever you want to send mail to someone. This option is available whether you're online or off—you can compose mail off-line and send it when you log on.

When the Compose Mail option is chosen, America Online responds with a window labeled Compose Mail (see Figure 11-1).

Note the position of the insertion point on your screen. It's located within the To field of the window. America Online, in other words, is waiting for you to provide the recipient's screen name. Type it in. (If you don't remember the screen name, use the Address Book, which we'll discuss later in this chapter.)

You may send mail to multiple addresses if you wish. Simply include multiple screen names in the To field, separated by a comma after each additional name. A space following the comma is optional. AOL will insert one for you. If you want to send mail to Steve Case, Tom Lichty and Kathy Parks, place "Steve Case, MajorTom, CoolKath" (without the quotes) in the To field.

Tap the Tab key and the cursor will jump to the "CC" (carbon copy) field. Here you can type the screen names of those people who are to receive "carbon copies" of your mail. Carbon copies are really no different than originals. Whether a member receives an original or a copy is more a matter of protocol than anything else. *Note*: Use only screen names in the To and CC fields. Do *not* put members' real names here. A member's screen name is his or her address, which ensures that mail will arrive at the correct computer location. Real names do not work unless they're actually the screen name as well.

Blind carbon copies

As is the case with the traditional "CC:" at the bottom of a business letter, the addressee is aware of all carbon copies. This is a traditional business courtesy.

On the other hand, you may want to send a copy of a message to another member without the addressee (or addressees or CCs) knowing you have done so. This is known as a "blind" carbon copy. To address a blind carbon copy to a member, place his or her screen name in the CC field, *enclosing it in parentheses*. No one but the recipient of the blind carbon copy will know what you've done. The ethics of this feature are yours to ponder; its use, after all, is voluntary.

Use the Tab key to move the insertion point to the Subject field, and enter a description of up to 32 characters in length, counting spaces and punctuation. *Note*: The Subject field must be filled in—AOL won't take the message without it.

Press the Tab key again. The insertion point will move to the message text area. Type your message there (see Figure 11-6).

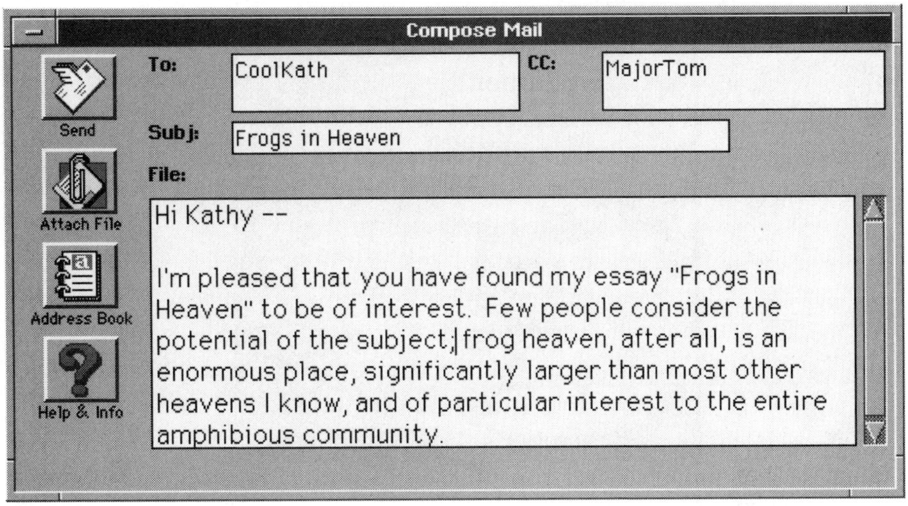

Figure 11-6:
The completed
message is ready
to send.

Compose Mail

| | To: | CoolKath | CC: | MajorTom |

Send

Attach File

Address Book

Help & Info

Subj: Frogs in Heaven

File:

Hi Kathy --

I'm pleased that you have found my essay "Frogs in Heaven" to be of interest. Few people consider the potential of the subject; frog heaven, after all, is an enormous place, significantly larger than most other heavens I know, and of particular interest to the entire amphibious community.

With the message completed, click on the Send icon if you're online. America Online will take care of your mail from there (see Figure 11-7).

Figure 11-7:
America Online
displays a box that
tells you your mail
has been sent.

Your mail has been sent.

OK

Preparing mail off-line

Consider preparing mail when you're off-line and the meter isn't running. You can linger over it that way, perfecting every word. When you complete a message, you'll notice that the Send button is dimmed (unavailable). You may choose Compose Mail from the Mail menu again to compose another message. A second Compose Mail window will appear on top of the first. Continue this until all desired messages are composed, each time layering a new window in front of the previous one. When ready to send, click on the Go To menu, select Set Up & Sign On, and complete the signing on process (see Figure 11-8).

Figure 11-8: You
may sign on from
the Go To menu
using the Set Up &
Sign On option.

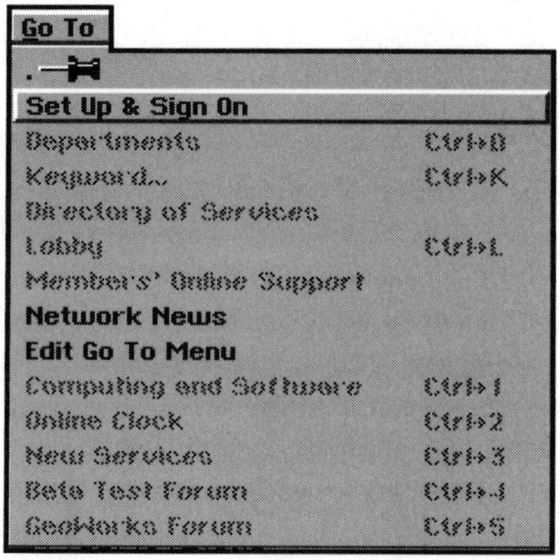

When completely signed on, the top message window's Send button
will be active. Click it and AOL will send the message. Continue to
click each successive Send button until all messages are sent. If you
decide you don't want to send a message, simply use the Close window box to close it. (We'll talk about saving messages later.)

Addressing a memo

Occasionally, you may want to send a text file to another member.
Perhaps it's a file you've created with the New command (File menu),
or a text file you captured online. Regardless of the source, you can
send text files as mail (rather than as a file). To do this, make sure the
file is open and is the topmost window on your screen. Then choose
Address Memo from the Mail menu.

When you do, America Online furnishes the Compose Mail window
(see Figure 11-1) and places a copy of your text file in the message area
for you. All you have to do is supply the name of the recipient and the
subject, and send it on its way.

This command is especially useful for those who prefer to use a word processor to compose messages. Word processors feature spelling checkers and productivity tools that AOL's Compose Mail utility doesn't offer. If you prefer to use your word processor, be sure to save the word-processing document as text only, then use the Address Memo command to send it as mail. Of course, if you prefer to copy and paste text messages between other GeoWorks applications and AOL, that works too. Just remember that any formatting contained in a specific application's file will be lost or altered when pasted into an AOL Mail window. (Refer to Appendix E for more information about using GeoWorks applications in conjunction with America Online.)

A pain in the neck

Because there's no eye contact nor voice intonation in e-mail messages, sometimes it's necessary to punctuate your conversation with textual "smileys," as they're called. Smileys clarify the sender's intention when it might otherwise be misinterpreted. The phrase "Just as I thought, Billy Joe: there are no forks in your family tree" could be interpreted slanderously. Follow it with a smiley, however, and most members will understand your attempt at depraved humor: "Just as I thought, Billy Joe: there are no forks in your family tree. ;)"

The semicolon-parenthesis combination at the end of the sentence above is a wink. Turn your head 90 degrees counterclockwise and you'll see a little "smiley face" with its right eye winking. It's a pain in the neck, but it's better than making enemies.

Below are some of the more common smileys. Some members use them more than others, but most everybody does eventually.

:)	Smile
;)	Wink
:D	Laughing out loud (also abbreviated "LOL").
:(	Frown
:/	Chagrin
{}	Hug (usually plural: {{{{}}}} Why hug just once?)

These are the smileys we see most often online. There are scores of others we've seen— :# (lips are sealed), :& (tongue tied), :[(pout), :* (kiss) and :0 (yell). But our favorite is :p (sticking out tongue). (We actually list more of our favorites in Chapter 13, "Ten Best.")

All of this is a little like those inane yellow smiley faces that punctuated the '70s, but it's justified here. Misinterpretation of text is easy; smileys help clarify the meaning. Go ahead: smile at someone today. ;)

Reading new mail

The next option on the Mail menu—Read New Mail—refers to mail you've just received (see Figure 11-9).

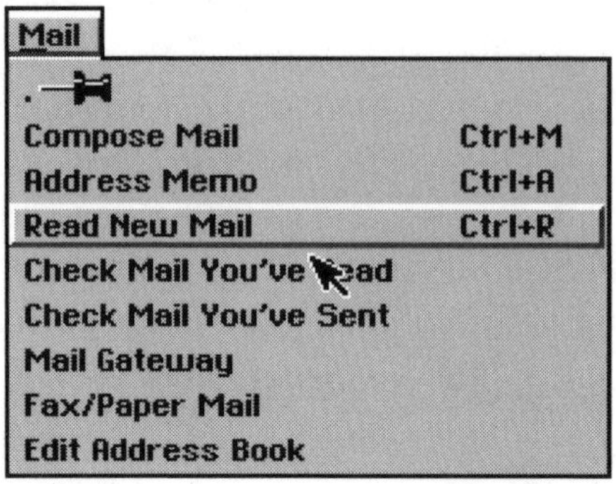

Figure 11-9: The Read New Mail option provides another opportunity to read unread mail.

Mail	
Compose Mail	Ctrl+M
Address Memo	Ctrl+A
Read New Mail	Ctrl+R
Check Mail You've Read	
Check Mail You've Sent	
Mail Gateway	
Fax/Paper Mail	
Edit Address Book	

In addition to accessing new mail by clicking on the envelope icon in the Welcome screen or the tiny mailbox on the Menu bar, you can also select Read New Mail from the Mail menu. In all cases, the New Mail window appears, allowing you to select the mail you want to read.

Mail is like Christmas morning to us. We can't wait to read it. Nonetheless, there are those who don't share our enthusiasm, choosing not to access the New Mail window immediately upon signing on. And that is probably why AOL provides this menu option. With it, mail can be read at any time.

A fourth option

You may have noticed the "Ctrl +R" on the menu next to the Read New Mail option. These are keyboard shortcuts to perform the function they describe. In addition to the three other ways to read new mail, you can also hold down the Ctrl key and press "R" (without the quotes) and access the New Mail window.

Though Figure 11-3 shows only one unread piece of mail, a number of e-mail messages may appear here. If more than one shows up, they will appear in the order in which they were received at America Online. The most recent mail will be at the bottom, the oldest at the top.

In other words, to read your mail in chronological order from oldest to most recent, read 'em from top to bottom. Double-click on the first one, and America Online displays that message (see Figure 11-10). When you are finished reading the first piece of mail and want to go on to the second piece without going back to the New Mail window, click once on the Next button at the bottom of that window.

Figure 11-10: The message window allows you to read, reply to and forward, or move on to the next piece of your mail.

```
┌──────────────────────── Frogs in Heaven ────────────────────────┐
│ ┌──────┐  Subj: Frogs in Heaven                                  │
│ │      │  Date: 92-07-26 17:32:06 EDT                            │
│ └──────┘  From: CoolKath                                         │
│  Reply    To:   CoolKath                                         │
│ ┌──────┐  CC:   MajorTom                                         │
│ │      │  P▭▭▭▭▭▭▭▭▭▭▭▭▭▭▭▭▭▭▭▭▭▭▭▭▭▭▭▭▭▭▭▭▭▭▭▭                  │
│ └──────┘                                                         │
│ Forward   Hi Kathy --                                            │
│ ┌──────┐                                                         │
│ │      │  I'm pleased that you have found my essay "Frogs in Heaven" to │
│ └──────┘  be of interest. Few people consider the potential of the subject; │
│ Reply to All  frog heaven, after all, is an enormous place, significantly larger │
│ ┌──────┐  than most other heavens I know, and of particular interest to the │
│ │      │  entire amphibious community.                           │
│ └──────┘                                                         │
│ Download File                                                    │
│ ┌──────┐                                                         │
│ │      │                                                         │
│ └──────┘                                                         │
│ Download Later                                                   │
│                        ┌──────┐                                  │
│                        │ Next │                                  │
│                        └──────┘                                  │
└──────────────────────────────────────────────────────────────────┘
```

Replying to Mail

Once you have read your mail, you can reply to it, forward it to another member, close the window or move on to the next piece. We'll tell you how to reopen it in a few moments. Each of these options is accomplished with a click of the mouse. To reply to a piece of mail, simply click on the Reply icon pictured in Figure 11-10. Actually, all the Reply icon does is call up a Compose Mail window with the To and the Subject fields already filled in with the appropriate information (see Figure 11-11). Aside from these two features, a reply is no different from any other message. You can add to the To and CC fields if you wish, and discuss any subject that interests you in the message text. You can even change the Subject field or remove the original recipient's screen name from the To field, though this somewhat defeats the purpose.

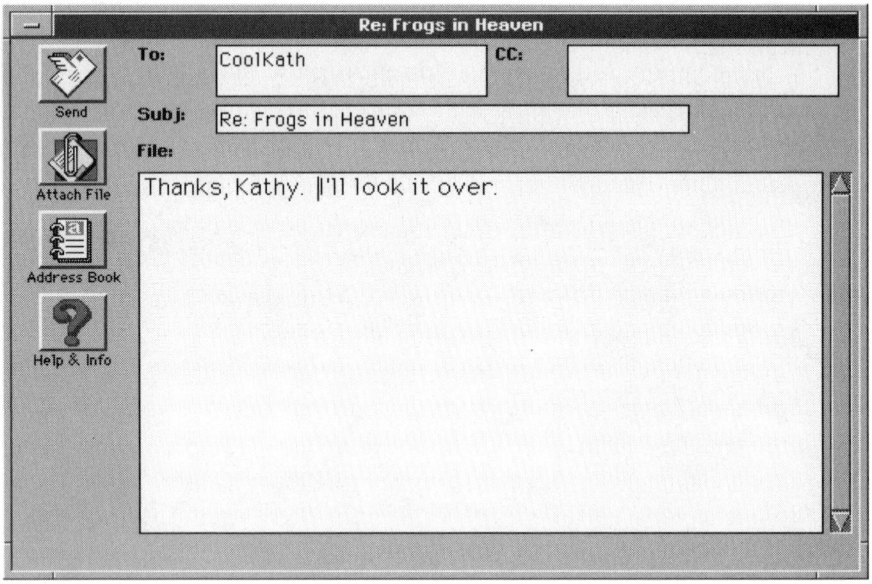

Figure 11-11: The Reply mail window. Note that the To and Subject fields are already filled in.

Re: Frogs in Heaven
To: CoolKath **CC:**
Subj: Re: Frogs in Heaven
File:
Thanks, Kathy. I'll look it over.

Send · Attach File · Address Book · Help & Info

Replying to all

Look once again at Figure 11-10. Note that there are two reply icons, including one marked "Reply to All." Reply to All allows you to reply to everyone who was sent a message, including any carbon-copy addressees. In other words, you have your choice of replying only to the original sender ("Reply") or to everyone who receives a message ("Reply to All").

Note: Reply to All does *not* reply to blind carbon-copy addressees. The rule here is: Reply to All replies to all whose screen names are visible to the recipients in the Mail window. If you don't see a name (which would be the case if someone received a blind carbon copy), that person won't receive your reply.

Replying with a copy of the original

Some people get lots of mail. Steve Case, for instance, gets 50 or 60 pieces a day. For Steve's benefit, we always include a copy of his original message when we reply. We do this to help him remember the subject of our discussion. Rather than copy and paste his message into a Reply window, we use the Forward icon. Remember that forwarded mail includes a copy of the original message along with your comment. If you add a comment to a piece of mail and forward it back to the sender, you have actually *replied*, with a copy of the original attached. This little trick also works when you want to reply to a message which the sender may not recall.

Since a copy of the original message gets sent along with the reply, replying by using the Forward icon is an inefficient way of handling mail. Most significantly, the Stratus has to store much more data for forwarded mail. Stratus storage problems, however, are not our concern. The people at AOL are gonna love us for telling you about this.

Forwarding mail

Occasionally you may get mail that was not copied (CC) to someone else you feel should see it. With a click of the mouse, you can remedy this. To forward a piece of mail to another member, simply click on the Forward icon pictured in Figure 11-10. America Online will respond with a slightly modified Compose Mail window (see Figure 11-12).

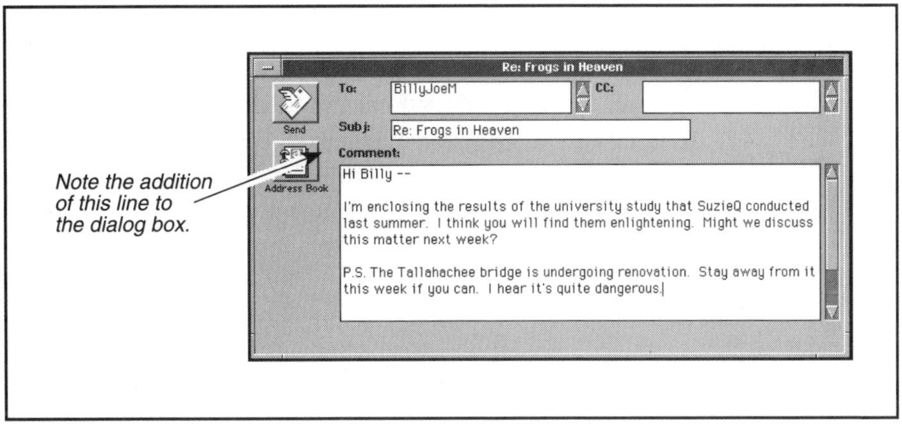

Figure 11-12:
The forward mail window provides an opportunity to add a comment to a piece of forwarded mail.

Note the addition of this line to the dialog box.

The window pictured in Figure 11-12 is where you enter your forwarding comment and the screen name of the person who is to receive the forward. The new recipient then receives the forwarded mail with your comment at the top. America Online clearly identifies forwarded mail by including a line at the top of the message which declares it as forwarded mail and identifies the person who sent it (see Figure 11-13).

Figure 11-13: Forwarded mail is identified to the recipient in the message winow by this line in the message header.

This addition to the message header tells you this is a forwarded message.

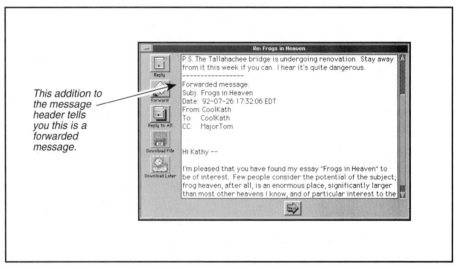

Checking mail you've read

We all forget things now and again: "What did Billy Joe say in that message he sent before he went to Tallahatchee?" That's why AOL provides the Check Mail You've Read option under the Mail menu.

When you choose this command, AOL responds with the Old Mail window (see Figure 11-14).

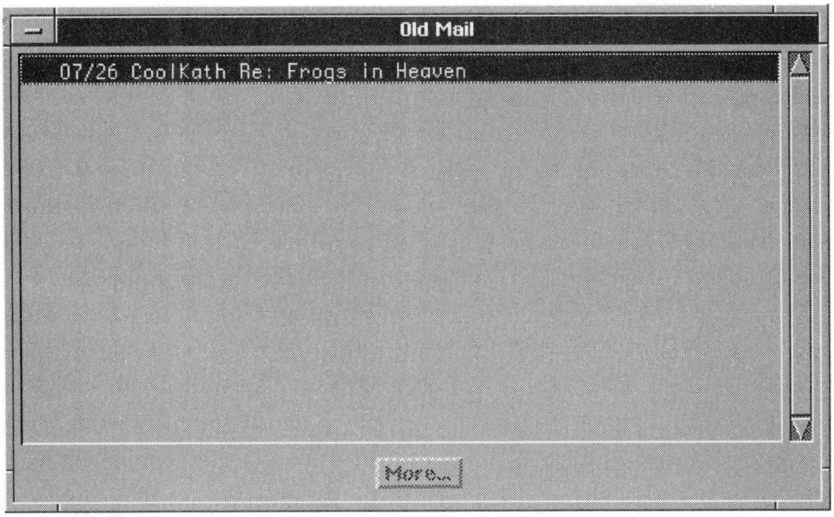

Figure 11-14:
The Old Mail
window lists all of
the mail you have
read, just in case
you forget.

Old Mail

07/26 CoolKath Re: Frogs in Heaven

More...

There are no surprises here. Double-click on any message in the window and you can re-read it. Re-read mail can be forwarded and replied to just like any other mail.

More likely, you will use this feature to recall things you've read for inclusion in other messages. This is an effective way of discussing an ongoing subject with another member: "When you said <<your demeanor reminds me of frog's breath>> what exactly did you mean?" In this example, material inside of the chevrons (<< >>) has been copied from a document you've read, then pasted into the current message. Direct quotes like this are hard to refute.

Checking mail you've sent

Occasionally you may want to review mail you have sent to other members: "What exactly did I say to Billy Joe McCallister that caused him to visit the Tallahatchee Bridge last night?"

Everything you send is retained for at least a week (or until the recipient reads it, if it goes unread for more than a week) and may be recalled by choosing Check Mail You've Sent from the Mail menu (see Figure 11-15).

Figure 11-15:
You may review
mail you have sent
with the Check
Mail You've Sent
option under the
Mail menu.

Mail
· ⊨
Compose Mail   Ctrl+M
Address Memo   Ctrl+A
Read New Mail   Ctrl+R
Check Mail You've Read
Check Mail You've Sent
Mail Gateway
Fax/Paper Mail
Edit Address Book

When you choose this option, America Online displays a listing of all the mail you have sent within the last seven days (see Figure 11-16).

Figure 11-16:
Double-click on
entries in this
window to read
outgoing mail.

```
┌──────────────────────────── Outgoing Mail ───────────────────────┐
│ → ·                                                               ▲│
│  07/26 CoolKath Frogs in Heaven                                   ║│
│  07/26 CoolKath Test                                              ║│
│                                                                   ║│
│                                                                   ║│
│                                                                   ║│
│                                                                   ║│
│                                                                   ║│
│                                                                   ║│
│                                                                   ║│
│                                                                   ▼│
│                       ┌─────────────┐  ┌─────────┐                 │
│                       │ Show Status │  │ More... │                 │
│                       └─────────────┘  └─────────┘                 │
└───────────────────────────────────────────────────────────────────┘
```

While you read mail you've sent, you can select and copy it, then paste it into other documents. This works especially well for reminder notices, clarifications and nagging. It may save you some typing as well: you may need to send a message that's a near-duplicate of one you sent four days ago. Rather than retyping text from the old message, re-open it using Check Mail You've Sent under the Mail menu, copy the sections you need, and paste them into a new message window.

Note: Even though you can review mail you've sent, you can't modify or cancel it. Just like the US Mail, once correspondence has been posted, it can't be changed or unmailed.

Checking the status of read mail

Look again at Figure 11-16. Do you see the Show Status button? If you ever need to know if and when a piece of your mail was read, click on this button (see Figure 11-17).

Figure 11-17:
You can check to
see when your
mail was read by
clicking on the
Status button in
the Mail You Have
Sent dialog box.

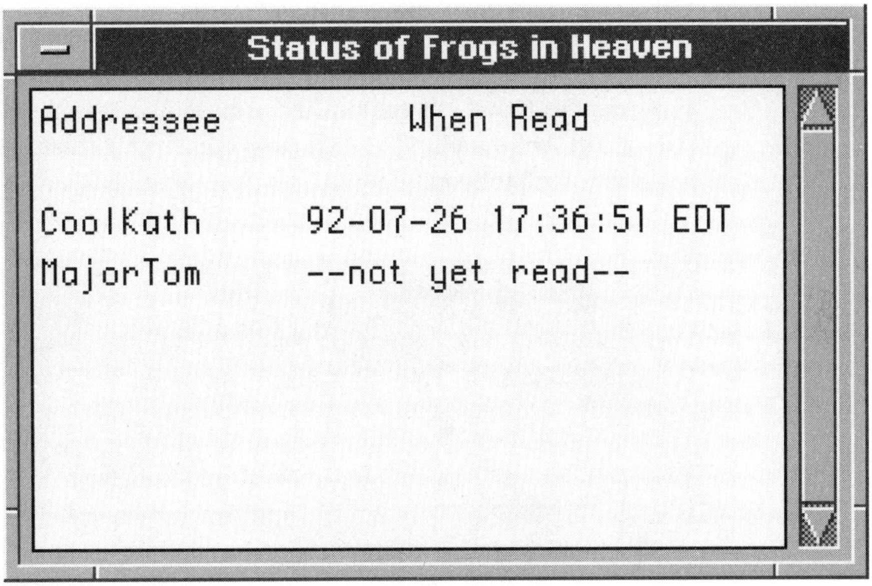

Status of Frogs in Heaven

Addressee	When Read
CoolKath	92-07-26 17:36:51 EDT
MajorTom	--not yet read--

Improve your status

The Show Status button in the Mail You Have Sent window not only reminds you of when you sent a message, it tells you when all the other addressees (primary and carbon-copy) read the message as well. If you sent the Tallahatchee message to Billy Joe and two other AOL members, and something untoward happened to him at 10:00 PM that night, you might want to know who read the message *before* then.

The Address Book

America Online provides an address book just like the address book next to your telephone. In effect, AOL's book is a cross-reference, listing people's real names and their corresponding screen names. Our recommendation is that you use the Address Book, even if you only have a name or two to put there now. Eventually, you'll have scores of entries in your Address Book, and you'll be glad they're there.

Adding a name to the Address Book

No one memorizes screen names. Screen names are eccentric composites of letters and numbers like "MikeQ4506" that AOL's sign-on software cooked up when the member first joined, or something cute like "DerringDo," which the member created later, when AOL's default screen name became insufferable. Either way, most screen names are eminently forgettable. That's why AOL provides an address book.

Of course, before you can use the Address Book, you have to put some names there. It's easy. Choose Edit Address Book, from the Mail menu and America Online will provide the Address Book Editor window (see Figure 11-18).

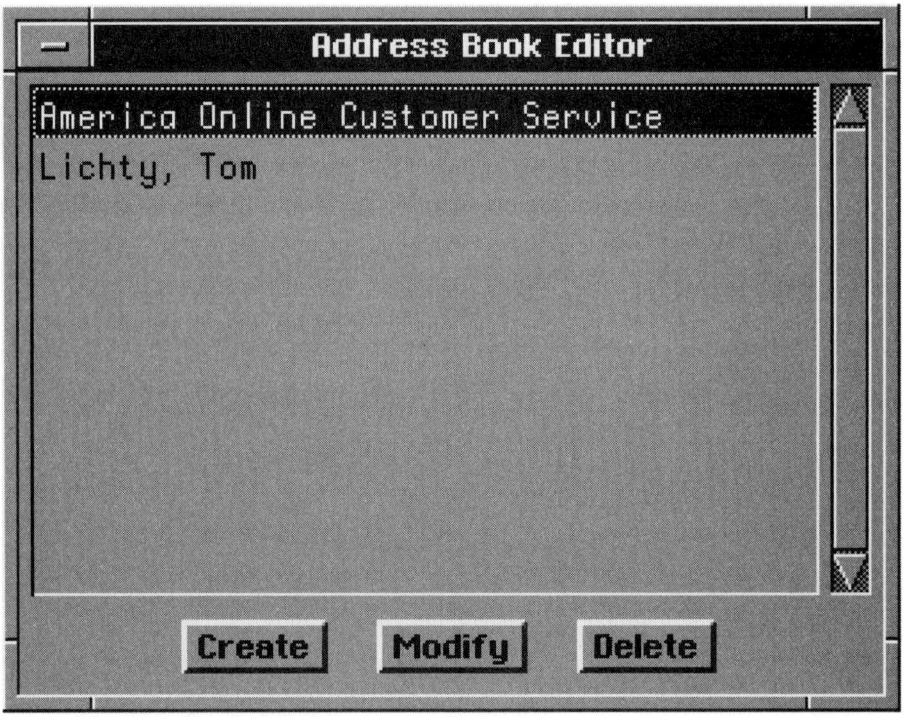

Figure 11-18:
The Address Book
Editor window
allows you to
create, modify and
delete entries.

To add an entry to your Address Book, click on the Create button. America Online will provide the editing form pictured in Figure 11-19.

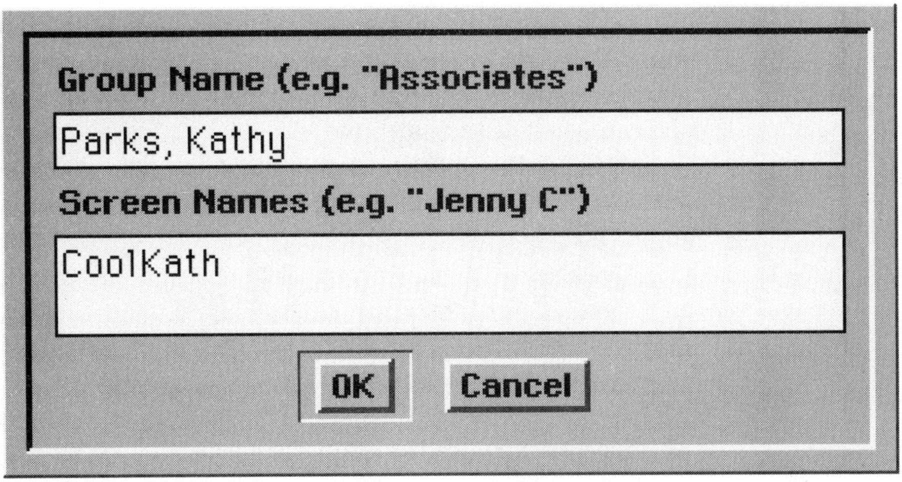

Figure 11-19:
The Address Book
editing form.

Group Name (e.g. "Associates")

Parks, Kathy

Screen Names (e.g. "Jenny C")

CoolKath

OK   Cancel

Type the person's real name in the Group Name field, last name first
(so your Address Book will look like a phone book), then type their
screen name in the Screen Names field. (Don't know the screen name?
Look it up using the Member Directory, discussed in Chapter 3,
"Online Help & the Members.") The next time you choose Edit Address
Book from the Mail window, the new name will appear there (see
Figure 11-20).

Figure 11-20:
The Address Book
Editor window
now includes the
additional entry.

Address Book Editor

America Online Customer Service
Lichty, Tom
Parks, Kathy

Create   Modify   Delete

Now you're ready to use the Address Book whenever you prepare mail. Look again at the Compose Mail screen (see Figure 11-1). Do you see the icon marked Address Book? If your Address Book is current, you can use it to look up people's screen names and plug them into the To and CC fields of the Compose Mail window. When you click on the Address Book icon, the "Address this memo to:" window appears (see Figure 11-21).

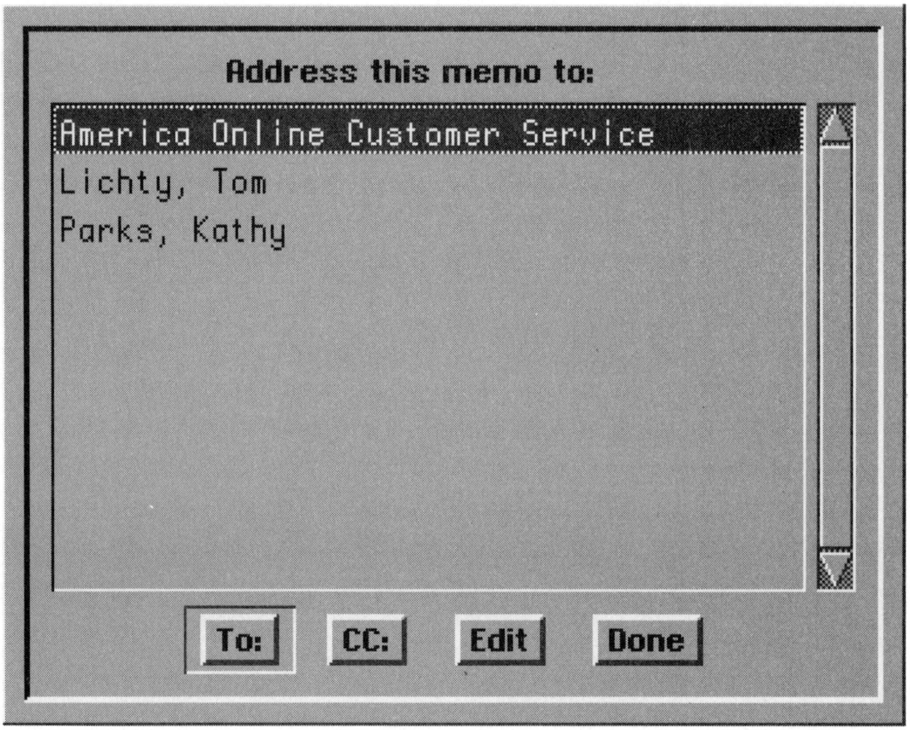

Figure 11-21:
The "Address
this memo
to:" window.

Address this memo to:

America Online Customer Service
Lichty, Tom
Parks, Kathy

| To: | CC: | Edit | Done |

Now all you need to do is click on the entry that you want, then click on the To or CC button at the bottom of the screen. When finished, click on the Done button. America Online will enter the properly spelled screen name at the desired point in the Mail window. All it takes is a few clicks of the mouse.

You'll notice an Edit button at the bottom of the "Address this memo to:" window as well. This takes you directly to the Address Book Editor window, where you can make changes or create new or delete existing addresses (see Figure 11-20).

Multiple accounts

If you look again at Figure 11-19, you'll notice that there's room for multiple screen names in the Screen Names field. You may wonder why.

Imagine that you're participating in an online discourse on frog's feet with three other esteemed biologists. Nearly every piece of mail on the subject has to be sent to all three of them. In this situation, you might want to create an entry in your address book called Froggers, and list all three screen names in the Screen Names field. Simply enter screen names separated by a comma, just as you would enter multiple names in the To and CC boxes in the Compose Mail screen. Once you have done so, all you have to do is select Froggers from your Address Book to send mail to all three.

Gorilla food

Okay, you e-mail Thunder Lizards: here's your raw meat. Read this section and you'll take your place among the e-mail illuminati. Mortals will climb mountains to seek your wisdom; the masses will genuflect as you pass by; your aura will illuminate the sky.

Saving your mail

A while back we mentioned that e-mail to us is like Christmas morning. We anticipate it with ardor. We descend into a pit of depression if a beep doesn't indicate mail when we sign on. Consequently, we've developed a cadre of online friends and correspond with them regularly. This means we get a lot of mail. Right now, as we're writing this book, we're sending and receiving a half-dozen pieces of mail a day. Filing mail is critical: we require access to it that's convenient, fast and *electronic*. We copy and paste messages frequently, and a paper filing system just won't do. We're also interested in environmental issues and the thought of paperless electronic mail is promising. Our e-mail filing system is the bedrock of our online experience.

You may be facing the same need. Because of the Christmas-morning quality of America Online's e-mail system, lots of people get lots of mail, and lots of people need to be thinking about a filing system. Now's the time to bring the subject into the open.

The process

Each piece of mail you send or receive can be saved as a file on any drive, in any directory or subdirectory you choose. Every time you read a new piece of mail, highlight the portion you want to save and choose Save As from the File menu. At the next window, you can select the drive, directory and subdirectory you want.

Once you have determined that, replace the "Untitled" file name with the file name of your choosing. Press Enter or click once on the Save button at the bottom of the box.

Filing strategies

If your mail is infrequent, a single subdirectory for all your mail may prove beneficial. Any time you save mail, save it to that subdirectory. If you have more frequent mail, you may want to create subdirectories by years, months or even weeks and store your mail there.

If you're like us, you may want to use a people-based strategy. We have subdirectories named after each person with whom we regularly correspond. Each time we receive mail, we save it into that person's subdirectory. If we receive mail from an infrequent correspondent, we have a miscellaneous file.

Another type of filing strategy is subject-based. You may choose this method if your online mail relates best to a number of subjects. Perhaps you use America Online to plan your travels. You may have developed some acquaintances in the Travel Club or be receiving confirmations from EAASY SABRE, AOL's online travel reservations service (see Chapter 7, "Travel & Shopping"). You may be clipping articles from Wine & Dine Online, the excellent restaurant, food and wine forum. If your interests are varied, you might develop a number of files for each of your destinations.

These strategies can be combined, of course, and they aren't the only ones. There are no doubt scores of others. What we're trying to do is convince you of the importance of filing your mail. Decide upon a method, set it up to your satisfaction and maintain it faithfully. You will become a better citizen of the e-mail community if you do.

File-naming conventions

Files can, of course, be named anything with eight or fewer characters and up to three characters in the extension. Each name must be unique within that subdirectory. If you don't use the date-based strategy, you

might want to include the date in your file names; if you don't use the people-based strategy, you may want to include the person's name or initials in your file names.

Accessing these files

The files you have been saving are in pure ASCII text. When you want to access and read these files in AOL later, the command is as simple as choosing Open from the File menu.

A file can also be opened through most other text-editing programs outside of AOL—a word processing program, for instance. Again, simply provide the drive, directory, subdirectory (if any) and file name with extension. There's your file, ready to be read or edited.

Save the header, too

Most of the filing strategies described here rely on the storage not only of received mail, but mail you have sent as well. All you need to do is copy each piece of mail you send and paste it into the appropriate file. Here's a tip: choose Read Mail You've Sent from the Mail menu and open the mail to be copied from there. Mail retrieved this way contains America Online's header information— date, time, CCs and blind CCs—the retention of which should be considered a necessity in any mail-filing system. If you simply Copy text from the message field of a Mail window, it won't contain all this information.

Attaching files to messages

Understand that we're not talking in the abstract here: files are files. Files may include text, graphics, data, sound, animation—even programs. Any of these files can be attached to a piece of e-mail. When mail is received with an attached file, the file is then downloaded in its native format.

Which is astounding. File transmission requires elaborate protocols and error-checking. Not a single bit or byte can be displaced. Most other telecommunications services make you decide upon one of many cryptic protocols with names like Kermit and XModem. You also have to determine the number of data bits, stop bits and the parity setting your system needs. There are about 50 potential configurations for file transfer and usually only one of them will work in a given situation.

Forget about all of that. You needn't become involved. America Online handles it all invisibly, efficiently and reliably. If you want to send a file, all you have to do is click on the Attach File icon (review Figure 11-1), choose the drive, subdirectory and file name of the file you want to send and AOL takes care of it from there.

Figure 11-22 follows a telecommunicated file from beginning to end. The journey spans half a continent—from Oregon to Mississippi—but only costs pennies.

Use attached files appropriately

Before the recipient can do anything with an attached file, it has to be downloaded, saved and (usually) viewed with some kind of program other than America Online itself. This is something of a nuisance for the recipient. In other words, don't send attached files when a simple e-mail message will do.

You may be tempted, for instance, to send a word-processed file to another member instead of a conventional message. Perhaps the message is long, or you want to format it, or you just prefer your word processor over AOL's text editor. Resist the urge. America Online can handle e-mail messages up to 8k in length (about 15 pages). No one expects fancy formatting when it comes to e-mail, and you can always send unformatted word-processed files by using AOL's Address Memo command under the File menu. Attached files should never be sent when simple messages will do.

Figure 11-22:
Across the country
and back via MG-
TD. (Illustration by
Rich Wald,
Computing and
Software Library.)

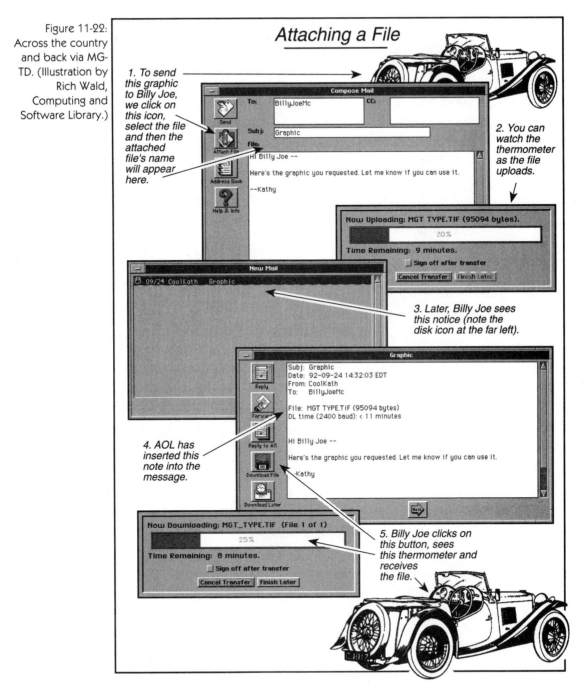

Attaching a File

1. To send this graphic to Billy Joe, we click on this icon, select the file and then the attached file's name will appear here.

2. You can watch the thermometer as the file uploads.

3. Later, Billy Joe sees this notice (note the disk icon at the far left).

4. AOL has inserted this note into the message.

5. Billy Joe clicks on this button, sees this thermometer and receives the file.

E-mail alternatives

The world is not a perfect place. No one can really predict the weather, computers don't always address envelopes reliably, and *some* people still aren't online. What if you want to communicate with these heathens? You could write them a letter, but that requires paper, an envelope (there's that word again), a stamp and a trip to a mailbox. You could phone them, but an answering machine will probably take the call (and your money as well, if it's long distance). You could try telepathy or ask Scotty to beam you there, but these are emerging technologies and you know how reliable they are (remember *The Fly*?).

Paper mail

Instead, use America Online to send 'em a letter. All you have to do is type the letter and click on a few buttons (see Figure 11-23). A few days later, a real paper letter in a real paper envelope will arrive at your declared destination, looking for all the world like you typed it yourself. The cost for this service is somewhere between the cost of the US Mail and the cost of a long-distance phone call, and it's no more difficult than sending e-mail. This brings such a convenience to communicating that it almost eliminates procrastination.

Speaking of procrastination, when was the last time you wrote to your mother?

Note that the only difference between sending regular e-mail and sending US Mail is the address. If America Online sees "@usmail" in an e-mail address, it automatically triggers the address-request dialogs you see pictured in Figure 11-23.

Note: Zip codes are required, and AOL verifies that the zip codes indicated match the cities in both the return and mailing addresses. If they don't, you'll receive an "invalid US Mail address" error and be sent back to the offending entry.

Figure 11-23:
Sending a message
via US Mail
involves
completing return
and mailing
address forms
before
confirmation.

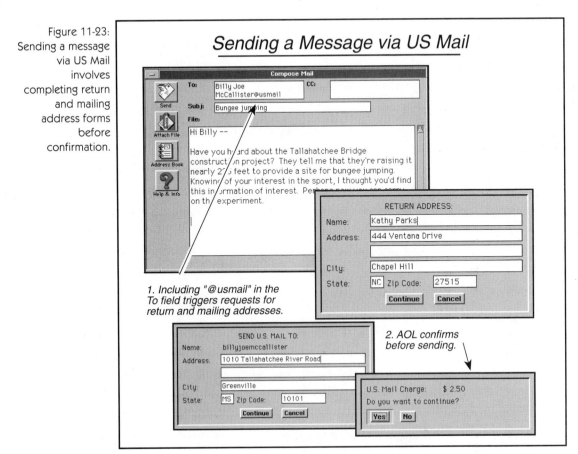

Figure 11-23: Sending a message via US Mail involves completing return and mailing address forms before confirmation.

Sending a fax

Perhaps your mother owns a fax machine (doesn't everybody?). You can save a few cents and a few days over paper mail by sending her a fax instead. Again, America Online stands ready to serve, even if you don't own a fax machine yourself. The process is no more complicated than sending paper mail—or e-mail, for that matter (see Figure 11-24). Again, an @ sign in an address triggers the dialog.

Figure 11-24:
Fax mail differs
little from
normal e-mail.

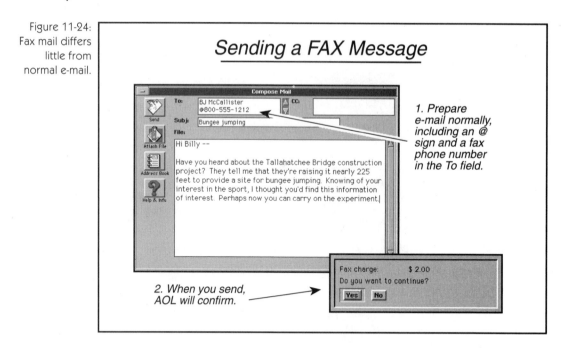

Within a few minutes after sending fax mail, America Online will send e-mail to you confirming the transmission of the fax message (see Figure 11-25).

Figure 11-25:
Once your fax has
been successfully
transmitted,
America Online
sends you this
message via e-mail.

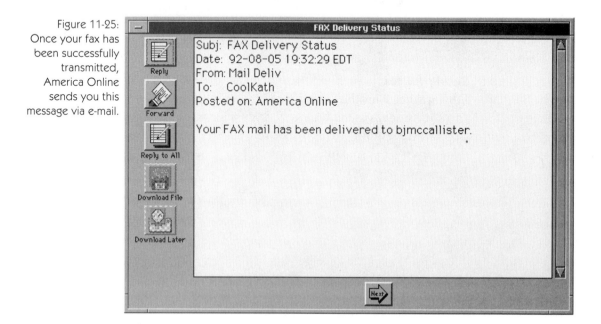

The fine print

- Fax and paper mail can be sent to multiple addresses. Complete the To field just as you would for e-mail, separating the recipients' names with commas. You will be charged for each address, however.

- All charges are billed to your online account.

- Paper mail requires a valid zip code.

- Fax addressee names cannot exceed 20 characters, including spaces and punctuation. Paper mail addressee names are limited to 33 characters.

- You cannot attach files to either fax or paper-mail messages. In other words, both services are plain text only.

- Both fax and paper-mail messages wrap to 70 characters on a line. Fax pages each contain a maximum of 60 lines. Paper-mail messages contain 40 lines on the first page (to make room for the address) and 53 lines on all others.

- Forced page breaks may be declared: Type ">>> PAGE BREAK <<<" (again, without the quotes) on a line by itself. This works for both fax and paper mail.

- Paper mail is limited to four pages. Fax mail is limited to 24k.

- Include your real name (as opposed to your screen name) in the text of both fax and paper mail.

- In either case, you will receive a confirmation identifying all charges before America Online sends your mail (refer again to Figures 11-22 and 11-23). If, after reviewing the charges, you decide you don't want to send the mail or the fax, you can cancel at that point.

The Internet mail gateway

Much as we loathe to admit it, America Online is not the world's only telecommunications service. In fact, the granddaddy of all telecommunications services is the Internet, the place where electronic mail was born. The Internet is an international linkage of thousands of systems like AOL, spanning millions of users in 33 countries. Since it is used heavily by government and educational institutions, the Internet is funded by federal subsidies and charges nothing for access.

As far as e-mail distribution goes, the Internet is to AOL as the Universe is to Walla Walla, Washington—and it has similar potential. Think about it—most of the world's telephone systems are linked together in such a way that nearly anyone can place a call from any phone in the world to any other phone in the world. Why can't the computers of the world do the same? No doubt they will someday, and the Internet may very well be their liberation.

Three years in search of 75 cents

Cliff Stoll is an astronomer. Since astronomers do a lot of computer modeling, Cliff is also fairly adept at computers. That's a good thing, because there isn't much work for astronomers, and there is for computer operators, especially at Cliff's level.

Which is how Cliff Stoll came to be involved with Internet and Milnet, an Internet branch which ties together thousands of unclassified computers in the Army, Navy and Air Force. When we asked Cliff to contribute to this book, he wrote:

"Hmmm... military computers on a network? A group of German programmers, adept at breaking into computers, decided to make money from their skills. For a year, they snuck into dozens of systems across the Milnet, copied data from them, and sold this information to the Soviet KGB. They were high-tech spies. With keyboards and modems, they exploited security holes in distant computers. Once on a system, they scanned for sensitive material, passwords or pathways to other computers. For a year, they went undetected. Then they bumped into me.

"In August 1986, while managing an astronomy computer in Berkeley, California, I noticed a 75-cent accounting error. Someone had used a few minutes of computer time without a valid billing address. Curious...just nickels and dimes, but worth checking into. *Zooks*, but what I found! Using a printer and several PCs I watched someone sneak through my system, onto the Milnet, and then steal information from military systems a thousand miles away.

"Instead of locking him out of my system, I let him prowl through it, quietly tracking him back to his roost. The trace took a year, but in the end, we proved that five guys were spying over the computer networks. They were convicted of espionage in 1990."

For the whole story, read Cliff's book, *The Cuckoo's Egg*. It's the true story of tracking a spy through the maze of computer espionage, and it ought to be required reading for any user of the Internet. Cliff's Internet and AOL addresses are in the front of his book and, like us, he loves to receive mail.

Buy a copy of his book, read it, then send him some e-mail telling him you heard about it here.

America Online includes an Internet mail gateway (keyword: Internet) that allows you to send electronic mail to anyone on any online service that has a similar gateway. It's like connecting the Walla Walla phone system to AT&T. Through the Internet, you can communicate to e-mail users on other systems throughout the world, including AT&T Mail, AppleLink, CompuServe and MCI Mail.

AOL doesn't charge extra for this service. All you pay is America Online's standard connect-time charges.

Internet e-mail is composed and sent just like any other, only the address is changed. To address an Internet user, simply place the recipient's Internet address in the To field of the Compose Mail form (see Figure 11-26). It's the same concept as adding the area code to a phone number when out of the local area.

Note: You may notice mysterious times, dates and places in the header and footer of your message. Ignore that. It's the Internet's record of how the mail was processed and is of little interest to the typical user.

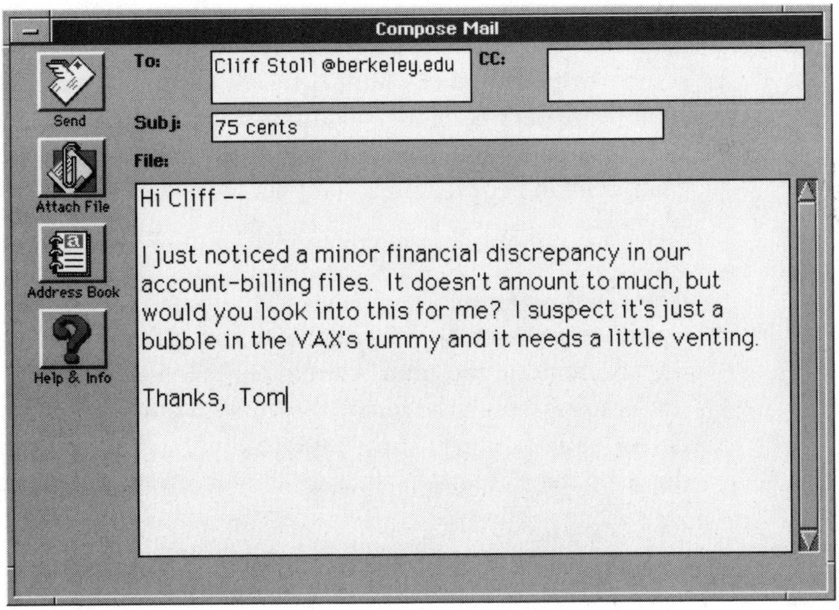

Figure 11-26:
Sending mail via
the Internet is no
different than any
other AOL e-mail,
only the address
has changed.

	Compose Mail
Send	**To:** Cliff Stoll @berkeley.edu **CC:**
Attach File	**Subj:** 75 cents
	File:
Address Book	Hi Cliff --
	I just noticed a minor financial discrepancy in our account-billing files. It doesn't amount to much, but would you look into this for me? I suspect it's just a bubble in the VAX's tummy and it needs a little venting.
Help & Info	Thanks, Tom|

To reach a few of the more common Internet-connected services, use the following address formats:

Location	Short Address	Example
CompuServe	cis	12345.678@cis
MCI Mail	mci	name@mci
AT&T Mail	att	name@att
AppleLink	apple	name@apple

Remember, besides what you'll find using the keyword: Internet, there's no formal documentation for the Internet, and that means there's no Internet membership directory. AOL's Internet gateway is like connecting Walla Walla to AT&T *without* a phone book. You must know the addressee's *exact* Internet screen name, including all the periods, dashes, underscores and @ signs. America Online can't help you with Internet screen names; you simply have to know who you're talking to. There's one thing we can tell you, however: if you're an AOL member, you already have an Internet address. Just provide your AOL screen name ahead of "@aol.com" (without the quotes): MajorTom@aol.com, for instance, or CoolKath@aol.com. They have a nice ring, don't you think? Put your Internet address on your business card: certain people will be *very* impressed.

Moving on

Could there be more? Oh yes. AOL can queue files for later download-ing and resume files that were interrupted during downloading.

These features are unique to America Online. They're known as the Download Manager. They're incredible, but not indescribable. And describe them is what we're about to do: just turn the page.... 🔜

The Download Manager

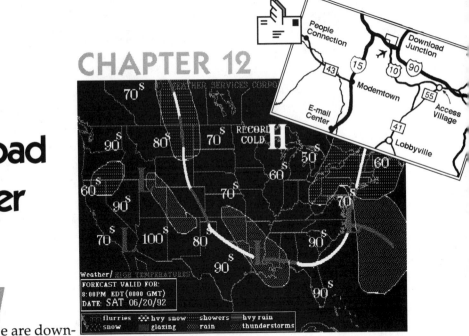

W e are down-loading zealots. We both beta-test software, some of which has to be downloaded. We collect utilities, fonts and graphics for desktop publishing ventures. We're constantly downloading snippets from the Writers' Forum and probably download three or four hours' worth of material a week.

Downloading a single item is one thing; Version 1.5 provides a "Log off when finished" button so the meter doesn't keep running while we've gone somewhere else during the process. But, if we wanted to group together a number of items to download, we'd have to sit there and wait for one to finish before we could start the next.

Additionally, as you learned in Chapter 11, you can receive mail from another member that includes a file they have attached to their document. When this occurs, your mail displays an icon of a 3.5-inch disk, giving you the option of downloading that file right then or later.

Happily, America Online lets you download multiple files in imme-diate succession and automatically sign off when you are finished—without you even having to be there.

You also can continue your current session and download later when you're almost ready to log off. All this is possible because of the Down-load Manager.

Frontispiece graphic by Weather Services Corporation, transmitted via satellite to America Online (keyword: Weather).

The Download Manager at Work

Downloads probably offer more potential than any other AOL feature. Tens of thousands of files reside on the Stratus's hard disks, with hundreds of new ones being added each week. And every one of them can be downloaded to your computer.

Using the Download Manager, you can establish a queue of files while you're online. Just before you sign off, you can instruct the Download Manager to download the files and the system to sign off when the download is complete.

After the process begins, you can walk away and the downloading will take place in the background. You'll automatically be logged off when the downloading is finished. If you are a GeoWorks user and have the complete GeoWorks software installed (not just the portion of it needed to run AOL), you can work on other GeoWorks applications while AOL downloads in the background. But be aware that any work you do while downloading will detract from the speed and efficiency of your modem and will therefore result in longer download times. (For more on using AOL wit GeoWorks, see Appendix E.)

Let's watch a typical Download Manager session to see what the screens look like. We'll schedule two files for downloading; then we'll instruct the Download Manager to handle the downloading process and sign off automatically.

Selecting files for downloading

Figure 12-1 illustrates the process of selecting a weather map for downloading. Weather maps arrive at AOL throughout the day via satellite and are never more than a few hours old. Moreover, they're small: they always download in five minutes or less.

Figure 12-1: The last step in selecting a weather map for delayed downloading is to click on the Download Later button, resulting in the dialog box at the bottom of the illustration.

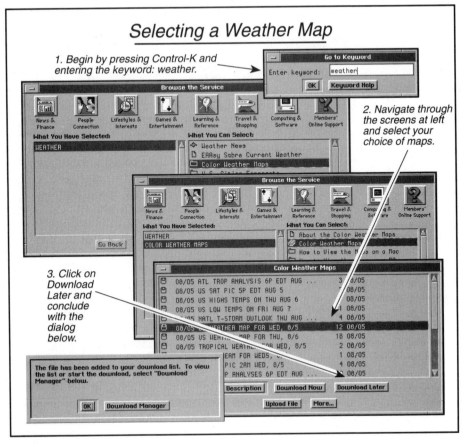

This prompts the next screen to appear, giving us the choice of continuing or going right to the Download Manager. We might as well give the Download Manager more than one thing to do; so let's select another file to add to the download queue. A Mike Keefe political cartoon seems appropriate (see Figure 12-2).

Figure 12-2:
Selecting a Mike
Keefe cartoon is
similar to selecting
a weather map.

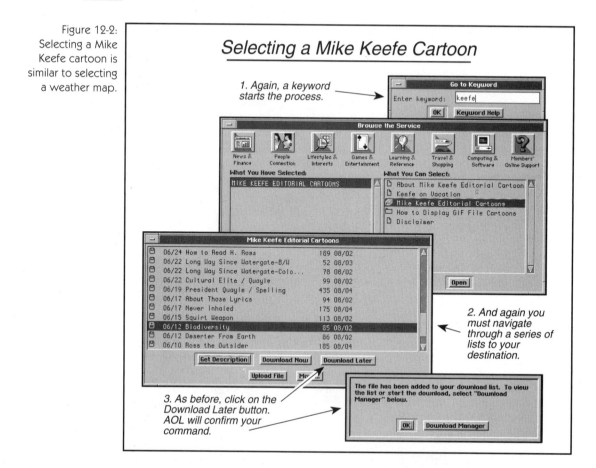

He's a blues musician, too

Mike Keefe has been drawing political cartoons for the *Denver Post* for 15 years. He won the 1991 Fischetti Editorial Cartoon Award, and has been recognized by Sigma Delta Chi and the National Headliners Club, winning its highest honors. His work also appears in *USA Today*, the *New York Times*, the *Washington Post*, *Time*, *Newsweek*, and *U.S. News and World Report*. His online cartoons are available Monday, Wednesday and Friday by 9:00 PM Eastern time. You can reach him online via the screen name "dePIXion." You can find his cartoons by using the keyword: Keefe.

When we asked Mike for permission to use a cartoon in this book, he sent the one pictured in Figure 12-3. Mike, if you think it's a rat race being a cartoonist, try writing books for a living.

Figure 12-3: Mike Keefe posts new cartoons every week on America Online.

Running the Download Manager

Meanwhile, back at the keyboard, we've decided to call it a day. Rather than sign off, we can click on the Download Manager button or choose Download Manager from the File menu.

Figure 12-4: The Download Manager window lists all files scheduled for download, including sizes, destinations and the estimated amount of time required to download the entire queue.

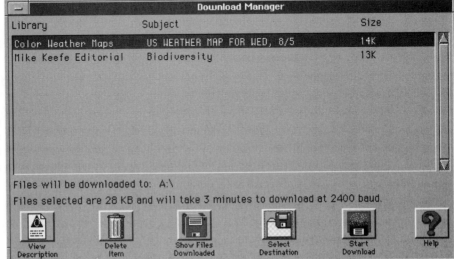

Note the icons across the bottom of Figure 12-4. This is an impressive array of commands. America Online wants you to have complete control over the downloading process, especially now that it's about to begin. Let's review those icons:

- *View Description* is the same as the View Description button when you're browsing a file library. It's handy to have this command here: though you may have read a file's description a half-hour ago, chances are you remember nothing about it now that you've reached the Download Manager window. Lots of things could have happened in the interim. This icon saves a long trip back to the file's original location to review its description.

- *Delete Item* allows you to remove a file (or two, or three) from the list. Sometimes, enthusiasm exceeds resources.

- *Show Files Downloaded* lets you review your past 50 downloads from within the last seven days, after which time, each is deleted. There is no value in downloading the same file twice. Though America Online will warn you if you try to download a file you have already downloaded, you can save yourself the trouble by checking this list first.

- *Select Destination* allows you to declare a destination directory or subdirectory other than the AOL Downloads subdirectory, which is the default. *Note*: All the files in the queue must download to the same folder.

- *Start Download* begins the download process. We will use it in a moment.

- A click on the *Help* icon produces the Download Manager help screens.

> ### Pick up where you left off
>
> Occasionally, the downloading process is interrupted. Lightning strikes. A power cord gets tripped over. The phone line develops a stutter. These kinds of things don't happen often; but when they do, they always occur when you're 80 percent of the way through a 47-minute download. *Poof!* There goes 38 minutes of connect time.
>
> That's why the "% Complete" column appears in Figure 12-4. If a file was interrupted during a download, this column declares the interruption and assures you that only the missing portion of the file will be downloaded, not all 47 minutes' worth.

The downloading process commences when the Start Download icon is clicked (see Figure 12-5).

Figure 12-5: The Download Manager session ends with a display of information like this.

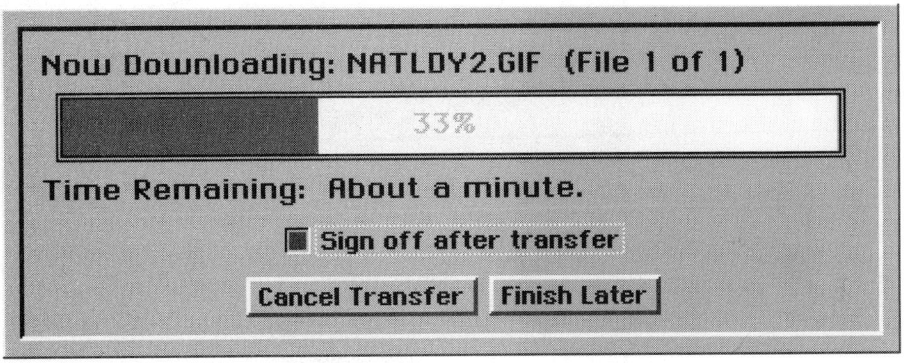

Now Downloading: NATLDY2.GIF (File 1 of 1)

33%

Time Remaining: About a minute.

■ Sign off after transfer

| Cancel Transfer | Finish Later |

Look again at Figure 12-5. When the "Sign off after transfer" box is checked, you can walk away from the computer while all this is going on, secure in the knowledge that you'll automatically be signed off when everything has been downloaded satisfactorily.

When it's all over, we have two nice, big graphics to tack to the wall (see Figure 12-6).

Figure 12-6: Tack a weather map and a political cartoon to your wall each day; people will think you're clever, erudite and urbane.

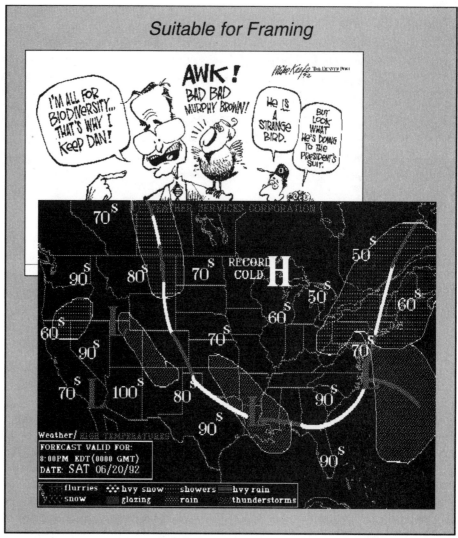

GIF files

Because America Online serves several different platforms of computers, it's imperative that different graphic formats are accommodated.

Fortunately, a number of generic graphic formats have emerged, including TIFF, EPS and GIF. Perhaps you noticed that the weather map and cartoons we just discussed were GIF (Graphics Interchange Format) files. These were developed specifically for the telecommunications industry. The format accommodates color, grayscale and black-and-white graphics with equal aplomb. It's also a very efficient format: more data is packed into each GIF byte than practically any other graphics format.

Moving on

After reading about the complexities of the Download Manager, you might think it's not for you—that it's more trouble than it's worth. But many users find it an invaluable feature, and once you get the hang of it, you'll be batch-downloading like a true professional. Now reward yourself for reading this far by turning the page. The "Ten Best" chapter follows; it's the pot of gold at the end of the rainbow.

Ten Best

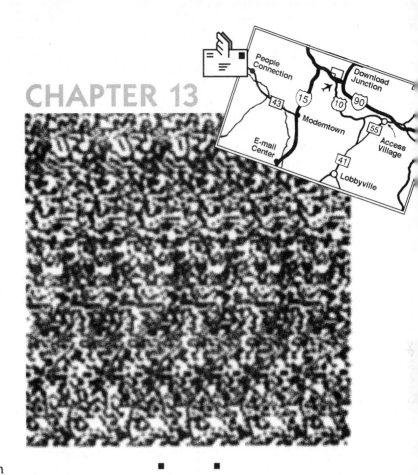

■   ■

CHAPTER 13

When Tom
was a boy, he believed that if he remained quiet and cooperative all day and all night Christmas Eve, Santa would be especially generous to him. For one 24-hour period every year, he was a model child. He did everything that was asked of him, exactly as requested. He must have been right: nowadays he receives paperweights and paisley ties on Christmas mornings rather than the electric trains and red wagons he received back in the days of deference.

Have you been naughty or nice? You haven't turned to this chapter first, have you? This chapter is a reward for faithful readers only. This is our Ten Best chapter, and we award it only to those who have read all of the preceding 12 chapters. If that's you, read on....

Frontispiece graphic by Jim Leftwich. Keywords: File Search; use the criterion "Bela Julesz" (the Bell Labs researcher who discovered the random-dot stereogram visualization method depicted here). To see the encoded image, stare at the two squares below the graphic, crossing your eyes slightly, until the two squares become three. Maintaining that focus, shift your gaze upward. You will see a circular contour of a three-dimensional terrain. This is arguably one of the ten-best graphics posted on AOL.

Ten best tips

Since we're discussing honor and privilege, let's begin with a list of the ten best tips for using America Online. Most of these tips represent methods by which you can save time online (so you save money); all of them will make your online experience more efficient and effective; and not a one of them is dishonorable.

1. **Read this book.**

   If you're reading this paragraph in spite of the admonition on the previous page, at least plan to read the rest of this book eventually. It's full of insights and techniques—not only ours, but those of scores of other members as well. You don't have to be online to use this book. Take it on your next blue-water cruise: people will think you're very erudite, recondite and jocose.

2. **Use keywords and keyboard shortcuts.**

   This tip is so important that we've included two appendices—Appendix A and B—listing AOL's keywords and keyboard short-cuts, respectively. Keywords can save you tons of time. Don't worry about committing them all to memory, just memorize those you use often. (Your most frequently used keywords should be added to your Go To menu, which is explained in Chapter 6, "Lifestyles & Interests.") Keywords take you to locations that normally require the navigation of menus within menus within menus, and they do it in less than a second. To enter a keyword, type Ctrl-K; to see an online list of keywords, type Ctrl-K and click on the Keyword Help button.

   Some of AOL's keyboard shortcuts are worth memorizing: Ctrl-K to enter a keyword, Ctrl-M to compose new mail, Ctrl-F to find a member, Ctrl-I to send an Instant Message—that's only four. It won't take long to learn them.

3. **Use Ctrl-X.**

   Speaking of Ctrl-key combinations, also learn Ctrl-X. Ctrl-X halts printing and halts long articles, downloads and lists as they are received online. That's important: sometimes you'll double-click on an article icon (articles are discussed in Chapter 6) only to find that you got yourself into a four-minute feed that you don't want to read after all. No problem: type Ctrl-X. The same goes for lists: Ctrl-X stops a list of Mail You Have Read, for instance, which may contain hundreds of entries.

4. **Compose mail off-line.**

   The Compose Mail command (Mail menu) works off-line as well as on. You can compose all of your mail off-line while the clock's not running, perfecting every phrase. You can even attach files while you're composing mail off-line. When you have finished composing a piece of mail, just leave the Compose Mail window open on your desktop. You can repeat this as often as necessary to accommodate multiple pieces of outgoing mail, accumulating Compose Mail windows like—well—junk mail (though we're hardly suggesting an analogy). When all of your composing is finished, sign on and start sending. It's that easy.

5. **Use help.**

   Whenever you have a question about AOL, try choosing Help from the menu bar (online or off), or using the keyword: Help (online only). AOL offers more avenues of help than Revlon has hair colors, and most of them are free of connect-time charges. Read Chapter 3 ("Online Help & the Members") if you haven't already.

6. **Keep track of your time and money.**

   It's easy to lose track of time and money when you're online, but no one—neither you nor AOL—benefits from unexpected charges when the bill arrives. You can always check your current (and previous) month's bill by using the keyword: Billing (which is free), and the keyword: Time tells you how long you've been online during any particular session.

7. **Log your sessions and save to disk.**

   Don't spend time reading material online that can just as easily be saved and read later while off-line, when the meter is no longer running. Logging is a mechanism that allows you to capture all the text you encounter online without stopping to read it—whether it's text from the encyclopedia, messages on a board, a discussion in a conference room—any text on your screen will be saved into a log if you open one before you start your online journey. (See Chapter 5, "News & Finance," for a discussion of logging procedures.)

   Logging is particularly valuable for new members. Start a log, sign on and visit a few areas, then sign off. Now review the log (use the Open command under the File menu to open logs). You'll learn a lot about America Online when you can review an online session at your leisure.

Of course, it's not easy to remember to open a log for each session, and sometimes you don't know you're going to run across something you want to save until you're there. Fortunately, all text on America Online can be saved onto your hard drive for later review off-line. Simply go to the File menu and select Save. This causes all the text in the article or message in the front-most window on your screen to be transferred to any disk drive you specify, where it will be saved as a plain text file that you can read using AOL or the word processor of your choice. Note that it isn't necessary for you to scroll through the entirety of an article in order to save it: even though you haven't seen the entire text of the article, your computer has, and everything is saved when you issue the Save command.

8. **Download when system activity is minimal.**
The AOL system—the Stratus and the long-distance carrier in your local area—gets very busy in the evenings and on weekends. Your time on the system is allocated in slices, and these time slices get smaller as the system becomes more active. Your computer spends more of its time waiting in line for data when time slices get small, yet the clock keeps running regardless.

Whenever you're planning a long download—say, anything over ten minutes—plan it for the time of day when the system is least active. Typically, that's the morning: the earlier the better. Read about the Download Manager in the previous chapter, and use it to tame your download time.

9. **Look for "More" buttons.**
Lots of AOL windows include buttons or folders marked "More." Don't neglect them. AOL doesn't tie up your system feeding you all 500 matching entries to a database search, for instance. Rather, it offers the first 50 or so, then waits to see if you want more. You may want to cancel at that moment, or you may want to see more. When the conditions are appropriate, AOL always offers the More option, but it's only useful if you choose to exercise it. AOL users who neglect the More buttons never know what they're missing.

10. **Manage your windows.**
AOL's "modeless" strategy allows you to wander all over the service, leaving a litter of windows behind you. A mess like this quickly becomes unmanageable: you may spend needless time

cleaning up after yourself or searching for a specific window on screen while the online clock keeps running. A number of techniques aid window management:

⚠ The bottom of the Window menu lists the titles of all open (or hidden) windows. Use this menu to find the one you want quickly and easily, no matter how messy the screen becomes.

⚠ Choosing Close from the Window menu (or Ctrl-F4) closes the front-most window, or you can close a window by double-clicking on the window's close box.

⚠ Ctrl-F9 (or Close All from the Window menu) closes *all* windows except the Browser, the Welcome screen and the Network News window. This is something of a crisis-oriented command, but it's very satisfying to watch.

Many thanks to Tom de Boor for his help with this list. Though Tom is an AOL employee (he is in charge of the Learning & Reference Department), he's always interested in finding ways to save members' money. The list above is a good example.

Ten best downloads

The list below is hardly objective and most certainly in no particular order. It is exclusive of fonts and graphics: you will have to explore those on your own. This is just a list of really great and useful stuff, all of which is available online for the cost of your connect time and perhaps a small shareware fee.

To find any of the downloads mentioned below, use the keywords: File Search, then specify the name of the file as your search criterion. If you find more than one version available of a particular program, be sure to download the one with the highest version number, since it's the most recent release of that program.

1. **PKZip**
   This is the software that compresses ("zips") files to significantly less than their original size. It's also the software that AOL prefers you use for compressing files before you upload them. PKZip is

discussed in Chapter 7, "Computing & Software." *Note*: Investigate PKLite as well: it compresses *programs* (rather than files). Programs compressed with PKLite typically occupy half their original space on your disk, yet remain fully functional.

2. **Paint Shop Pro and Graphics Workshop**

    These are graphics conversion and viewing shareware programs. Paint Shop Pro (by Robert Voit) is a Windows program of remarkable functionality and quality. Graphics Workshop (by Alchemy Mindworks) is available for either the Windows or the DOS environments. Most of the really spectacular graphics available on AOL are in GIF—Graphics Interchange Format—format. Few PC programs are compatible with GIF files, so GIF files invariably have to be converted to some format your software can read. Both programs handle the task well, providing conversion from (and to) dozens of common PC graphics formats.

3. **Alchemy**

    Even though GIF files are relatively small compared to others, they're still huge. A full-screen, 256-color GIF file typically measures one-quarter of a megabyte. If you're willing to sacrifice a tiny bit of quality, then store your graphics in JPEG (Joint Photographic Experts Group) format. Unlike GIF (and most others), JPEG is a "lossy" compression technique, where some of the original data gets lost during compression. The sacrifice is worth it: JPEG files are usually one-tenth the size of GIF files, and the data loss is all but invisible. To convert to and from the JPEG format, use Alchemy. *Note*: Paint Shop Pro (mentioned above) features a proprietary lossy compression format that is as efficient as JPEG. If you use Paint Shop Pro (and you don't need to convert the JPEG files of others), you won't need Alchemy.

4. **SPEAKER**

    This is the speaker driver that Microsoft left out of Windows 3.1. It was just one of those things that had to wait until later. It's available now, and it allows your internal PC speaker to play all of the WAV files found in the Computing & Software Department. The Control-Panel sound icon even lets you assign these sounds to various Windows functions, like start-up, exclamation, error and shut-down. Freeware from Microsoft.

5. **AOLDBF and the weekly file listings**

   More than 25,000 files are available for downloading from America Online. Searching the libraries for a specific entry can be time consuming, all the more so when *you're* paying for the time. That's the bad news. The good news is that listings for all 25,000 files are posted online and compressed with PKZip, so they may be downloaded quickly. Moreover, the listings are updated weekly, so the downloaded database on your hard disk is never over a week old. AOLDBF is a program that reads and searches through these listings, so you can search the libraries while off-line and save online time charges. The program is a simple little database viewer, providing the searches, sorts and appends (weekly listings are appended to the master database on your disk) that help you peruse the libraries. There's no charge for either AOLDBF or the file listings, other than the connect time required to download them.

6. **AOL.PIF**

   Use this file to run the GeoWorks version of AOL under Windows. The program will run much faster and there's less chance you'll encounter resource conflicts when you minimize AOL while you are online.

7. **Emoticons**

   Here's an exhaustive list of all the "smileys" you're likely to encounter online. With this list at your side, you can smile with the best of 'em. ;)

8. **DR6WIN**

   Use this utility to run Windows 3.1 under DR DOS.

9. **Wolfenstein 3-D**

   This landmark shareware game features the fastest 3D visuals ever seen on the IBM PC in 256 colors and VGA. The music is intense, and the digitized effects are mind-boggling. Your perception of IBM games (and shareware) will be forever changed. Captured behind enemy lines while on a secret mission during WWII, you're taken to a prison camp for questioning. If you can escape, you'll move smoothly through a stunning 3D environment with amazing details, secret chambers, traps and treasures, intelligent moving opponents and a boss creature menacing enough to warrant a Stephen King novel. (Shareware from Apogee Systems.)

10. **Fairy Godmom**

If you don't care for carnage (Apogee willingly rates Wolfenstein as "PC," for "Profound Carnage"), try Fairy Godmom (file search for FGODMOM). Armed with only a Magic Wand, Godmom can temporarily convert her pursuers (most take the form of somewhat befuddled crabs) into things like brick walls. The game features 50 levels of play and should challenge even the most avid arcade-game player. Good sound, great graphics and animation. Try animating a Godmom in a full-length gown as she climbs a ladder and you'll appreciate the author's creativity. (Shareware from John Blackwell.)

11. **I Laughed So Hard I Cried**

We know this is number 11 on a list of 10, but it's not really a download either. Rather, "I Laughed So Hard I Cried" is a search criterion (keywords: File Search) for a series of humorous stories and anecdotes discovered online and compiled by Sandy Brockman (AFLSandyB). This is spirit-lifting stuff, and we can all use a lift of spirits now and again.

Many thanks to Kate Chase (PC Kate) for her assistance with this list. We had to spend immeasurable hours testing the games she submitted for review, but it was worth the effort.

Ten most frequently asked questions of Customer Relations

As you might expect, the people at Customer Relations spend 90 percent of their time answering the same questions over and over again. Perhaps it will help if we answer them for you here: it may save you the trouble of contacting Customer Relations (and save them the trouble of replying).

1. **Where can I get help?**

   ⚠ Read Chapter 3, "Online Help & the Members." You might also look up the topic in the index of this book to see if your question is answered here.

   ⚠ Run the AOL software and choose Help from the Help menu.

   ⚠ Go online and use the keyword: Help.

- Ask a Guide for help. Enter the Lobby by typing Ctrl-K, and look for someone there with the word "Guide" in his or her screen name.

- Ask Customer Service Live. Use the keywords: CS Live. You can get live, online support this way.

- Ask Customer Relations for help. Use the keyword: Help, then double-click on any of the topics in the category box.

- Use the keyword: MHM. This takes you to AOL's Members Helping Members bulletin boards.

- Call Customer Relations at 800-827-6364. This should be your last resort.

2. **Where can I ask questions?**
   We know this question is answered above, but it's asked so often that we're including it as a separate item here.

   - Ask Customer Relations for help. Use the keyword: Help, then double-click on any of the topics in the category box. There's an envelope icon at the bottom of every Support Center topic window just for the purpose of sending questions to Customer Relations.

   - Ask Customer Service Live. Use the keywords: CS Live. It's open during the evenings.

   - Use the keyword: MHM. This takes you to AOL's Members Helping Members bulletin boards, where you can get help from your peers. Peer help is often the best of all.

3. **How do I find additional or closer access numbers?**
   SprintNet (discussed in Chapter 1, "Starting the Tour") is always adding additional access numbers. To stay in touch, use the keyword: Access.

4. **Can I use AOL from multiple computers?**
   No problem, even if they're different kinds of computers. All you need is software for each, and the software is free. Use the keyword: AskAOL to request additional copies of AOL software.
   When you receive the additional copy of the software, do *not* use the certificate number and password in the packet. Rather, enter the

screen name and password you normally use. This will configure the new software to your existing account.

5. **Where do I begin?**
   🔺 We suggest you visit the New Member Lounge first. Use the keyword: Lobby, then click on the Rooms icon. The New Member Lounge is open every evening at 9:00 Eastern time, except Monday and Wednesday.

   🔺 You might also visit the Lifestyles & Interests or Computing & Software departments. (Lifestyles & Interests is the subject of Chapter 6; Computing & Software the subject of Chapter 7.) Find a forum there that interests you, read and reply to messages posted on boards (described in Chapter 6), and visit the forum's chat room (most have one—chat rooms are discussed in Chapter 10) when it's available.

   🔺 Use the keyword: Help, then check out "Hints for New Members." Online help is free.

   🔺 Perhaps most important, though, is that you do what you enjoy. There's no right or wrong place to begin your AOL travels. Feel free to explore uncharted territory. You can hardly get lost when you never leave home.

6. **How can I see how much time I have used and check my bill?**
   The keyword: Time displays the online clock; the keyword: Billing displays your charges, exclusive of the current session. You can get a complete explanation of charges here as well, and change your billing method if you want. The keyword: Billing is a free area.

7. **How do I change my screen name?**
   Though you cannot change your original screen name, you can add up to four additional names and use them as you wish. Use the keyword: Names. This is a free area as well.

8. **How do I change my profile?**
   Use the keyword: Help, then click on the Account & Billing Options icon. Alternatively, choose Edit Your Online Profile from the Members menu. The first method is free; the second is not.

9. **How do I disable Call Waiting?**
   Call Waiting can disrupt online sessions, often resulting in a disconnect. To disable it, choose Setup from the Welcome window when you're not online. In most areas, you need only check the box labeled "Use this command to disable call waiting." In some places, you may need to change the command from "*70" to "1170." If you have trouble, ask Customer Relations (see item #1 on this list) or consult your local phone company .

10. **How do I turn off my modem speaker when dialing?**
    Again, click on the Setup button from the Welcome screen when you're not online. Now click on "Advanced Setup." Add "M0" (that's a zero, not an O) to the end of your Post-Modem String. Click on OK, then click on Save Changes. If you have trouble, ask Customer Relations (see item #1 on this list).

Thanks to Jay Levitt and the Customer Relations Department for help with this list.

Ten best ways to make friends online

Perhaps above all, AOL is a community. If you're not a part of it, you're missing a wealth of opportunity. As in any community, you're ahead of the game if you know how to break into it. Here's how:

1. **Visit the Lobby.**
   Read Chapter 10 ("People Connection"), then press Ctrl-K. Say hello when you arrive. The Lobby is probably the greatest resource for online friends.

2. **Find a favorite room and hang out there.**
   Chapter 10 describes the Event Rooms Guide (keyword: PC Studio). Look it over, find a room that interests you and visit that room when it's available. You might also find a favorite room by visiting any of AOL's forums (forums are described in Chapter 6, "Lifestyles & Interests").

3. **Visit the New Member Lounge.**
   If you're new to AOL, you'll find comfort in numbers in the New Member Lounge. It meets every evening at 9:00 Eastern time, except Monday and Wednesday.

4. **Post your profile.**

   Don't neglect to post a profile for yourself. Use the keyword: Help, then click on the Account & Billing Options icon. (You can also edit your profile by using the appropriate command under the Members menu, but the keyword method described above is free.) Talk about yourself. Make your personality irresistible. People in chat rooms often peek at other occupants' profiles, and if you haven't posted a profile, you're a *persona non grata*.

5. **Use an effective screen name.**

   You can use the Help-keyword technique described above to add a screen name to your account if the one you're using now isn't very effective in a social situation. People have a hard time relating to a screen name like "Mike6734," but many find "MajorTom" and "CoolKath" worthy of comment. If nothing else, include your first name or nickname in your screen name so people can address you like a friend.

6. **Search the membership for others with similar interests.**

   Choose Search the Member Directory from the Members menu and search the directory for others with interests similar to yours. Read their profiles and send them e-mail. You'll be surprised at the number who reply.

7. **Read messages and reply.**

   Find a forum that interests you (Chapter 6 discusses forums), go to its message boards and start reading. Eventually, you'll see some that provoke a response. Go ahead: post your comment. It gives you a sense of purpose the next time you sign on: you'll scramble to that message board to see if anyone responded to your posting.

8. **Post a message soliciting replies.**

   Members Helping Members (keyword: MHM—see Chapter 3, "Online Help & the Members") is a great place to go for message-posting, but any forum will do. Post a message asking for help or an opinion. People love to help, and everyone has an opinion.

9. **Read articles and reply.**

   This is similar to number 7, above. In forums like the Writer's Forum, people pour their hearts out in their articles, and they're always hoping for a little positive feedback.

10. **Download a file and reply.**
    This goes especially for fonts and graphics. Download a few files (downloading is discussed in Chapter 7, "Computing & Software," and Chapter 12, "The Download Manager") and reply to the originator via e-mail. In selecting the graphics for this book, we sent e-mail to dozens of online artists, and every one of them replied within a day or two—most with two or three pages of enthusiastic banter.

Ten best smileys

Let's be frivolous. Though smileys are discussed more formally in Chapter 11, "Electronic Mail," here are our ten favorite informal smileys. (For a complete list of Smileys, use the keyword: File Search, and search for a file named "Emoticons.")

1.	@--->->-	A rose
2.	=:-()	Scared smiley
3.	0:-)	Innocent smiley (halo)
4.	:-)8	Bow-tie smiley
	8:)	Bow-in-hair smiley
5.	:-8	Smiley who just ate a pickle
6.	C|:-=	Charlie Chaplin
	=|:-)=	Abe Lincoln
7.	:-!	Bronx cheer
8.	:-@	Screaming smiley
9.	:-$	Orthodontics smiley
10.	C|:)	Sombrero smiley

Best Ten-Best list

From Scudamour, "Top Ten Things I Don't Like About My PC":

- Tends to short out when used in shower.

- Doesn't keep hot side hot, cool side cool.

- Uses the modem to call 1-900-HOT-MAMA when I'm away at work.

- Leaves little floppies all over the carpet.

- Doesn't slice or dice, let alone make julienne fries.

- Annoying dialog box keeps appearing that reads, "Do you have Prince Albert in a can?"

- Pull-down menus never feature tasty snack items.

- Third eye caused by screen radiation is making it harder than ever to get a date.

- That scary red button on the keyboard marked "Explode."

When he's not compiling lists, Scudamour (aka Patrick Wynne) illustrates books. Look for Ursula K. Le Guin's latest children's book, *Fish Soup*, published by Atheneum, for an example of his work.

Everybody out!

Our tour has concluded. Typical of tours everywhere, ours has been an abridgement—a synopsis of things we find most interesting about AOL. You will find your own favorites, and in so doing discover things we not only didn't mention, but may not even know about ourselves. Moreover, AOL is a moving target: like most online services, America Online is almost a fluid—flowing from opportunity to opportunity, conforming to trends and advances, relentlessly expanding to fill new voids. We'll try to keep up, and no doubt there will be a second edition of this book someday to describe an even bigger and better America Online than the one we know today.

Meanwhile, this edition has reached its end. While you're waiting for the next one, sign on to America Online and send us some e-mail. Tell us what you want included (or excluded) in the next edition. Tell us what you liked or disliked about this book. Send us logs, files, articles—anything you think might complement *The Official America Online Tour Guide*. We look forward to hearing from you.

—*MajorTom and CoolKath*

APPENDIX A
Keywords

Keywords are the fastest way to get from one place to another on America Online. To go to a specific forum or area, you just select Keyword from the Go To menu (or type Ctrl-K), and enter the keyword.

Of course, you need to know the keyword before you can enter it. The most current list of keywords is always available by clicking on the Keyword Help button in the Go To Keyword window. It's a long list, so long that it's divided into sublists by department. Because of its length, you might have trouble finding the keyword you want by consulting the list online.

We'd like to suggest two alternatives:

⚠ Use the keywords: Dir of Services (or choose Directory of Services from the Go To menu). From here, choose Search the Directory of Services. This is a searchable database of services offered by America Online (and it's discussed in Chapter 3, "Online Help & the Members"). Because it's searchable, the directory is a faster method of locating an online area than reading through the list of keywords, and the directory always lists keywords when they're available.

⚠ Use the following lists of keywords. Each is organized differently than the lists you'll find under the online keyword list, and they may save you the trouble of printing a list of your own.

The Official AOL Tour Guide

Keyword tips

The three little keyword tips below may be of help to you.

🔺 Like screen names, keywords are neither case- nor space-sensitive. Typing "dirofservices" works just as well as "Dir of Services." *Note*: Keywords are limited to 18 characters.

🔺 Many windows identify their associated keywords in the lower-left corner of the window. Look for these.

🔺 Add frequently used keywords to your Go To menu. Editing the Go To menu is described in Chapter 6, "Lifestyles & Interests."

General Keywords

Billing	Check your current billing or change your billing method
Dir of Services	Searchable database of services available online
File search	Searchable database of downloadable files available online
Help	Members' Online Support (free)
Internet	Learn about sending mail to subscribers of other services
MHM	Members Helping Members (free)
Names	Add, delete screen names
Password	Change your password
Profile	Add or edit your member's profile
Time	Time of day and time online for the current session

Keywords (Sorted by forum)

Forum	Category	Keyword
4D Developers	SIGS	mbs
Aatrix Software, Inc.	Industry Connection	aatrix
Academic Assistance Center	Learning & Reference	homework, tutoring, research
Academic Research Service	Learning & Reference	research
Access Software	Industry Connection	access software, links
Activision	Industry Connection	activision
AD&D	Games & Entertainment	oadd, neverwinter, nwn, add
Adult Literacy	SIGS	aed, med
Adult Literacy Forum	Learning & Reference	read
Advanced Software, Inc.	Industry Connection	advanced
Advertising	SIGS	mbs, mdp, mgr
Affinity Microsystems	Industry Connection	affinity
Afterwards Coffeehouse	Learning & Reference	afterwards, arts
Aladdin Systems, Inc.	Industry Connection	aladdin

Forum	Category	Keyword
Altsys Corporation	Industry Connection	altsys
Alysis Software	Industry Connection	alysis
American Airlines	Travel & Shopping	eaasy sabre, sabre, easy sabre
Apple Classrooms of Tomorrow	Learning & Reference	acot
Apple Classrooms of Tomorrow	SIGS	aed, med
Apple Professional Exchange	SIGS	mcm
Applications	PC Forums	pap, PC applications
Applied Engineering	Industry Connection	applied, ae
APX	SIGS	mms
Ariel Publishing	Industry Connection	ariel
Argosy	Industry Connection	argosy
Art & Graphics	Apple II Forums	agr, a2art, a2graphics
Articulate Systems	Industry Connection	asi, articulate
Asimov/Analog Forum	Lifestyles & Interests	asimov, analog
Ask the Doctor	People Connection	ask the doctor
Astronomy Club	Lifestyles & Interests	astronomy
AutoVantage	Travel & Shopping	auto
Aviation Club	Lifestyles & Interests	aviation
Awakened Eye	SIGS	mcm
Baby Boomers' Club	Lifestyles & Interests	baby boomers
Baseline Publishing	Industry Connection	baseline
BBS Sysop's Club	SIGS	acm
Beagle Bros.	Industry Connection	beaglebros, beagle, bb
Beginners	Mutual Interest	abf, newlink
Bering Bridge Project	SIGS	aed, med
Berkeley Macintosh User Group	SIGS	ugf
Berkeley Softworks	Industry Connection	berkeley
Berkeley Systems	Industry Connection	berksys
Bicycle Network	Lifestyles & Interests	bikenet, bicycle
BioScan	Industry Connection	bioscan
BLOC Publishing	Industry Connection	bloc
Boston Computer Society	SIGS	ugf
Bowers Development (AppMaker)	Industry Connection	bowers, appmaker
Broderbund	Industry Connection	broderbund
Bull Moose Tavern	Learning & Reference	bull moose, politics
Bulls & Bears	Games & Entertainment	bulls and bears, bullsandbears
Business	Macintosh Forums	mbs, macbusiness
Business & Finance	News & Finance	business
Business News	News & Finance	business news
Byte Works	Industry Connection	byteworks, byte
Career Center	Learning & Reference	career, careers
Cartoons	People Connection	cartoons, yourtoons

Forum	Category	Keyword
CE Software	Industry Connection	cesoftware
Celebrity Cookbook	People Connection	celebrity cookbook, cookbook
Center Stage	People Connection	centerstage, auditorium, shows
Chicago Online	Lifestyles & Interests	chicago online
Claris	Industry Connection	claris
Classifieds	People Connection	classifieds
College Board	Learning & Reference	college board
Color Weather Maps	News & Finance	color weather maps, weather maps
Comedy Club	People Connection	comedy, comedy club
Communications	Apple II Forums	acm, a2telecom
Communications	Macintosh Forums	mcm, maccommunication
Comp-u-Store Online	Travel & Shopping	compustore
CompileIt	SIGS	mhc
Computer Express	Travel & Shopping	computer express
Computer Gaming World	Industry Connection	cgw
Computing Forums	Online Area	forums
CompuToon	People Connection	computoon
Cooking Club	Lifestyles & Interests	cooking
CoStar	Industry Connection	costar
CP/M & MS-DOS	SIGS	adv
Crystal Ball, The	People Connection	crystal ball, tarot
Cultural Resources, Inc.	Industry Connection	cultural
DacEasy, Inc.	Industry Connection	daceasy
Darts	Games & Entertainment	darts
Davidson & Associates	Industry Connection	davidson
Dayna Communications	Industry Connection	dayna
Debate Forum	News & Finance	debate forum
DeskMate	PC Forums	des, deskmate
Desktop Publishing/WP	Macintosh Forums	mdp, macdesktop
Development	Apple II Forums	adv, a2development
Development	Macintosh Forums	mdv, macdevelopment
Digital Vision	Industry Connection	digital
Direct Software	Industry Connection	direct
DisABILITIES Forum	Lifestyles & Interests	disabilities
Dolby Audio/Video Forum	Lifestyles & Interests	dolby
Dollars & Cents	News & Finance	dollars, dollarsandcents, dollars&cents, dollars and sense
DOS	PC Forums	dos
Dove Computer Corp.	Industry Connection	dove

Forum	Category	Keyword
Download Interactive Games	Games & Entertainment	games download, download games
Dubl-Click Software, Inc.	Industry Connection	dublclick
EAASY SABRE	Travel & Shopping	sabre, american airlines, eaasy sabre
Education	Apple II Forums	aed, a2education
Education	Macintosh Forums	med, maceducation
Education Connection	SIGS	aed, med
Electric Image	Industry Connection	electric
Emergency Response Club	Lifestyles & Interests	emergency
Emigre Fonts	Industry Connection	emigre
Encyclopedia	Learning & Reference	encyclopedia, comptons
Entertainment	Games & Entertainment	entertainment, games&entertainment
Environmental Forum	Lifestyles & Interests	earth
Ethics & Religion Forum	Lifestyles & Interests	religion
Exam Prep Center	Learning & Reference	exam prep
Exchange, The	News & Finance	exchange
Express Music	Travel & Shopping	express music
Express Yourself	Lifestyles & Interests	debate
Express Yourself	News & Finance	debate, express yourself, opinion
Farallon	Industry Connection	farallon
Fax/Paper Mail	Mail	fax, us mail, paper mail
Fifth Generation	Industry Connection	fifth
Fight Back	News & Finance	fight back
FirstClass	SIGS	mcm
Flower Shop	Travel & Shopping	flower shop, flowers
FontBank	Industry Connection	fontbank
Forum Auditorium	Mutual Interest	rotunda
Free-Form Gaming Forum	Games & Entertainment	rdi, ffgf
Gadget Guru Electronics Forum	Lifestyles & Interests	electronics
Gallery, The	People Connection	gallery
Game Designers	SIGS	mdv, adv, mgm, agm
Game Resort	People Connection	resort
Games	PC Forums	pgm, PC Games
Games & Entertainment	Apple II Forums	agm, a2games
Games & Entertainment	Macintosh Forums	mgm, macgame
Gaming Information Exchange	Games & Entertainment	gix
Gay & Lesbian Forum	Lifestyles & Interests	gay, lesbian
GCC Technologies	Industry Connection	gcc
Genealogy Club	Lifestyles & Interests	genealogy
GeoWorks	Industry Connection	geoworks
Giftedness Forum	Learning & Reference	gifted, mensa
Global Village Communication	Industry Connection	global village, global, teleport

Forum	Category	Keyword
Grandstand, The	Games & Entertainment	grandstand
Graphic Arts & CAD	Macintosh Forums	mgr, macgraphics
Graphics	PC Forums	pgr, PC graphics
Graphisoft	Industry Connection	graphisoft
Groupware	SIGS	mbs, mcm, mdv
GS+ Magazine	Industry Connection	gsmag
Ham Radio Club	Lifestyles & Interests	ham radio
Hardware	Apple II Forums	ahw, a2hardware
Hardware	Macintosh Forums	mhw, machardware
Hardware	Online Area	hardware
Hardware	PC Forums	phw, PC hardware
Hatrack River Town Meeting	Lifestyles & Interests	orson card, hatrack
Helix	SIGS	mbs
Home Office Computing	Industry Connection	home office
Home Shopping	Travel & Shopping	shopping, the mall, stores
HyperCard	Macintosh Forums	mhc, machypercard
HyperStudio Network	SIGS	aed, apr, ams, apr
inCider	Industry Connection	incider
Independent Traveler	Travel & Shopping	traveler
Industrial Computing Society	SIGS	mbs
Infocom	Industry Connection	infocom
Inline Design	Industry Connection	inline
Interactive Education Services	Learning & Reference	ies, courses, classes
International House	Learning & Reference	international
Investor's Network	News & Finance	investing, investor's network, investments
Issues in Mental Health	Lifestyles & Interests	imh
IYM Software Review (It's Your Money)	Industry Connection	iym, iym software reviews
Job Listings Database	Learning & Reference	jobs
Kent*Marsh	Industry Connection	kentmarsh
Kiwi Software	Industry Connection	kiwi
Koala: Featuring MacVision	Industry Connection	macvision, koala
Language Systems	Industry Connection	language sys
LaPub	People Connection	lapub
Laserdirect	Travel & Shopping	laser, laser printing, laser direct
Leading Edge Information Center	Industry Connection	leading edge
Legal	SIGS	mdp, mbs, mcm, acm
Letraset	Industry Connection	letraset
Lucasfilm Games	Industry Connection	lucasfilm
MacArtist	Industry Connection	macartist
MacAvenue	Industry Connection	macavenue
MacroMind, Inc.	Industry Connection	macromind
MacSciTech	SIGS	mbs
Mall, The	Travel & Shopping	mall, store, stores, shopping & travel

Forum	Category	Keyword
Market Master	Industry Connection	market
Marketfield Software	Industry Connection	marketfield
MasterWord	Games & Entertainment	mw, mword, word library
Maxis	Industry Connection	maxis
MECC	Industry Connection	mecc
Meridian Data	Industry Connection	meridian
Micro Dynamics, Ltd.	Industry Connection	micro dynamics
Microcom	Industry Connection	microcom
MicroMat Computer Systems	Industry Connection	micromat
Micron Technology	Industry Connection	micron
MicroProse	Industry Connection	microprose
Microseeds Publishing, Inc.	Industry Connection	microseeds
Microsoft Small Business Center	News & Finance	business center, small business, msbc, msbiz Center
Microsoft Support	Industry Connection	microsoft, ms solution
Military & Vets Club	Lifestyles & Interests	military
Milliken	Industry Connection	milliken
MiniCad	SIGS	mgr
Mirror Technologies	Industry Connection	mirror
Movies	Games & Entertainment	movie reviews, movies
Multimedia Exchange, The	Learning & Reference	multimedia
Music & Sound	Apple II Forums	ams, a2music
Music & Sound	Macintosh Forums	mms, macmusic
Music Programmers	SIGS	mms, mdv
Music/Sound	PC Forums	pmu, PC music
National Education Association	Learning & Reference	nea
National Geographic Online	Learning & Reference	geographic, ngs
National Space Society	Lifestyles & Interests	nss, space
Neverwinter	Games & Entertainment	oadd, ad&d, nwn, add
New Era, Inc.	Industry Connection	new era
News Watch	News & Finance	newswatch
News/Finance	News & Finance	finance, news, news room, news&finance
Newsbytes	News & Finance	newsbytes
NewsLink	News & Finance	headlines, newslink, our world, topnews
Nibble Magazine	Industry Connection	nibble
Nomadic Computing	SIGS	mcm
Now Software	Industry Connection	now
Object Factory	Industry Connection	object factory
ON Technology	Industry Connection	on
Online Gaming Forums	Games & Entertainment	gaming
Online Tonight	People Connection	online tonight
Operating Systems	Macintosh Forums	mos, system 7
OptImage Interactive Services	Industry Connection	optimage
Other Sports	Games & Entertainment	tennis, golf, boxing

Forum	Category	Keyword
PC AO	Mutual Interest	pcforums
PC Classifieds	News & Finance	pcclassifieds
PC Novice & PC Today Online	Industry Connection	pcnovice, pctoday
PC Studio	People Connection	pcstudio
People Connection	People Connection	chat, people connection, pc, people, talk
Personal Computer Peripherals	Industry Connection	pcpc
Pet Care Club	Lifestyles & Interests	pet care
Peter Norton Computing	Industry Connection	symantec
Photography Forum	Lifestyles & Interests	photography, kodak
Photoshop	SIGS	mgr
Play-By-Mail & Strategy	Games & Entertainment	pbm, play by mail
Portfolio Systems, Inc.	Industry Connection	dyno
Power Up Software	Industry Connection	power up
PowerDraw	SIGS	mgr
Powershift	SIGS	mms
Productivity	Apple II Forums	apr, a2productivity, awp
Programmer U	SIGS	adv, mdv, pdv
Programming	Online Area	programming
Programming	PC Forums	pdv, PC development
ProVUE Development	Industry Connection	provue
Punchlines	People Connection	punchline
Quantum Que	People Connection	que
Quantum Space	Games & Entertainment	qspace, quantum space
Quark, Inc.	Industry Connection	quark
RabbitJack's Casino	Games & Entertainment	casino, rabbitjack's casino
Radio Control Club	Lifestyles & Interests	radio control
Real Estate Online	Lifestyles & Interests	real estate, mls, mortgage rates
Registration Center (IES)	Learning & Reference	register
RockLink	Games & Entertainment	rocklink
Role-Playing Games Forum	Games & Entertainment	rpg
Romance Connection	People Connection	dating, romance
Salient Software	Industry Connection	salient
Science & Engineering	SIGS	mbs
Science Fiction Forum	Lifestyles & Interests	science fiction
Scuba Club	Lifestyles & Interests	scuba
SeniorNet	Lifestyles & Interests	seniornet
Service Bureau	SIGS	mdp
Shiva Corporation	Industry Connection	shiva
Shopping	Travel & Shopping	mall, store, stores, shopping&travel
Sierra On-Line	Industry Connection	sierra
Small Business	SIGS	mbs
Softek Design	Industry Connection	softek

Forum	Category	Keyword
Softsync, Inc.	Industry Connection	softsync
Software Center	Mutual Interest	computing, software center
Software Center	Online Area	software
Solutions, Inc.	Industry Connection	solutions
Spectrum HoloByte	Industry Connection	spectrum
Specular International	Industry Connection	specular
Sports	Games & Entertainment	sports talk, grandstand
Sports Link	Lifestyles & Interests	sports
Sports News	Games & Entertainment	sports news
Sportslink	Games & Entertainment	sports, sportslink, sports club
SSI	Industry Connections	ssi
Star Trek Club	Lifestyles & Interests	star trek
StockLink	News & Finance	portfolio, stocklink, stocks, stock portfolio, stock quotes
Strata, Inc.	Industry Connection	strata
Strategic Simulations	Industry Connection	ssi, strategic
Strategies for Business	News & Finance	businessknowhow
Student Access Online	Learning & Reference	student
Study Skills Service	Learning & Reference	study
Substance Abuse Forum	Learning & Reference	substance abuse, prevention
Supercard	SIGS	mhc
SuperMac	Industry Connection	supermac
Symantec	Industry Connection	symantec
T/Maker	Industry Connection	tmaker
TACTIC Software	Industry Connection	tactic
Tammys Tips	People Connection	tips
Tax Forum	News & Finance	gotax, tax
Teacher Pager	Learning & Reference	teacher pager
Teachers' Forum	Learning & Reference	ttalk
Teachers' Information Network	Learning & Reference	tin, teacher, teachers
Technology Works	Industry Connection	techworks
Teen Scene	People Connection	teen, teens, teen scene
Telecom	PC Forums	ptc, PC telecom
TeleFinder	SIGS	mcm
Television	Games & Entertainment	television, tv
TGS Systems	Industry Connection	tgs
Time	News & Finance	time
Today's News & Weather	News & Finance	top news
Travel	Travel & Shopping	shopping&travel, travel
Trivia Club	People Connection	trivia, trivia club
USA Today	News & Finance	usatoday
User Group Forum	Mutual Interest	ugc, ugf, user groups
Utilities	Macintosh Forums	mut, macutilities
Utilities & Desk Accesories	Apple II Forums	aut, a2utilities

Forum	Category	Keyword
Virtus Corporation	Industry Connection	virtus, walkthrough
Virus Info Center	SIGS	virus, mut
Voyager Company, The	Industry Connection	voyager
Windows	PC Forums	win, windows
Wine & Dine Online	Lifestyles & Interests	wine, restaurant, beer
WordPerfect Support Center	Industry Connection	wordperfect
Working Software	Industry Connection	working
Writers Club	Lifestyles & Interests	writers
XCMD Developers	SIGS	mdv, mhc
XNet SIG	SIGS	mhc
Zedcor, Inc.	Industry Connection	zedcor

Keywords (Sorted by category)

Category	Forum	Keyword
Apple II Forums	Art & Graphics	agr, a2art, a2graphics
Apple II Forums	Communications	acm, a2telecom
Apple II Forums	Development	adv, a2development
Apple II Forums	Education	aed, a2education
Apple II Forums	Games & Entertainment	agm, a2games
Apple II Forums	Hardware	ahw, a2hardware
Apple II Forums	Music & Sound	ams, a2music
Apple II Forums	Productivity	apr, a2productivity, awp
Apple II Forums	Utilities & Desk Accessories	aut, a2utilities
Games & Entertainment	AD&D	oadd, neverwinter, nwn, add
Games & Entertainment	Bulls & Bears	bulls and bears
Games & Entertainment	Classifieds	classifieds
Games & Entertainment	Darts	darts
Games & Entertainment	Download Interactive Games	games download, download games
Games & Entertainment	Entertainment	entertainment, games&entertainment
Games & Entertainment	Free-Form Gaming Forum	rdi, ffgf
Games & Entertainment	Gaming Information Exchange	gix
Games & Entertainment	Grandstand, The	grandstand
Games & Entertainment	MasterWord	mw, mword, word library
Games & Entertainment	Movies	movie reviews, movies
Games & Entertainment	Neverwinter	oadd, ad&d, nwn, add
Games & Entertainment	Online Gaming Forums	gaming
Games & Entertainment	Other Sports	tennis, golf, boxing
Games & Entertainment	Play-By-Mail & Strategy	pbm, play by mail
Games & Entertainment	Quantum Space	qspace, quantum space
Games & Entertainment	RabbitJack's Casino	casino, rabbitjack's casino
Games & Entertainment	RockLink	rocklink

Category	Forum	Keyword
Games & Entertainment	Role-Playing Games Forum	rpg
Games & Entertainment	Sports	sports talk, grandstand
Games & Entertainment	Sports News	sports news
Games & Entertainment	Sportslink	sports, sportslink, sports club
Industry Connection	Aatrix Software, Inc.	aatrix
Industry Connection	Access Software	access software, links
Industry Connection	Activision	activision
Industry Connection	Advanced Software, Inc.	advanced
Industry Connection	Affinity Microsystems	affinity
Industry Connection	Aladdin Systems, Inc.	aladdin
Industry Connection	Altsys Corporation	altsys
Industry Connection	Alysis Software	alysis
Industry Connection	Applied Engineering	applied, ae
Industry Connection	Ariel Publishing	ariel
Industry Connection	Argosy	argosy
Industry Connection	Articulate Systems	asi, articulate
Industry Connection	Baseline Publishing	baseline
Industry Connection	Beagle Bros.	beaglebros, beagle, bb
Industry Connection	Berkeley Softworks	berkeley
Industry Connection	Berkeley Systems	berksys
Industry Connection	BioScan	bioscan
Industry Connection	BLOC Publishing	bloc
Industry Connection	Bowers Development (AppMaker)	bowers, appmaker
Industry Connection	Broderbund	broderbund
Industry Connection	Byte Works	byteworks, byte
Industry Connection	CE Software	cesoftware
Industry Connection	Claris	claris
Industry Connection	Computer Gaming World	cgw
Industry Connection	CoStar	costar
Industry Connection	Cultural Resources, Inc.	cultural
Industry Connection	DacEasy, Inc.	daceasy
Industry Connection	Davidson & Associates	davidson
Industry Connection	Dayna Communications	dayna
Industry Connection	Digital Vision	digital
Industry Connection	Direct Software	direct
Industry Connection	Dove Computer Corp.	dove
Industry Connection	Dubl-Click Software, Inc.	dublclick
Industry Connection	Electric Image	electric
Industry Connection	Emigre Fonts	emigre
Industry Connection	Farallon	farallon
Industry Connection	Fifth Generation	fifth
Industry Connection	FontBank	fontbank
Industry Connection	GCC Technologies	gcc
Industry Connection	GeoWorks	geoworks
Industry Connection	Global Village Communication	global village, global, teleport

Category	Forum	Keyword
Industry Connection	Graphisoft	graphisoft
Industry Connection	GS+ Magazine	gsmag
Industry Connection	Home Office Computing	home office
Industry Connection	inCider	incider
Industry Connection	Infocom	infocom
Industry Connection	Inline Design	inline
Industry Connection	IYM Software Review (It's Your Money)	iym, iym software reviews
Industry Connection	Kent*Marsh	kentmarsh
Industry Connection	Kiwi Software	kiwi
Industry Connection	Koala: Featuring MacVision	macvision, koala
Industry Connection	Language Systems	language sys
Industry Connection	Leading Edge Information Center	leading edge
Industry Connection	Letraset	letraset
Industry Connection	Lucasfilm Games	lucasfilm
Industry Connection	MacArtist	macartist
Industry Connection	MacAvenue	macavenue
Industry Connection	MacroMind, Inc.	macromind
Industry Connection	Market Master	market
Industry Connection	Marketfield Software	marketfield
Industry Connection	Maxis	maxis
Industry Connection	MECC	mecc
Industry Connection	Meridian Data	meridian
Industry Connection	Micro Dynamics, Ltd.	micro dynamics
Industry Connection	Microcom	microcom
Industry Connection	MicroMat Computer Systems	micromat
Industry Connection	Micron Technology	micron
Industry Connection	MicroProse	microprose
Industry Connection	Microseeds Publishing, Inc.	microseeds
Industry Connection	Microsoft Support	microsoft, ms solution
Industry Connection	Milliken	milliken
Industry Connection	Mirror Technologies	mirror
Industry Connection	New Era, Inc.	new era
Industry Connection	Nibble Magazine	nibble
Industry Connection	Now Software	now
Industry Connection	Object Factory	object factory
Industry Connection	ON Technology	on
Industry Connection	OptImage Interactive Services	optimage
Industry Connection	PC Novice & PC Today Online	pcnovice, pctoday
Industry Connection	Personal Computer Peripherals	pcpc
Industry Connection	Peter Norton Computing	symantec
Industry Connection	Portfolio Systems, Inc.	dyno
Industry Connection	Power Up Software	power up
Industry Connection	ProVUE Development	provue
Industry Connection	Quark, Inc.	quark
Industry Connection	Salient Software	salient
Industry Connection	Shiva Corporation	shiva

Category	Forum	Keyword
Industry Connection	Sierra On-Line	sierra
Industry Connection	Softek Design	softek
Industry Connection	Softsync, Inc.	softsync
Industry Connection	Solutions, Inc.	solutions
Industry Connection	Spectrum HoloByte	spectrum
Industry Connection	Specular International	specular
Industry Connection	SSI	ssi
Industry Connection	Strata, Inc.	strata
Industry Connection	Strategic Simulations	ssi, strategic
Industry Connection	SuperMac	supermac
Industry Connection	Symantec	symantec
Industry Connection	T/Maker	tmaker
Industry Connection	TACTIC Software	tactic
Industry Connection	Technology Works	techworks
Industry Connection	TGS Systems	tgs
Industry Connection	Virtus Corporation	virtus, walkthrough
Industry Connection	Voyager Company, The	voyager
Industry Connection	WordPerfect Support Center	wordperfect
Industry Connection	Working Software	working
Industry Connection	Zedcor, Inc.	zedcor
Learning & Reference	Academic Assistance Center	homework, tutoring, research
Learning & Reference	Academic Research Service	research
Learning & Reference	Adult Literacy Forum	read
Learning & Reference	Afterwards Coffeehouse	afterwards, arts
Learning & Reference	Apple Classrooms of Tomorrow	acot
Learning & Reference	Bull Moose Tavern	bull moose, politics
Learning & Reference	Career Center	career, careers
Learning & Reference	College Board	college board
Learning & Reference	Encyclopedia	encyclopedia, comptons
Learning & Reference	Exam Prep Center	exam prep
Learning & Reference	Giftedness Forum	gifted, mensa
Learning & Reference	Interactive Education Services	ies, courses, classes
Learning & Reference	International House	international
Learning & Reference	Job Listings Database	jobs
Learning & Reference	Multimedia Exchange, The	multimedia
Learning & Reference	National Education Association	nea
Learning & Reference	National Geographic Online	geographic, ngs
Learning & Reference	Registration Center (IES)	register
Learning & Reference	Student Access Online	student
Learning & Reference	Study Skills Service	study
Learning & Reference	Substance Abuse Forum	substance abuse, prevention
Learning & Reference	Teacher Pager	teacher pager
Learning & Reference	Teachers' Forum	ttalk
Learning & Reference	Teachers' Information Network	tin, teacher, teachers
Lifestyles & Interests	Asimov/Analog Forum	asimov, analog

Category	Forum	Keyword
Lifestyles & Interests	Astronomy Club	astronomy
Lifestyles & Interests	Aviation Club	aviation
Lifestyles & Interests	Baby Boomers' Club	baby boomers
Lifestyles & Interests	Bicycle Network	bikenet, bicycle
Lifestyles & Interests	Chicago Online	chicago online
Lifestyles & Interests	Cooking Club	cooking
Lifestyles & Interests	DisABILITIES Forum	disabilities
Lifestyles & Interests	Dolby Audio/Video Forum	dolby
Lifestyles & Interests	Emergency Response Club	emergency
Lifestyles & Interests	Environmental Forum	earth
Lifestyles & Interests	Ethics & Religion Forum	religion
Lifestyles & Interests	Express Yourself	debate
Lifestyles & Interests	Gadget Guru Electronics Forum	electronics
Lifestyles & Interests	Gay & Lesbian Forum	gay, lesbian
Lifestyles & Interests	Genealogy Club	genealogy
Lifestyles & Interests	Ham Radio Club	ham radio
Lifestyles & Interests	Hatrack River Town Meeting	orson card, hatrack
Lifestyles & Interests	Issues in Mental Health	imh
Lifestyles & Interests	Military & Vets Club	military
Lifestyles & Interests	National Space Society	nss, space
Lifestyles & Interests	Pet Care Club	pet care
Lifestyles & Interests	Photography Forum	photography, kodak
Lifestyles & Interests	Radio Control Club	radio control
Lifestyles & Interests	Real Estate Online	real estate, mls, mortgage rates
Lifestyles & Interests	Science Fiction Forum	science fiction
Lifestyles & Interests	Scuba Club	scuba
Lifestyles & Interests	SeniorNet	seniornet
Lifestyles & Interests	Sports Link	sports
Lifestyles & Interests	Star Trek Club	star trek
Lifestyles & Interests	Trivia Club	trivia
Lifestyles & Interests	Wine & Dine Online	wine, restaurant, beer
Lifestyles & Interests	Writers Club	writers
Macintosh Forums	Business	mbs, macbusiness
Macintosh Forums	Communications	mcm, maccommunication
Macintosh Forums	Desktop Publishing/WP	mdp, macdesktop
Macintosh Forums	Development	mdv, macdevelopment
Macintosh Forums	Education	med, maceducation
Macintosh Forums	Games & Entertainment	mgm, macgame
Macintosh Forums	Graphic Arts & CAD	mgr, macgraphics
Macintosh Forums	Hardware	mhw, machardware
Macintosh Forums	HyperCard	mhc, machypercard
Macintosh Forums	Music & Sound	mms, macmusic
Macintosh Forums	Operating Systems	mos, system 7

Category	Forum	Keyword
Macintosh Forums	Utilities	mut, macutilities
Mail	Fax/Paper Mail	fax, us mail, paper mail
Mutual Interest	Beginners	abf, newlink
Mutual Interest	Forum Auditorium	rotunda
Mutual Interest	PC AO	pcforums
Mutual Interest	Software Center	computing, software center
Mutual Interest	User Group Forum	ugc, ugf, user groups
News & Finance	Business & Finance	business
News & Finance	Business News	business news
News & Finance	Color Weather Maps	color weather maps, weather maps
News & Finance	Debate Forum	debate forum
News & Finance	Dollars & Cents	dollars, dollarsandcents, dollars&cents, dollars and sense
News & Finance	Exchange, The	exchange
News & Finance	Express Yourself	debate, express yourself, opinion
News & Finance	Fight Back	fight back
News & Finance	Investor's Network	investing, investor's network, investments
News & Finance	Microsoft Small Business Center	business center, small business, msbc, msbiz center
News & Finance	News/Finance	finance, news, news room, news&finance
News & Finance	News Watch	newswatch
News & Finance	Newsbytes	newsbytes
News & Finance	NewsLink	headlines, newslink, our world, topnews
News & Finance	PC Classifieds	pcclassifieds
News & Finance	StockLink	portfolio, stocklink, stocks, stock portfolio, stock quotes
News & Finance	Strategies for Business	businessknowhow
News & Finance	Tax Forum	gotax, tax
News & Finance	Television	television, tv
News & Finance	Time	time
News & Finance	Today's News & Weather	top news
News & Finance	USA Today	usatoday
Online Area	Computing Forums	forums
Online Area	Hardware	hardware
Online Area	Programming	programming
Online Area	Software Center	software
PC Forums	Applications	pap, PC applications
PC Forums	DeskMate	des, deskmate

Category	Forum	Keyword
PC Forums	DOS	dos
PC Forums	Games	pgm, PC games
PC Forums	Graphics	pgr, PC graphics
PC Forums	Hardware	phw, PC hardware
PC Forums	Music/Sound	pmu, PC music
PC Forums	Programming	pdv, PC development
PC Forums	Telecom	ptc, PCTelecom
PC Forums	Windows	win, windows
People Connection	Ask the Doctor	ask the doctor
People Connection	Cartoons	cartoons, yourtoons
People Connection	Celebrity Cookbook	celebrity cookbook, cookbook
People Connection	Center Stage	centerstage, auditorium, shows
People Connection	Classifieds	classifieds
People Connection	Comedy Club	comedy, comedy club
People Connection	CompuToon	computoon
People Connection	Crystal Ball, The	crystal ball, tarot
People Connection	Gallery, The	gallery
People Connection	Game Resort	resort
People Connection	LaPub	lapub
People Connection	Online Tonight	online tonight
People Connection	PC Studio	pcstudio
People Connection	People Connection	chat, people connection, pc, people, talk
People Connection	Punchlines	punchline
People Connection	Quantum Que	que
People Connection	Romance Connection	dating, romance
People Connection	Tammys Tips	tips
People Connection	Teen Scene	teen, teens, teen scene
People Connection	Trivia Club	trivia, trivia club
SIGS	4D Developers	mbs
SIGS	Adult Literacy	aed, med
SIGS	Advertising	mbs, mdp, mgr
SIGS	Apple Classrooms of Tomorrow	aed, med
SIGS	Apple Professional Exchange	mcm
SIGS	APX	mms
SIGS	Awakened Eye	mcm
SIGS	BBS Sysop's Club	acm
SIGS	Bering Bridge Project	aed, med
SIGS	Berkeley Macintosh User Group	ugf
SIGS	Boston Computer Society	ugf
SIGS	CompileIt	mhc
SIGS	CP/M & MS-DOS	adv
SIGS	Education Connection	aed, med
SIGS	FirstClass	mcm

Category	Forum	Keyword
SIGS	Game Designers	mdv, adv, mgm, agm
SIGS	Groupware	mbs, mcm, mdv
SIGS	Helix	mbs
SIGS	HyperStudio Network	aed, apr, ams, apr
SIGS	Industrial Computing Society	mbs
SIGS	Legal	mdp, mbs, mcm, acm
SIGS	MacSciTech	mbs
SIGS	MiniCad	mgr
SIGS	Music Programmers	mms, mdv
SIGS	Nomadic Computing	mcm
SIGS	Photoshop	mgr
SIGS	PowerDraw	mgr
SIGS	Powershift	mms
SIGS	Programmer U	adv, mdv, pdv
SIGS	Science & Engineering	mbs
SIGS	Service Bureau	mdp
SIGS	Small Business	mbs
SIGS	Supercard	mhc
SIGS	TeleFinder	mcm
SIGS	Virus Info Center	virus, mut
SIGS	XCMD Developers	mdv, mhc
SIGS	XNet SIG	mhc
Travel & Shopping	American Airlines	eaasy sabre, sabre, easy sabre
Travel & Shopping	AutoVantage	auto
Travel & Shopping	Comp-u-Store Online	compustore
Travel & Shopping	Computer Express	computer express
Travel & Shopping	EAASY SABRE	sabre, american airlines, eaasy sabre
Travel & Shopping	Express Music	express music
Travel & Shopping	Flower Shop	flower shop, flowers
Travel & Shopping	Home Shopping	shopping, the mall, stores
Travel & Shopping	Independent Traveler	traveler
Travel & Shopping	Laserdirect	laser, laser printing, laser direct
Travel & Shopping	Mall, The	mall, store, stores, shopping & travel
Travel & Shopping	Shopping	mall, store, stores, shopping&travel
Travel & Shopping	Travel	shopping&travel, travel

Using the Keyboard

Some online services expect you to learn complex commands and
cryptic code words to get around. Not America Online!

Like any graphical user interface (GUI), America Online has been
designed for use with a mouse, and you should definitely take advantage of AOL's mouse capabilities if you intend to get the most of your
time online. If you don't have a mouse, you can still navigate the service
from your keyboard—and even if you do have a mouse, there will be
times when it makes sense to use the keyboard instead. Some simple
guidelines are provided here for quick reference.

To select buttons...

A current button is the button that contains the cursor. You can move
the cursor by pressing the Tab key. To select the current button, press
the spacebar.

A default button is activated if you press the Enter key without
selecting another button. You can tell a default button by its thick
double outline; pressing Enter *always* selects the active button.

To access a department...

Tab to advance to the department icon of your choice, then press the
spacebar. The What You Have Selected list box lists the title of the
department you selected, and the What You Can Select list box fills
with all the areas that are ahead of you.

Note: Pressing the Shift and Tab keys at the same time moves the
cursor in the opposite direction.

To enter an area of a department...

Press the Up or Down Arrow key to move the cursor to the selected
area in the list box, then press the spacebar.

To pull down a menu...

The menu bar appears at the top of the America Online window. The Help, File, Edit, Go To, Mail, Members and Window menus appear with an underlined letter. To pull down a menu, hold down the Alt key and press the underlined letter from the menu of your choice. A rectangle appears around the menu item you selected. Press the Down Arrow key to move the rectangle to the menu option of your choice, then press the spacebar to choose the menu option.

Keyboard shortcuts...

Some menu items have an associated keyboard shortcut denoted by an underscore. Other shortcuts use one key. To use the keyboard shortcut, press the designated key or the combination of keys. (For example, instead of pulling down the Edit menu to cut a section of text, highlight the text you want to cut, then press the Shift and Delete keys simultaneously. The highlighted text is cut from the current window display.)

Scrolling text with Page Up/Page Down

When you scroll text, you'll first need to press the Tab key until the dotted outline (which is normally on one of the buttons) disappears. This means that the text field in your window is currently selected. You can then use the Page Up/Page Down keys to scroll.

Control keys

You can accomplish a lot online by using a few simple key combinations, and every second you save by using a keyboard shortcut is another second you can spend downloading files or chatting with friends online. To execute the keyboard shortcuts shown below, you'll often need to hold down a modifier key and then type another key. For instance, to find a member online, you would hold down the Control key and then press the F key (while still holding down the Control key). Even though the letters that follow are capitalized to avoid confusion, you don't need to press the Shift key to capitalize them when using them online.

Access the Browse the Service window—Enter
Stop incoming text—Ctrl-X
Close a window—Ctrl-F4
Copy—Ctrl-Ins
Cut—Shift-Del
Disk utilities—Ctrl-U
Find a member online—Ctrl-F
Get member info—Ctrl-G
Move to previous button—Shift-Tab
Move to next button—Tab
Open a new text file—Ctrl-N
Open an existing file—Ctrl-O
Open Browse the Service window—Ctrl-D
Open Keyword window—Ctrl-K
Open Lobby window—Ctrl-L
Open Mail window—Ctrl-M
Overlap windows—Ctrl-F5
Paste—Shift-Ins
Read new mail—Ctrl-R
Save a file—Ctrl-S
Scroll up a page—Page Up
Scroll down a page—Page Down
Send an instant message—Ctrl-I

Control-X

Press Ctrl-X at any time to stop incoming text. For instance, if you are
reading a message and don't want to read the rest of it, press Ctrl-X.

The Menu Bar

The programmers at America Online go to great lengths to make sure their software always complements the look and feel of the GeoWorks graphic environment they have established. This is particularly evident in the easy-to-use pull-down menus. Let's look at each of the menus, one at a time.

The Help menu

Use the Help menu to access the Help Index. See Chapter 3, "Online Help & the Members," for more information about using the Help Index.

About AOL provides a screen revealing the version of AOL currently in use. This can be handy to use if an upgrade is released and you are not sure what you have.

The File menu

The America Online File menu has unique items specially designed to help you capture and save the information you gather when you are online.

New (Ctrl-N)

This option allows you to create a new document in which you can type notes or paste text you found online that you want to print or save. A text document can be up to 24k in size. If you want to mail a new file you created, you can transform any text document into a Mail memo by making that document the topmost window on your screen and selecting "Address Memo" from the Mail menu on your horizontal menu bar.

If you prefer, you can save and close the text file, and then attach it to a Compose Mail memo using the Attach File option.

TIP: Unless you're sending a very long document (or one that is formatted in a word processor) to an America Online member, consider transforming your text document into a Mail document as described above. This will make the recipients of your mail happy, since they won't have to go to the trouble of downloading your memo before reading it—they can read it and respond to it online!

Open... (Ctrl-O)

Use this option to open any text file. If the file is less than 24k long, you can edit the document as well; if the file is longer, you can view it in 24k "chunks" and use the More button at the bottom of the window to move forward in the file.

Save (Ctrl-S)

Save writes the contents of a modified file to your disk. If you've never saved this file before, you will be prompted to choose a file name. You can use this option to save text that you read online.

Save As...

Save As saves the current file under a new name or in a new location that you specify.

Disk Utilities (Ctrl-U)

The disk utilities allow you to create directories, open, delete and rename files.

Print

Use this to print text found on America Online windows. Any text window can be printed; menus and other lists cannot.

Logging

An America Online Log is like an online tape recorder; it allows you to open a file and keep a record of everything that happens during your session.

Opening a Conference Log while you're in a People Connection or conference room will record all conversation that goes on in the room (as long as you are in it while your log is open).

You can open a Session Log to keep track of message board text, articles read—any text that is "incoming" while you're on America Online. (Electronic mail will not be logged.) Outgoing text (mail you send, for example) is not logged.

When you open a log, you'll be prompted to choose a name and destination (where it will be stored) for the text file.

You can read your log file from within America Online only *after* you close it.

Download Manager

This menu option takes you to the Download Manager, where you can view and edit the list of files you have ready to download. For detailed help, read Chapter 12, "The Download Manager."

File Transfer Log

The File Transfer Log lets you know the status of downloads that occurred during your most recent session.

Stop Incoming Text (Ctrl-X)

This command allows you to immediately stop incoming text (such as a news article or piece of mail) so that you can move on to your next online activity.

Exit

When you select "Exit" while you're online, a box will appear on your screen asking if you're "sure you want to sign off." If you select "Yes," you will be disconnected from America Online but will remain in the application. Selecting "Exit Application" will take you out of the AOL application and back to DOS.

The Edit menu

The Cut, Copy and Paste options on the Edit menu allow you to move text from a text window into an electronic "clipboard," or holding place, and back again.

You can copy and paste any of the online text you see on America Online. Use these commands to get the most from the information you find on America Online; for example, you might wish to copy and paste encyclopedia or news articles, or the contents of message boards, into other documents to manipulate and use off-line.

Copy Text

This option enables you to copy text from any document and place it in another document. For example, if you wanted to copy text from a paragraph into mail that you're composing, you would highlight the text that you wish to copy and select Copy from the Edit menu. Then you would press Ctrl-M to open a Compose Mail form, click in the main text field and select Paste from the Edit menu to paste text into your mail message.

Cut Text

The Cut option lets you cut text from one area of a document for placement in another area, or cut text from one document for placement in another document. On America Online, you can only cut text from files that you have created (although you can copy from almost any document).

Paste (Shift+Ins)

The Paste option is used in conjunction with either the Cut or Copy options to place cut or copied text.

The Go To menu

The Go To menu is designed to help you move around on America Online. You will be able to customize certain options on your Go To menu so that you can use it to go directly to the online areas that you visit frequently.

Although you can access the Go To menu whether you're online or off-line, certain options on the menu will be dimmed (unavailable to you) when you're off-line.

Set Up & Sign On

If you select this option when you're off-line but within the America Online application (composing mail or reading Help, for example), the "Set Up & Sign On" screen will appear; then you can immediately sign on to America Online, or change your communications configuration (modem and access telephone numbers).

When you select Set Up & Sign On from within the America Online

application, any windows or mail that you have open on your screen
will remain open as you sign on to America Online.

Departments

This option will bring up the Browse the Services window—the graphic
screen with icons that represent the eight departments of America
Online. To go to any of these departments, click on the icon that represents them.

Keyword... (Ctrl-K)

Keywords allow you to "jump" directly to many areas of America
Online. Using a keyword is simple: just pick Keyword from the Go To
menu, or type Ctrl-K. Then type the keyword of your choice—you'll
move directly to the area of your choice without having to traverse
through multiple windows.

    Choose Keyword List from the screen where you enter your Key-
word for a list of America Online keywords. (AOL will mail you a
Keyword Card with a list of favorite America Online keywords the
next business day after you sign on for the first time.) For more keywords, see Appendix A, "Keywords."

Directory of Services

The Directory of Services is a searchable database that helps you find
where to go online to see topics of interest to you. To use the Directory
of Services, choose "Search the Directory" from the list on the Directory
of Services window. Then type in a clue or keyword that describes
what you're looking for. You'll get a list of associated areas, and each
will contain a brief description of each area, its location and the keywords you'll need to move there quickly.

Lobby (Ctrl-L)

If you select this option, you'll go directly to the Lobby of People
Connection, America Online's social center.

Members' Online Support

This option will take you directly to the Members' Online Support
department, where you can find out what's happening online, what

new services are available, the status of your current bill, answers from our Customer Relations department—and just about anything you need to know as an America Online member. Use of this area is free of connect charges.

Network News

Every so often while you're online, America Online will send you "Network News"—small windows at the top of your screen that will let you know what's happening on America Online. If you select Network News from the Go To menu, you'll be able to scroll through all the Network News items that have been sent to you during your current online session.

Edit Go To Menu

This feature allows you to customize the Go To menu to suit your needs and interests. You can choose the areas you frequently visit and add the appropriate keyword to this menu, no matter where the area is online. Once you know the keywords to your favorite areas, personalize the Go To menu using this feature, and you'll make it easier than ever to move around.

AOL has preselected a few keywords for your Go To menu—items they think you'll want to try. If, however, you would like to remove or change any of these, just select Edit Go To Menu.

The Mail menu

America Online has a full-featured electronic mail system that's easy to use yet powerful.

Compose Mail (Ctrl-M)

You can compose and address a piece of mail using the same form whether you're online or off-line within the America Online application. If you select Compose Mail from the Mail menu, a blank mail form will appear on your screen.

From the Compose Mail form, you'll construct your memo and mailing information. To address your mail, simply type in the screen names of the recipients in the "to" field. If you have more than one recipient, be sure to separate the screen names with a comma; for example, MarshallR1, SallySue8, Robin.

Or, choose the Address Book from your Compose Mail form to access your personalized list of accounts.

America Online provides a "blind" carbon copy feature. That means that you can send a copy of your mail to someone without anyone else on the distribution list knowing about it. To do this, simply insert parentheses around the name of the secret recipient, as in (John1), and add that name to the CC field of your Compose Mail window.

You can also send any file—including a formatted word processor, spreadsheet, graphic or sound document—to another America Online member. Simply click the Attach File icon; then locate the name of the file you want to send on the standard file list. There's no limit on the size or type of file that you can attach. When you select the file you want to send, the name of the file will appear on the mail form, and the Attach File icon will change to Detach File. If you change your mind about sending the file, you can click on the Detach File icon and the file will be removed from the form.

Address Memo (Ctrl-A)

If you have a plain text document open (online or off), which you "Opened" from within the AOL application or created using the New option on the File menu, you can transform the text into a mail format so you can easily address and send it. Selecting the Address Memo option accomplishes this—then all you have to do is fill out the address portion of the memo and send it.

Read New Mail (Ctrl-R)

When you select Read New Mail from the Mail menu, a window will appear that lists your new (unread) mail. From this window, you can read each piece of mail by double-clicking, or by selecting with your arrow keys and the spacebar.

Check Mail You've Sent

This convenient online feature allows you to review mail you've sent and check to see if it has been read. Select the Status button to see who read it and when.

Check Mail You've Read

America Online stores your mail for one week after you've read it. You can use this option to review mail that you may have already read, or to check the status of mail you've read (to see if others on the distribution list have read it, too).

Mail Gateway

Select this option to find out how you can use AOL's Mail Gateway to send mail to friends and associates on CompuServe, MCI Mail, AT&T Mail, AppleLink and any other service connected to the Internet.

FAX/Paper Mail

America Online allows you to send FAX (no special equipment needed) and US Mail. If you select the FAX/Paper Mail option while you're online, you will find instructions and a list of prices for this service.

Edit Address Book

Your personal Address Book is a handy way to organize the mail addresses you use on a regular basis. Use this feature to compile an America Online "rolodex" to keep track of your online associates.

This is how it works. Suppose you meet a new friend online named Bart Simpson. His screen name on America Online is "BartS," and you want to add him to your personal Address Book. To do so, you would take the following steps:

- Select Edit Address Book from the Mail menu.

- Click on the Create button. A form will appear on your screen.

- In the Group Name field, type the name of your friend: Bart Simpson

- In the Account field, type the screen name of your friend: BartS

The next time you want to send a piece of mail to Bart (or anyone else in your Address Book), simply bring up the Compose Mail form, click on the Address Book icon on the left side of the form and click on the name of the person whose account address you would like to enter in the field.

You can even list group addresses in your Address Book. For example, let's suppose you have a group of online colleagues to whom you regularly send mail—your staff at work or your favorite Forum Leaders on America Online. This is how you'd create a group of addresses in your Address Book:

△ Select Edit Address Book from the Mail menu.

△ Click on the Create button. A form will appear on your screen.

△ In the Name field, type the name of your address group (for example: My Forum Leaders).

△ In the Accounts field, type the screen names of everyone you would like in that address group (for example: PC Kate, PCC Rowena, AFL Pete).

You have set up a group address, and every time you select My Forum Leaders from your Address Book, the names of those accounts will appear on the field you designate on your Compose Mail form.

You can also modify your address lists and delete names from your lists.

TIP: As you meet new friends and associates online, be sure to add their names to your Address Book. This way, you won't lose track of anyone by forgetting their "real" name or account address.

The Members menu

Send Instant Message (Ctrl-I)

Instant Messages are instant "for your eyes only" messages that you can send to anyone who is signed on to America Online at the same time as you.

When you select Send Instant Message from the Members menu, a form will appear on your screen where you can type the screen name of your intended recipient and your message. Then select Send, and the message will be on its way. To verify that the person is currently online, enter his or her screen name and click on the Available? button.

Get a Member's Profile (Ctrl-G)

This option will allow you to get basic information about the member whose screen name you specify. If a member has created an online profile (see below), this is a quick way to view it.

Locate a Member Online (Ctrl-F)

Using this option, you can find out if a member you're interested in talking to is online. If the person is in a "chat" area (People Connection, or a conference room), you'll be told where he/she is. If they're online but not in a "chat" area, you will simply be told that they're online.

Search Member Directory

This option will take you to America Online's Member Directory. Once you're there, you can look up detailed information about other members, enter a profile of yourself or search for the account names (screen names) or real names of other members.

Edit Your Online Profile

Use this option to create or modify your own online profile in the Member Directory.

Preferences

By selecting this feature, you can customize several America Online functions to suit you. You received the AOL software with preferences preselected for you ("defaults"). AOL thinks that most members will like them the way they are; but they know we, as members, are independent thinkers and like to make these decisions for ourselves! Don't worry about experimenting—you can always select this menu item and try something else if you don't like your changes.

   To turn a preference on or off, simply click on the box to the left of the preference.

General Preferences

△ Notify me immediately of Network News: (default is on). From time to time (about every 30 or 45 minutes when you're online), informational bulletins called "Network News" are sent to members with information about special events happening on the service "right now." For example, if the Graphics Forum is getting ready to start a meeting while you're online, you'll see a "Network News" notice to let you know when and where online it is happening. You don't need to do anything to get these messages—they will automatically appear at the top of your screen. If you'd prefer not to receive these messages while you're online, select Ignore Network News.

△ Double-space text in conference areas (default is off).

△ Automatically scroll documents as they're received: (default is off). If you select this option, incoming text (for example, a news article or electronic mail) will automatically scroll on your screen as it is sent from the America Online host computer. If you leave the option as is (the default), you'll still be able to manually scroll text using the scroll bar on the right on your incoming text window, even before the text has completely arrived.

Downloading Preferences

△ Decompress ZIP and ARC files when I sign off: (default is on). You will find that many AOL files that are available for downloading are "zipped" or "archived"—that is, they have been compressed so that they take up less space. The advantage to this is that they take less time to download, which saves you time and money.

△ Before you can use these files, however, they must be decompressed using the utility that comes free with your America Online software. AOL will automatically decompress any compressed files that you've downloaded when you sign off from America Online. This is a very convenient feature. If you'd prefer that these files not be decompressed, you can take care of that by turning off this preference. (But remember—the first time you try to use a file that is compressed, you will have to take the time to decompress it.)

⚉ Delete ZIP and ARC files after decompression: (default is off). If you turn on this preference (which is defaulted to off), America Online will automatically delete the compressed version of any file that is decompressed. This will save space on your hard drive.

⚉ Retain information about my last xx downloads: You can change the number of downloads that you store information about by clicking on the numbers.

⚉ Confirm additions to my download list: (default is on). If you leave this on, America Online will acknowledge every addition to your download list in your Download Manager.

Font & Color Preferences

⚉ Where possible, display text as __ Small __ Medium __ Large (default is medium).

⚉ Set background color of documents to gray: (default is off).

Edit Screen Names

This option allows you to add or delete new screen names to your "master account" (the name you created the first time you signed on). Although the screen name of your master account cannot be changed, you can use this option to add or delete "alter egos" for yourself, or create up to four additional subaccounts for yourself or members of your family. (Keep in mind that only one of these accounts can be signed on to America Online at any given time.)

You can have these additional accounts (each with their own password) at no additional charge. All online charges incurred by these accounts will be charged to the billing method the master account holder selected when first signing on.

The Window menu

The Window menu contains options for manipulating the workspace on your screen. You have the option to close one or all windows, hide a window and change the size of windows.

In addition to the commands at the top of the Window menu, you can select any open window by choosing the name of the open window from the list at the bottom of the Window menu.

APPENDIX D
On the Road

This appendix shows you how to change your America Online software's configuration and how to log on to America Online using a computer other than your own, or your own computer in another location. It also gives you some tips for solving problems and calling America Online while traveling.

Changing your Setup

The first time you log onto America Online, the software asks you several questions as part of the software installation process. Your answers determine such things as the speed of the modem, the local access telephone numbers to use and so on. However, you might need to change this information: for example, if you upgrade your modem or if you need to use different local access numbers while traveling.

To change your set-up options, launch the America Online software. Instead of signing on as you normally would, click on the Setup button at the bottom of the sign-on screen. The software displays a new window with a number of options. You can use this screen to change any of the following options:

- Phone Type—Touch-tone phones are standard equipment today in homes and hotels. However, there are still a few local phone exchanges (or homes) that do not support tone-dialing. If your AOL software seems to be having trouble when first dialing the local access number, use the Phone Type option to change your software to "Pulse" dialing.

- Phone Numbers—The First Try and Second Try fields contain the phone numbers your AOL software uses to connect with the Stratus. The Second Try number is used only if the First Try number is busy or does not respond properly. You will need to change these numbers if you're moving to a new area, if you're traveling or if you want to try a different local access number.

- To find a new number, you can remove both phone numbers from this screen and AOL will dial the 800 number and allow you to select new access numbers.

- Remember, any long-distance charges you incur reaching the AOL access number are your responsibility. They're not included as part of your monthly America Online fee.

- Baud Rate—You only need to change this if you get a modem with a different speed than your current modem, or if you're currently using a local access node that doesn't take full advantage of your modem's speed capabilities. For instance, you may use a local access number that can only handle 1200 baud. But if you later switch to a different number that can serve 2400-baud modems, and you have a 2400-baud modem, then you'll need to change the baud rate setting that your AOL software uses. Set the Baud Rate option to the highest speed your modem can handle.

- Network—This option is used to select which phone carrier handles your phone calls from the local access computer to AOL's Stratus. SprintNet is the most widely used carrier for AOL, but you can use the Network option to select the appropriate network as specified for the access number in the Members' Online Support Department.

- Outside Line Prefix—Some telephone systems, particularly in hotels or businesses, require you to dial a "9" or other prefix to get an outside line. Enter the number you want AOL to dial; then enter a comma. The comma tells the modem to wait two seconds before dialing the next number. If it takes longer than two seconds for your phone system to access an outside line and generate a dial tone, you might want to add a second comma just to be sure.

- Disabling Call Waiting—When you're connected to AOL and someone tries to call you, he or she would normally get a busy signal. But if you have Call Waiting, the caller hears a normal ring and AOL hears the beeps that normally let you know you've got a call waiting. As you can imagine, this tends to confuse your computer (not to mention the Stratus). This interference can corrupt file downloads and may even cause your modem to be disconnected from AOL. If you use Call Waiting, you can (and should) temporarily disable it on most phone systems by entering a code such as *70 or 1170 before dialing AOL. Be sure to include the comma after the string of numbers: it tells the modem to wait two seconds before dialing the next number. Note that the AOL software has already entered *70 and the comma for you in the Disable Call Waiting field. To configure your software to turn off Call Waiting whenever you dial AOL, all you have to do is click on the check box next to the words, Disable Call Waiting. If you aren't sure what numbers you should enter to disable Call Waiting, check with your local telephone company.

Solving common connection problems

If you have problems with line noise (static on your phone line while signed on to AOL), the result may be file-transfer errors, strange characters on the screen or occasional disconnections from America Online. One step you can take to cut down on line noise is temporarily to set your baud rate to a lower speed. Try the speed one step down from your current setting.

Another common problem is a phone cord with a bad connector (or jack) on one or both ends, or a faulty wall jack. If you hear lots of static when you're talking on the phone, odds are the same amount of static (line noise) is present when you use AOL. Check with your telephone company or an electrician to find out what can be done to improve your line quality.

Sudden disconnections can also be caused by Call Waiting. The click that indicates a call is waiting on the line sounds like a "break" (disconnect immediately) signal to the modem, which obligingly hangs up. If this is a problem, select the Disable Call Waiting option on the Setup screen (but only if you are indeed using Call Waiting).

Using America Online on the road

Using America Online when you are traveling is easy if you make a few preparations:

- Look up the local access numbers in the Members' Online Support Department for the area you'll be visiting. Do this *before* you leave; you can't use the directory unless you're signed on.

- If you're going to be staying in a hotel, ask for a "computer-ready" room: one with an extra phone jack for your modem. If the hotel doesn't have phones set up for computer users, you can usually remove the phone cable from its phone jack and connect your modem cable.

- Inexpensive kits are available that help in setting up your modem when traveling. It's also a good idea to travel with an extra length of standard phone line with modular (RJ-11) jacks on each end.

You can use America Online for backing up your work while traveling. Send mail to yourself and attach the file you want to save. If you need to restore the file, you can read the mail and download the saved file. If you lose your work while you're on the road, or even after you return, you'll have a backup waiting online when you get home.

Signing on as a Guest

When you install your America Online software, you also set up the screen names you'll use. You can store up to five names.

If you're logging on to AOL using a friend's computer, however, it won't have your screen names available on the sign-on screen. In that case, select the "Guest" screen name from the list of names on the sign-on screen and then click on the Sign On button. (The "Guest" name appears at the bottom of the list of screen names, no matter whose machine you're using or what kind of computer it is.) The software will dial the local access number and connect to AOL.

After you've made the connection, you'll see a dialog box that asks for a screen name and the password. Enter your screen name and password. America Online will connect using your account. Charges you accrue during the session will be billed to your account rather than your friend's.

Note: Data such as your Address Book information is stored locally on your computer rather than online. As a result, you will not be able to see this information when you are logged on as a Guest on another computer.

APPENDIX E
Running AOL Under GeoWorks

Although America Online is a standalone application and fully functional as such, it can also be run under GeoWorks as a GeoWorks application. (See the Glossary for a definition of GeoWorks.) Remember, AOL comes with a special run-time version of GeoWorks that is custom-designed for America Online. If you want to run AOL as a standard GeoWorks application, you'll need to buy and install the fully functional version of GeoWorks. If you'd like to find out more about GeoWorks, sign on to AOL and visit GeoWorks, which is in the Industry Connection Forum.

If you run AOL under GeoWorks, you will not only be able to fully operate AOL, you will also be able to work with other GeoWorks applications simultaneously. Because of the multitasking capabilities of the GEOS environment, you can work in GeoWrite and GeoDraw even while America Online is connected to the Stratus.

Switching between applications

To get to another GeoWorks application while in AOL, simply click on the Express button. The Express button is the button with an "E" on it at the very top of your screen near the left corner.

You'll see that the diamond next to America Online is blackened. Click on GeoManager to switch from AOL to the Advanced Workspace in GeoWorks. From this point, you will be able to click on any GeoWorks application icon to open that application and work within it.

There are several things to remember when switching applications:

   ▲ Unless you specifically logged off, you are still adding time to your AOL session and are getting charged for that time. AOL has no way to tell that you switched from that application, and the meter doesn't stop running.

⚠ You can't get back to AOL by clicking on its icon in the GeoManager workspace because AOL is still running in the background; it's in a window underneath the GeoManager. To return to AOL, click on the Express button and choose America Online from the list.

⚠ If you choose Exit to DOS from the Express Button menu, you will be disconnected from AOL and GeoWorks will be closed.

Switching to other GeoWorks applications while downloading

If you have the full-featured version of GeoWorks installed on your PC (not just the run-time portion of GeoWorks that comes as part of your AOL software), you can work in other GeoWorks applications in the foreground while AOL downloads files for you in the background.

First, before you start downloading, take AOL out of full-screen mode, and make sure that an open window from the other GeoWorks application that you want to use is visible. (This is necessary because you won't be able to use the Express menu to switch out of AOL.) Once your download begins, click on the background application window that you want to use; this will move AOL to the background and your other GeoWorks application to the foreground. Remember, though, that any processor- or disk-intensive tasks you perform in the foreground will slow down AOL's background downloading, and if you haven't set AOL to sign off automatically once the download is complete, your account will remain logged on in the background—running up charges—while you work away in another application in the foreground.

Using GeoWrite documents in AOL Mail

If you already have GeoWrite documents that you would like to use in America Online e-mail, or if you would like to spell-check your e-mail, you may create the document in GeoWrite. Any special character or type formatting you add will not be recognized by AOL, because the file you take into AOL will be nothing more than an ASCII text file with no formatting.

When you are finished composing and spell-checking and are ready to take your memo to AOL, you can either save it as a text file (under the File menu) or copy all the text using the Edit Copy command.

Now switch back to AOL using the Express button. If you saved the file as text, choose Open from the File menu to open the file. Then, if you want to send the file as e-mail, choose Address Memo from the Mail menu. The letter you wrote in GeoWrite will be attached to the Compose Mail screen and all you have to do is add the screen name and subject lines.

If you copied the text while in GeoWrite, you can start the Compose Mail screen (under the Mail menu), place your cursor where you want the GeoWrite text to begin and select Paste from the Edit menu. The text you copied will now appear in the Compose Mail window.

Running AOL under Microsoft Windows

America Online can be used with Microsoft Windows 3.x as a DOS application. Because AOL is unlike many other DOS applications in that it requires an uninterrupted connection to your phone line, special care must be taken when running America Online under Windows.

First, America Online is a full-screen graphic application. For that reason, Windows will not permit it to run in the background while other applications are used. Invoke the task-switching features of Windows with care; if you leave America Online unattended for too long, or if you switch tasks at all during communication-intensive operations such as file transfer, you may lose your connection. Also, note that you will continue to be billed for connect time while you are switched out of the America Online software; the host computer is unable to detect whether you have task-switched to another application. As a rule of thumb, we recommend not leaving America Online for more than five minutes while you are signed on.

Additionally, certain safety features of Windows must be disabled in order to achieve maximum performance from America Online. If you simply run the "AOL.BAT" file from the Windows File Manager, America Online may appear to be sluggish. Fortunately, a PIF file can be used to alert Windows to the special requirements of the America Online software. The needed PIF file, as well as a Windows-compatible America Online icon, is included with your AOL software. The PIF file provided assumes that you installed America Online in the suggested "AOL" directory on drive C. If your copy of America Online is elsewhere, you will need to use the PIF Editor accessory (included with Windows) to modify the PIF file.

Installing America Online into the Program Manager

To add America Online to your Program Manager:

🔺 Within the Windows Program Manager, create the program group to which you want to add America Online current.

🔺 Select New from the Program Manager File Menu.

🔺 Select the Program Item button; then select OK.

🔺 Enter a description for the Program Item: America Online is what we used.

🔺 Enter the following into the Command Line input field: C:\AOL\AOL.PIF. Alter the path appropriately if your copy of America Online is on a different drive or in a different directory.

🔺 Select the Change Icon button.

🔺 When the new window appears, type the following into the File Name input field: C:\AOL\AOL.ICO. Again, alter the path if needed.

🔺 Select the View Next button. The America Online logo should appear. If it does not, verify that you entered the path correctly.

🔺 Select OK to close both windows.

Now the America Online icon will appear in the program group that you chose, and using America Online becomes as simple as double-clicking on its icon. Consult your Windows manual for more information on the Program Manager and Windows functionality in general.

Modifying your America Online PIF file

You will only need to modify your PIF file if you installed America Online onto a drive other than C, or a directory other than AOL. If this is the case:

 Open the PIF Editor from the Accessories program group.

 From the File menu, open the PIF file contained in your America Online directory.

 Change the path on the line marked "Start-up Directory" to reflect the drive and directory that contains your AOL software.

 Select Save from the File menu.

Glossary

access number — A telephone number (usually a *local* telephone number) by which your modem may access America Online. See also *SprintNet*.

AFK — Common shorthand for "away from keyboard." The phrase is used in chat rooms and with Instant Messages to notify others that queries may not be answered for a while.

analog — Analog information is information composed of varying intensities of measurement. Sound and light, for instance, are examples of analog information, composed of waves of varying amplitude. Most real-world information is analog; most computer information is not. Contrast with *digital* and *binary*.

ANSI characters and graphics — American National Standards Institute characters represent an extension of the ASCII definition. ASCII represents the 128 characters (plus command characters) that a standard keyboard can produce. ANSI represents an additional 128 characters—things like foreign-language characters, trademark and registration symbols, and footnote symbols. While ASCII text transfers reliably across all kinds of computers, ANSI does not: the DOS ANSI set of characters differs from the Window's ANSI set, and the Window's ANSI set differs from the Mac's. See also *ASCII*.

article — Articles are textual documents intended, primarily, to be read online. Any article may be printed or saved, however, for later examination off-line. Contrast with *file*.

ASCII — The American Standard for Computer Information Interchange provides a numeric code for all the characters available using a standard keyboard. This code is common among all computers in this country (and in many other parts of the world), thus data in ASCII format is compatible with nearly every computer system. See also *ASCII text* and *ANSI characters*.

ASCII text — Textual data represented as ASCII numbers. Most e-mail is ASCII text (sometimes called "plain text") and is thus compatible with a wide variety of machines.

asynchronous communication — In asynchronous communication via modems, characters do not need to be transmitted constantly. Therefore, the start and end of a character need to be identified by use of a start bit and one or more stop bits.

attached file — America Online allows you to attach computer files of any nature—graphics, text, animation, sound—to an e-mail message. When mail with an attached file is received, the attached file is downloaded to the recipient's hard drive. Recipients must be members of AOL, however, since attached files are ignored when e-mail is sent from AOL to other electronic mail networks.

auto-answer — A modem configured to answer the phone when called is said to be set to auto-answer.

baud rate — This is an industry-accepted method of measuring modem speed. Roughly translated, baud rate divided by 8 equals transmission speed in bytes per second. If you are using a 2400-baud modem, for instance, data transmission to and from your computer will theoretically occur at 2400/8, or 300 bytes per second. Because of error-checking signals and data-identification protocols, about half to two-thirds of these bytes represent actual transmitted data; the rest of the data are confirmation and transmission commands and messages, and are discarded once they've served their purpose. A 2400-baud modem, in other words, actually transfers data at 150 to 200 bytes per second. See also *byte* and *modem*.

BBS — A Bulletin Board System (BBS) is any central system accessed via modem and phone lines and where data is posted for dissemination among the users. As such, America Online is a (large) BBS. Typically BBSes are much smaller than AOL and only offer a few—usually specialized—features. Features may include searchable databases, message boards and libraries. There are many more of these than most people expect: more than 200 are in operation in Portland, Oregon— typical for a community of 1 million residents.

binary — Literally, a binary condition is one where only two conditions may exist. In their heart of hearts, all computers are binary: nothing but on's and off's, 1's and 0's, yes's and no's. A *binary file* is one composed of 1's and 0's (as opposed to a *text file*, which is composed of text). Most graphics files are binary. A *binary graphic* is pure black or white: no gray and no color. Contrast with *ASCII text*. See also *digital* and *analog*.

bit — This is the smallest measure of computer information—literally a BInary digiT. A bit is binary: it can either be on or off—and nothing else. A string of eight bits is said to be a *byte*. Refer to *byte* for further information. See also *binary* and *digital*.

blind carbon copy — America Online provides the capability to send a blind carbon copy: a copy of an e-mail message sent to an AOL member other than the primary recipient without the recipient being aware of the copy. This is done by placing the name of the member who is to receive the blind carbon copy in parentheses within the CC address box. Compare with *carbon copy*.

board — See *message board* and *BBS*.

BRB — Common shorthand for "be right back." It is used by AOL members when participating in chat rooms or other online group discussions.

browse — Typically used in association with *message boards* and *libraries*, the term browse refers to a casual examination of message or file subject lines, rather than a detailed examination of the messages or files themselves. See also *message board*, *library*, *file* and *message*.

bulletin board — See *message board* and *BBS*.

byte — Roughly speaking, a byte is the amount of storage—either in random access memory or on disk—that's required to store one keystroke of information. This sentence, in other words, requires 60 bytes of storage. America Online's maximum "field length" is 32,000 bytes, or 32k. This means that theoretically, messages posted on AOL can be as large as 32k. In fact, AOL limits messages to 24k, leaving room for header information like date, time, sender and receiver. This also means that your America Online software cannot open files larger than 32k. This entire glossary contains about 25k to 30k of text information.

carbon copy — Though e-mail messages may be addressed to multiple recipients, carbon copies may be sent to those for whom the message is of secondary interest. The primary addressee is aware of the copy, similar to the CC: convention used in business correspondence. Compare with *blind carbon copy*.

chat — Whenever a number of people are simultaneously connected to America Online (or any other telecommunication service), they may chat, or type messages to one another in real time. AOL has numerous *chat rooms* for this purpose.

chat room — Chat rooms are where members gather to type messages to one another in real time, receiving immediate responses—none of the store-and-forward encountered in electronic mail. America Online offers "public" chat rooms (the names of which are published on the network and thus easily accessed by all members) and "private" chat rooms, which are open only to those who create them or know their names and meeting times. See also *chat*.

close box — The close box is the little box with the hyphen-type bar in the upper-left corner of a window. Clicking on this box closes the window.

club — See *forum*.

common carrier — See *packet-switching network*.

CompuServe — One of the first commercial online services, similar to America Online, though with less of an emphasis on community and graphical interface. CompuServe is now owned by H & R Block.

CPU — The Central Processing Unit is the heart of a computer. It's actually a small "chip" of electronic components.

Ctrl key — The Control (Ctrl) key on a PC is usually located near the space bar. Like the Shift key, the Ctrl key is held down while another key is pressed, thus issuing a command.

database — A database is an organized collection of information, usually maintained by a computer. Think of your telephone book as a database of people with telephones, organized alphabetically, and including a name, address and phone number for each person in the database. A *searchable* database would be like a telephone book that would let you say, "Give me a list of all of the people on Elm Street," or "Show me all of the people with 555 as the first three digits of their phone numbers." Most of America Online's databases are searchable.

data bit — Not all bits within a telecommunications byte represent data. In some systems, the eighth bit (the *parity bit*) is used to determine the integrity of the other seven. The other seven, then, would be the *data bits* for that byte. See also *parity*.

DataPac — DataPac is a packet-switching network operated by Bell Canada. See *SprintNet* and *packet-switching network* for a thorough explanation.

department — This is the broadest category of information into which America Online divides its material. At this writing there are eight departments: Computing & Software, Games & Entertainment, Learning & Reference, Lifestyles & Interests, News & Finance, People Connection, Industry Connection and Travel & Shopping. See also *forum*.

digital — Digital signals are those composed of binary information, typically 1's and 0's. Digital devices are those that respond to these signals. All computer data is digital. Contrast with *analog*. See also *binary*.

DOS — The Microsoft Disk Operating System (usually called DOS, or MS-DOS) is the most popular operating system for IBM-PCs and compatibles. DOS is required for running all DOS-based programs on a PC and requires the use of codes and proper syntax to correctly issue a command.

download — In the America Online context, downloading is the transfer of stored information from the Stratus to your computer. Usually, downloads are *files*, which are intended for review once you're off-line. You download graphics and programs, for instance. See also *file*; contrast with *upload*. Download is used often as both a noun and a verb. For instance, you might *download* a graphic file to your hard drive, where you store your latest *downloads*.

e-mail — Electronic mail is private mail sent from one computer to another. America Online's e-mail can be sent to multiple recipients, carbon-copy recipients and blind-carbon-copy recipients. It can be replied to and forwarded and even include attached files. Electronic mail can be sent to other AOL members as well as members of other popular online services and telecommunications networks. E-mail is private and every bit as inviolable as US Mail. Compare with *voice mail* and *message*.

emoticons — Characters, mostly consisting of punctuation, which are meant to be viewed sideways, and which give information on the writer's emotional state. The symbol :) is a smile (turn your head 90 degrees counterclockwise to see it). Also referred to as *smileys*.

external modem — External modems are housed in their own case and are located outside the computer. They often are capable of serving any kind of computer, not just a DOS-based PC.

fax (facsimile) — A method for sending images over telephone lines. Fax images may be sent from computer to computer as well (without the use of fax machines), using the appropriate software and modem. America Online will send any e-mail message to a designated fax machine if you wish. The process is described in Chapter 11, "Electronic Mail."

fax modem — Modems equipped to send and receive fax messages as well as standard telecommunication. Nearly any computer-generated document can be sent as a fax: just select the fax modem as the "printer." Received fax documents are stored on the computer's hard disk for viewing on-screen or printing on a printer. See also *fax*.

file — In this context, a file is a computer file (text, graphics, program, sound, animation) that is intended to be *downloaded* to a member's computer for review off-line. Files may be attached to e-mail or stored in *libraries*. See also *download* and *library*. Contrast with *article*.

file compression — As if by magic, many computer files can be reduced to half (or even less) of their original size by using file-compression techniques. Though they must be decompressed to be used, compressed files take up much less storage space than their uncompressed counterparts, and require far less time to transfer via the America Online system or any modem. Files compressed using a product called PKZip are decompressed automatically by the AOL software.

flow control — A method used to synchronize communications between two computers. Computer A may be sending information faster than computer B can receive it. To accommodate the problem, computer B sends a signal to computer A asking it to stop sending until B can catch up. The protocol employed by the two computers to facilitate this synchronization is called flow control. See also *protocol*.

forum — America Online's forums (or *clubs*) are places where people with similar interests visit to exchange ideas, opinions and comments. Most forums offer *message boards*, *articles*, *chat rooms* and *libraries*. Wine & Dine Online, for instance, is a club. So are the Online Home Companion and BikeNet. See also *article*, *chat room*, *library* and *message board*.

forum leader/consultant/assistant — America Online employs a number of knowledgeable members to coordinate and maintain the myriad complexities of its forums: checking uploaded files for viruses, responding to mail and messages, organizing public-room appearances and monitoring message traffic. Normally, only one forum leader serves as "chairperson" of the forum, with a number of *forum consultants* and *forum assistants* to serve as aides. These people are recognizable by their screen names, which contain the letters "AFL," "AFC" or "AFA"—worn like the stripes of military uniforms to identify their expertise and position within the AOL hierarchy.

gateway — America Online offers a number of links to other telecommunications services. The EAASY SABRE travel reservations service, for instance, is an entirely separate system—independent of AOL, as are the Internet electronic mail system and StockLink investment tracking service. Connections made to these other services are referred to as gateways. See also *Internet*.

GeoWorks — GeoWorks is the graphical user interface upon which PC AOL is housed. It is a very sophisticated multitasking, windowing environment and is marketed as a high-performance, cost-effective alternative to MS Windows, easily running on all PCs from XTs to 486s.

Guide — Guides are America Online members who specialize in helping other members and are chosen for their helpful and friendly online personalities. You can usually find a Guide in the Lobby after 6:00 PM Eastern time. See also *Lobby*.

hacker — Generally speaking, hackers are computer aficionados who take delight in unlocking the conundra of mysteries in a computer system. More specifically, hackers have come to be associated with computer "pirates," sailing the oceans of global networks and plundering their riches. Read Cliff Stoll's *The Cuckoo's Egg* (see bibliography) for an engrossing, if not alarming, true story of international espionage at the hands of an expert hacker. See also *virus*.

Hayes compatible — A Hayes-compatible modem is one that implements the Hayes Command Set—a series of commands for controlling a modem introduced with the Hayes Smartmodem 300 in the early 1980s. These commands have become standardized and are used by America Online's software to issue commands such as to lift the phone off the hook, dial and hang up. You will need a Hayes-compatible modem to use America Online.

icon — A pictographic representation of a command, request or thing. Usually, you can click on an icon with a mouse and the computer will take some form of action. The America Online Welcome screen features a series of icons along its right side to alert members to significant features posted on the system.

initialization string — The sequence of characters sent to a modem in order to set it up for subsequent communications. Accessed through America Online's Setup command.

insertion point — The flashing vertical bar representing the cursor whenever text is being edited. Any typing will appear at the insertion point. An insertion point may be moved using either the mouse or the arrow keys.

instant message — Instant messages may be exchanged between two AOL members logged on to the service at the same time. By choosing Send Instant Message from the Members menu, you may enter the recipient's screen name and a short message, then send the message to another member who is currently signed on. The recipient will see the message within a few seconds and will be provided with the opportunity to respond. Instant messages may be exchanged at any time, from nearly any portion of the service.

interface — The method by which a computer communicates with a human and vice-versa. The *textual* interface (or command line interface) has been the primary interface for years on the PC, whereby all communication was accomplished with a series of textual commands and menus. The Macintosh was the first widely accepted consumer-oriented computer with a graphical user interface (GUI), which includes a mouse, pull-down menus and dialog boxes. Since then the Windows and GeoWorks environments have brought a similar graphical interface to PCs. Pen-based interfaces are now common, as are audible menu-driven interfaces, such as those used by voice-mail systems.

Internet — The Internet is a network of computer networks, which are interconnected at all times. It spans the globe, connecting more than 100,000 machines, many of which serve as hubs for local networks, serving scores—even hundreds—of users each. The Internet is maintained by the National Science Foundation. AOL offers an Internet e-mail service; use the keyword: Internet. See also *gateway*.

keyword — Keywords are shortcuts to specific destinations within America Online. You can jump directly to your stock portfolio, for instance, by using the keyword: Portfolio. To use a keyword, type Ctrl-K and then the keyword, followed by the Return or Enter key.

kilobyte — 1024 bytes of data. Often abbreviated by "k," as in "a 32k text file."

library — In the America Online context, a library is a vehicle for the storage of *files*. If you want a graphic of Bart Simpson, for instance, you will probably want to search a library for it. Indeed, some libraries are searchable (see *database*), while others must be *browsed*.

line noise — You have heard line noise before but probably haven't thought much about it: line noise is that extraneous noise on telephone lines that we usually hear as clicks, pops and hisses. While line noise is usually only a nuisance to voice communication, it wreaks havoc with telecommunications signals.

Lobby — The Lobby is America Online's primary public *chat room*. Members can stop by the Lobby at any time to chat with other members or to see a listing of other public rooms. As such, the Lobby is somewhat analogous to the lobby of a hotel. See also *chat room*.

LOL — Common shorthand for "laughing out loud." Used during chat sessions while online with other users.

megabyte — 1,048,576 bytes of data.

message — Messages are posted on *message boards* by members for other members to read and as such are public. See *message board*; contrast with *e-mail*.

message board — Analogous to a cork bulletin board, message boards (or simply *boards*) are places where members post messages, typically to solicit a reply or to comment on a prior message. Because messages accumulate quickly, America Online organizes boards using folders, wherein a number of messages on a specific subject are contained. Message boards are sometimes called bulletin boards.

modem — This is a contraction of MOdulator/DEModulator, a device for converting digital information (which your computer requires) into audio information (which your telephone requires) and back again. You need a modem to communicate with America Online. See also *auto-answer*, *baud rate* and *Hayes compatible*.

node — As used in the America Online context, a node is a single telephone number used by several people in a particular region to access the AOL system. Most nodes are local and do not involve long-distance charges. See also *packet-switching network* and *SprintNet*.

online — The condition of a computer when it is connected to another machine via modem.

operating system — The underlying program that coordinates all of the invisible operations necessary for a computer's operation: finding, reading and writing disk files; accepting keyboard input; managing memory; and sending output to the screen and printer. In many ways, an operating system is to a computer what the autonomic nervous system is to a human. The operating system for IBM-PCs and their clones is usually MS-DOS; AOL's Stratus computer uses an operating system called VOS. The Macintosh operating system is "the System," or "System 7."

packet-switching network — Packet-switching networks (PSNs) are networks of computers that communicate via a defined packet format. Let's say computer A is talking to New York and computer B is talking to Washington, DC. Both A and B are in California. By using *packets* of information, computer A can send a packet, then computer B, then A, and so on. The computer in New York "sees" all of the incoming packets, but only receives those intended for it. If all of the computers on the network agree on a definition of a packet, they can all share the same telecommunications circuit—usually a telephone line. This is how a single telephone line (node) in, say, Sacramento, can handle hundreds of computer conversations simultaneously. America Online uses a variety of PSNs to supply local nodes (local telephone numbers) for members' access. See also *SprintNet*.

parity (parity bit) — An early technique for error correction that utilizes one extra bit per character—the parity bit—to validate the integrity of the received data. Few telecommunications services use the parity bit any longer. Contrast with *data bit*.

PKZip — PKZip is PC file-compression software written by PKWare, Inc. It includes the ability to zip and unzip files, verify authenticity, create self-extracting files and more. PKZip is distributed via both shareware and commerical channels. Files compressed with PKZip are automatically "unzipped" when downloaded from America Online or when opened using the AOL software. PKZip files (called "archives") are often identified by the ".ZIP" filename extension. A PKZip archive can contain many individual files combined into a single archival file. Use the keywords: File Search and enter PKZip. See also *file compression*, *self-extracting archive*, *download* and *shareware*.

protocol — Telecommunication protocols are techniques by which sender and receiver validate the integrity of received data. Using mutually agreeable protocols, the receiver can notify the sender of garbled transmissions and request the data in question to be resent. AOL's telecommunications protocols are especially elaborate, allowing for the interruption (and subsequent resumption) of data transfer without damage to the file in question. See also *line noise*.

screen name — Screen names are the names used by AOL members to identify themselves online. Screen names may contain no fewer than three and no more than ten characters and must be unique. Any one account may have up to five screen names, to accommodate family members and/or alter-egos.

searchable database — See *database*.

self-extracting archive — Most compressed files must be decompressed using the same software that compressed them. Most PKZip files, for example, must be decompressed using PKZip software (or the AOL software, which includes portions of PKZip for decompression). Self-extracting archives, on the other hand, contain not only the compressed data, but also the routines necessary to decompress themselves. Self-extracting archives are often identified by the ".sea" filename extension. See also *file compression* and *PKZip*.

shareware — Shareware is software that's typically posted on services like AOL for distribution (via downloading) directly to the user. Since the producer (or programmer) usually posts shareware and the user downloads it, distribution is direct and nearly without cost. Users are generally encouraged to make copies and give them to friends—even post them on other services. This method of "pass-around" distribution gives rise to the term "shareware." Payment is voluntary and relatively small ($5 to $50), sent directly to the producer. Shareware survives on the honor system. A number of permutations have developed, among them freeware (no payment) and postcardware (send a picture post-card to the producer).

smileys — See *emoticons*.

SprintNet — SprintNet (a service of US Sprint—formerly called TeleNet) is a long-distance carrier offering local "nodes," or local telephone numbers, to remote services. Local nodes mean no long-distance charges: America Online pays SprintNet and other carriers, not you. These services are leased by a number of public and private companies: when you dial up AOL, you may be sharing a node with users of other commercial services, small companies feeding their daily financial reports to service bureaus, banks—all kinds of telecommunications users. Node sharing brings the cost of the service down. That's why America Online doesn't run long-distance lines of its own: large carriers like SprintNet are simply less expensive. Another carrier—Datapac (a subsidiary of Bell Canada)—serves Canadian members. All carriers used by AOL are properly called *packet-switching networks*.

stop bit — A bit that follows a byte of data to signify the end of a character.

Stratus — America Online's online computer is a Stratus, manufactured by the Stratus Corporation in Marlboro, MA. The Stratus features a "redundant" operating system and hardware configuration. Multiple processors, disks and memory banks process and store everything twice. This is an expensive process (Stratus is one of the most expensive computer systems you can buy), but it doubles the system's reliability. The Stratus runs 365 days a year, 24 hours a day, and it's backed up by a standby diesel generator in case the power fails.

telecommunications — Two-way communications between computers via modems and telephone lines.

upload — In the America Online context, uploading refers to the transfer of files from your computer to AOL's Stratus. Uploaded files may be attached to e-mail (therefore, typically intended for a single recipient, and more frequently referred to as attached files), or they may be uploaded for inclusion in a *library*, for all to see and use. See also *file* and *library*; contrast with *download*.

Windows — Microsoft's Windows is a graphical extension to DOS, the operating system for IBM-PCs and compatibles. Using standards partially licensed by Apple Computer, Windows offers pull-down menus, dialog boxes and mouse-oriented operation similar to that of the Macintosh. See also *DOS*.

virus — A computer virus is a program that travels from machine to machine via floppy disks, networks or telecommunications services. Analogous to biological viruses, computer viruses are unwelcome intruders and may be destructive. All software uploaded to America Online is checked for viruses, and you can download antiviral software programs from America Online for use on your own PC. Computer viruses are usually written by hackers who take delight in spawning progeny and seeing them replicate throughout the electronic universe. See also *hacker*.

voice mail — Many telephone systems and telephone companies now offer voice mail, a system of leaving voice messages when no one answers the phone or the phone is busy. Voice mail systems offer most of the advantages of e-mail systems, and one major disadvantage: if the addressee lives some distance away, voice mail delivery usually involves a long-distance call. Compare with *e-mail*, which usually does *not* involve long-distance charges.

Bibliography

Aboba, Bernard. *The BMUG Guide to Bulletin Boards and Beyond.* Berkeley, CA: BMUG, 1992.

Though BMUG is an acronym for the Berkeley Macintosh Users' Group, this book is not particularly Macintosh-specific. Aside from the 100 or so pages devoted to use of the BMUG Bulletin Board System (BBS), this book is a thorough presentation of telecommunications subjects, including a quick-start chapter; using USENET UUCP and FidoNew netmail; a BBS Network Guide; sending mail around the world; jargon; buying a modem; how to save money on your phone bill; file transfer between Macs, PCs and Unix; and file compression. Excellent basic reference for any telecommunicator, especially the Internet user.

Banks, Michael. *The Modem Reference.* New York: Brady, 1988.

If you're looking for a basic handbook on using a modem, this book offers plenty of sound advice. It also features a complete guide to several commercial online services (including America Online) and has lots of tips and suggestions for trouble-shooting your modem.

Dvorak, John C. *Dvorak's Guide to PC Connectivity.* New York: Bantam, 1991. 3 disks.

As its title suggests, this book is more about connectivity, not telecommunications (Dvorak's telecommunications book appears below). It is divided into four parts: cables, hardware (modems, fax, scanners, storage, printers), connectivity software and networks.

Dvorak, John C. and Nick Anis. *Dvorak's Guide to PC Telecommunications.* Berkeley, CA: Osbourne-McGraw Hill, 1990. 2 disks.

A comprehensive examination of telecommunications, divided into four parts: layperson's view, technical view, user guides (to the programs on the enclosed disks) and appendices.

Glossbrenner, Alfred. *The Complete Handbook of Personal Computer Communications: Everything You Need to Know to Go Online With the World* (3rd ed.). New York: St. Martin's Press, 1989.

This is the book to get if you're after a listing of all the commercial online services available and what they have to offer. Includes CompuServe, Delphi, Dow Jones, Huttonline, Investor's Express, NewsMet, MCI Mail and, of course, America Online.

Nelson, Kay. *Voodoo DOS: Tips & Tricks With an Attitude*. Chapel Hill, NC: Ventana Press, 1992.

DOS demystified. This book offers DOS users tips on everything from making backups to customizing the Shell. A tip-filled chapter on memory management is particularly valuable.

Pournelle, Jerry and Michael Banks. *Pournelle's PC Communications Bible*. Redmond, WA: Microsoft Press, 1992.

More of a practical view of telecommunications than a technical one, this book features chapters on online research, doing business by modem, international communications (with emphasis on Japan and Europe), how it works and modems.

Rittner Don. *EcoLinking: Everyone's Guide to Online Environmental Information*. Berkeley, CA: Peachpit Press, 1992.

The first guide to the rapidly growing phenomenon of activists and researchers using personal computers to link up with each other and their resources. Excellent guide to online research—including the Internet—in the layperson's lexicon.

Robinson, Phillip. *Delivering Electronic Mail*. San Mateo, CA: M&T Books, 1992.

A thorough treatise on electronic mail, including chapters on terminology, security, choosing an e-mail system, using an e-mail system, managing an e-mail system, LAN e-mail programs, public e-mail systems and the Internet. Excellent resource for the person in charge of a local e-mail system.

Stoll, Cliff. *The Cuckoo's Egg*. New York: Pocket Books (Simon & Schuster), 1990.

Reads like a spy novel, but it's a true story of computer espionage via Internet. This is great reading, regardless of whether you're interested in telecommunications. It's required reading if you want to know more about the Internet. Cliff nailed the spy (after three years of tracking— when the CIA, FBI and NSA could not—and made the front page of the *New York Times*).

Index

A

Academic Assistance Center 219–21
Address Book 275–77
    adding names 275–76
Airline reservations 192–96
    booking 196
    finding cost 195
    finding flights 194–95
Alchemy 306
America Online
    description of 2–14
    examples of use 10–12
    using away from home 1–5, 310
America Online (software) 8–10
    installing 28–41
        to Microsoft Windows 360
        requirements for 22–28
        See also Installation
    loading from DOS 41
AOLDBF 307
AOL.PIF 307
Archives, Online Russian 210–12
Archives, self-extracting 185
Articles 117–18
ASCD Online 228–29
Authors' Cafe 239–41
AUTOEXEC.BAT 32
Automobiles
    buying 201–3
AutoVantage 201–3

B

Baird, Andy 221
Barwick, Tim 171
    uploading tips 189
Baud rates
    changing 2, 352
    defined 24
    installing modem 39

Bicycling
    BikeNet Forum 143–45
Billing
    account status 68, 188, 303, 310
    See also Payment
Book
    how to use *See* Using this book
Book Bestsellers Forum 76–77
Boolean searching 121–23, 174–75
Box Office 253
Break key 112, 302, 337
Brockman, Sandy
    humorous stories 308
Bulls & Bears Game 104
Business, small *See* Small business
Buttons
    selecting 335

C

Call Waiting
    disabling 311, 352–53
Carbon copies
    blind 264
    electronic mail 264
Career Center 213–16
Cartoons 77–79
Case, Steve 13
    letter from 49
Categories
    keywords 326–33
Center Stage 253–56
    schedules 253
Chat rooms 69–70
    excluding comments 248
    highlighting comments 248
    hints for new members 244
    list of people in 246–47
    techniques 245–48
    See also Rooms, private; Rooms, public

Chats
    composing   245–46
Clancy, Tom   239–41
College Board Handbook   222–23
    searching   222–23
College Board Online   221–24
Colleges & universities
    courses   212–13
    guidance   221–24
Comedy Club   82–84
Compressing   See Files, compressing
Compton's Encyclopedia   206–8
    searching   207
Computer Express   199–200
Computers
    consumer information   199–200
    using multiple   310
Computing & Software Department   147–90
    forums   161–70
    Home-Office Computing
        (periodical)   152
    Microsoft Knowledge Base   152–53
    Networker's Journal   153
    New Product Information   153
    News & Reference   150–56
    Newsbytes News
        Network   153, 155–56
    online to computer industry   156–61
    PC World Online (periodical)   148–50
Conference calls
    private rooms as   245
CONFIG.SYS   32
Configuring
    software   8–10
    telephone connection   41–42, 351–52
Connecting   21–50
    errors   42, 353
    first time   42–49
Control keys   336–37
Copy & paste
    electronic mail messages   267, 358–59
Credit cards   26, 45–47
    entering information   47

Crossman, Craig   151–52
Ctrl-X   112, 302, 337
Customer Relations   57, 63
    most frequently asked
        questions   308–11
Customer Service Live   61–63
Cut & paste
    chats   245–46

D

Databases, online
    searching   107–8, 119–24
        expressing criteria   120–23
    See also specific names of databases
        (PC World Online, Microsoft
        Knowledge Base, etc.)
Datapac   7
de Boor, Tom   218
    tips for using America Online   302–5
Decompressing   See Files, decompressing
Definitions
    financial terms   104–5
    terms used in book   363–76
Departments
    accessing   335
    entering area   335
    See also specific name of department
Diamond Computer Systems
    online support   158–59
Directory
    for America Online installation   30–31
Directory of Services   58–61
    accessing   61
    keywords   317
    searching   59–61
Documentation
    using this book as   14–17
DOS, DR   162–63, 307
DOS Forum   161–64
DOS prompt
    loading America Online   41

Download Manager 291–99
    commands 296
    deleting files from list 296
    help 296
    logging off 297
    percentage completed 297
    selecting destination 296
    sign off, alternative to 295–96
    starting downloading 297
    viewing descriptions of files 296
    See also Downloading
Downloading 137–38, 171–85
    defined 171–72, 179
    finding files for 172–78
        shareware 307
    hardware & software
        requirements 177
    judging efficiency of 179
    number times file downloaded 177
    preferences 349–50
    process of 179–80
    reply to creators 313
    resume after interruption 297
    selecting files 292–95
    ten best shareware 305–8
    time
        estimate 176–77
        taking too long 179
    timing 304
    See also Download Manager
DR DOS *See* DOS, DR
Drivers
    deleting 40
DR6WIN 307

E

E-mail *See* Electronic mail
EAASY SABRE gateway 192–96
Ecology
    Environmental Club 139–41
Edit menu 341–42

Electronic mail
    Address Book 275–77
    addressing 263
        multiple addresses 263–64
    advantages of 259
    alternatives 283
    carbon copies 264
        blind 264
    checking mail already read 272
    checking mail sent 273–74
    composing 263–66
        off-line 265–66, 303
        word processor, on 267
    copy & paste 267
        from GeoWorks 267, 358–59
    defined 258
    FAXes, sending 284–86
    features of 258
    files
        attaching to message 280–81
        sending as memo 266–67
    filing 278–80
        date-based 279
        mail sent 280
        people-based 279
        single subdirectory 279
        subject-based 279
    forwarding 271
    international 286–89
    Internet 286–89
    off-line preparation 265–67
    paper mail, sending 283–84, 286
    process of 259–63
    reading
        chronological order 269
        new mail 261–62, 268–69
    replying to 269–71
        sending original
            message with 271
    sample exercise 259–63
    saving 278–79
    sending
        multiple addresses 278

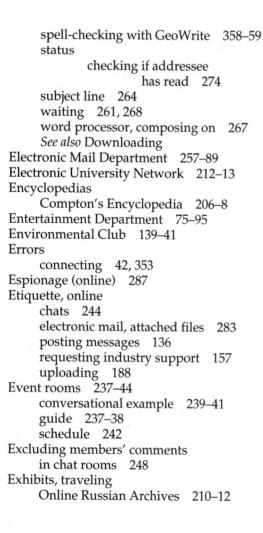

spell-checking with GeoWrite   358–59
status
    checking if addressee
        has read   274
subject line   264
waiting   261, 268
word processor, composing on   267
See also Downloading
Electronic Mail Department   257–89
Electronic University Network   212–13
Encyclopedias
    Compton's Encyclopedia   206–8
Entertainment Department   75–95
Environmental Club   139–41
Errors
    connecting   42, 353
Espionage (online)   287
Etiquette, online
    chats   244
    electronic mail, attached files   283
    posting messages   136
    requesting industry support   157
    uploading   188
Event rooms   237–44
    conversational example   239–41
    guide   237–38
    schedule   242
Excluding members' comments
    in chat rooms   248
Exhibits, traveling
    Online Russian Archives   210–12

F

Facial expressions
    finding list of smileys   313
    symbols for   267
    ten best smileys   313–14
Fairy Godmom   308
FAXes   284–86
File menu   339
File Search   172–78
Files
    attaching to messages   280–81

compressing   182–85
    lossy   306
    shareware   306
decompressing   184–85, 349–50
descriptions of   173–79
    saving   178
downloading   137–38, 171–85
    selecting for   292–95
    shareware   307
    See also Download Manager;
        Downloading
electronic mail   279
    attaching to messages   280–81
    memo, as   266–67
finding   172–78
    keywords, using   177
    search criteria   174–75
format   172, 181–82, 299
GIF   *See* GIF files
names   180, 279–80
    extensions   181–82
PIF   *See* PIF file
reading   280
saving electronic mail   278–79
stuffing   *See* Files, compressing text
    printing   58
    saving   57–58
unstuffing   *See* Files, decompressing
uploading   186–89
    See also Uploading
ZIP   *See* ZIP files
Finance   98–105
    definitions of terms   104–5
First session online   42–49
Folders   117–18
    browsing   131
    reading messages in   127–28
Fonts
    preferences   350
    Windows Forum   168
Forums   115–45
    articles & folders   117–18
    Computing & Software
        Department   161–70

finding help online   164
keywords   318–26
Lifestyles & Interests
        Department (list)   116
See also specific names of forums

G

Game shows
        Center Stage   253–56
Games   89–94
        Bulls & Bears   104
        Fairy Godmom   308
        Neverwinter Nights   90–93
        PC Games Forum   169–70
        play-by-mail   94
        Quantum Space   94
        RabbitJack's Casino   93
        Wolfenstein 3-D   307–8
Gateway 2000 (hardware)
        online support   159
Gateways
        defined   192
GeoWorks   9
        running America Online
                shareware   307
GeoWorks Ensemble
        Center Stage feature   254–56
        copy & paste for electronic
                mail   267, 358–59
        GeoWrite   358–59
        installing America Online   29–30
        online support   159
        running America Online   357–58
                switching between
                        applications   357–58
GeoWrite   358–59
GIF files   172, 299
        converting to PC format   172
                shareware   306
Glossary   363–76
Go To menu   342–44
        editing   125
Gralow, Nancy   124

Grandstand   79–82
Graphics
        availability   1
        Graphics Meeting Room   165
        Macintosh Graphics Forum   1, 165
        PC Animation & Graphics
                Forum   164–65
        transferring   10
Graphics Interchange Format   *See* GIF files
Graphics Workshop   172, 306
Guides   68–70, 236–37
        defined   68

H

Hanley, Stuart   155–56
Hard disks
        recovery after disaster   155–56
Hardware
        buying   200
        problem-solving   156–61
        used by America Online   5–6
        See also Computing & Software
                Department
Help   51–70, 308–11
        Customer Relations   57, 63
        Customer Service Live   61–63
        Directory of Services   58–61
        forums   164
        keywords   59
        Members Helping Members   63–70
        methodical approach   52
        off-line   53–54
        online   55–70
                See also Members Online
                        Support
        online to hardware & software
                vendors   156–61
        screens
                saving   58
        ten best tips   303
        topics
                printing   58
                saving   57–58

Help menu   339
Highlighting members' comments
     in chat rooms   248
Home-Office Computing (periodical)   152
Homework
     assistance   219–21
Houses, buying and selling
     Real Estate Forum   141–42
Humorous stories   308

I

Independent Traveler   196–99
Industry Connection   156–61
Initial session online   42–49
Installation   28–41
     GeoWorks, using   29–30
     to Microsoft Windows   360
     modems   38–39
     mouse   35–38
     printers   40
     requirements for   22–28
     subdirectory for America
          Online   30–31
     video adapter   33–34
Instant Messages   249–53
     defined   249
     phone calls, instead of   249
     sending   250–51
Internet mail gateway   286–89
Interrupt key   112, 302, 337
Investing   98–105
IYM Software Review (periodical)   152

J

Jobs
     Career Center   213–16
JPEG   306

K

Keefe, Mike   294–95
Keyboard   335–37
     shortcuts   336
          ten best tips   302
Keywords   318–33
     accessing online   59, 317
     category, sorted by   326–33
     Directory of Services   317
     forums, sorted by   318–26
     general   318
     searching for files   177
     ten best tips   302
     tips   318

L

Learning & Reference Department   205–31
Lectures
     Center Stage   253–56
Levitt, Jay   62–63
     most frequently asked
          questions   308–11
Libraries   137–38
     defined   137
Lifestyles & Interests Department   115–46
     forums, list of   116
Lobby   234–36
     conversation in   236
     entering   234–36
     making friends online   311
Logs   105–6, 303–4
     message boards   129
Lossy compression
     shareware   306

M

Macintosh Graphics Forum   1, 165
Magazines   *See* Periodicals
Mail   *See* Electronic mail; Paper mail
Mail menu   263–77, 344–47

Market News   102–3
Member Directory   70–72
Members
    directory of   70–72
    locating online   247
    new
        beginning explorations   310
        hints for chatting   244
        New Member Lounge   243–44
    photographs   247
    profiles   70, 72–74, 312
        chat room users   247
        creating & editing   72–73, 311
    similar interests, finding   71–72, 312
    See also Members Helping Members;
        Members Online Support
Members Helping Members   63–70
Members menu   347–50
Members Online Support   55–70
    Customer Relations   57, 63
    Customer Service Live   61–63
    Directory of Services   58–61
    Guides   68–70
    Members Helping Members   63–70
    topics available   57
    windows closing when chosen   56
Menu bar   339–50
Menus
    Edit   341–42
    File   339
    Go To   125, 342–44
    Help   339
    Mail   263–77, 344–47
    Members   347–50
    pulling down   336
    Window   350
Message boards   65–68, 124–36
    adding messages   135–36
    browsing   129–31
    date of last visit   133
    defined   65
    finding messages   132–34
    finding new messages   132

logging messages   129
making friends online   312
messages posted since
        specific date   134
posting messages   135–36
reading messages   126–34
    first message   129–30
selecting a board   126–27
subject of messages   130–31
Messages   *See* Instant Messages;
    Message Boards
Microsoft
    online support   159
Microsoft Knowledge Base   152–53
Microsoft Small Business Center   108–13
Microsoft Windows
    running America Online   359
Miller, Peter G.   142
Modems   4, 23–24
    buying   24–25
    connecting   25–26
    defined   23
    installing   38–39
    speakers   24–25
        turning off   311
More button   61, 304
Mouse
    choosing during installation   35–38
    problems   37
Movie reviews   87–88
MS DOS   *See* DOS
Music
    RockLink Forum   84–86

N

Names
    adding to Address Book   275–76
    files   180, 279–80
        extensions   181–82
    screen   260
        adding or deleting   350
        Address Book   276–77

changing   311
choosing   26–27, 47–48
entering   48
finding   71, 276
guest   354
making friends online   312
National Education Association   227–28
National Geographic Online
    (periodical)   209–10
NEA Online   227–28
Network News
    ignoring   349
Networker's Journal   153
Neverwinter Nights   90–93
New Member Lounge   243–44
    making friends online   312
New Product Information   153
News
    finding specific items   107–8
    See also Databases, online
News & Finance Department   97–113
News & Reference   150–56
News & Resources   154
News Search   107–8
Newsbytes News Network   153, 155–56

O

Oakley, Peter   78
Online databases   *See* Databases, online
Online Gaming Forum   89–94
Ontract Data Recovery   155–56
Organization of this book   15–17
Overview of book   18–20

P

Paint Shop Pro   306
Paper mail   283–84, 286
Parents
    assistance for   229–30
Parents' Information Network   229–30

Passwords   44–45
    choosing   27–28
    entering   48
Payment
    method of   26, 45–47
PC Animation & Graphics Forum   164–65
PC Games Forum   169–70
PC Kate
    ten best shareware   305–8
PC World Online (periodical)   148–50
People Connection Department   233–56
Periodicals
    Home-Office Computing   152
    IYM Software Review   152
    National Geographic   209–10
    PC World Online   148–50
Photographs
    members   247
PIF file   360
    modifying   360
PKZip   184, 306
Portfolios
    building   100–101
    charting in spreadsheets   101–2
    saving to disk   102
Preferences   348–50
    downloading   349–50
    fonts   350
    scrolling   349
Premium services
    AutoVantage   201–3
Printers
    installing   40
Printing
    help topics   58
    text files   58
Profiles   70, 72–74, 312
    creating   72–73
    editing   72–73, 311
    people in chat rooms   247
Program Manager
    installing America Online into   360
Programming
    Visual Basic   167

Q

Quantum Space   94

R

RabbitJack's Casino   93
RAM   22
Real Estate Online   141–42
Recording to disk   105–6, 129, 303–4
Reference works   205–31
Résumés   215–16
Reviews
        movies and videos   87–88
Rittner, Don   141
Rock and roll music
        RockLink Forum   84–86
Romance (online)   252
Rooms
        defined   61–62
        See also Chat rooms; Event rooms;
                Rooms, private; Rooms, public
Rooms, private   244–45
        conference calls   245
        See also Chat rooms
Rooms, public
        creating   243
        Event rooms   237–44
                See also Event rooms
        finding   237–43
        Guides   236–37
        list of available   243
        lobbies   234–36
                See also Lobby
        See also Chat rooms
Russian Archives, Online   210–12
Ryan, Kathy   89

S

Sabre   192–96
Saving
        to disk   105–6, 129, 303–4
        file descriptions   178

help screens   58
portfolios   102
Schedule
        Center Stage   253
        Event Rooms   242
Scrolling   336
        preferences   349
Self-extracting archives   185
Setup
        changing   351–53
                telephone numbers   178, 351–52
        See also Installation
Shareware
        defined   168–69
        ten best   305–8
Shopping   199–204
Sign off
        using Download Manager   295–96
Small business   108–13
Smileys   267
        finding list of   313
        ten best   313–14
Software   8–10
        buying   200
        configuring   8–10
        installing   28–41
                requirements for   22–28
                See also Installation
        problem-solving   156–61
        See also Computing & Software
                Department; Shareware
Sounds
        finding and installing
                shareware   306–7
SPEAKER   306–7
Spell-checking   358–59
Splitters (telephone)   26
Sports
        Grandstand   79–82
SprintNet   7
Starter kit   23
Status button   274
StockLink   98–104

Stocks 98–105
    buying and selling 103–4
    finding symbols 99–100
    Market News 102–3
    portfolios *See* Portfolios
Stoll, Cliff 287
Stop key 112, 302, 337
Stratus computer 5–6
Student Access Online 217–18
Students
    assistance for 217–24
Stuffing *See* Files, compressing
StuffIt 185
Subdirectory
    for American Online
        installation 30–31
Subject listings
    organization of book 16–17
Supervision and Curriculum Development,
    Association for 228–29

T

Teachers
    assistance for 224–29
    helping students 219–21
Teachers' Information Network 224–26
Telecommunications
    defined 4
    Networker's Journal 153
Telecommunications service 4–5
Telephone
    access numbers 2, 42–44, 310
        switching setup 178, 351–52
    connection
        configuring 41–42
    disabling Call Waiting 311, 352–53
    lines 2, 23, 352
    modular jack 23
    networks 2, 6–8, 352
    rotary vs. pulse 1, 351
    splitters 26

"Ten best" lists 301–15
    making friends online 311–13
    most frequently asked
        questions 308–11
    shareware 305–8
    smileys 313–14
    tips for using America Online 302–5
Terms
    financial 104–5
    used in book 363–76
Time
    downloading
        estimate 176–77
        taking too long 179
    duration online 70, 303, 310
Tips for using America Online 302–5
TradePlus gateway 103–4
Travel 191–204
    airline reservations 192–96
    talking with other travelers 198–99
    tips for using America Online 354
    using America Online 351–56
Travel & Shopping Department 191–204
Trivia Club 86–87

U

Universities *See* Colleges & universities
Unstuffing *See* Files, decompressing
Upload File Information form 187–88
Uploading 186–89
    defined 186
    information form, filling in 187
    process of 186–88
    tips 189
    virus checking 177
Using this book 14–18
    as documentation 14–17
    organization of 15–17
    overview of chapters 18–20

V

Vendors
    contacting online   156–61
Video adapter
    choosing during installation   33–34
Video reviews   87–88
Virus checking   177
Visual Basic   167

W

Williams, Robin   252
Window menu   350
Windows
    closing when enter free area   56
    managing   305
    sizing   245–46

Windows Forum   166–68
Windows (software)   *See* Microsoft
    Windows
Wine & Dine Online   115–24
Wolfenstein 3-D   307–8
Word processing
    electronic mail messages   267

Y

Your Money   104–5

Z

ZIP files   184

This book was produced on a Macintosh IIci using PageMaker 4.01. It was output directly to film using a Linotronic 330 imagesetter.

The body copy is set in Palatino, the heads are set in DTC Kabel, the sidebars are set in Adobe Futura Condensed.

More
Sourcebooks &

Sorcery from Ventana Press

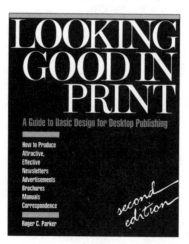

Available from bookstores or Ventana Press. Immediate shipment guaranteed. Your money returned if not satisfied. To order or for more information, contact:

Ventana Press, P.O. Box 2468, Chapel Hill, NC 27515
919/942-0220   Fax 919/942-1140

DOS, WordPerfect & Lotus Office Companion, Second Edition
$19.95
401 pages, illustrated
ISBN: 0-940087-80-4

The Bible for business software users is now updated and expanded to include new versions of DOS (5) and Lotus (2.3). This book will boost productivity for anyone who uses the most popular PC-compatible software programs.

The Makeover Book: 101 Design Solutions for Desktop Publishing
$17.95
282 pages, Illustrated
ISBN: 0-940087-20-0

"Before-and-after" desktop publishing examples demonstrate how basic design revisions can dramatically improve a document.

Newsletters From the Desktop
$23.95
306 pages, illustrated
ISBN: 0-940087-40-5

Now the millions of desktop publishers who produce newsletters can learn to improve the design of their publications. Filled with helpful design tips and illustrations.

Looking Good in Print, Second Edition
$23.95
410 pages, illustrated
ISBN: 0-940087-32-4

With over 100,000 in print, **Looking Good in Print** is looking even better. More makeovers, a new section on designing newsletters and a wealth of new design tips and techniques to broaden the design skills of the ever-growing number of desktop publishers.

Voodoo DOS
$19.95
320 pages, illustrated
ISBN: 0-940087-95-2

Increase your productivity with the "magic" of **Voodoo DOS**! Packed with tricks for DOS 5 and earlier versions. This lively book offers a wide range of time-saving techniques designed for all users.

Desktop Publishing With WordPerfect, Second Edition
$21.95
306 pages, illustrated
ISBN: 0-940087-95-2

WordPerfect offers graphic capabilities that can save users thousands of dollars in design and typesetting costs. Includes invaluable information on creating style sheets for consistency and speed. Covers versions 5.0 and 5.1.

Harvard Graphics Design Companion
$23.95
300 pages, illustrated
ISBN: 0-940087-78-2

An instructive companion guide to the dozens of Harvard Graphics tutorials, this book explores the graphic design capabilities of the software.

T

O ORDER additional copies of *The Official America Online Tour Guide* or any other Ventana Press book, please fill out this order form and return it to us for quick shipment.

	Quantity		Price		Total
The Official America Online Tour Guide: PC Edition	_____	x	$19.95	=	$_____
Voodoo DOS	_____	x	$19.95	=	$_____
Looking Good in Print	_____	x	$23.95	=	$_____
Newsletters From the Desktop	_____	x	$23.95	=	$_____
The Makeover Book	_____	x	$17.95	=	$_____
Desktop Publishing With WordPerfect 5.0 & 5.1	_____	x	$21.95	=	$_____
DOS, WordPerfect & Lotus Office Companion, 2nd Edition	_____	x	$19.95	=	$_____
Harvard Graphics Design Companion	_____	x	$23.95	=	$_____

Shipping: Please add $4.50/first book for standard UPS, $1.35/book thereafter; $8.00/book UPS "two-day air," $2.25/book thereafter.

For Canada, add $8.10/book. $_____

Send C.O.D. (add $4.20 to shipping charges) $_____
North Carolina residents add 6% sales tax $_____

                                                  Total $_____

Name _____ Co. _____

Address (No P.O. Box) _____

City _____ State _____ Zip _____

Daytime telephone _____

____ VISA ____ MC Acc't # _____

Exp. Date _____ Interbank # _____

Signature _____

Please mail or fax to:
Ventana Press, P.O. Box 2468, Chapel Hill, NC 27515
919/942-0220; FAX: 800/877-7955

TO ORDER additional copies of *The Official America Online Tour Guide* or any other Ventana Press book, please fill out this order form and return it to us for quick shipment.

	Quantity	Price	Total
The Official America Online Tour Guide: PC Edition	_____	x $19.95 =	$_____
Voodoo DOS	_____	x $19.95 =	$_____
Looking Good in Print	_____	x $23.95 =	$_____
Newsletters From the Desktop	_____	x $23.95 =	$_____
The Makeover Book	_____	x $17.95 =	$_____
Desktop Publishing With WordPerfect 5.0 & 5.1	_____	x $21.95 =	$_____
DOS, WordPerfect & Lotus Office Companion, 2nd Edition	_____	x $19.95 =	$_____
Harvard Graphics Design Companion	_____	x $23.95 =	$_____

Shipping: Please add $4.50/first book for standard UPS, $1.35/book thereafter; $8.00/book UPS "two-day air," $2.25/book thereafter. For Canada, add $8.10/book. $_____

Send C.O.D. (add $4.20 to shipping charges) $_____
North Carolina residents add 6% sales tax $_____

                                                                                    Total $_____

Name _____ Co. _____

Address (No P.O. Box) _____

City _____ State _____ Zip _____

Daytime telephone _____

_____ VISA _____ MC Acc't # _____

Exp. Date _____ Interbank # _____

Signature _____

Please mail or fax to:
Ventana Press, P.O. Box 2468, Chapel Hill, NC 27515
919/942-0220; FAX: 800/877-7955

MORE ABOUT VENTANA PRESS BOOKS...

If you would like to be added to our mailing list, please complete the card below and indicate your areas of interest. We will keep you up-to-date on new books as they're published.

Yes! I'd like to receive more information about Ventana Press books. Please add me to your mailing list.

Name_____

Company _____

Street address (no P.O. box)_____

City _____ State_____ Zip_____

Please check areas of interest below:

_____ Macintosh	_____ PC compatible
_____ Desktop publishing	_____ Networking
_____ Desktop design	_____ Facsimile
_____ Presentation graphics	_____ Business software

Please return the card to Ventana Press, P.O. Box 2468, Chapel Hill, NC 27515, 919/942-0220, FAX 919/942-1140. (Please don't duplicate your fax requests by mail.)

VENTANA PRESS
PO BOX 2468
CHAPEL HILL, NC
27515